Rebels and Radicals

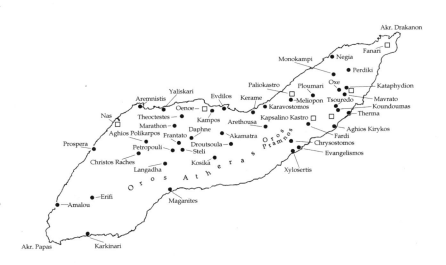

Rebels and
Radicals

ICARIA 1600–2000

Anthony J. Papalas
author of *ANCIENT ICARIA*

Bolchazy-Carducci Publishers, Inc.
Wauconda, Illinois USA

Editor
James T. McDonough, Jr.

Associate Editor
Patrick Romane

Cover Design
Adam Phillip Velez

Page Design & Typography
Dom Roberti

**Rebels and Radicals
Icaria 1600–2000**

Anthony J. Papalas

Bolchazy-Carducci Publishers, Inc.
1000 Brown Street
Wauconda, IL 60084 USA
www.bolchazy.com

Printed in Canada
2005
by Friesens Corporation

Paperback: ISBN-13: 978-0-86516-606-6
Paperback: ISBN-10: 0-86516-606-4
Hardbound: ISBN-13: 978-0-86516-605-9
Hardbound: ISBN-10: 0-86516-605-6

Library of Congress Cataloging-in-Publication Data

Papalas, Anthony J., 1939-
  Rebels and radicals : Icaria 1600-2000 / Anthony J. Papalas.
    p. cm.
  Includes bibliographical references and index.
  ISBN-13: 978-0-86516-605-9 (hardbound : alk. paper)
  ISBN-10: 0-86516-605-6 (hardbound : alk. paper)
  ISBN-13: 978-0-86516-606-6 (pbk. : alk. paper)
  ISBN-10: 0-86516-606-4 (pbk. : alk. paper)
  1. Ikaria Island (Greece)--History. I. Title.

DF901.I4P36 2005
949.5'82--dc22

2005007050

To my wife Françoise

Enfin!

And my daughter Mary Laura and my son John Anthony,

who grew up with "both Icarias."

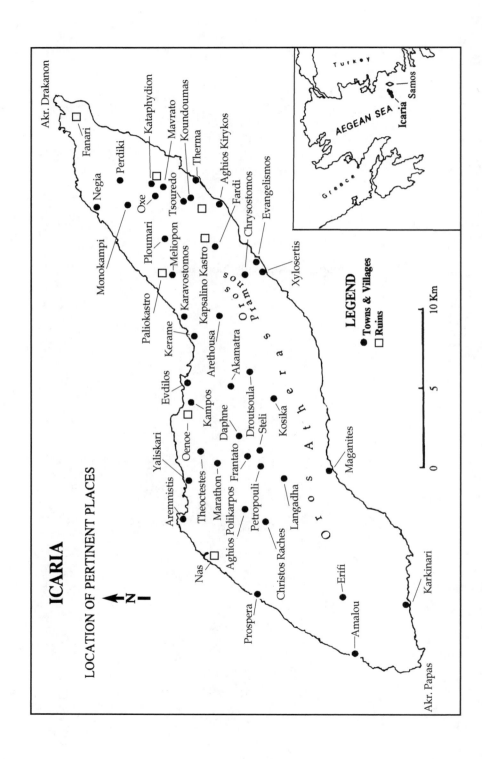

ICARIA

LOCATION OF PERTINENT PLACES

LEGEND
● Towns & Villages
□ Ruins

Akr. Drakanon
Fanari
Negia
Perdiki
Kataphydion
Mavrato
Koundoumas
Therma
Oxe
Tsouredo
Aghios Kirykos
Monokampi
Ploumari
Meliopon
Fardi
Karavostomos
Paliokastro
Karavostomos
Kapsalino Kastro
Chrysostomos
Evangelismos
Kerame
Xylosertis
Oros Pramnos
Paliokastro
Arethousa
Akamatra
Evdilos
Kampos
Daphne
Droutsoula
Kosika
Oros Atheras
Yaliskari
Oenoe
Steli
Aremmistis
Theoctestes
Marathon
Frantato
Maganites
Nas
Aghios Polikarpos
Petropouli
Langadha
Prospera
Christos Raches
Erifi
Amalou
Karkinari
Akr. Papas

Turkey
AEGEAN SEA
Icaria
Samos
Greece

0   5   10 Km

Introduction

In a sense this work began in 1961 when I first visited Icaria and started learning Greek, hearing stories passed down through many generations, and discovering a society totally different from anything I had imagined. By the middle of my summer stay, I decided to write a book about the island. The one I eventually did, *Ancient Icaria*, was very different from the one I had planned.

The present book corresponds more with my original goal, to combine some of my experiences and interviews with a traditional scholarly study of the island. My focus originally was on the 20th century, but I decided to begin where I had left off in the previous volume. By covering the last four hundred years, I cast a wider net than I had intended and took more years than I had anticipated. Furthermore, there were many perils for a specialist in ancient Greek culture to undertake a work dealing with Ottoman and Modern Greek history, and countless hazards in writing the recent history of a turbulent and controversial period. But the opportunity of moving into a new realm without really leaving home and discovering answers to questions that haunted me was a temptation I could not resist.

I had many goals. By exploiting unusual sources I intended to provide a detailed analysis of a frontier province in the Ottoman Empire from the period of 1600 to 1912. I hoped to explain and understand the main questions Icaria faced in the 20th century—poverty, emigration to America, the nature of the Axis occupation, the rise of Communism, the Civil War and the rightwing reaction to the radical movements of the postwar period. On an island where most people are connected by ties of blood or friendship, a clear picture emerges, and this knowledge will hopefully contribute to a better understanding of what happened throughout Greece in the 20th century where people confronted the same issues.

Perhaps my chief aim was to establish the importance of the history of one of the most remote regions of Greece, and to give significance to its people. I was seeking to rescue the Icarian shepherd, the obscure charcoal maker, and the immigrant factory worker from the great condescension of posterity.

Acknowledgements

I am deeply indebted to my wife Françoise and to Gene Ryan who coped with a messy manuscript replete with foreign tongues. I owe much to John Iatrides who read and commented on chapter 6, "The Red Island," and to Themistocles Speis who introduced me to Icaria in 1961 and commented on parts of the manuscript. I am obliged to Jim McDonough who provided his professional services as copy editor. I am grateful to my publisher Lou Bolchazy who not only took a chance on publishing a local history of an obscure island, but also visited Icaria to see whether it merited a book.

The influence of my parents, who were born in Ottoman Icaria, immigrated to America, and never passed a day of their new life without expressing nostalgia for their native land, pervades this book. Angelos Kalokairinos has been a mine of information and a source of inspiration. This book is considerably richer for the documents and insights provided so generously by John Pyke. I am much indebted to John Melas who preserved so much important material in his 1955 history of Icaria, and who spent time with me and stirred my interest in the culture of the island when I first visited it nearly a half century ago.

There are no public archives for the history of Icaria. I cannot begin to thank the countless people in Greece, particularly Icaria, Samos, Athens, and in North America, especially New York, San Francisco, Detroit, Pittsburgh and Toronto, who searched through trunks for old documents such as dowry agreements and judicial decisions from Ottoman officials, and patiently sat through lengthy interviews. I am especially thankful to Nicholas Diamantides who not only gave me boxes full of old newspapers and documents, but also was delighted to see me carry out a task that he had once contemplated undertaking. Likewise, I owe special gratitude to Christos Malachias who provided me with unusual material and photographs. When I doubted the value of such a study, I found support from two Hellenists, Peter Green and Nicholas Purcell, who have carefully explored the island and have found it as fascinating as I did, and provided me with important insights. My colleagues, Bodo Nischan and Michael Enright, although specialists in areas of European history not related to Greece, took an interest in my research and encouraged me to finish the work. I am, of course, responsible for all errors in this book.

Contents

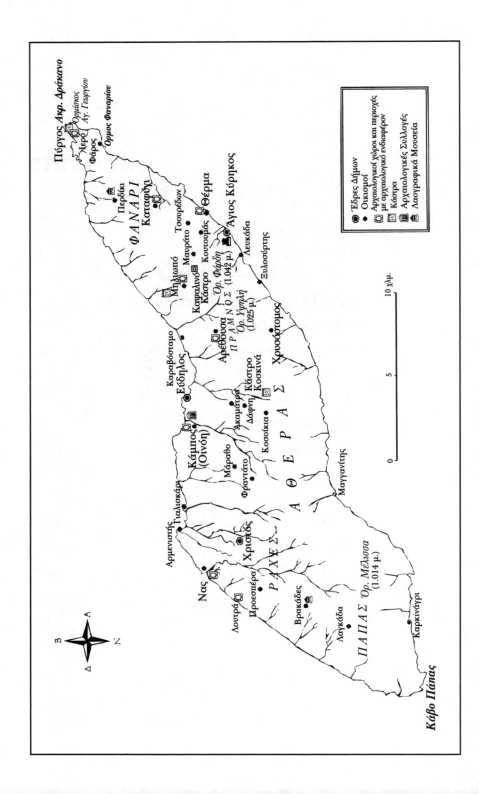

CHAPTER 1

Ouloi Emeis Efendi
"It's all of us, Sir."

The Environment

ICARIA, an island of the Aegean Sea, is about 40 kilometers (25 miles)
long and 3 to 9 km (2 to 6 miles) wide, with an area of 255 sq. km (98
sq. miles). It is part of the Sporades chain. In contrast with the
Cyclades, which cluster around Delos, the Sporades have no specific orientation. The Northern Sporades lie northeast of Euboea, while Icaria
belongs to the Anatolian group which stretches along the coast of Asia
Minor and includes Patmos and Leros. Samos, with its imposing Mt.
Cerkis, some 15 miles east, has been traditionally Icaria's proud and prosperous neighbor. Icaria had always more in common with Patmos, and
Leros, the former about 20 miles and the latter about 40 miles southeast.
These islands, along with Icaria, were considered among the poorest
regions of the Ottoman Empire's Aegean possessions. Icaria has an unbro-
ken coastline. There are no projecting arms from its jagged edges to create wide harbors. Thus seafarers had to settle for small roadsteads and
coves. While Patmos and Leros have indented coasts and natural ports,
they do not have adequate water resources or good soil. Icaria generally
receives sufficient rainfall, indeed more than the prosperous islands of
Mytilene and Samos, and has some—though not abundant—arable land.
The bulk of the rain comes in December and January, but the rains of April
can be heavy and occasionally destructive, wiping out sections of roads
and cutting craters into modern asphalt surfaces. The northern section,
which the natives refer to as *sofrano*, receives more rainfall than the

1

southern, *stafenti*. The area around the village of Christos Raches in the north is distinct with forests of fir trees and is therefore greener than the bald, steep, and long escarpment that stretches along the southern shore. The amount of rainfall fluctuates enormously. Records in the capital, Aghios Kyrikos, include 1104 millimeters (43.5 inches) of rainfall in 1988, the peak for the decade, but only 314 (12.4 inches) in 1989. Between 1983 and 1988 the average rainfall amounted to 821 millimeters (32.3 inches), while the figure dropped to 564 (22.2 inches) for the period between 1989 and 1995.[1]

Water runs profusely into the sea, but a considerable amount is absorbed by the island's karst, underground hollowed out limestone formation. The pools of water which collect beneath the surface feed springs and rivers. However, in the 19th century the destruction of much of the forest (undertaken chiefly to make charcoal) lowered the water table and thus reduced wells, springs, and rivers. The people cultivated most of the arable land, about 5% of the island, although after 1960 agriculture went into gradual decline.[2]

In the summer, the *meltimi,* the Etesian winds (annual winds, from Greek *etos,* "year") of classical antiquity coming from the northeast, make the Icarian Sea, the section of the Aegean encompassing Icaria, the most turbulent in the Aegean. The lee of Icaria afforded only limited shelter at Fanari where ships were somewhat less exposed when the strong winds of the Aegean roared. Around 300 BC the Icarians built a fine tower on this low-lying area. Among other functions, this structure aided pilots who navigated through these dangerous straits and marked the roadstead, now called Aghios Georgios from the small church in the vicinity, below the tower. Only the most intrepid mariners ventured near the high cliff-bound Icarian coast, and it was not until the end of the 19th century that steamers began to make regular visits to the island, but did not endeavor to approach shore. Boatmen ferried passengers and cargo to land in small shallow-bottomed rowboats. The Greek government constructed a mole, a massive stone wall jutting into the sea and providing shelter for ships, at the capital Aghios Kyrikos in the 1980s, but the absence of such a facility in the past partially explains the peculiar development—or lack of development—of Icaria.[3]

When the *meltimi* hits the northern side of Icaria, it replaces surface air without any atmospheric disturbance. Thus there is scarcely any land breeze. People stroll in calm weather on the northern beaches between the villages of Aremistis and Yaliskari while great waves hit the shore.

Crossing the Atheras mountain range, which separates northern Icaria from the southern half of the island, the *meltimi* encounters warmer ground air. The contrast in temperatures produces a vertical displacement of air generating surface gusts and eddies. These winds whisk dishes and bottles off modern outdoor café tables, damage crops, and bend saplings. This peculiar phenomenon was noted even in antiquity. Theophrastus (*De Ventis* 34), the third century BC Peripatetic, observed that there was little land breeze on the windward side of Aegean islands while the lee region was subject to windy weather. These turbulent gales played a role in the catastrophe of the summer of 1993 when they fanned flames that ignited the parched maquis, the dense growth of small trees and shrubs so typical of Mediterranean lands. The fire spread through the underbrush, reached villages, burned houses, and killed thirteen people.[4]

The Early History

Despite the lack of arable land and harbors, and the role of fierce winds, the inhabitants of Icaria flourished in classical antiquity. They built a famous temple for Artemis at Nas, which gets its name from the word *naos*, meaning "temple," now a tourist village on the northwest coast, and established two *poleis,* Oenoe on the north coast, and Therma on the south. In the middle of the fifth century BC the combined annual taxes of Oenoe and Therma to the Delian league were eleven thousand drachmas, a substantial sum for that time, ranking Icaria in the upper thirty percent of tax-paying regions in the Athenian Empire. The Greeks described the island as either Makris, for its long shape, or Ichthyoessa, for the rich supply of fish off its coast. The origin of the name Icarus (the ancient name of Icaria) is not clear, but apparently, by the fifth century BC the inhabitants began to associate the name of their island with Icarus, the son of Daedalus, and identified a natural landmark with the tomb of Icarus. The alleged sepulcher was conspicuous from the sea and became part of the navigational topography for sailors negotiating the straits between Icaria and Samos, some fifteen miles to the east. Icarians from the classical to the modern period shared the pride in the Icarus connection. Indeed, many Icarians in the modern period believe that Icarus was a historical figure who experimented in aviation and fell on the island.[5]

In the fifth and fourth centuries BC, Icarian wine became famous, and in the following century Therma, with its radioactive warm springs, gained a reputation as a health spa. For a short time Therma took the name of the god of health, Asklepieis, an appropriate appellation for a city claiming to be a healing center. But at the end of the Hellenistic Age, piracy became endemic, driving the people of Icaria from their coastal settlements, and beginning a period of decline that lasted for the next two thousand years. A barter economy, dictated by poor land and lack of harbors, reasserted itself. At the end of the first century BC, Samians resettled Oenoe and exploited the plains of Campos, the rich bottomlands on the north coast a few miles east of Evdilos, to graze their flocks. By the beginning of the *Pax Romana*, Icaria was a backwater.[6]

Civilization revived somewhat in the Byzantine era. The Byzantine emperors established naval *themata*, military spheres, and until the 10th century, the *thema* of Samos furnished ships to the emperor and patrolled the region. Evdilos, a town adjacent to Oenoe, flourished as part of this important naval *thema,* and may have served as a provincial shipyard. At that time Icaria had one of the best supplies of oak needed for the keel of the *dromon,* the Byzantine military ship. Around 1050 the Byzantine government closed its Aegean shipyards and shifted its main naval construction to Constantinople, the principal imperial port as well as the capital. Samos ceased to be a naval center, and thus the entire region again went into decline. The inhabitants of Icaria tended to retreat into a forested, impenetrable interior. The encroachment of the Turks into the Byzantine Empire at the end of the eleventh century began a process that forced many Greeks of Asia Minor to flee westward to seek refuge on islands in the Aegean. As the Turkish menace grew in Asia Minor, Icaria became a safe haven.[7]

In the fourteenth century, the Aegean became a patchwork of various interests. Byzantine authorities had granted certain islands to Venice and Genoa as part of a policy to keep the Turks, who were beginning to establish naval strength, out of the Aegean. Icaria was in the possession of Genoa from 1325 to 1481, almost three decades after the fall of Constantinople itself. There remain some indications of this occupation. For example, there are two fortifications on Icaria associated with the Genoese, and perhaps some of the many Italian surnames which survive on the island today go back to the 14th century. When the Genoese evacuated Icaria, some Icarians decided to abandon the island. The Knights of St John, who took Rhodes in 1309 and flourished as merchants and warriors, coveted Icaria as an Aegean base. The aim of the Knights was to carve out an Aegean empire, and prevent the Turks from establishing a foothold on the islands. Their fleet, which originally consisted of four large galleys and a number of smaller vessels, grew into a force to rival the Genoese in the Aegean and was vastly superior to the embryonic Ottoman navy. In 1312, the Knights destroyed a Turkish fleet near Amorgos, and by 1319 controlled the Anatolian Sporades as far as Leros.[8]

Between the Hospitallers and the Turks

In 1403 the Castilian Ruy González de Clavijo, on a diplomatic mission to Samarkand, passed by Icaria, and, ignoring the Genoese fortifications, reported that the ruler of the island was a woman and that the land was extensively cultivated. He was mistaken on both counts. While Icaria was not deserted, as many islands were, it maintained only small settlements in its inaccessible interior. Hardly any of the land was cultivated. Akamatra rather than Evdilos was now the main populated area. The communities in the western region, the most important of which was Langadha, remained protected because they were remote. If there are any Icarians on the island today descended from the inhabitants of the Byzantine era, they are offspring of people from this region. In 1453 Constantinople fell to the Ottomans, and the Turks proceeded to take possession of some of the islands. Many, however, were deserted. Samos remained without visible settlements throughout the 15th century. About 1500 a Turkish official landed there to hunt and was so taken by the beauty of the island that he ordered its resettlement, establishing a village with Greeks from Mytilene on the island of Lesbos. This village, also called Mytilene, in the eastern part of Samos, is not visible from the sea. Later in that century, the Ottomans encouraged settlements of Samian coastal areas, and apparently some Icarians from Akamatra claimed land near Karlovassi. By the mid-seventeenth century there were eighteen villages on Samos, and unlike the Icarians who considered settlements of several dwellings as villages, Samian counterparts generally consisted of at least fifty houses.[9]

As the Porte—the French title for the government of the Ottoman Empire, short for La Sublime Porte, "the High Gate"—repopulated Samos and brought it back into the mainstream of Aegean history, Icaria remained a backwater. When the Genoese abandoned Icaria, the inhabitants turned to the Knights of St. John for help. According to Marcos Coronelli, a Venetian historian of the 16th century, Icarians in 1481 petitioned the Knights for land in Rhodes. Wishing to elude Turkish pirates who were allegedly kidnapping their children and converting them to

Islam, they offered to surrender their freedom and live as serfs. In 1483 the people of Nisyros, an island about fifty miles north of Rhodes, petitioned the knights in Rhodes for the same privilege. The desire of the denizens of these islands to abandon their homes is connected to the growth of Ottoman sea power. Turkish raiding parties roamed the islands seeking young men to impress into the nascent Turkish navy. Deploying such means, the Ottoman authorities eventually amassed around seventy thousand sailors, mostly Greeks, for their unsuccessful siege of Rhodes.[10]

The richest inhabitants of Akamatra would have been better off economically even in some menial capacity in Rhodes. However, the Knights, after repulsing the Turkish siege, rejected the Icarian request to settle them in Rhodes, but did send a garrison to Icaria, and converted the island into a protectorate, 1481–1522. Icaria served as a frontier outpost in the Knights' Sporades Empire. The names of several Roman Catholic bishops, who probably never came to Icaria, survive. We may assume the Knights occupied the same fortified points held previously by the Genoese, and protected the Icarians from piratical invasions, particularly from attempts to impress the young men into the Ottoman navy.[11]

If the Knights had been successful in curtailing piracy in the eastern Sporades, they quickly reemerged after the Knights pulled out of the area. In 1544 Jerome Maurand, a priest from Antibes and the almoner for the French galleys operating in the area, noted that Myconus, an island about thirty miles west of Icaria, had been utterly destroyed by pirates. A few years later, it seemed to Pierre Belon, a French naturalist and traveler who sailed past Icaria, that it was uninhabited. He reported that Turkish corsairs operating in the area made it impossible for people on the island to cultivate the land or keep animals. But Icaria, unlike Myconus and other smaller islands, enjoyed a remote, forested interior. Belon, therefore, was unaware of Akamatra, Steli, Langadha, and other villages of five or six houses that were not visible from the sea. They took care to conceal any signs of life, going so far as to block the chimneys in their hearth to prevent smoke from escaping and thus providing pirates with a reference point. To avoid asphyxiation most of the family, apparently, remained outdoors while the food was being cooked. Travelers like Belon would assume the island was desolate but pirates knew better. Around the time Belon voyaged in the vicinity of Icaria, a man from Langadha betrayed his fellow villagers by informing pirates where shepherds were grazing their animals. The Icarians, however, stole a march on the pirates. They ambushed the marauders, killing some and driving the rest away. Such a defense system was only possible in the interior where the inhabitants, relying on *viglas*, a system of observation points, kept a watch for intruders. On the other hand, no such defense system could be deployed on the coast. Thus the best land in Icaria, like Campos, a very fertile area, was abandoned and, through neglect, riddled with stagnant pools that made it unsafe because of malaria. We may conjecture that Icaria had then a population of about three thousand, located entirely in the interior of the island.[12]

The Beginning of Ottoman Rule
and Bishop Georgirenes

The Ottoman Turkish Sultan Selim I (born 1467, ruled 1512–1520) built a fleet to support a successful campaign in Syria and Egypt. His son, Suleiman I the Magnificent (born 1494 or 1495, reigned 1520–1566) enlarged Ottoman naval forces, and in 1522 deployed the new vessels in his successful campaign against the Knights in Rhodes. At this time the Knights withdrew from the Aegean and abandoned Icaria. We hear nothing of Icaria during Suleiman's three-year war (1537–1540) with Venice. By the middle of the 16th century the Porte controlled most of the Aegean. Suleiman wished to have a detailed knowledge of this area, and encouraged naval officers to make maps of the region. Piri Reis (died about 1554), the nephew of the great admiral Kemal, was the most successful of these naval cartographers. Best known for his 1513 map of the New World, he also made a detailed map of the Aegean with a commentary, the *Book of Sea Lore*. In this work Piri Reis included a map of Icaria with a brief description of the island. According to the Ottoman cartographer, Icaria was a long mountain with a perimeter of seventy miles. In the western portion he noted a strong fortress and at the eastern extremity a small bay with a copious supply of fresh water for sailors. Piri Reis oddly listed Icaria among the possessions of Genoa though the Genoese had pulled out of Icaria in 1481. Piri's reference to Genoese fortifications in Icaria suggests that Genoa repossessed the island after 1522 when Suleiman drove the Knights out of the Aegean. The sultan esteemed Genoese merchants, approved of their activity on Chios, and perhaps permitted them to place a garrison in Icaria to support Genoese ships sailing to Chios. The second Genoese dominance of Icaria, apparently, did not last long.[13]

Sultan Murad (or Murat) III (born 1546, reigned 1574–1595) made perhaps the first attempt to impose Ottoman authority on the settlements perched high in the mountains of Icaria. Murad endeavored to increase the tax base in the Aegean by establishing mints in the region, and increasing the circulation of silver coinage. To further this policy, the sultan issued a series of firmans, imperial decrees, related to Naxos, Andros, Paros, Melos, and Santorini. The sultan granted the people of these islands rights to bequeath property, repair churches and generally to improve conditions. Although none of these decrees referred to Icaria, they attest to a general attempt to improve conditions in the Aegean islands. It was perhaps during this time that the village society that Georgirenes was to describe in the middle of the 17th century began to emerge. These developments were brought to a temporary halt when the Ottoman Empire went to war with Venice (1645–1664) under Sultan Ibrahim I (reigned 1640–1648 and Sultan Mehmed IV (1648–1687).[14]

During this conflict Venetians, Turks, and pirates raided the island. The Icarians again took refuge in their forested interior, and forbade outsiders to settle on the island. The impact of the recent war was evident in 1670 when the bishop Joseph Georgirenes arrived. Georgirenes' *Description of Patmos, Samos, Nicaria and Mt. Athos,* (London, 1677), is the most comprehensive 17th century source for Icaria. It is undeniably genuine and, allowing for some hyperbole, rather accurate. Unlike non-Greek visitors, he did not base his reflections on what he saw as he sailed past the island, or on what he heard from persons on neighboring islands, but mainly on what he witnessed as he ranged through the rugged island. While the Icarians made a strong impression on him, his stay was the subject of conversation on the island for many years after. Three hundred thirty-five years later, the elders in Raches and Akamatra recounted stories handed down about the prelate's sojourn. Born in Melos around 1630, he became bishop of Samos and Icaria in 1666, holding the position until 1672. The bishop, with revenues drawn mainly from Samians, lived the life of a relatively wealthy man. Apart from his ecclesiastical substantial salary, he received an allowance of milk, cheeses, wine, sheep, and goats from the Samians and Icarians.[15]

Although the rewards of office were plentiful, risks were considerable. During the Venetian-Turkish war (1645–1664), the Venetians made his predecessor, Bishop Christophoros, a native Samian, serve as a galley slave because he was unable to raise enough money to satisfy a Venetian war levy. Georgirenes, who became bishop at the end of the war, when the Ottomans had resumed control of the Aegean, was mindful of how quickly he might fall from his lofty station. He was under pressure to collect the *cizye* or *kharadj* (a Turkish tax), which the Icarians called *hatach*, and in addition to make a contribution to the patriarch in Constantinople who had appointed him bishop. By the end of the 17th century, not only did the patriarch have to raise 20,000 groschen, (a large European silver coin) for a *peskes* (supposedly a voluntary gift) for the sultan, but he also had to pay an annual involuntary tax of that amount. As one contemporary source reported, as soon as the patriarchs were promoted, "they sent to all their bishops, to contribute to the sum they have disbursed for their preferment, and such as deny, they depose and send others to their charge . . . and they are forced to do this to the poor people, to take food out of their wives and children's mouths." Generally they could not raise the required sum. In the seventy-five years between 1625 and 1700 the sultan appointed fifty patriarchs, an average tenure of only eighteen months. The patriarch was unable to hold his position long because his bishops like Georgirenes had difficulties raising funds to help him defray the expense of his office.[16]

We may digress for a moment to consider Georgirenes' later career. As bishop he had unspecified difficulties with Turkish officials who came to Samos from Crete. He cryptically referred to their abusive behavior that forced him to retire to the monastery of St. John on the island of Patmos. He probably had not raised all of the expected head tax. The monastery in Patmos did not prove to be the haven he had hoped. Despite charters from the Pope, the King of France, the Doge of Venice, and the Grand Masters of Malta, threatening anyone who raided the monks with dire consequences, corsairs were a bane to the monastery.[17] Georgirenes fled to France and then to England where he became a prominent member of the Greek community in Soho on Greek Street. His cousin, Lawrence Georgirenes, was a London businessman who had invented a method for pickling mackerel and was trying to make his fortune in England with his new method. The bishop was enterprising in his own right. He met Charles II and his brother the Duke of York, who became a patron of sorts, and encouraged Georgirenes to undertake a collection of funds for the first Greek Church in London. He raised the huge sum of eight thousand pounds sterling. Unfortunately, a subordinate absconded with some of the funds, but with the remaining cash, the Greeks of London endeavored to purchase land and then build a church. Due to legal complications they did not acquire title to the land they thought they had possessed, and thus the building, which survived until 1934, reverted to the owner of the land. It never served as a Greek Orthodox Church. Georgirenes sought solace in intellectual pursuits. He toyed with converting to the Anglican Church,

and planned to have a work on theology printed in England. Though that
venture never materialized, he collaborated with Henry Denton, the chap-
lain to the Levant Co. in Constantinople, to compose a *Description of
Patmos, Samos, Nicaria and Mt. Athos.*[18]

For Samos, Patmos, and Mt. Athos, Georgirenes chiefly describes the
topography and monuments, but in his chapter on Icaria he reveals a fas-
cination with the people and a talent for unbyronic observation.
Georgirenes described Icarians in the way that other European travelers
portrayed Greeks in general, namely as inferior and wretched specimens
of the human race. The clergyman from Samos noted conditions that were
more primitive than in other parts of the Aegean. With the exception of a
few charcoal merchants who made boats and went to Chios to exchange
their product for grain, and the shepherds with the greatest flocks, the
Icarians were the most destitute people of the islands. He complained that
they did not even have the means to support a suffragan, a diocesan bishop subordinate to Georgirenes. He wrote, "there is not a bed on the island,
the ground is their tick," and the only clothing they possessed, they wore
on their back. He could have added that some slept in the same room with
their animals. While most went without shoes, some had footwear made
of thin copper, perhaps the *petromachi* of the Papas dialect spoken in the
western part of the island, where people wore shoes of pigskin reinforced
with thin copper plates. They baked a type of pita bread on a stone just
before meals. The head of the household divided it equally, but pregnant
women and guests received a double share. They added one-third water to
their wine, diluting it more than other Greeks. They did not keep wine in
wooden caskets, but rather in jars, the *pithoi* we encounter in legal documents, and they siphoned it out with a straw. Each family possessed one
hand mill for grinding grain, but kept no furniture or property in the
house. Unlike their neighbors on other Greek islands they did not develop, even in the modern era, a reliance on closets, cupboards, and keys to
lock their belongings. As we have noted, they kept their valuable possessions, even food, hidden outside in *chostokelia.* Georgirenes based his
account to some extent on the practices he encountered in the main villages. Akamatra boasted one hundred houses, and Steli and Raches were
about half that size.[19]

There were a number of small settlements each consisting of several
houses. Unlike the Samians, the Icarians did not build their domiciles
close to one another, even in the main villages, but lived apart with houses encircled by gardens, and vineyards, and grazing land for animals.

These small Icarian settlements were like islands on dry land cut off from their neighbors by pathless mountains and valleys. The Icarians might have developed antisocial traits if priests had not arranged marriages for their offspring with eligible persons in distant villages. Neighborly visits, however, were rare, and difficult. According to the bishop, the Icarians often conducted their "visits" at great distances. "Guests" and "hosts" yodeled their news through winding valleys. "Such were the distances that it required a quarter of an hour for the message to arrive. And yet they make distinct and proper answers both audible and intelligible without the help of a stentophonical trumpet."[20]

Despite their low status in the Aegean, the Icarians were the only Greeks not to accept strangers from other islands in marriage, "for they believed they were descendants of the Byzantine emperors, and did not want to mix their noble blood with inferior peasants, *choriates,* as they called other islanders." On the other hand, they exploited their beggarly appearance abroad to practice the profession of the pauper. Georgirenes' account of Icarian manners bristles with such irony and criticism. Apart from giving the Icarians credit for providing the rare visitor with double portions at meals, he does not acknowledge any other virtues or generous behavior. While there is no hint of any refinements in 17th century Icaria, it must be said that the fear of pirates prevented people from developing some of the positive qualities they exhibited a century later. Quite contrary to Georgirenes, the monk Nephon, who settled in Icaria in 1750, found the Icarians the kindest and most hospitable people in the Aegean. By the end of the 19th century, visitors invariably commented on their extraordinary hospitality. Icarians offered guests goat meat, olives, and wine. Plates were never taken from the table so the guest might not presume he was being asked to leave. At mealtime in many houses, women set an extra plate with a piece of bread in case a visitor appeared, and, if a stranger passed by their home while they were eating and was reluctant to join them, they forced him to partake of their meal.[21]

Georgirenes, however, came a century too early to witness this open-handed behavior, and concluded that they were the poorest people with the most barren soil in the Aegean, but blessed with robust bodies and long lives. We should not dismiss his remarks about their exceptional good health, which he attributed to the air and water, as overstatement. In the fourth century BC Therma acquired the name Asclepieis, a healing center, and even today the health spa is in use, and the island enjoys a reputation for its air, thanks to the purifying force of the *meltimi,* and its good drinking water. Georgirenes saw people allegedly one hundred years old hale and hearty, and wills of that period reveal people reaching an advanced age. While there are not enough figures to bear this out statistically, the Icarians from 1400 to 1800 seemed more *makrobioi* than other Greeks whose adult longevity was 34 years for males and 28 for females. The well being of the population was not entirely the result of good air and water, but rather also the consequence of inhabiting the interior where they were relatively safe from coastal malaria and the plagues that ravaged the Aegean. Furthermore, houses, constructed of stone and clay mortar and without beds or furniture, were relatively hygienic. In such an environment, bacteria for deadly diseases did not thrive. Finally, these houses were not built contiguous to one another, as Georgirenes observed, and thus disease did not spread easily. Despite these buffers against plague, one ravaged the island in the late 18th century. In 1950 the local historian, Melas, who was collecting information for his history of Icaria, interviewed a man about 80, who in his youth had heard from his elders that a deadly disease, *skordoulon,* characterized by pimples that blister and form pockmarks on the face, ravaged the island. This elderly gentleman, apparently, was referring to the 1788 great plague of smallpox that killed some fourteen thousand people in Chios. This epidemic may partially explain the decline of Akamatra, the only village where houses were clustered together, in the 18th century.[22]

Georgirenes' chief aim in visiting Icaria was to evaluate the tax base, and the Icarians no doubt exaggerated their penury in order to maintain a low assessment. How could people who considered the ground their bed, had one set of tattered clothes, were cursed with barren soil, and had no ports, pay taxes? The deficiencies of intervillage lanes provided protection from pirates and tax collectors alike, but prevented the bishop from visiting certain parts of the island. Where he did go, he saw a barter economy in which everyone was his own baker and cobbler. The Icarians made exactly the impression they wished to make, and thus dodged some of the taxes they were expected to pay. For the 16th and much of the 17th century, Icarians avoided the head tax. In subsequent centuries, they paid this tax but were not assessed a custom excise, taxes on houses, wax, baths, and salts, or a tithe on agricultural products. The Porte was successful in collecting such taxes on other islands.[23]

The bishop reported, "once they slew a Caddee, sent by the grand Signior." The cadi, as the Greeks then referred to most Ottoman officials connected with taxation, were often arrogant. In 1687 one of them threatened the people of Myconus, if they delayed further in remitting their taxes, he would burn the entire island, hang some people and put others in galleys. He warned them that it was no use fleeing for he knew every hiding spot on the island.[24]

In 1669, a year or so before Georgirenes came to Icaria, the sultan made a tax assessment of many of the Aegean islands, dispatching officials, "cadis," who behaved in a haughty manner as they attempted to register all of the agricultural and industrial production including honey, beehives, and olive presses. In addition to such taxes, on Naxos they attempted to seize boys for service in the janissaries, the sultan's elite military force. It was, apparently, at this time that the Icarians bore a cadi in a type of settee, over Mt. Atheras at Kako Katavasithi, and there tilted the conveyance, and thus hurled the man over a precipice. Georgirenes reports that they were summoned to answer for their crime, and they "by common consent owned the fact." According to the oral version of the event, passed down from one generation to the next, the Turks sent an expedition but could not find the culprits, who took refuge in caves. Presumably, the Turkish force seized hostages and threatened to harm them if the responsible men did not appear before a Turkish judge. Apparently, the most prominent Icarians came forth and accepted collective responsibility for the act, "*ouloi emeis efendi.*" "It's all of us, Sir." We may surmise that this gathering of Icarians to deal with the emergency was the origin of the Icarian *demogerontia,* council of elders. Georgirenes adds that the judge saw "there was neither gain nor glory in punishing such miscreants, and that in justice they must punish all, or none, he dismissed them untouched."[25]

The community took responsibility for the criminal behavior of some of its members and thus escaped mass executions. It was not in the interest of the Ottoman government to invest in the extermination of the insignificant inhabitants of this remote island. Some of the people could retreat to the old Genoese strongholds, forcing the Turks to take the expensive, if not impossible, maneuver of dragging cannons into the mountains to besiege remote fortresses. Others could simply conceal themselves in caves. If the Ottomans had succeeded in massacring a portion of the population, the semi-deserted island would have become a pirate haven. These people had committed a serious crime, but by appearing in an Ottoman court they demonstrated that they were not lawless, and had the potential to pay taxes. At this time the Ottomans were endeavoring to repopulate deserted areas of their realm. Apparently, the Icarians were given amnesty from a capital crime on condition that they dutifully collected their own head tax. From the time the Icarians did away with the cadi, until some time in the middle of the 18th century, no Turkish official had stepped onto the shores of Icaria.[26]

According to Georgirenes the Icarians paid three hundred crowns, apparently one crown for each adult male. We may assume the bishop tallied three hundred adult males, doubtless an undercount, not being able to tally the people who lived in the "stentophonical" regions of the island. The bishop probably meant a *kurus,* an Ottoman silver coin, for three hundred gold coins would have been impossible to squeeze out of Icaria every year. The Icarian documents of the period mention silver and not gold coins.[27]

Icaria was in grade three, the lowest *hatach* category. A generation later, about 1700, Pitton de Tournefort, a botanist and medical doctor commissioned by Louis XIV to study the plants, history, geography and the religion of the Aegean, reported a *hatach* (head tax) of 525 crowns; again we may assume silver coins. An undated document, probably from the end of the 18th century, mentions a *hatach* of 1,500 groschen, about two groschen for each male. The head tax was levied on all adult males except the old, insane, and those who provided special services. This tax did not take into account economic disparities between people, and was especially hard on the poor in most islands. In Icaria it was relatively fair because most people were on equal footing. Furthermore, by being free of Turkish administrators, the Icarians were able to conceal much of their population and assets. Thus by taking collective responsibility for sending the cadi careening down a mountainside, the Icarians gained certain tax advantages.[28]

The Icarians while generally believing in their superior pedigree exploited their low economic status. According to local lore a fictional George Trouletes went to Constantinople to persuade the sultan to lower taxes. Too poor to equip his ship with regular sails, he outfitted it with tree branches laden with leaves. Gazing from the window of the imperial palace, the sultan saw this strange vessel sailing through the straits and upon learning that the owner was an Icarian and could not afford proper sails, decreed lowering the taxes of the Icarians by 30 groschen.

We may compare Icaria's tax situation with that of some of the neighboring and more prosperous islands. In Chios it was not a cadi, but rather a private entrepreneur, a Jew, who in 1625 acquired the right to collect taxes. With the thriving *mastika* (a very valuable aromatic resin) and silk trade, each adult Chian male paid a head tax of eleven groschen. Samos produced silk, pitch, cotton, and wheat, and boasted of large villages with as many as three-hundred houses. The cadi went to every village, charged the priests to provide a register of adult males, and collected three groschen from each male. Unlike the Chians, Samians had difficulties paying their tax. Georgirenes maintained that the high tax in Samos kept the people in poverty and ignorance. There was no point in maintaining an official on an island like Icaria where there was little husbandry, where most villages consisted of less than six houses, and only a few priests were literate enough to help register the male citizens on the tax ledger.[29]

The 17th century Icarian economy, as documents from the period attest, was based largely on barter. There was, however, a lively Aegean commerce, and Icarians, according to Georgirenes, traded in wood, boats, sheep, goats, pigs, wax, and honey. Unlike the products of many of the other islands, Icarian products were not taxed, and therefore it must have been easy enough for them to sell their ware to neighboring islands and raise the requisite crowns for their head tax collected by a native designated as a *muchtar,* or headman. The first Icarian *muchtar* on record was Papas (the title of a priest) Nikolaos Kouloulias who undertook in 1676 to raise the *hatach* of one and one-half groschen per adult male. A century later the Ottoman government replaced the *muchtar* system with a *kaimakames,* governor, who resided in Akamatra, and from there collected taxes and administered justice. He had culprits caned, and apparently, conducted a hanging or two, for today the Akamatrians point to a plane tree in the village square where Turks executed malefactors. The governor mainly punished men who had committed crimes against their fellow Icarians.[30]

Social and Economic Life

Georgirenes' animadversions on Icaria confirmed what the Samians long believed, and were doubtless the source for more unfavorable accounts. Bernard Randolph, a British adventurer who visited Samos shortly after the bishop's trip, reported that the Icarians were so poor that they went out naked on their boats to fish and thus saved wear and tear on their clothing. The Samians told Randolph not to visit Icaria, because when God made the world he created Icaria for its trash heap. Around 1700 Tournefort passed by Icaria. On Myconus he met an Icarian priest, ragged as Lazarus, who told him that the Icarians were barbarous. Judging from the priest's appearance, Tournefort believed it, but discouraged by bad weather, the *meltimi,* he was unable to confirm this opinion by visiting the island.[31]

With such a reputation, Icaria did not entice the few travelers who ventured into the Aegean to step onto its shores. About 1740 William Perry, a medical doctor, was weather-bound on the western tip of Icaria for several days. Perry had heard that there were few inhabitants on the island and those were "almost naked and seldom seeing or conversing with any of the human species except those of their isle." Perry's party met no one on the first day, but on the second, members of the crew who went on a hunting expedition encountered some natives, dressed in rags. The Icarians fled, thinking they had stumbled into pirates. Later, realizing that this was no raiding party, they exchanged meat for bread.[32]

Cut off to some degree from the world, the Icarians developed a distinctive dialect. It was, oddly enough, not Georgirenes, but rather Tournefort who commented on this, characterizing the language as "*plus du Grec literal,*" (ancient Greek) perhaps basing this opinion on his conversation with the Icarian priest in Myconus. This dialect survived well into the 19th century. In 1892 Professor Hatzidakis, the founder of the chair of linguistics at the University of Athens, published an article on the subject, concluding that the Icarians preserved more classical usages than any other Greeks.[33]

The archaic language raises the question of the origin of the Icarians. Georgirenes met people who claimed Byzantine aristocrats, who had fled from Constantinople in 1453, for ancestors. The reliability of an oral tradition of two centuries is not unreasonable, but not guaranteed either. While the names of the great Byzantine aristocratic families, Palaeologoi, Comnenoi, and Catacuzene, are not represented in Icaria, there are some surnames which derive from uniquely Byzantine family names.[34]

An anthropologist, Aris Poulianos, argues that the present Icarians are the lineal descendants of the people who inhabited the island in classical antiquity and perhaps even the Bronze Age. He bases his view on the survival of pagan beliefs and skeletal remains, and maintains that the skulls of present Icarians resemble five thousand-year-old skulls from Crete. His use of skeletal evidence seems highly arbitrary and is difficult to assess. The survival of alleged pagan rituals is common throughout Greece. On several occasions, the population on Icaria nearly vanished, and over the centuries there were waves of new settlers. At best we may conclude that the island was relatively isolated from 1500 to 1600. Perhaps some Icarians from the western interior are descendants from people who inhabited the island in ancient times, but the bulk of the present population is descended from settlers who came from Asia Minor, the other islands, particularly Crete, and from the Peloponnese during the years 1500 to 1825.[35]

Many of the present inhabitants of the island can trace their ancestors back to the 17th century when the first written documents appear. Dowry agreements, bills of sale, and wills of this period record the names of prominent families of the present era—Vlachos, Mamatas, Kazalas, Kefalos, Kouloulias, Koutsophlakes, Kastanias, Glaros, Tsembides, Tripodis, Loukatsos, Karemalis, Kouvdos, Kouvares, Poulos, Lakkios, Raptes, to mention only a few. The few literate Icarian priests (whose signature legitimized the legal document) drafted most of these items.

These wills, dowry agreements, and bills of sale deal with property in the interior, Akamatra, Steli, and Langadha, where a few silver coins— groschen and aslania (akce)—and vineyards, beehives, a plot of land, a pithos (a clay jar about four feet high with a girth of three feet) of wine or grain, sheep, and, in exceptional cases, a cow were priceless possessions. Families subsisted on a small plot of land, with a few animals and an apiary. Beehives, vineyards, and *pithoi* filled with grain and wine, items generally listed in dowries, were powerful lures for suitors. We know little about family life during this period. Georgirenes reports that pregnant women received a double portion of food. Wills from the 17th and 18th century often make provisions for offspring on the basis of services rendered to the parents. It is possible that in such difficult economic circumstances offspring were viewed largely as an asset, and the deep bonds between parents and children, which are so evident in the modern era, had not fully developed.

In 1601 a certain Anna, born in 1521, when the Knights of St. John were lords of Icaria, left land and a vineyard to her son, Papas Xenos, and divided three groschen among two friends. Anna, who apparently was relatively prosperous because she could make a will, possessed some cash. Money came to the island from commerce in wine, charcoal, and timber exported to neighboring islands, but in Icaria itself money for daily needs was almost superfluous. Apart from land transactions based upon four or five silver coins, or fees paid to a priest for services, money rarely changed hands in what Georgirenes accurately saw as a barter economy based on the exchange of sheep, goats, beehives, walnuts, and *pithoi* of wine and grain. The 1610 testament of Angeloudakes of Vrakades, a man from the northwestern part of the island, referred to his possessions in Amalou and Vrakades, but did not mention groschen. The absence of money is more noteworthy in the 1640 wedding gift of Papas Georgios Katzimates to his daughter Kale betrothed to Kur (Sir) Xenon, the son of Papas Ioanniou. It seems that priestly families, the wealthiest members of the community, endeavored to arrange marriages within their group. Papas Katzimates gave his daughter as a dowry property in Myliopo, a remote village in the northeastern section of the island, Raches, Proespera, Langadha, and Amalou. He was one of the most prosperous men of his time and thus able to provide his daughter with three *pithoi* of wine, two *pithoi* of grain, eight beehives, ten sheep, fifteen goats, a bull, and a half a cow. We wonder whether Katzimates butchered the cow and presented half the meat to his daughter or earmarked half the milk to her. In 1643 Papas Gerasimos Gardias—who enjoyed the position of director, *hegoumenos,* of the monastery, without actually being a monk himself, of Saint Theoctestes—bequeathed three large fields in Raches and his sawmill in Campos to heirs in Icaria and his four beehives to the monastery of St. John in Patmos. Presumably, the monastery would lease or sell the beehives to someone in Icaria.[36]

The settlement of the coast depended on assurances that pirates were not a constant menace. Around 1670 pirates drove Georgirenes from Patmos. At that time pirates captured an English gunner named Roberts who described how his subjugators made Icaria an occasional base. Piracy, however, was sporadic rather than a continual problem. Although an occasional pirate raid deterred Icarians from settling coastal areas, it did not prevent them from going to sea. Georgirenes referred to Icarian boat building and trade with Chios, about thirty miles north. There were men, like the Icarian priest whom Tournefort met on Myconus selling timber, who set off by themselves on small boats with modest cargoes. Trade was conducted by *cabotage,* by men setting off with wine, honey, or charcoal in rowboats or small sailboats, and not on large vessels requiring crews, ports, and coastal communities. Piracy was as ineffective at ending this type of trade as the Italian and German forces of the Second World War were when they occupied the Aegean islands and attempted to control Aegean traffic. Icaria was never absolutely isolated from the rest of the world but it was not as integrated into the Aegean community as other islands.[37]

Venturing toward the Coast

At the end of the 17th century, a man named Perdikis, apparently, settled in the village of that name, and a certain Tsimbedes left Kouniado, traveled across the entire island, and allegedly built the first house in Fanari. Papas Gardias' investment in the monastery of Theoctestes, near Campos, and a wood sawmill at Campos suggests a growing sense of security from pirates. By the beginning of the 18th century, references to coastal property become more frequent in the bills of sale, dowries, and wills. Often one person owned property in several villages attesting to an increased interaction between various sections of the island. Men used the few rich plains mainly as grazing land, lived in temporary shacks, and returned to their villages in the interior after their work was finished. A new wave of settlers at the end of the 17th century was a further impetus to colonize the coast. When the Turks took Crete in 1669, and destroyed Candia (Herakleion), which remained in ruins into the next century, some fugitives settled in Icaria. Some of the Italian surnames on Icaria perhaps derive from people arriving from Venetian Crete. The best known of these settlers, however, was renamed when he arrived in Icaria. According to oral tradition this man arrived in Armenistis, where the natives labeled him Kochilas, a derisive sobriquet (*paratzungle*) apparently connected to his survival on crabs and sea urchins. His descendants flourished in Raches and, acquiring new *paratzunglai*, established themselves in southern regions of the island. In 1701 the Turks reconquered southern Greece, producing another wave of refugees leaving the Peloponnese and settling in the islands. Names such as Vassilaros and Moraitis appear in documents. And people from other islands continued to arrive as the names Andriotes (the man of Andros), Kassiotes (the man of Kassos), Parianos (the man of Paros), Creticos (the man of Crete), and Cyprios (the man of Cyprus) indicate. Land was available near the precarious coast, and a few ramshackle structures appeared in these areas. The population also increased in the interior, and price for land nearly doubled. There was a building boom in Langadha with the development of a new section opposite *Paliochora,* the old district.[38]

As piracy waned in the 18th century, the Icarians resettled Evdilos. Permanent coastal settlements established better connections between Icaria and other islands, permitted the use of larger sail vessels rather than small craft which had to be constantly hidden on shore, and brought some measure of prosperity. The improved conditions, which in part were the result of new settlers bringing ideas from the mainland and Crete, are

reflected in the relatively grammatically correct language of the legal documents of the 18th century. Furthermore, these documents reveal more
possessions. Papas Gardias, one of the most prosperous Icarians of the
mid-17th century would have envied the wealth of Papas Zacharias
Malachias who in 1737 bequeathed his house in Kosikia, a village in the
center of the island, gardens, vineyards, five *pithoi* of wine, one of grain,
a bull, a cow, and eleven sheep to his children. By this time such property could now be converted into good sums of cash. In 1791 Nikolaos
Beles sold two fields in *viglas* for fifty groschen.[39]

Religious Life and Superstitions

Judging from the wills of Papas Gardias and Papas Malachias, the
Icarian clergy were the most important and prosperous members of society. Georgirenes, however, was surprised that an Icarian priest visiting
Samos refused to sleep in a bed, and when he visited Icaria, he saw nothing to change his view of the Icarian clergy. Tournefort, who met an ignorant Icarian priest selling timber in Myconus, assumed all Icarian priests
were illiterate. According to Tournefort, there were twenty-four priests in
Icaria, and one monastery. Papas Malachias and Papas Gardias were probably a cut above their twenty-two colleagues who memorized part of the
Liturgy, and were among the few who could read the Liturgy aloud, and
did so, perhaps learning this skill in Patmos where they acquired bibles.
Priests earned money or goods by performing marriages, baptisms, funerals, and, if they were literate, drafting legal records. They also worked
their fields, and engaged, as Tournefort notes and Papas Gardias' will indicates, in commerce.[40] It was not, however, until the end of the 18th century, when Papas Georgios Rhodios came to the island, that Icaria would
have a genuinely educated priest.[41]

Monasteries had an important function on the island not only for religion, but in economics, and education as well. The Icarians, apparently,
took the first steps to honor Saint Theoctestes in the early 17th century.
Around 950 pirates seized Theoctestes, a native of Mytilene. She eventually escaped from her captors and found refuge on Paros where she lived
in isolation and achieved a reputation for her saintly ways. Several centuries later priests, allegedly taking the bones of Theoctestes from Paros
to Mytilene, were forced by storm to seek shelter in Icaria. Natives stole
the bones and hid them in a cave near the village of Marathon, on the
north central part of the island. After many years a peasant, who dreamed

of their whereabouts, discovered them in a valley near the village of Marathon. Pious men chiseled a chapel out of a huge boulder to house the relics. Papas Gardias, it seems, took control of the new religious institution, and did much to promote the bones as relics. Muttering appropriate incantations and carrying the relics through infertile fields or bringing them into the vicinity of sick people, the relics allegedly produced miracles. There were no doctors or medicines on the island so even water from the monastery was highly prized for therapeutic purposes. For such services there was a fee. With proceeds from the relics he built the monastery into the adjacent boulder. An artist from Chios, apparently paid from the earnings of Theoctestes' relics, painted the image of Papas Gardias and his mother on the chapel wall, along with depictions of sinners suffering in hell. The relics and monastery became a very profitable business. Some envious Icarians wished to deprive the entrepreneurial priest of the moneymaking relics. Papas Gardias apparently did not fear the torments of hell as illustrated on his chapel wall for fraud. To his rivals he displayed a charter in the name of the Patriarch Callinicus, granting himself full control of the relics, chapel, and monastery. Melas examined the document and concluded it was a forgery.[42]

The icons in the chapel of Theoctestes depict people undergoing the most horrific tortures the Icarian imagination could summon. Visitors to the chapel saw adulteresses entwined with snakes and other similar punishments meted out to sinners who gossiped, lied, and blasphemed. These images were as forceful as the execration language in legal records of the time. The 17th century will of Papas Malachias warns his legatees not to sell or give away any share of their patrimony lest they incur the testator's malediction and curse, *anathema kai katara,* from the other world. By the end of the century, this type of threat is strengthened. Any heir who does not adhere to the terms of the last will and testament "shall enjoy no joy or success in life *chaeri kai prokope na men di.*" Many documents began with the formula "since we all must pay a common debt and do not know the terrible hour of death," and end with blessings and curses to those who adhere to or reject the terms of the will.[43]

Papas Gardias could make good use of a saint's relics among people whose religious beliefs contained a strong pagan component. For instance, they considered a field where a man had been slain as eternally barren, and endeavored to control high winds by puffing into a vase, cursing the trapped air, then burying the vessel with the imprisoned wind. At the end of the 19th century, the Samian historian Stamatiades remarked that the Icarians were the most superstitious and religious people of the Aegean. An excommunication document drawn up in 1818 supports his view. A thief stole some olives and sheep and vandalized property. The injured party commissioned a priest to draw up an *aphorismos,* a writ of excommunication, condemning the culprit and anyone concealing knowledge of the crime to a tortured existence in hell. Furthermore, the descendants of the thief were destined to endure leprosy, the fate of Judas, and behold all their earthly ventures fail.[44]

The Icarians continued to believe in the efficacy of curses and relics into the 20th century. In 1909, when a blight attacked the Icarian vineyards, cultivators paid 24,000 groschen to the monks of Patmos to bring the relics of St. John to bless the diseased plants. In a time when a family could survive on one hundred groschen a month, this was an enormous sum, and represented more than three times the Icarian annual ecclesiastical tax paid to the patriarch. While the use of relics in such a way has pagan roots, a more clearly pagan practice was an attempt to control the winds, which church officials ended sometime in the 18th century. The villagers of Kataphyion, Negia, and Monokampi met annually at Anemotaphia, presumably in July before the *meltimi* season. They appointed the eldest in the group to blow into a vase that was then buried. Casting curses and stones upon the entombed vessel, they sought to curb the destructive force of summer windstorms.[45]

In some cases, the priests, who provided these services, tended to be less superstitious than their flock. When a plague of caterpillars invaded the vineyards of the island in 1907, the cultivators paid a priest to carry icons, burn incense, and chant prayers in their infested vineyards. After the ritual, the cleric directed his children to remove the caterpillars manually from the vines and destroy them. Even construction plans gave way to superstitious practices. In Raches a man who went to great expense to purchase a lot and prepare the foundations, unearthed bones that smelled like rotten flesh. Discarding his expenditures, he donated the site for a church that was built immediately on the spot.[46]

At memorial services the Icarians differed from their neighbors by offering boiled meat to the congregation rather than *koliva,* boiled wheat, to commemorate the dead. The wealthy shepherds doubtless took the lead in this ritual, but such a practice may also be connected to the *raskoi,* wild goats which were common property. At the end of the 20th century, there were about 8,000 goats on the island but there were doubtless more in the 17th and 18th centuries. The frequent ritual consumption of meat resembled a pagan rather than a Christian ceremony. The custom prescribed the regular distribution of the most precious commodity on the island, a way of sharing the resources of the island, and thus renewed constantly the *ouloi emeis efendi* spirit.[47]

A Way of Life

The Icarians did not construct any significant structures until the 18th century. The inhabitants of Kosikia were rather typical of the 17th century, living in a house cum stable with their animals. This was an improvement over some of the early homes, the *theoctesta,* abodes similar in appearance to the monastery and chapel at Theoctestes, which were cave dwellings. Several of the *spitia,* houses, referred to in the 17th century records, are extant. They are extensions of the granite landscape representing a primal architecture—sturdy, short, and rooted like their inhabitants. On average, these houses were no more than 12 meters by 12 meters, essentially one-room domiciles. Mud was used for mortar. A few had a second story, a *pyrgos,* attached to the lower story and connected by an outside staircase—resembling Byzantine houses depicted in icons. Such was Georgirenes' residence in Raches, the so-called Skirianos house, used in the 1980s as a stable, and in the 1990s as a shelter for Albanian farm workers. Judging from the fact that Georgirenes sojourned there, this house was considered a mansion. The 17th century roof made from local slate laid over timber is still intact. Attempts at imitating this style have failed because contemporary hardwood is inadequate and roof beams made from it rot after a few years. The roof sharply descends to a line parallel to an encircling wall. Upon entering through doors about four and one-half feet high, one sees a niche in the wall for a torch, a circular hearth for an oven, a vent behind the hearth which functioned as a chimney, and a stone bench built into the wall. Contemporaries reported that there was no moveable furniture. The soot-covered walls bear testimony to the practice of blocking the vent to prevent the release of smoke, which might provide pirates with a reference point. This house, like most dwellings of the era, was placed in a secluded spot and could not be seen from the coast, in part because the builder put walls, which blended in with the landscape, between the house and the sea. The bed was simply a board on the earth, the blanket a goatskin. There were no attractive items in the houses except possibly for a stringed musical instrument and a *phylaki,* a shepherds' backpack, made of goatskins.[48]

The toponym *Vigla,* lookout, exists in several places on Icaria. Most of the 17th century settlements depended on *viglas* for security from either a quick sea raid or from corsairs who had temporary bases on the coast.[49] Sentinels with strong voices warned people of impending danger. In Cyprus at that time each village appointed guards to man the *viglas* day and night. When they observed intruders they informed their village by a fire signal. Icarians perhaps were not so efficiently organized for their valuable possessions, *pithoi* full of wine or grain and other such items, were hidden in the earth outside their houses, and pirates were not as likely to raid villages where booty was nearly impossible to locate.[50]

Except for paying taxes, Icaria scarcely felt the hand of the Ottoman government until the early decades of the 18th century. About that time Ottoman authorities divided Icaria into three districts, Peramerias, Fanari, and Mesaria. Peramerias covered the western part of the island stretching from the recently resettled Evdilos to Papas. While Evdilos was the administrative center, Christos Raches, well in the interior, was the largest village. Fanari covered the eastern section. Aghios Kyrikos was not yet founded, and the main villages of this district, Meliopon, Plumari, and Monokampi, were near the Genoese fortifications of Palio Kastro and Kapsalino Kastro. Akamatra, Georgirenes refers to it as *"Ka- Chora,"* was the largest village on the island with about one hundred houses and served as the center of Mesaria and the capital of the island. Akamatra was situated near the villages of Daphi, Petroupoli, Kosika, Langadha, and Frantato, where eighty percent of the people lived. Eventually Akamatra became the residence of the Turkish governor and of the few Turkish officials on the island.[51]

The first evidence of a judicial system comes at the end of the 17th century when the *demogerontia* of Mesaria appointed a five-man jury to adjudicate legal cases, apparently for the entire island. The bulk of the litigation must have been connected to property disputes complicated, as wills and bills of sale from the period attest, by men owning land in various parts of the island. The *demogerontia* of Mesaria appointed *kastellanoi,* gendarmes, to enforce the law for the entire island. The authorities confined some offenders to their homes, others to stockades, and administered 39 lashes for theft or damage to the forests or even capital punishment for murder. In the late 18th century, the *demogerontia* condemned a certain Kalogeros to death for the murder of Papas Koutsouphlakes.[52]

We do not know when such an official first arrived, but there are records of one at the end of the 18th century. There was no Turkish population on the island, and thus the Ottoman officials were not disposed to interfere in local matters. When Icarians wished to appeal the decision of the local council, they did not resort to the resident official, but rather invited a Turkish judicial official, a *tzaoutes,* to investigate the matter. Such procedures were rare for the unsuccessful party paid not only the value of the disputed property, but also for the travel expenses of the *tzaoutes.* The mere threat of an appeal was enough to make one hesitate about litigation, and the risk of such intervention may have prevented the *demogerontia* from behaving in an arbitrary or tyrannical way.[53]

This very minimal system of government provided all the administrative needs for a rural society. Georgirenes, supported by Tournefort, reported that people who lived on this island were more primitive and backward than other people in the Aegean. Haralambos Pamphylis, an Icarian lawyer and politician who published an Icarian newspaper in the mid-1920s, argues that Tournefort was mistaken about Icaria because he was trying to write amusing stories to please M. le comte de Ponchatrain, the official in the French government who supervised his voyage. According to Pamphylis, in the era of Ponchatrain a feudal society prevailed in France that prevented men from understanding their sources, or in fact from reporting the truth. Thus Tournefort perversely misjudged the Icarian priest. Had the French savant stepped onto Icarian shores, he would have found a community more liberal, orderly, and advanced than Tournefort's France. Melas contends that Georgirenes did not stay long enough in Icaria to assess the real conditions of the people. Though there was poverty, Melas argues that the cultural level of Icaria was comparable to that of Athens described in Pericles' funeral oration. If a parallel for 17th and early 18th century Icaria is to be made with the ancient world, Homeric Greece rather than classical Athens would be more apt. A 17th century traveler stepping onto Icarian shores might think he was entering the Cyclops' den rather than Plato's Academy. Alexis Poulianos, however, maintains that conditions in Icaria at this time inspired the utopian scheme of Étienne Cabet (1788–1856). Cabet's *Voyage en Icarie* (1840), which he called a "philosophical and social romance," was a precursor to Marxian ideology, and has features resembling Stalin's totalitarian state. Such a political ideology was appealing to a majority of Icarians in the 20th century, but Cabet had nothing to do with 19th century Icaria, and it is a mystery why he named his utopian community Icaria. The travel accounts and legal documents from the island of that period depict an illiterate, xenophobic people who, despite some cooperative instincts, could not have provided Cabet with a model for his perfect state.[54]

The Reign of the Zambetes

By the middle of the 18th century, Icaria had taken steps to become a respectable member of the Ottoman Empire. Not only was there an Ottoman official on the island, but also the *demogerontia* seemed to function efficiently, and shepherds were now grazing their flocks on the coastal plains. But there were temporary setbacks brought about by the Turko-Russian Wars (1768–1774 and 1787–1792). In the first conflict, Catherine the Great (1729–1796; empress, 1762–1792) sent a small naval force from its base in the Baltic to the Mediterranean. Led by Admiral Alexei Orlov, who relied heavily on British officers, the Russians trapped the main Turkish fleet in the Bay of Chesmé near Mytilene. On July 6, 1770, the Russians stripped the Ottoman Empire of its navy. Shortly after this naval victory, the Russians at a conclave of allies in Chios proclaimed the freedom of the Greek islands, and appealed to Greek sailors to enlist in the Russian navy. The Icarian *demogerontia* sent a delegate to Chios, some 40 miles north, to congratulate the Russians on their victory. Orlov proceeded to occupy Patmos and a few other islands while poorly armed irregular Greek forces attacked with little success various Turkish garrisons along the coast of Asia Minor. Despite the easy victory at Chesmé and showy proclamations about Greek freedom, the Russians did not intend to make the Aegean a major war theater, and aid a Greek insurrection against the Turks. The Russian indifference to the Greeks was revealed in the peace treaty of July 1774. Russia took territory north of the Black Sea, and withdrew from the Aegean, leaving the Greeks in the lurch. The defeated Ottoman navy reentered the Aegean, descended on the islands that had most conspicuously collaborated with Orlov, and took vengeance on pro-Russian elements.[55]

Icaria was slightly compromised by the events of 1770. The *demogerontia* had angered the Porte by sending a delegation to Orlov but the Ottoman authorities let matters slide until 1787 when the second war with Russia broke out. As a precautionary measure the Porte withdrew its official from Akamatra and replaced him with a *zambetes,* a local with dictatorial power. The *zambetes* answered to the Ottoman Grand Admiral of the Aegean, who had placed the islands under military law in anticipation of a second Russian fleet that never appeared. Around 1790 a certain

Stamatis Kastanias assumed the position of *zambetes tes Ikarias*. He clearly enjoyed broader power than the Turkish official he had replaced. According to oral tradition, pirates had kidnapped Kastanias from Icaria at the age of seven, and reared him in the Peloponnesus. The grand Admiral, who commanded a fleet of twenty-two ships of the line and fifteen frigates, prized Greek sailors. Recruited into the Ottoman navy, Kastanias apparently learned Turkish and won the respect of the Grand Admiral who decided to deploy Kastanias to curb the power of the *demogerontia*. He held this office well into the first decade of the 19ᵗʰ century. He collected taxes, issued proclamations in the name of the *demogerontia*, and possessed veto power over the decisions of this body. While the document which allegedly made him *zambetes* does not exist, there are references in contemporary records to a sultan's *firman* that gave him extraordinary power. At times he used his authority wisely. On September 13, 1795, the Icarian *zambetes* proclaimed that whoever hewed a fir tree for the purpose of manufacturing charcoal had to compensate the owner of the land and pay a tax as well. While this enlightened measure may not have been fully appreciated by his subjects, other unspecified acts were perceived as extremely oppressive. This doubtless explains the otherwise unintelligible decree of Papas Christodoulos Kaphakos who in 1795 unilaterally deposed the *haratzomani* of the sultan, apparently a synonym for *zambetes,* in the name of the *Reaya,* (the Ottoman term for non-Muslims). Papas Christodoulos' efforts to oust Kastanias proved unsuccessful, and conditions on the island only returned to normalcy after the death of the *zambetes* at some unknown date. In the late 1930s Stamatis Kastanias known as Captain Stamatis, a lineal descendant of the *zambetes tes Ikarias,* presented the firman to the Greek dictator, Ioannes Metaxas. Kastanias claimed that all of Icaria was his *tzifliki,* private estate. Metaxas replied, "Captain Stamatis, I don't give a damn what the firman grants. You cannot have Icaria."[56]

A Taste of the Greek Enlightenment

After the demise of the *zambetes,* the Ottoman government dispatched an official to Akamatra, and restored local rule to the *demogerontia*. During the first two decades of the 19ᵗʰ century, the Icarians were shedding their poverty as they basked in the glow of nearby prosperity. Icaria was poised for takeoff. An excellent high school had emerged in Chios; the islands of Hydra, Psara, and Spetze developed a merchant fleet of several hundred vessels. The stability of the Aegean was reflected in the practices of the businessmen of these islands. They lent money without a note, and never locked their stores. Captains sailed without fear of pirates, and did not secure valuable cargoes on their ships while in port. A sign of the new sense of security in Icaria was the construction of the monastery of Evangelismos at Levkada, on the southern coast, the first impressive structure built near the sea since the Byzantine period.[57]

Icarians capitalized on opportunities outside their island more than ever. Some Icarians must have settled in Patmos. Around 1750 a family named Kariotes appeared there. Other Icarians found work in Samos. Chios, however, was an El Dorado for the Icarians, and represented in that era what America signified to later generations. They went for menial work, and a few stayed and prospered. The emigration apparently began in the middle of the 17th century when a certain Xenos Makkas left Icaria for Chios, did so well there that he decided to stay, and in 1650 sold his Icarian property. It was no light matter for these alleged descendants of the Palaeologoi to acquiesce to a lowly status in foreign lands, to be mentored, *kybernetai,* by the Chians.[58]

The most successful Icarian immigrant to Chios was the eminent mathematician, Ioannis Tzelipis. Born around 1760, he went to Chios as a young boy. Somehow he managed to study mathematics in Italy, and to become a professor in the famous gymnasium at Chios, the so-called Chian school, one of the main educational institutions for the Greeks of the Ottoman Empire. He translated several important works of mathematics from Italian and French into Greek. We do not know how this destitute boy from Ploumari, a village then of about five houses, obtained the means to study in Italy. In the 1920s some octogenarians in Icaria had heard from their elders, contemporaries of Tzelipis, that the scholar went to Chios to work as a servant for an affluent merchant. According to this tradition the Chian, impressed with the young man's intelligence and dependability, sent him to Italy to serve his sons who were studying at a university. He perused their books, acquired much knowledge, and eventually matriculated in the university himself. There is another possible explanation for this rags-to-riches story. The learned monk Nephon, who had settled in Icaria, was from Chios and knew prosperous people there. Perhaps he ascertained the boy's great intelligence, and arranged for wealthy Chians to help Tzelipis study in the Chian School where Italian and Latin were taught. Arriving in Chios in the 1780s, he soon distinguished himself in his studies, and went to Italy with the aim of obtaining a degree and returning to teach in the high school.[59]

Chapter 1

In 1792, Tz...is petitioned members of the affluent Chian community living in...e arrived in Italy with a thorough grounding in Euclid,
reported...d Galen, but knew little of Newton and recent trends in math-
Aris...geometry, algebra, and optics. Tzelipis intended to introduce the
...cience in Greece, and write about these subjects in plain Greek.
...parently the issue of *katharevousa* versus the simpler *demotike* Greek
was current in the Chian School, and Tzelipis, true to his unpretentious
background, opted for an unadorned written language close to the spoken
idiom. The young scholar, however, needed three more years in Italy,
specifically in Florence and Pisa, to obtain his degree. He, therefore, was
requesting funds to assist him in completing his studies, but this money he
argued was not for himself but for Greece *tou yenou mas.* Appended to the
petition was a letter of recommendation signed by prominent Chian merchants, including the wealthy Lukkas Rallis. We may assume the Chians
in Livorno responded positively to this letter, for he completed the works
outlined in the epistle, and returned to Chios to teach in the celebrated
school which foreigners compared to a European university.[60]

Tzelipis and his family perished in the Turkish punitive expedition to
Chios in 1822. In Chios all traces of him vanished, but in Icaria one of his
letters survived. On October 16, 1814, the Icarian savant had written to
the priest Georgios Rhodios about a property dispute in Icaria. A relative
of the professor had settled in Samos, and returned to Icaria to sell property; it allegedly belonged to two orphaned boys, who were also related to
the professor. Tzelipis, assuming the part of protector for the two brothers, threatened to contest the transaction by appealing to a *tzaoutes,* an
Ottoman official, to adjudicate the matter. Tzelipis warned that such a procedure would be very expensive for the litigants who lost the case. Not
only would they have to reimburse travel expenses but provide a fee for
the Turkish official. While Tzelipis wanted to protect the interest of the
orphans in the land matter, he could not offer them financial support for
he had his own children to sustain, owned no land in Chios, and thus had
to purchase his food. After the orphans resolved their legal problems, he
invited them to Chios to learn a trade or to do menial work. While he was
willing to offer them some minimal protection, Tzelipis warned the boys
that if they were lazy and unwilling to work, they would go hungry.[61] The
letter of the professor, which survived in Icaria, possibly dispels the theory that he married into a thriving Chian family. At any rate, he claimed
that he owned no land in Chios, and therefore must not have received a

dowry. Such a statement, however, must be taken with grain of salt, for it was the standard ploy, much used a century later by an-Americans, to dodge requests for money from poor relatives on the by stress- ing their own financial limitations. We do not know the e the let- ter, but we may assume that Tzelipis was revered in Icaria for com- plishments, and the boys prevailed in this case.

Tzelipis' career as teacher and writer raises the question of li and education in Icaria. Had he received any schooling before going Chios? Though there were then no village schools in Icaria, by the late 18 century monks and priests taught the rudiments in return for chores or a monthly payment of three groschen, and a loaf of bread. Among the pos- sible Icarian teachers of Tzelipis was the monk Nephon, who established the monastery of Evangelismos in the last decades of the 18th century. Born in Chios in 1740 as Nikolas Nikolaras, he was orphaned at an early age. He went to Constantinople to eke out a living as a child worker. After witnessing the death of his closest friend, Nikolaras took monastic vows, assumed the name Nephon, and entered the monastic community at Mt. Athos. Eventually, he came to Icaria where he built, with funds collected in Chios and Smyrna, the monastery Evangelismos in Levkada. Sometime after the completion of the monastery, he left Icaria to serve elsewhere, but returned to spend his last days at Evangelismos, his home, and among the Icarians, the most hospitable of all the people he had known.[62]

Among the first secular educators was George Mavrogenes who came from Istanbul and taught in the Fanari region about 1780. In the next cen- tury, teachers trained in the Evangelical School in Smyrna arrived with textbooks and taught in several villages. Eventually, the *demogerontia* supervised the development of village schools and arranged for the salary of teachers which consisted of money and clothing. The focus was on reading and not writing, and the period of schooling was six years.[63]

The Greek War of Independence

At the beginning of the 19th century, Greece was moving toward inde- pendence from the Ottoman Empire. In 1814 Greek patriots formed the *Philike Hetairia,* Society of Friends in Odessa. The aim of the "Friends" was to free Greece from Ottoman rule. Numbered among the "Friends" was Stavros Klitos, a member of the *demogerontia.* Ioannes Logothetes, whose mother was a Kouloulia from Icaria and who took the unusual step

Chapter 1

of marrying ολ̈ος.[64] the island, was one of the leaders of the independence

movement event leading to independence took place on March 6, 1821, Alexander Ypsilanti, a Greek officer in the Russian army, led forces Moldavia. Though the Turks easily crushed Ypsilanti's troops, the uprising sparked a revolt in the Morea (Peloponnesus) on March 25, 1821. The war quickly spread to all corners of the Greek world, and on April 18, 1821, the Greek flag was raised in Samos. Soon after declaring their independence, a mob of Samians slaughtered Turkish merchants who had recently arrived in Vathi. The Turks retaliated by massacring Samian residents in Asia Minor. The sultan, who considered Samos a necessary naval base through which troops and supplies would be shipped to Greece, dispatched five Turkish ships-of-the-line and four frigates to that island. The Greeks quickly converted commercial vessels into military ships. The bulk of these "war" vessels came from Psara, and the Greeks immediately deployed them to prevent the Turkish fleet from assaulting Samos. The Ottoman navy, however, eluded their adversary and arrived at Samos early in May 1821. The Turkish forces shelled Tigani, driving the populace to the mountains. Dimitrius Ypsilanti, the brother of Alexander, hastened to the Aegean. In Patmos he rendezvoused with the ragtag Greek fleet and in organizing the defense of the islands appointed Ioannes Logothetes to command the Greek forces in Samos.[65]

Greek forces drove the Turkish vessels not only from Samos but also temporarily from the Aegean. This was not entirely a favorable development for the Greeks. Since 1770 the Ottoman navy had been effective in suppressing piracy, but now Greek privateers, many of them former pirates, emerged plundering Turkish possessions on the coast of Asia Minor and then turning on their fellow Greeks in the Aegean islands. The leading citizens of Chios, wealthy merchants who had done much to promote Hellenism, were disturbed by the emergence of violent elements that were plundering Turks and Greeks alike. A sort of class warfare threatened to emerge as a secondary theater to the main conflict. Logothetes recruited a motley force drawn mainly from Samos but including a few Icarians, and proceeded to raid Chios. There he butchered several hundred Turks, and then fled the island. In April 1822, the Turks retaliated, sending an expeditionary force to Chios that slaughtered twenty thousand people. With the exception of a few Icarians who volunteered for the Greek navy, and some who joined Logothetes' force, the Icarians did not play a prominent part in these events, and resisted efforts to be recruited into the

Greek armed forces. After the war the sultan acknow~~~~lged Icaria's non-violent position in the turbulent decade.[66]

Accounts of the massacre in Chios swept through Ica~~ island took on the aspect of a forsaken land. On May 18, 18~~nce the after the catastrophe in Chios, a Greek warship moored nea~~ ~~nth George Jarvis, an American volunteer serving in the Greek ~~ observed that the coastal area, which appeared to have had some rece~~ habitation, now was deserted because the people, out of fear of the Turks, had fled to the "mountains and ravines." Jarvis saw a few miserable stone houses abandoned on the coast, and only the great herds of sheep roaming near the shore, suggested the existence of people somewhere on the island. He hiked into the interior where he met four men in pitiful garments, the standard attire of Icarians according to all travel accounts from Georgirenes to Jarvis. These natives, when ascertaining he was not hostile, approached him. He remarked that they lived in extremely primitive conditions, and it may have been possible to lure some of them to join the fleet. On other occasions officers endeavored to recruit or impress natives into naval service, but on this instance the men of Jarvis' ship were more interested in taking on animals than new sailors, and in the course of the next two years, other Greek ships anchored at Fanari and also plundered Icarian shepherds. Icaria served as the foodbasket for the Greek navy, and the depredations of the Greeks were bitterly remembered on the island for more than a century.[67]

At times, Patmos was the base for the Greek fleet, but goats, sheep, and even water were in short supply there. Thus the Greek fleet continually cruised to Icaria seeking victuals. The people in the interior of the island were less vulnerable to assaults than those on the coast, but they were well aware of what was taking place in Fanari. Around 1823 armed Greeks carrying a Greek flag marched to Raches and conferred with the *demogerontia*. They appealed for men and provisions, and were offering promissory notes from the new Greek government for supplies. By now the Icarians had grown weary of the war. The *demogerontia,* aware of the damage inflicted by the Greek fleet on the shepherds of the island, was unimpressed with the request. They informed the delegation that they had no problems with the Turks, and had nothing to contribute to the war. The deputation left empty-handed but the following year, on July 23, 1824, Admiral Sachtouris, in command of seven vessels, took shelter in Fanari where he used the tower for target practice, perhaps thus registering a protest about Icarian apathetic support of the war. Needing funds to pay his sailors one month's salary in advance, he undertook to exact one thousand groschen, apparently one from each adult male in the Fanari district. The shepherds, who were being ruined by "contributing" sheep to the Greek fleet, petitioned the admiral to distribute the burden of maintaining the fleet more evenly throughout the island, but Sachtouris, as the failed mission to Raches indicates, did not have the ability to make a levy on the more remote parts of the island. The admiral's tax on the Icarians was modest in contrast to the exaction of August 15, 1824, on Kalymnos 10,000 groschen, Karpathos 20,000 groschen, Patmos 8,000 groschen and Leros 2,500 groschen.[68]

The new Greek government, with headquarters in Hydra, an island off the coast of the Peloponnese, encouraged Sachtouris to continue his efforts to collect revenues necessary to maintain a fleet for the protection of the inhabitants of the islands from Turks and pirates. He, therefore, raised his next levy on the Icarians to 8,000 groschen. The Icarian response, which is not extant, may have been similar to the Patmian letter addressed to the government in Hydra in that year. "Because our land is infertile, and the inhabitants impoverished, we cannot pay the tax." The Patmians concluded with the bold assertion that they did not believe that any benefits would accrue from such taxes.[69] The Patmians had a point. The Ottoman navy had done a better job of suppressing piracy than the Greek fleet. Coastal areas of most Aegean islands were unsafe. Evdilos had nearly vanished by 1830, and shepherds feared to graze their flocks on the rich bottomlands. Pirates established temporary bases in coves on the island. The British navy, which operated in the region, regarded Icaria as a pirate base. In 1826, while Sachtouris was moored at Fanari, a British ship pursued a pirate craft to some point in Icaria where the pirates hid their vessel and themselves. They were not as a matter of fact native Icarians, but the British sailors considered them Icarians, and indeed some pirates slipped into villages. Sailors took stories back to Britain about Icarian pirates, and English adventure novels for boys described Icarian villages teeming with pirates.[70]

The sultan's firman of 1835 refers to pirates having ravaged the island during the War of Independence (1821–1830), and Jarvis' description reveals a devastated land during that period. The Icarians had not only lost control of their coastal region, but desperadoes were infiltrating the villages of the interior. An example illustrating how this took place is the case of an alleged refugee from the slaughter of Chios. He settled in a village, and then seduced a girl. The family took matters to the *demogerontia* which ordered the *kastillianoi* to administer the customary thirty-nine lashes to the seducer. Though he eventually married her, the newcomer resented the punishment, and induced his brother, a pirate, to raid the village. It proved to be a destructive foray because the pirates had inside information on where the people kept their property. In response to this attack, the *demarch* of Fanari banned any stranger from settling in the district. Anyone harboring a non-native Icarian would be punished, and his house burned. A newcomer from Symi, who had arrived before the alien law was enacted, invited some of his relatives to join him. The people formed a local militia and in expelling the aliens killed several of them. A folk song deals with an incident from this period. A band of men, we do not know whether they were natives or aliens, came from Perameria to raid the flocks of Papas Koutsoflakes in Petropouli. They murdered the priest, but were apprehend by the men of the village who burned them alive.[71]

The decade of 1820 to 1830 was similar to the half-decade of World War II (1940–1945). The Icarians, cut off from the outside world, suffered privations, degenerated to a degree of anarchy, and resorted to vigilante justice. Men slept in their fields during harvest-time to protect their crops. Homicide, previously a rare occurrence, became more common. For instance, in 1828 a man murdered the seducer of his wife. The *demogerontia* imposed a one-year exile on the malefactor. Returning with arms before the year of exile expired, he intended to murder several members of the *demogerontia*. Arrested before he could consummate the homicides, he was again tried, and during the proceedings there was a reference to one of his relatives, who had also killed someone, and to a general history of the family's violence. The council of elders sentenced him to death, and confiscated his property, which was given to the victim's family.[72]

Turkish rule had begun in Icaria with the murder of a cadi and it ended some two hundred years later when the Icarians ferried the Turkish governor of Icaria, a certain Karampournou, who apparently spent the war in custody, to Chesmé, a city in Asia Minor across from Chios. In 1826 the Icarians began the new era by shifting the capital from Akamatra to Marathon.[73]

1. D. Walker, *The Mediterranean Lands* (London, New York, 1962), p. 28, compares wind activity and rainfall on the lee and windward sides of Aegean islands. Rainfall figures: *Nea Ikaria,* Jan. 1994. Comparative rainfall figures: C. Berghold and K. Styrein, *Surface Water Storage on the*

Island of Ikaria, Greece: A Preliminary Feasibility Study (Stockholm, Royal Institute of Technology, 1993), appendix B, p. 1.

2. J. Melas, *Istoria tou Nesou Ikarias* (Athens, 1958), II, p. 196, cites a decree of the *demogerontia,* Sept. 13, 1795, stipulating that no one, including priests, was allowed to cut trees without a permit. All references to Melas' history are from volume two. In the northern part of the island, there is a higher percentage of arable land; see K. Spyridakis, "Laographike Apostole eis Ikaria," *Epeteris tou Kentrou Ereunes Laographias,* 15–16 (1962–1963), 230, who provides 1960 figures for Raches where 823 acres, out of 10,000 were under cultivation.

3. For the difficulty of ships finding sheltered anchorage off Icaria in antiquity, see *Anth. Pal.* 7. 699, and in the modern era, *New Pilot Directions for the Mediterranean,* Great Britain Admiralty Hydrographic Department (London, 1831), p. 249. H. Kyrieleis, "The Heraion at Samos," in N. Marinatos and R. Haag, *Greek Sanctuaries: New Approaches* (London, 1993), pp. 125–128, reports that the column left standing at the Heraion in Samos, like the tower at Fanari, served as a reference point for sailors. The temple of Artemis at Nas, near a small harbor on the northwest promontory of Icaria, guided sailors along the northern shore. For the maritime function of temples, see Ingrid E. M. Edlund-Berry, *The Gods and the Place: Location and Function in the Countryside of Etruria and Magna Graecia (700–400 B.C.)* (Stockholm, 1987), p. 48. It was not only the absence of harbors that shaped the history of the island. In antiquity it was recognized that there were great differences in climate, resources, topography, and geography among the Aegean islands, and these variations produced distinct social traditions; see G. Reger, *Regionalism and Change in the Economy of Independent Delos* (Berkeley, Los Angeles, and Oxford, 1994), p. 273. In the first half of the 20th century, technological developments tended to minimize the physical differences and thus produce a more homogenized culture within the Aegean islands, but Icaria was untouched by these changes until the 1960s.

4. For an explanation of wind turbulence on the lee side of Aegean islands, see J. Morton, *The Role of the Physical Environment in Ancient Greek Seafaring* (Leiden, 2001), pp. 57–58. The *New Pilot: Great Britain Admiralty Hydrographic Dept., New Piloting directions for the Mediterranean Sea* (London, 1831), p. 249, notes that these winds were especially severe on the lee of Icaria.

5. A. J. Papalas, *Ancient Icaria* (Wauconda, Illinois, 1992), pp. 46–48. Pausanias (9. 11. 15), a second century A.D. Greek author, referred to the tomb of Icarus on the island. Many people on the island today believe that Icarus was a historical person who had dabbled in aviation with unfortunate results. For instance, one person told the author she feared that Icaria might lose some credit for its role in aviation because inaccurate reports were circulating that Jewish engineers in classical antiquity had designed Icarus' wings; interview with an elderly lady, Aghios Kyrikos, May 26, 2002.

Morton, *The Role of the Physical Environment,* pp. 195–197, discusses the
tendency of the ancient Greeks to designate a prominent site as the tomb of
a mythological figure and use it as a navigational landmark. Ichthyoessa:
The contours of the seabed near Icarian shores provide the best breeding
grounds for lobster in the Aegean; interview Antonis Phournos, a thriving
fish merchant, Aghios Kyrikos, June 2, 2001.

6. L. Robert, "Les Asklepieis de l'Archipel," *Revue des Études Grecques,* 46
   (1933), 423–441. Papalas, *Icaria,* pp. 91–94. Despite its mountainous terrain and lack of harbors, Icaria was interdependent on the economy of the
   region. For an explanation of how such regions are integrated in a larger
   area, see P. Horden and N. Purcell, *The Corrupting Sea: A Study of
   Mediterranean History* (Oxford, 2000), pp. 80–81.

7 For Byzantine sea power during this period, see H. Ahrweiler, *Byzance et la
   mer: la marine de guerre la politique et les institutions maritimes de
   Byzance aux VIIe XVe siècles* (Paris, 1966), 159–163. D. Koumparos, *The
   Communal Management of the Radi Forest on Icaria Island Greece,*
   Department of Environmental Studies, University of the Aegean (Mytilene,
   2001), p. 7, notes the uniqueness of the thick Icarian oak forest, vestiges of
   which survive today. Joseph Georgirenes, *Description of Patmos, Samos,
   Nicaria and Mt. Athos* (London, 1677), p. 60, reports that the Icarians,
   despite their alleged isolation, were expert at making boats and other small
   vessels. This skill may have been a survival from their Byzantine tradition.
   S. Vryonis, *The Decline of Medieval Hellenism in Asia Minor* (University
   of California, 1971), pp. 168–170, describes a brutal displacement of
   Greeks from Anatolian urban and rural areas. Apparently, the Aegean was a
   refuge for Greeks and remained predominantly Greek.

8. For a discussion of the Genoese in the Aegean, see H. Ahrweiler, *Byzance
   et la mer,* pp. 230–234. An Icarian ballad, dealing with the Genoese con-
   quest of Icaria, preserves a tradition of Icarian resistance; see W. M.
   Ramsay, "A Romaic Ballad," *Journal of Hellenic Studies,* 1 (1888),
   293–299. For the Knights' Aegean Empire, see Anthony Luttrell, *The
   Hospitallers of Rhodes and their Mediterranean World* (Aldershot,
   Hampshire, Great Britain and Brookfield, Vermont, 1992), and H. J. A. Sire,
   The Knights of Malta (New Haven, 1994), pp. 27–36. Ottoman navy: P.
   Brummett, "The Overrated Adversary: Rhodes and Ottoman Naval Power,"
   Historical Journal, 36, 3–4 (1993), 520. Melas, *Ikarias,* pp. 75–76, pro-
   vides a register of Italian surnames and toponyms.

9. R. Gonzalez, *Embajada a Tamolorán* (Madrid, 1943), pp. 22–24.
   Buondelmonti, in C. Legrand's *Description des îles de l'Archipel* (Paris,
   1897), p. 70, reports Turkish refugees in Samos about 1400. They, apparently, did not become permanent settlers. For Buondelmonti, see R. Stoneman,
   Land of Lost Gods: Search for Classical Greece (Norman, Oklahoma,
   1987), p. 23. Mytilene: J. Georgirenes, *Description,* p. 3. Mytilene: M.
   Margarones, *Geographia Nomou Samou* (Karlovasi, Samos, 1966), pp.
   66–71. Akamatra: Georgirenes, *Description,* p. 2, maintains that the Turks

brought to Samos families "from the voisinage." J. Melas, *Ikarias* 21–25, 55, claims that there are areas near Karlovasi called Kariotika and Akamatra, but there is no mention of them in Margarones' *Geographia Nomou Samou.* Palio-Karlovasi is near the coast but not visible from the sea, doubtless to elude the notice of pirates. Pierre Belon, *Les observations de plusieurs singularités et choses mémorables trouvées en Grèce* (Paris, 1553), p. 86, observed mainly Turkish corsairs, probably based in Fourni, operating near Samos. Georgirenes, *Description,* pp. 3–4, states that these pirates came from Malta, Leghorn, Savoy, and Sardinia.

10. P. Coronelli, *Dell'archipelago* (Venice, 1688), p. 160. As the Turks developed their navy, the need for skilled sailors and oarsmen increased. For the shortage of naval personnel, see Brummett, "Overrated Adversary," 520–553. Sire, *Knights of Malta,* p. 39, says that the Greeks considered the Knights to be "benign overlords." Genoa in Icaria: Papalas, *Ancient Icaria,* pp. 166–168. Raid on Nisyros: Richard Economakis, *Nisyros: History and Architecture of an Aegean Island* (Athens, 2001), p. 85.

11. Turkish fleet: Brummett, "Overrated Adversary," 519–520. Icarian bishops: Pius Bonifacius Gams, *Series Episcoporum Ecclesiae Catholicae* (Washington, 1969, reprint of 1873 original), pp. 448–449. Siege of Rhodes: A. Sire, *Knights of Malta,* pp. 27–36, 53–54.

12. The antipirate policy of the Knights in the Aegean is reflected in a charter cited by Georgirenes, *Description,* p. 81, issued by the Grand Master of Malta to protect Patmos against pirates. The document, which proved to be ineffective about 1650, suggests that at one time the Knights were useful in patrolling the Sporades area. J. Maurand, *Itinéraires d'Antibes à Constantinople 1544* (Paris, 1901), pp. 155–161. Pierre Belon, *Les observations* p. 86. Apostolos Euangelou Vakalopoulos, *Istoria tou Neou Hellenismou,* Volume II, part 1, *Tourkokratia, 1453–*1669 (Thessaloniki, 1964), pp. 41, 182–183, and *Origins of the Greek Nation* (New Brunswick New Jersey, 1970), pp. 221–222, takes Belon's account at face value. For a bibliography on Belon, see S. Yerasimos, *Les voyageurs dans l'Empire ottoman, XIVe–XVIe siècles: Bibliographie, itinéraires, et inventaire des lieux habités* (Ankara, 1991), pp. 188–193. Pirates at Langadha: Alexis Poulianos, *Laika Tragoudia tes Ikarias* (Athens, 1964), p. 260. Population: Jean de Thévenot, *Voyage en Europe, Asie et Afrique* (Amsterdam, 1727), Volume I, pp. 349–352, a French botanist, who passed through the Aegean in 1655, reported that there were about three thousand inhabitants on the island, a high estimate. Thevenot's authority on Icaria is dubious. He reports an implausible Icarian *rite de passage* of naked young men presenting themselves in a public square before the population, women included, marching to an elevated point near the shore, and plunging into the sea. The best divers won the fairest and wealthiest maidens. The tale reveals, however, the separation of Icaria from the rest of the Aegean, an isolation that obliged travelers to invent material when writing about the island. At the time Paros, a much more prosperous island, had a population of around

3,000; see B. J. Slot, *Archipelagus turbatus: les Cyclades entre colonisation latine et occupation ottomane c. 1500–1718* (Leiden, 1982), p. 286. Malaria in coastal regions: J. Lawrence Angel, *The People of Lerna: Analysis of a Prehistoric Aegean Population* (Princeton, 1971), pp. 77–84; L. W. Hackett, *Malaria in Europe: an Ecological Study* (London, 1937), who generally argues that Greece was one of the areas in the Mediterranean most distressed by malaria, and that the affliction was not eradicated until the 20th century. D. Koumparos, *The Radi Forest,* p. 7, notes the value of the Icarian oak forest in providing a screen against pirates.

13. For Selim's naval policy, see the comments of A. C. Hess, "The Ottoman Seaborne Empire, 1453–1525," *American Historical Review,* 75, no. 7 (1970), p. 1911. Piri Reis: S. Soucek, "A propos du livre d'instruction nautique de Piri Reis," *Revue des Etudes Islamiques,* 32, 2 (1971), p. 240, and P. Brummett, *Ottoman Seapower and Levantine Diplomacy in the Age of Discovery* (Albany, 1994), pp. 105–106. For Piri Reis' description of Icaria, the original Turkish text and a Modern Greek translation, see D. Loupes, *O Piri Reis (1465–1553), Chartographei to Aigaiou: E Othomaniki Chartographia kai E Lemne tou Aigaiou* (Athens, 1999), p. 223. For Suleiman's tax policy in the Aegean, see A. M. Andréades, "L'administration financière de la Grèce sous la domination Turque," *Revue des Études Grecques,* 23 (1910), 127. J. Guilmartin, *Gunpowder and Galleys: Changing Technology and Mediterranean Warfare at Sea in the 16th Century* (Cambridge, Massachusetts] 1980), p. 79, notes the special relationship between Suleiman and Genoa. For the prosperity of Chios under Genoese rule and its positive role in the region, see J. Heers, *Gênes au XVe siècle* (Paris, 1961), Volume II, p. 215. The Turks took Tenos in 1715. It was the last island to fall to the Turks.

14. Melas, *Ikarias,* p. 27. For this and the chronology of Aegean islands passing into Ottoman hands, see E. Rouzos, *O Aigaiopelagitikos Politismos Sta Chronia tes Tourkokratias* (Athens 1978), pp. 6–7. Mints: Ş. Pamuk, *A Monetary History of the Ottoman Empire* (Cambridge, England 2000), p. 90.

15. Georgirenes, *Description,* pp. 60–62. Piton de Tournefort, *Relation d'un Voyage au Levant, Fait par ordre du roi* (Amsterdam, 1703), p. 256. Anna and Katzimates: Melas, *Ikarias,* pp. 132–134. Poulianos, *Laika Tragoudia,* p. 260, records a folksong from Langadha which depicts pirates basing their assault on information provided by a resident. Georgirenes, *Description,* p. 66, wrote that "they admit no stranger to settle with them"; it represents an effort to eliminate the fifth-column element, allies of corsairs.

16. For Christophoros: Georgirenes, *Description,* p. 36. Peskes: S. Runciman, *The Great Church in Captivity: A Study of the Patriarchy of Constantinople from the Eve of the Turkish Conquest to the War of Independence* (Cambridge, 1968), pp. 200–202. Fifty patriarchs: A. K. Fortescue, *The Orthodox Eastern Church* (London, 1916), p. 242. Remarks about patriarchs: Sir George, Wheeler quoted by P. Sherrard, *The Greek East and the*

Latin West (London, 1959), pp. 102–103. For the violence of the Venetian-Turkish War, see Rouzos, *Aigaiopelagitikos,* p. 10. Value of groschen: Pamuk, *Monetary,* p. 134.

17. Georgirenes, *Description,* pp. 60–61.

18. Georgirenes, *Description,* pp. 80–83. Runciman, *Great Church,* pp. 33–37, 81, who cites a broadsheet in the British Museum: *Tracts Relating to London,* 1599–1760, pp. 33–37.

19. Georgirenes, *Description,* pp. 63–65.Oral tradition has it that he celebrated the Mass in Saint Basil's Church at Akamatra; see S. Salothas, *Ikariaka* 2 (1976), p. 29. Kosoika, goat houses, suggests that in this village people lived with their animals in their houses; see G. Hatzidakis, "Peri tes Ikarias Dialectou," *Messaionika kai Nea Ellenika* (Amsterdam, 1990), 2, 407. Tournefort, *Relation,* p. 254, notes that some villages consisted of one house. Acquiring health benefits from sleeping on the ground was not entirely an Icarian custom. Pilgrims going to Tenos to pay homage to Panaghia, the Virgin Mary, lay down on the earth to benefit from its curative powers; see Richard H. Blum and Eva Maria Blum, *The Dangerous Hour: The Lore of Crisis and Mystery in Rural Greece* (London and New York, 1970), p. 25. *Petromachi:* suggestion of A. Kalokairinos, e-mail message, March 14, 2003. For the use of keys and cupboards, see M. E. Kenna, *Greek Island Life: Fieldwork on Anafi* (Netherlands, 2001), p. 37.

20. Stentophonical trumpet: Georgirenes, *Description,* p. 65. Horden and Purcell, *The Corrupting Sea,* p. 124, note this as "not an extreme example" of how microregions cohere unassisted by technology. The Icarians deployed their unique combination of mountainous terrain and heavy forest as protection against pirates and tax collectors. Mitropolitos Siderokastros Ioannos, *E Ekklesia tes Ikarias apo tes Idreseos Autes Mechri Semero* (Siderokastros, Greece, 1978), p. 130, cites the 1640 dowry agreement of Kale, the daughter of Papas Georgios Katzimates betrothed to Xenos, son of Papas Ioanniou. The villages of these priests are not recorded, but the father of Kale provided his daughter with property in Raches, Proespera, Langadha, Amalou, and Meliopon. For this document he is indebted to Melas.

21. Georgirenes, *Description,* p. 70. Nephon: I. D. Tsarnas, "Istoria tes Ieras Mones tou Evangelesmou Levkadas, *Ikariaka,* 37 (1966), pp. 11–13. Tsarnas, *Ikariaka Phoné,* 7 (1976), p. 11. Hospitality: Spyridakis, "Laographike," 234–235; Stamatiades, *Ikariaka,* p. 101. Extra plate: A. Plakidas, *It Could Happen Only in America* (Athens, 1966), p. 23. Dilys Powell, *Remember Greece* (New York, 1943), pp. 15–18, each morning found fruit at the door of her house provided by anonymous Icarians. Force strangers to eat: H. Hauttecoeur, "L'île d'Icaria," *Bulletin de la Société Geographiques d'Anvers* 25, (1900), 348.

22. Life span: L. Angel, *The People of Lerna,* p. 77. People on the island seem to have had a longer life span than those on the mainland. James Dallaway,

Constantinople Ancient and Modern, with Excursions to the Shores and Islands of the Archipelago and the Troad (London, 1797), pp. 284–285, met a man in Chios allegedly 120 years old and commented that such "longevity was not uncommon in the Greek islands." Great plague in Chios: Guillaume Olivier, *Voyage dans l'Empire Ottoman, l'Egypte et la Perse fait par ordre du gouvernement, pendant les six premières années de la République* (Paris, 1801–1807), pp. 123–124. In the Aegean, plagues seem to have been a reoccurring problem in the 18th century. When Alexei Orlov issued his proclamation of independence for the Greek islands, he appealed for sailors to man his fleet, but specified that men from plague-infested areas were unwelcome; see T. E. Evangelidos, *E Mykenos: Istoria tes Nesou apo ton Archaiotaton Chronon Mechri ton Kath Emas,* (Athens, 1914), p. 143. Interview of octogenarian: Melas, *Ikarias,* p. 59. Construction of houses: W. McNeil, *Plagues and People* (New York, 1976), pp. 173, 253.

23. The Icarians were not the only islanders to hide assets to evade taxes. The Chians concealed their wealth by forbidding women to wear expensive clothing or jewelry, Philip P. Argenti, *Chius Vincta or the Occupation of Chios by the Turks (1566) & Their Administration of the Island, 1566–1912* (Cambridge, England, 1941), p. ccxxiii. Assessment of taxes: A. Andreades, "L'administration financière de la Grèce sous la domination Turque," *Revue des Études Grecques* 23 (1910), 27–28. Georgirenes, *Description,* p. 18, reports that village priests in Samos kept lists of adult males for tax purposes. Tax of 1669–1670: Slot, *Archipelagus Turbatus,* pp. 213–214. See B. Lewis, *The Emergence of Modern Turkey* (Oxford, 1966), p. 33, for the rapacious practices of tax-farmers and their ruinous effects on the economy.

24. Georgirenes, *Description,* pp. 66–67. Trial in Icaria: Bürchner, "Ikaros," 980.

25. Georgirenes, *Description,* pp. 66–67. K. Tsapaliares, *E Nesos Ikaria* (Athens, 1927), pp. 144–145, mistakenly put this event about 1690, after Georgirenes' visit. Ch. Th. Parianos, *Kai O Demokratikos Stratos Ikarias* (Athens, 2000), pp. 60–61, recounts the oral version. An old lady told him the tale in 1948 when he was a guerrilla and temporarily concealed in her house. The reliability of the oral tradition is borne out by the topographical details in the story that helped Parianos find and hide in the same cave as that in which the cadi's slayers took refuge.

26. The concept of corporate liability was recognized on other islands as well; see Philip P. Argenti, *Chius Vincta,* pp. cxlv–cxlvi. Canons: Guilmartin, *Gunpowder and Galleys,* pp. 77–78. Taxes: Aegean Doomsday Book: Slot, *Archipelagus Turbatus,* p. 302. Repopulate deserted areas: C. Imber, "The Navy of Suleiman the Magnificent," *Archivum Ottomanicum,* 1980, p. 276.

27. Georgirenes, *Description,* pp. 68–69. Testaments: see note 36. Value of gold coins: Pamuk, *Monetary History,* p. 69.

28. Tournefort, *Relations,* p. 255. Melas, *Ikarias,* 132. For various grades of hatch see Andreades, "L'administration," 146. Groschen: Foreign travelers

called it a piaster while the Icarians later referred to the coin as groschen, or aslania, akce. The groschen remained the standard monetary unit until 1912 when Icaria became independent. One hundred groschen equaled a Turkish lira. Melas, *Ikarias,* 125. Georgirenes, *Description,* pp. 66–67. For the importance of the head tax, see the comments of A. Andreades, "L'administration financière" 148.

29. Georgirenes, *Description,* pp. 66–67. Ronald Jennings, "The Population, Taxation, and Wealth in Cities of Cyprus According to the Detailed Population Survey (Defter-I-Mufasial of 1572)," *Journal of Turkish Studies,* 10 (1986), 175–189, analyzes the Turkish agriculture survey made in Cyprus in 1572. For the Byzantine period and the Genoese adoption of the Byzantine tax system, see F. Dölger, *Beiträge zur Geschichte der byzantinischen Finanzverwaltung besonders d. 10 u. 11 Jahrhundert* (Leipzig, 1917), pp. 47, 107, 147. Aegean doomsday book: B. J. Slot, *Archipelagus Turbatus,* pp. 302–309. H. Gerber, "Jewish Tax Farmers in the Ottoman Empire in the 16th and 17th Centuries," *Journal of Turkish Studies,* 10 (1986), 143–145, contrasts the Chian economy with that of the other islands where the *Reaya* struggled to raise taxes. Eleven groschen (piasters): Lord Charlement, *The Travels of Lord Charlement in Greece and Turkey,* ed. by W. B. Stanford and E. J. Finopoulos (London, 1984), pp. 31–32. Lively Aegean trade: Slot, *Archipelagus Turbatus,* pp. 217–218. Mastic: In 1292 the Catalan-Aragonese fleet raided Chios confiscating its mastic production which was worth 11,529 ounces of gold, more than needed to operate the fleet for an entire year; see Lawrence V. Mott, *Sea Power in the Medieval Mediterranean: The Catalan-Aragonese Fleet in the War of the Sicilian Vespers* (Gainesville, Florida, 2003), p. 255.

30. First Turkish official: Melas, *Ikarias,* p. 132. Samian economy and Icarian products: Georgirenes, *Description,* pp. 30–32; 60–61. Hangings: Interview with villagers in Akamatra, June 2, 2001.

31. Bernard Randolph, *The Present State of the Islands in the Archipelago, (or Arches) Sea of Constantinople, and Gulph of Smyrna; with the islands of Candia, and Rhodes. Faithfully Described by Ber. Randolph. To Which is annexed an index, shewing the longitude and latitude of all the places in the new map of Greece lately published by the same author (*Oxford, 1687), pp. 53–54. Tournefort, *Relation,* p. 254. For Tournefort, see D. Constantine, *Early Greek Travellers and the Hellenic Ideal,* (Cambridge, [England 1984), p. 55; O. Augustinos, *French Odysseys: Greece in French Travel Literature from the Renaissance to the Romantic Era* (Baltimore, 1994), p. 70.

32. Charles Perry, *A View of the Levant Particularly of Constantinople, Syria, Egypt, and Greece* (London, 1743), p. 485.

33. Tournefort, *Relation,* p. 254. For the dialect, see G. Hatzidakis, "Peri tes Ikarias Dialectou," 2, 397–460. One of Hatzidakis' aims was to refute Fallmaeyer's thesis that Modern Greeks were essentially descendants of

Slavs. Hatzidakis' tour of the various Icarian villages on donkey left a vivid impression on the people. Ep. Stamatiades, *Ikariaka* (Samos, 1893), p. 62.

34. A. Vakalopoulos, *Istoria tou Neou Ellenismou* (Thessaloniki, 1964), p. 107, is mistaken in his view that a great number the names from the Byzantine aristocracy persisted in Icaria. He bases his view on certain 19th century travel accounts of the Aegean which he considers unreliable elsewhere, *Istoria,* p. 43. In Icaria, our extant records begin to appear in the early 17th century unlike Chios, where documents with names of present-day families go back to the 14th century; see Argenti, *Chius Vincta,* p. clxxxiii. Melas, *Ikarias,* pp. 76–77, suggests that the Icarian family names of Maurice, Pardos, Lascaris, and Klekas are connected to great Byzantine families. This is unlikely. Melas does not appreciate the irony of Georgirenes, who contrasted the ill-clad Icarians with their *porphyrogenetoi,* born-to-the-royal-purple, pretensions and takes the bishop's observation as evidence that some 17th–century Icarians were descendants of the Byzantine nobility. In local lore a man named Kounias, allegedly a noble from Konya, settled in Kouniado sometime in the 13th century. Perhaps Georgirenes heard such stories. At any rate, the bishop was the source for the subsequent reports on this connection, but the reference to the alleged Byzantine relationship is a key element in his satirical treatment of the Icarians. Georgirenes insinuated that these self-professed *porphyrogenetoi* were the real *choriates, "red-necks"* of the Aegean.

35. Aris Poulianos, *E Proeleuse ton Ellenon* (Athens, 1982), pp. 66–67, 101–102, takes issue with Fallmaeyer and argues that the same race occupied Greece from the Neolithic to the present period, and that foreign infusions in the original Hellenic racial stock were minimal. Poulianos offers Icaria as a case study for his position. He notes the alleged practice of Icarians wrestling with Charon to save the life of sick friends. Poulianos does not cite any folktale or any other evidence for this. I have never encountered or heard of such a ritual in Icaria, and it does not seem to have ever been widely practiced. But there is such a tradition in other parts of Greece observed in folk literature. M. Alexiou, "Modern Greek Folklore and its Relation to the Past: The Evolution of Charos in Greek Tradition," in S. Vyronis, ed. *The "Past" in Medieval and Modern Greek Culture,* (Malibu, California, 1978), pp. 221–236, notes Euripides (*Alkestis* 843–849), as the origin of the wrestling story, but the version which appears in modern Greek tradition has the hero wrestling Charon for his own soul.

36. Documents: A. Tzelikas, *Ikariaka Engrapha: Tou 16[ou] kai 17[ou] Aiona apo to Archeio tes Panikariakes Adelphotetas Athenon* (Athens, 2000), pp. 18, 19, notes the sale of a field, probably a terraced plot, for four *aslania (akce)* silver coins. At that time in the Ottoman navy, an oarsman made 3 to 4 akces a day; see Imber, "The Navy of Suleiman," p. 267. Other such documents are in the collection of J. A. Papalas, *Icarian Documents* (unpublished, 1962) in possession of the author. The parchment for these documents probably came from Patmos; see D. G. Davais, *Patmos: The Sacred Island.*

Icarian wine: Francesco Lupazzolo's comment, about 1630, cited in F. W. Hasluck, "Depopulation in the Aegean Islands," *Annual of the British School at Athens,* 17 (1922), 153–154. Wooden boats, and charcoal: Georgirenes: *Description,* pp. 60–61; Piton de Tournefort, *Relation d'un voyage au Levant, fait par ordre du roi* (Amsterdam, 1703), p. 254. Anna and Katzimates: Melas, *Ikarias,* p. 366. Garidas: Spyridakis, "Laographike Apostole eis Ikaria," p. 237; Melas, *Ikarias,* pp. 132–134. E. Stamatiades, *Ikariaka* (Samos, 1893), pp. 68–74.

37. Georgirenes, *Description,* pp. 64–65. Mr. Roberts, *Adventures among the Corsairs of the Levant. His Account of their Villainous Ways of Living. Description of the Archipelago* (London, 1694), pp. 117–118.

38. George Jarvis, *Americans in the Greek Revolution,* edited by George G. Arnakis (Thessaloniki, 1965), pp. 47–48, saw such poorly built structures on the coast of Icaria as late as 1822. For the consequences of the Turkish-Venetian war, see Stamatiades, *Samiaka* (Samos, 1882), 2, 59. Georgirenes, *Description,* p. 81, discussed Christian pirates harassing the monks of Patmos. Apparently, in the previous century the remains of John the Evangelist protected the monks from such raids by Muslim pirates. Pirates who endeavored to loot the monastery received mysterious wounds; see A. Adorno, *Itinéraire d'Anselme Adorno en Terre Sainte: (1470–1471),* edited by Jacques Heers (Paris, 1978), p. 362. Tournefort, *Relations,* p. 137, describes the result of the devastation of Herakleion in 1700. The few remaining inhabitants found shelter in shanties. Perdiki: Tselikas, *Ikariaka,* (doc. 11). Increase in price of land: Tselikas, *Ikariaka,* documents 5, 7, 10, 12, 16, 17, 18, 19, 20, 25, 36, 38, 43, 45, 48, 51, 53, 96, 101, 117. Paliochorafia in Langadha, Tselikas, *Ikariaka,* document 4. See Rouzos, *Aigaiopelagitikos,* p. 17 for immigration to islands to escape Turkish oppression.

39. New blood: Rouzos, *Aigaiopelagitikos,* p. 17. Andreades, "L'Administration," p. 66, n. 1, marks 1700 as the beginning of a gradual decline of piracy. Wills: Tselikas, *Documents,* 18–19. Beles' will prepared by Papas Rhodios, Jan. 20, 1791.

40. Georgirenes, *Description,* p. 63, Tournefort, *Relation,* p. 254, and Melas, *Ikarias,* pp. 89–91. It was not until late in the 19th century that notaries appeared in Icaria. Function of notaries on islands: see Argenti, *Chius Vincta,* pp. cxc–cxci.

41. J. Melas, "Georgios Rhodios," *Ikariaka* 8 (1959), pp. 6–15. Tsarnas, *Ikariaka,* 7 (1976), pp. 16–17.

42. According to the *Vita S. Theoctestae,* 12–15, *Acta Sanctorum,* an ambassador of Leo VI about 900 heard on Paros about Cretan pirates transporting Theoctestes' relics from Mytilene to Paros. When the people of Mytilene decided to bring back the saint's bones is not clear. For the monastery see Spyridakis, "Laographike apostole eis Ikaria," p. 237; C. Stavrinou-Baltogianni describes the paintings, see *Archaologikon Deltion,* 20 (1965),

502–504. Also see the comments of Melas, *Ikarias,* pp. 132–134; Stamatiades, *Ikariaka* (Samos, 1893), pp. 68–74. Gardias was not only the hegoumenos but also the only monk. The Icarians calling a village a place with one house and a monastery a dwelling with one monk amused Tournefort, *Relation,* p. 254. Forged document: Melas, *Ikarias,* p. 266. For the alleged curative power of these relics, see Mitropolitos Siderokastros Ioannos, *E Ekklesia tes Ikarias apo tes Idreseos Autes mechri Semero,* pp. 126–127. Blessed water: H. Hauttecouer, "L'île d'Icaria," 358.

43. There are similar icons in the church of St. John in Kosika; see Melas, *Ikarias,* pp. 252–254, and P. Baliotes, "Kosikas" *Ikariaka* 7 (1958), 12–15.

44. Stamatiades, *Ikariaka,* pp. 68–74; 103–104, 116–119, who notes, among other beliefs, a lively fear of vampires. Although Stamatiades is an excellent source for Aegean practices, we should not assume that neighboring islands were considerably more enlightened. See C. Stewart's remarks on Naxos, *Demons and the Devil* (Princeton 1991), pp. 103–104, 258–259. Aphorismos: A. Plakidas, "Allo Ena Palio Kariotiko Engrapho," *Ikariaka* 37 (1966), 188.

45. Relics of St. John: A. G. Plakidas, "Icarian Phytopathological Remedies," *Pan-Icarian Convention Book* (Youngstown, Ohio 1935), no pagination. Witnessing the ineffective application of the relics was a turning point in Plakidas' life. Several years later he went to the United States, and eventually acquired a Ph.D. in botany specializing in phylloxera and other genera of plant lice. Rather than returning to Icaria he taught for many years at Louisiana State University. Ecclesiastic tax: in 1903 the Icarians paid 6,500 groschen annually to the Metropolitan in Samos; see G. Lombardas, *Ikaria eto Geographike tes Nesou Perigraphe* (Syros, Greece, 1903), p.38. Ceremony of the winds: G. Megas, "Ta Anemotaphia tes Ikarias," *Deltion tes Ellenikes Laographikes Etaireias,* 16, 1 (1956), 250–256.

46. A. Plakidas, *Pan-Icarian Convention Book* (Youngstown, Ohio, 1935) in Icarian Archives, (Verona, Pennsylvania). Melas, *Ikarias,* pp. 132–135.

47. For the establishment of the church, monastery, and boiled-meat practice, see Spyridakis, "Laographike Apostole," pp. 237–242. *Raskoi:* D. Koumparos, "The Communal Management of the Radi Forest," p. 7. One may compare the practice of distributing meat at Icarian memorial services with similar customs at pagan festivals; see M. H. Jameson, "Sacrifice and Animal Husbandry in Classical Greece," in C. R. Whitaker, ed., *Pastoral Economies in Classical Antiquity,* Cambridge Philosophical Society Supplementary Volume 14 (Cambridge, England 1988), p. 107.

48. Theoctesta: Hatzidakis, "Dialectou," p. 407. See J. Tsarnas, *Ikariaka,* 20 (1993), pp. 11–12, for the dimensions of the standard Icarian house. A. Hatzimichalis, "L'Art populaire Grec. L'île d'Icarie," *Byzantinische-neu-griechische Jahrbücher,* 6 (1927/1928), 211–213 provides a more detailed discussion of Icarian dwellings. Also see the comments of Melas, *Ikarias,* pp. 48–49. For the oral tradition about Georgirenes, see S. Salotas, *Ikariaka*

7 (1976), p. 29. The owner of the house, Christos Spanos, heard the story from his father who was born around 1860. Interview with C. Spanos, June 7, 1984, Raches, Icaria.

49. Mr. Roberts, *Adventure among the Corsairs,* p. 36. Hiding money outside the house remained a practice well into the 20th century. In Raches around 1920 a certain Skirianos, one of the most prosperous men in the area, concealed his life savings, gold sovereigns, in a wall enclosing one of his fields; interview Ch. Spanos, June 7, 1984.

50. Our best example of a pirate raid comes from an earlier period but provides us with a model for such incursions. About the year 1200, pirates raided Patmos, took food from the monks, and then came to Icaria. Apparently, watchmen in a lookout spotted them, alerted the people to the danger, and a force met them as they landed and exterminated the marauders; see Vranoussis, *Ta Agiologika Keimena tou Osiou Christodoulou Idrytou tes en Patmo Mones Philologike Paradoses kai Istorika kai Martyriai* (Athens, 1960), pp. 70–75 Viglas in Cyprus deployed against pirates in a similar manner: Louis, Conte de Mas-Latrie, *Histoire de l'île de Chypre sous le règne des princes de la maison de Lusignan* (Paris, 3 volumes, 1852–1861), 3, 238. By the late 17th century, pirate attacks into the interior had ceased. Georgirenes, *Description,* p. 63, writes "their few possessions are hid underground, not so much for fear of the corsairs, from whom their poverty is a sure guard, as out of custom." P. Savorinakes, *Nesiotikes Koinonies Sto Aigaio: E Periptose ton Ellenon tes Rodou [Rhodou?] kai Ko 19ou 20ou Aionas* (Athens, n.d.), p. 106, discusses the shifting Ottoman administrative centers in the Sporades and Dodecanese.

51. Georgirenes, *Description,* p. 61. Stamatiades, *Ikariaka,* pp. 64–65; Melas, *Ikarias,* pp. 125–126.

52. Melas, *Ikarias,* pp. 91, 125–126. Various punishments: C. Makkas, *Atheras,* Nov. Dec. 1994. Stamatiades, *Ikariaka,* 64–65.

53. For the role of the Tzaoutes, see I. Tsarnas, "I. Tzelipis O Mathematikos," *Ikaria* 9 (1959), 9.

54. Haralambos Pamphylis' editorial in Pandeki, December 15, 1928, issue 5, p. 76. Periclean Athens: Melas, *Ikarias,* p. 105. Alexis Poulianos, *Laographia Ikarias* (Athens, 1976), Volume I, 11–13, makes the unreasonable argument that Cabet had sources, no longer extant, which revealed that Icarians did not exploit Icarians. Poulianos asserts that he, as a simple Icarian, has no need to cite sources to prove his view about Cabet. He concludes that he will leave this task to pompous scholars.

55. Chesmé: N. E. Saul, *Russia and the Mediterranean 1797–1897* (Chicago, 1970), pp. 6–7. Turkish reprisals against islands: Rozos, *Aigiaopelagitikos,* p. 11, asserts "many islands paid a high price for their cooperation with the Russians." T. E. Evangelidos, *E Mykenos: Istoria tes Nesou apo ton Archaiotaton Chronon Mechri ton kath Emas* (Athens, 1914), pp. 142–143,

cites the diary of a British officer in the service of Russia who recorded the Icarian delegation to Orlov. Also see M. Malandrakes, "Nesiotika Chronia," *Ellenika* 10 (1937/1938), 69–116.

56. Kastanias: Melas, *Ikarias,* pp. 115–116. Melas cites a conversation with his friend T. Sophoulis, member of the Metaxas government and later prime minister, as the source of the Capitanios Stamatis story. For problems controlling local despots, see Argenti, *Chius Vincta,* pp. cxlv–cxlvi. The Ottoman navy in the Aegean: C. Anderson, *Naval War in the Levant: 1559–1853* (Princeton, 1952), pp. 318–347; S. J. Shaw, "Selim III and the Ottoman Navy," *Turcica: Revue d'études turques,* 1, (1969), 213. Zambetes and Christodoulos: Melas, *Ikarias,* p. 148.

57. For the practices of merchants and captains, see the remarks of Mavrocordatos to Howe, Samuel Gridley Howe, *An Historical Sketch of the Greek Revolution,* edited by George Georgiades Arnakis in the series Americans in the Greek Revolution (Austin, Texas, 1966; [reprint of New York 1828 edition]), p. 172, and D. Dakin, *The Greek Struggle for Independence, 1821–1833* (Berkeley and Los Angeles, 1973), pp. 75–76. For the decline in piracy, see, A. A. Andreades, "L'administration financiere," 66. The reduction of piracy after 1770 may be attributed to the modernization of the Ottoman navy; see S. J. Shaw, "Selim III and the Ottoman Navy," *Turcica: Revue d'Études Turques,* I (1969), 210. Piracy, however, did not disappear, and there was an outbreak of piratical activity in the northern Sporades around 1813 when a depression hit Aegean trade; see K. Papathanasopoulos, "Greek Shipping in its Historical Context," *Greece and the Sea* (Amsterdam, 1987), p. 106. Monastery: I. D. Tsarnas, "Istoria tes Ieras Mones tou Evangelesmou Levkadas," *Ikariaka,* 37 (1966).

58. Xenos Makkas: signed by a friend, George Kouvares; see Tselikas, *Ikariaka,* document 22. *Kybernetai:* letter of Tzelipis, in I. D. Tsarnas, *Ioannes Tzelipis: O Mathematikos Didaskalos tou Genous kai Ethnomartyras* (Athens, 1998), pp. 24–25. Kariotes: S. Asdrachas and I. Asdracha, "Baptistika kai Oikogeneaka Onomata se mia Nesiotike Koinonia: Patmos" in *Ste Mneme P. Apostolopoulou* (Athens, 1984), 66.

59. Oral tradition: L. Spanos, *Ikariaka Chronica* (Syros, Greece, 1925), pp. 70–71. Kybernetai: I. Tsarnas, *Ioannes Tzelipis* pp. 18–19. *George Jarvis; His Journal and Related Documents. Edited with Introduction, Prologues, Sequel, and Notes, by George Georgiades Arnakis. With the Collaboration of Eurydice Demetracopoulou* in his series "Americans in the Greek Revolution" (Thessaloniki, Greece 1965), pp. 47–48. Jarvis, who wrote in English, French, Greek, and German, described the gymnasium as "eine Universität." Europeans who visited Chios at the end of the 19th century noted that Italian and Latin were taught in the high school; see P. Argenti, S. P. Kyriakidis, *E Chios Para tois Geographois kai Perigetes* (Athens, 1946), p. 82–83.

60. Some of these enlightened Chian merchants who supported the type of work Tzelipis was doing were in Russia; see P. Herlihy, "The Greek Communities in Odessa, 1816–1917," *Journal of Modern Greek Studies* 7, 2 (1988), 242–244. Also see P. Argenti, *Chius Vincta,* p. ccx. For the change in the scientific curriculum in Greek schools in the 18th century, see T. Evangelidis, *E Paideia epi Tourkokratias* (Athens, 1936), I, 3–24. For comments on the type of teachers in Chian schools, see T. Ware, *Eustratios Argenti: A Study of the Greek Church Under Turkish Rule* (Oxford, 1964), pp. 45–47.

61. I. Tsarnas, *Ioannes Tzelipis,* pp. 24–25.

62. Spyridakis, "Laographike Apostole," 234–235; Stamatiades, *Ikariaka,* p. 101. The proportion of Greeks who could read and write was comparable to that of any other contemporary European nation; see the remarks of G. Finlay, *A History of Greece* (Oxford, 1877), 5, 283. Nephon: I. Tsarnas, "Istoria tes Ieras Mones tou Evangelesmou Levkadas, *Ikariaka,* 37 (1966); I. Tsarnas, *Ikariaka Phoné,* 7 (1976), 11.

63. Secular teacher: I. Tsarnas, *Ikariaka,* 1991, p. 38. Influence of Smyrna: G. Augustinos, *The Greeks of Asia Minor: Confessions, Community, and Ethnicity in the Nineteenth Century* (Kent, Ohio 1992), p. 222, n. 53.

64. Logothetes' mother was a Kouloulias from Icaria: Kosta I. Ptinis, *E Samos kai to 1821* (Samos, 1990), 36–37. Slaughter of Turks and reprisals: Ptinis, *Samos,* pp. 45, 62.

65. Ptinis, *Samos,* pp. 71–75; 84.

66. The Chians as the most prosperous people in the Aegean: Argenti, *Chius Vincta,* pp. 208–227, and Argenti, Kyrakidis, *E Chios,* pp. 832–833. Logothetes: Ptinis, *Samos,* p. 84. M. Kastanias, from Galiskari, led the Icarian contingent in Logothetes' force; see K. Tsapaliares, *Ikaria,* pp. 147–148, who apparently had some reliable oral sources a century after the event. Limited role of Icaria: see Ptinis, *Samos,* pp. 8, 40–44. Sultan's firman: G. Lombardas, *Ikaria etoi Geographike tes Nesou Perigraphe* (Syros, Greece, 1903), p. 42, who writes, "they have remained faithful to my empire." For an English translation, see C. D and I. B. Booth, *Italy's Aegean Possessions* (London, 1928), pp. 203–204.

67. *George Jarvis, His Journal and Related Documents,* pp. 47–48. Sachtouris, July 26, 1842, refers to the petition of Icarians from Fanari for damages done by the two previous fleets. The officers of these fleets probably rustled the bulk of the grazing animals noted by Jarvis; see K. Tsapaliares, *Ikaria,* pp.147–148, who provides long excerpts from the admiral's diary. Employment in the Greek fleet was an opportunity for Icarians such as Captain Ioannes Malachias depicted in the novel of T. G. Malachias, *O Gero Kapetan Giannis Malachias* (Athens, 1985). Based on oral tradition, this work deals with the revolutionary-war period and the rise of the Malachias family.

68. The Greek fleet in the 1820s: E. Protopsaltes, "E Tyche ton Notion Sporadon kata ten Epanastasin kai met' auten," *Karpathiakai Meletai* 2 (1981), 287–307; see Daikin, *Greek Revolution,* pp. 75–76, and K. Alexandris, *The Greek Marine in the War of Independence* (Athens, 1968). K. Tsapaliares, *Ikaria,* pp. 147–153, provides excerpts from Sachtouris' diary. Taxes: Tsapaliares, *Ikaria,* pp. 149–150. Patmos: E. Rozos, *Oi Nesiotes tou Aegaiou ston Agona* (Athens, 1971), p. 275. See the work of Theologos Malachias, *Anekdota Diegmata* (Athens, 1967), 1, 15–17, who ironically describes the appetite of the Greek sailors being whetted by the fresh sea air, and how their officers gave them a free hand in Icaria. Christos Spanos remembers hearing stories from old men about 1920 about the recruiters who came to Raches around 1823, interview Raches, June 12, 1961. The tradition confirmed by Angelos Kalokairenos: e-mail note Icaria, June 28, 2002, who heard the story from Stamatis Malachias, born in Raches about 1890.

69. Howe, *An Historical,* p. 172, argues that the Greek fleet performed an effective military barrier against the Turkish fleet and protected the islands from Captain Pasha. Patmos: Melas, *Ikarias,* pp. 109, 168. Spanos, *Ikaria,* pp. 96–97, who cites entries from Sachtouris' diary.

70. C. G. Pitcairn Jones, *Piracy in the Levant, Selected Papers of Admiral Edward Codrington* (Navy Records, London, 1934), p. 62. Also see the anonymous *Life of a Midshipman: A Tale Founded on Fact and Intended to Correct an Injudicious Predilection in Boys for the Life of a Sailor* (London, 1829), who notes how Icarian pirates captured and held young Frank Hartwell, a fictional character, and forced him to participate in raids on ships sailing between the Greek mainland and Asia Minor. The author's description of pirate life in an Icarian village is sheer fantasy.

71. Sultan's firman: G. Lombardas, *Ikaria eto Geographike tes Nesou Perigraphe* (Syros, Greece, 1903), p. 42, "they have undergone great losses by the acts of evil-doers, rebels and pirates." Pirates and Legislation: Melas, *Ikarias,* pp. 157–159, and Stamatiades, *Ikariaka,* p. 102. Also see Hatzimichalis, "L'Art populaire," 37, who apparently embellishes Stamatiades' account. Raid from Peramerias: Alexis Poulianos, *Laika Tragoudia,* 1, 35. The foray may have consisted of outsiders led by a local similar to a 16th-century occurrence; see Poulianos, ibid., p. 260. Such tactics went back to classical antiquity; see J. Osborne, *Classical Landscapes with Figures: The Ancient Greek City and its Countryside* (London, 1987), p. 154.

72. Melas, *Ikarias,* pp. 162–163. People pilfered crops in times of peace; see Argenti, *Chius Vincta,* p. ccxxi, who notes that in 1861 the *demogerontia* appointed eight night watchmen to protect crops. Such measures were more necessary in big islands such as Chios where fields were far from houses. Raid: Poulianos, *Laographia,* 1, 35.

73. Melas, *Ikarias,* pp. 165–166.

CHAPTER 2

In the Twilight
of the Ottoman Empire

Turkish Administration
and the Development of Agriculture

IOANNES Capodistria, the future president of Greece, arrived in Nauplia in the eastern Peloponnese early in 1828 to help establish the new Greek nation. At that time Greece consisted of only the Peloponnese, and a few adjacent islands. Capodistria succeeded in expanding Greek frontiers on the mainland, but was unable to acquire any of the Aegean islands near the coast of Turkey. When French philhellenes, representing Greek interests in the Aegean, failed to seize Chios, the fate of the islands near the coast of Turkey was sealed. The people on these islands, nonetheless, remained hopeful that they would join the emerging Greek nation. The Icarians had previously expelled all Turkish officials and the *demogerontia,* assuming that the island would become part of Greece, conducted business with a seal bearing the insignia of the Greek nation. An official of the Greek government established his residence in Marathon, a village in central Icaria. He endeavored to persuade the Icarians to populate coastal areas. In light of the recent piratical raids and the Greek navy's confiscation of goats and sheep along coastal areas, the Icarians rejected the idea. Gradually, however, people began to resettle Evdilos.[1]

The war between Greece and Turkey was formally concluded with the treaty of London signed on May 11, 1832. Epirus, Thessaly, Crete, Samos, Chios, Icaria, and several other islands reverted to Turkish rule, but were to be administered by Ottoman Greek governors. Some of these officials, Greeks living in the Ottoman Empire, were men of high caliber. For instance, the governor of Samos at the end of the 19th century was Miltiades Pasha Alexander Dosios, the son of the sultan's physician, and a man of distinction in his own right. Such eminent officials did not serve in Icaria, but the men who did were capable Ottoman Greeks.[2]

In 1832 Greece withdrew its official from Icaria, and Turkey did not send a replacement until 1836. During these four years, the *demogerontia* administered the island, and, as the Icarians began to reestablish their links with the Ottoman cities of the coast of Turkey, the customs official became a man of great importance. He enjoyed an income of 100 groschen for issuing passports, collecting custom fees, and supervising a quarantine station in Evdilos. Despite the quarantine procedures, the Icarians did not entirely escape a smallpox epidemic that devastated neighboring islands.[3]

During these years of isolation Icaria provided a haven for Greeks fleeing Turkish authorities. On July 4, 1834, the grand admiral of the Ottoman fleet, which was stationed in Vathi, Samos, sent a letter to the Icarian *demogerontia* threatening the island with dire consequences if a number of Samians, among them a bishop, were not delivered to the admiral in Vathi. Stavros Klitos, *proestos,* that is, headman in Icaria, involved in anti-Ottoman activities, advised the *demogerontia* to persist in sheltering the refugees. Klitos proceeded to find means to send them to the Peloponnese, which was the heart of free Greece. In the meantime, Klitos counseled the Icarians to amass huge amounts of walnuts and honey for the Turkish admiral who was so delighted with the *peskes,* bribe, that he temporarily forgot about the refugees. Eventually, the admiral summoned Klitos and other members of the *demogerontia* to Samos. The Icarians ignored the order, and for the next two years continued to harbor refugees and avoid taxes.[4]

Late in 1834, a representative from Icaria joined those from Symi, Nisyros, Astypalae, Patmos, Telos, Kalymnos, and Leros seeking to negotiate a semi-independent status within the Ottoman Empire. In 1835, the sultan Mahmud II (born, 1784; ruled, 1827–1839) issued a firman placing Icaria in the *evalet* (province) of the twelve Sporades. The sultan directed representatives of these islands to meet in Rhodes, which was the Turkish administrative seat of the region, to work out a tax arrangement.[5] Mahmud followed up with a second firman designating Icaria, Patmos, Leros, and Kalymnos as the four islands of the "White Sea". The Turks considered this region as not only the poorest section of the Aegean Sea, but also the most turbulent: rendered white with storm-driven waves. The firman of 1835 assured a great measure of local autonomy and became a sort of Icarian bill of rights. The sultan proclaimed that these four islands, while not participating in the recent rebellion, had suffered great harm from pirates and rebels. The sultan assessed these islands a light annual tax: eighty thousand groschen. The Icarian share was nineteen thousand, to be paid in two installments. In return for their taxes, the sultan announced "the inhabitants of these poor and arid islands would have the privilege of reposing every night tranquilly in their beds under my protection."[6]

In 1836, the Icarians resumed their second period as Ottoman subjects when a *kaimakames,* a Greek Orthodox layman, arrived to serve as the Porte's chief official. Upon stepping ashore, the *kaimakames* expected to meet officials with the first installment of the nineteen-thousand-groschen tax, but no one seemed to know anything about it. After being ignored for several days, he sent a message to the council of elders complaining that he was tired of waiting. He threatened that, if the taxes and a register of the adult males were not forthcoming, he would fine each adult male thirty groschen. Eventually, the *kaimakames* managed to register the men for tax purposes. Within a few years, however, there were problems. The *kaimakames* managed to raise half the required taxes.[7] The Icarians, in a petition to the governor of Rhodes, maintained that they had not been fully credited with an earlier payment, but admitted they were nonetheless in arrears because the villages of Peramerias, the western part of the island with the capital at Raches, did not contribute their quota, while the villages in the districts of Fanari and Mesarias had raised their portion. The governor of the Sporades wondered why the other islands of the White Sea had met their obligations, and the Icarians had not. Finally, the Icarians produced the requisite groschen, but pleaded for a tax adjustment because the people in the isolated and impoverished western part of the island could not raise their share.[8]

The Icarian tax of nineteen thousand groschen was a paltry sum compared to the hundred fifty thousand groschen the Porte assessed Mytilene. But even wealthy Mytilene had difficulties paying its taxes. In May 1841, the Mytileneans asked for tax relief pleading poverty brought on by a severe winter. The Turks were receptive to such arguments, for this petition came at the beginning of the Tanzimat period, 1839–1876, a time of reform in the Ottoman Empire. The Porte took measures to guarantee life and property to all its subjects. The sultan's aim was to shear his sheep not to flay them.[9]

Icaria enjoyed a favored-province status and was never to be crippled by Ottoman taxes. Shortly after the firman of 1835, the sultan reduced the Icarian head tax from nineteen thousand to eighteen thousand groschen, assessing each adult male fifteen groschen. The Turkish counted twelve hundred adult male Greeks on Icaria, although there were actually about twice that many. Despite the light tax burden the Icarians were notoriously dilatory in paying it. On March 11, 1843, the governor of the Sporades warned the *demogerontia* that unless taxes were immediately delivered, the Ottoman authorities would release several Icarian goat thieves from prison and allow them to return to Icaria. In 1848, the burlap bag containing the Icarian tax arrived in Rhodes—thirty groschen short: a member of the council of elders was summoned to Rhodes to make good this trifling sum.[10]

In the first two decades of this second phase of Ottoman rule, the Porte was especially concerned about anti-Ottoman activities. The *kaimakames* had the right to detain natives for treason, but could make no search and seizures or lengthy imprisonment without a warrant from the governor of the *evalet*. The governor of the Sporades urged the Icarians not to appoint any radicals to the *demogerontia,* and decreed that only good Christians not under the influence of a foreign government were acceptable to the Porte. The governor probably had Klitos in mind. In 1838, a warrant arrived in Icaria for the arrest of Klitos. He was sent to Rhodes to answer for his role in the bishop's escape. Ottoman authorities kept him in confinement for two years. With his health broken, he returned to Icaria in 1840 and died the following year.[11]

Despite the sultan's grant of autonomy, the *kaimakames* as representative of the sultan influenced legislation, issued fines, and imposed physical punishment. The Porte's intervention in Icaria was often for enlightened reasons. In 1838, the *kaimakames* threatened charcoal merchants, who were destroying forests, with a fine of two hundred and fifty groschen, which represented approximately the annual earnings of a farmer, and a flogging of one hundred lashes. The Porte maintained that the forests belonged to the Turkish government and made efforts to preserve them. In 1842, the Turkish authorities raised the fine to five hundred piasters and again a flogging of one hundred lashes. In 1865, the *kaimakames* threatened a particular charcoal merchant with corporal punishment if he persisted in violating the forest laws. The repetition of measures to save the timberland indicates the Ottoman inability to enforce this law. By the end of the 19th century, when the Icarians had relentlessly depleted their forests, the Ottoman government, acknowledging a fait accompli, surrendered the forests to the communities.[12]

Ludwig Ross, a German scholar who was making an archaeological tour of the Aegean, visited Icaria in August 1841, and witnessed Turkish efforts to improve the island. Ross as he traveled through the Aegean heard reports about this strange island, and upon stepping ashore was surprised not to find savages dressed in animal skins, but rather civilized people aware of the progressive ideas that had led to the Greek War of Independence. He approved of the recent trend to cultivate the land, which had doubled the wealth of the island, and liberated the Icarians from being exclusively exporters of charcoal. Ross believed that not only agriculture, but also the development of the health spas at Therma, which were already attracting people from Samos and Turkey, would bring Icaria into the modern world.[13]

Ross observed a society in a state of transformation. Aghios Kyrikos was a new village with twenty houses built closely together, while there were two hundred houses in Evdilos most of which had recently been built. With crewmembers, he walked from Aghios Kyrikos westward to the monastery of Panagia Evangelismos, founded some fifty years earlier. There he admired the recent efforts to plant olive trees and the introduction of peach and pear trees as well. Ross noted that the largest and most arable plain on the island was at Fanari where he saw herds consisting of four hundred sheep and goats, and other large herds in various parts of the island. The owners of these immense flocks, the *archontes* or "aristocrats," came into conflict with farmers, "democrats." They did not want this fertile land cultivated, and were opposed to the "democrats" who were farming it and introducing new crops, such as the type of fruit trees recently cultivated at the monastery of Evangelismos, and extensive vineyards. A few years after Ross' visit, the Icarians began to cultivate the potato and became one of the main producers of the potato in the Aegean. The dispute between the two factions had become so acute that the *demogerontia* requested the governor of Rhodes to send an arbiter, probably the dreaded *tsaoutes,* to settle the matter. The Icarians paid this official four hundred seventy-five groschen for a month's service, about eight percent of the Icarian tax liability. He ruled in favor of the cultivators.[14]

Apparently, the issue was not resolved, and the shepherds, the so-called "aristocrats," continued to graze their flocks on the land cultivated by the "democrats." The clash between the two groups led not only to raids on cultivated land, but to rustling animals as well and in 1843 Turkish authorities intervened, arresting the most notorious malefactors and imprisoning them in Rhodes. On May 25, 1844, the governor of Rhodes, Hasan Pasha instructed the council of elders to take measures to control the unfettered animals, mainly goats and sheep, which were damaging the tilled fields of "the poor reayas (non-Muslim subjects]." Properly tended animals were under the full protection of the law, but unrestrained animals were subject to seizure by any interested person without compensation. He urged the Icarians to cultivate vineyards, various fruits and vegetables, and sell the surplus.[15]

The agricultural advancements that had come to Icaria in the 1830s were largely a result of new settlers. Captain Georgios Damales, who had served in the Greek navy during the War of Independence, had brought an orphan, Georgios Spanos, back from Chios and raised him as a son. The Icaria to which this boy came had been sparsely populated for centuries. Because of their isolation and poverty, Icarians found it difficult to reproduce themselves and cultivate the land. Spanos was about to change all this. Shortly before Spanos arrived, raids of the Greek navy and pirates had driven the shepherds inland from the few plains along the sea. These rich bottomlands remained unexploited for the next five years. Thus when Spanos reached manhood he proceeded to put tracts of land in Campos under cultivation, and others copied his methods. He, apparently, became the leader of what Ross described as the "people's" party, a faction bringing grazing land, which had been considered communal property, under cultivation in private plots. A talented and energetic individual, he urged the Icarians to convert from a subsistence to a market economy. Such methods clashed with the owners of flocks of sheep and goats, the party Ross called "aristocrat" who were now returning to Campos and Fanari with their animals. The shepherds had neither the desire nor the skill to produce a cash crop. Dominating the *demogerontia,* they opposed fences that Spanos and his supporters were erecting to protect cultivated land from roving animals. Spanos, by relying on support from the Ottoman authorities, persuading some Icarians of the benefits of agriculture, and having his children intermarry into the leading families, particularly the Stenos family, was able to challenge the authority of the shepherd-dominated *demogerontia.* The clash is reflected in the proverb *"Vre Spanades,*

Vre Stenedes, giate maches tes aiges". (Why O why has the damned Spanos and Stenos clan on goats decreed a ban?) Spanos and his descendants, he had approximately six surviving children, were revered for their intelligence and innovations but occasionally disparaged for assertive commercial practices.[16]

The Ottoman government's support for the development of cash crops came at a time when urban areas, cities ready to consume Icarian agricultural products, were developing on the coast of Turkey. Most of the terraced walls that pervade the island are monuments to the wearisome labor of this first and nearly forgotten generation of 19th century tillers. They enclosed portions of the rich bottomlands and also fields surrounding the interior villages. According to an oral tradition, a man named Mamatas came from Chrysostomos and began to cultivate the fertile land in Maganitis, and was joined by others from Akamatra. A certain Malachias came from Chrysostomos and settled what was to become the coastal village of Xyloserti. Some of these farmers probably had very little land and only a few animals in the interior, and so they thus found opportunities to till plains near the coast. The clash between the new families that cultivated the land and the old families that had large herds persisted into the late 19th century when agriculture survived despite the presence of nearly thirteen thousand goats.[17]

Coastal areas, some of which had been considered communal property used by shepherds to graze animals, now were valuable agricultural land, and men who had been cultivating it claimed ownership. On March 23, 1847, a successful charcoal manufacturer invested fifty groschen in a plot of land at Fanari. He apparently wanted to diversify his operation by planting vineyards in this highly fertile area. Fear of living on the coast, however, had not entirely disappeared. Pirates often operated single-handedly, arriving at night to kill people simply for their clothes. Thus men living in new villages, such as Tsouredo and Perdiki, tilled Fanari, and returned to their secure homes at night. A growing network of village lanes that joined most villages to either Evdilos, Raches, or Aghios Kyrikos, by the middle of the 19th century increasingly connected Icarians who had been isolated from one another in previous centuries and who had been forced to communicate by "stentophonical voices." Hence property values in those villages soared. On July 20, 1868, a man purchased a plot of land in Tsouredo for seventy groschen; a generation later, such a piece of land with a house surrounded by terraced strips, vineyards, and olive trees, was worth anywhere from one thousand to fifteen hundred groschen.[18]

In the mid-19th century, Icaria experienced several crises. Only a few years after the sultan's magistrate rendered a verdict favoring farmers over shepherds and encouraging Icarians to intensify agriculture, a cold wave, beginning in November 1849 and lasting until March 1850, devastated the region. The Samians, who had a highly developed agricultural economy, were unable to pay their taxes to the Ottomans and were reduced to starvation. They lost many of their olive trees, vineyards, and grain fields. Some Samians resorted to raiding the coast of Asia Minor for supplies. The Icarians also lost many new fruit trees, and vineyards, but because their economy was not yet as heavily dependent on agriculture as was the case in Samos they took the crisis in stride.[19]

The Aegean area had barely recovered from the crisis of 1850 when the Crimean War (1853–1855) broke out. Turkey, which allied itself with Britain and France against Russia, requisitioned great amounts of produce from its rural population. The war economy created shortages in Samos and perhaps in Icaria as well, but the Icarians with their large herds of goats and sheep were still relatively self-sufficient. The real crisis for Icaria came after the war when the Russians forced large numbers of Crimean Tartars from the region of the Caucasus into the Ottoman Empire. Some lived in camps waiting for permanent homes, others roamed through Turkey raiding farmers for food. The Ottoman authorities, assuming from the tax roll that Icaria was underpopulated shipped some refugees to the island. When they approached shore, the Turkish authorities took the Tartar homesteaders from the steamship, and placed them on smaller boats. As they approached the "virgin land," an angry mob began hurling stones that sank one boat, forced the others back, and prevented the shipwrecked refugees from swimming ashore.[20]

Autonomy

By the end of the 1860s, Turkish authorities practically ceased to intervene in local matters. The decline of the Porte's intercession in Icarian affairs came at a time when the great European powers were championing the interest of the Ottoman Christians and were ready to provoke an incident for political purposes. For example, in August 1867, the Porte dispatched a warship to Symi, a small island some one hundred miles southeast of Icaria, to enforce its policies. In September, the

Symiotes sent a delegation to London to present Lord Stanley, the Secretary of Foreign Affairs to the Porte, a copy of the privileges granted by the sultan to Symi and other islands (Icaria was included), and to assert that the Porte was in violation of this agreement. Lord Stanley put pressure on the Turks to guarantee local autonomy in these islands. Apparently, the British intervention of 1867 had its effects in Icaria. After this date, the *kaimakames* put aside the rod and sought the good will of the people. These officials yielded the supervision of all internal affairs to the *demogerontia.* They accepted small bribes to overlook modest smuggling operations and permitted other minor infractions of Ottoman law. The chief Icarian transgression was undercounting the population to minimize the head tax. In the middle of the 19th century, the Icarians claimed to have about three thousand inhabitations while the Turkish authorities suspected there was twice that number. Thus the Icarians never paid their fair share of taxes until the end of the 19th century when the Ottoman government made a relatively accurate census.[21]

The Icarians had a long tradition of managing their own affairs, and enjoyed good local government through the *demogerontia,* one council of elders in each of the three districts. Justice was administered by a local judge appointed by Turkish authorities who sat with two members of the council of elders. It usually met the day after a party initiated a case, and presented a decision the following day. If one of the parties did not accept the decision of this body, the Turkish gendarmerie enforced the judgment. A litigant enjoyed the right to appeal his case in the provincial capital, which, depending on the period, was either in Rhodes or Chios, but this was an expensive procedure beyond the means of most Icarians. In situations involving chronic criminals, mainly habitual animal thieves, this judicial body would instruct the gendarmes to dispatch malefactors to prison in Rhodes.[22]

At the end of the 19th century, there was a Greek *kaimakames,* a Turkish customs official, and about twelve Turkish gendarmes serving in Icaria. They were extremely congenial people compatible with the Greek community. Only the customs official had his family in Icaria. Asir Efentis, who held this position in Evdilos, was well-respected, and his children were fully integrated into the village, going to Greek school, speaking Greek like natives, and playing with the Icarian children. Asir himself spoke passable Greek but with an accent and under stress, as when pirates raided Evdilos and stole his watch, he could not match the gender of articles with nouns making such blunders as "to pater sou."

These few Turkish officials wore a fez, a Turkish type of hat, the only mark visibly distinguishing them from the natives, but soon the more successful Icarians such as members of the *demogerontia,* aping Ottoman officials, took to wearing this apparel, thus proclaiming their loyalty to the regime.[23]

As prosperity came to the island, taxes increased. By 1890, the head tax reached thirty-five thousand groschen, thirty for each adult male. There was also a tax of twenty-three thousand groschen for judicial services, and one thousand Turkish pounds for administrative expenses covering the pay of the local governor and twelve gendarmes. In addition, the Icarians paid an ecclesiastical tax of sixty-five hundred to nine thousand groschen to the bishop in Samos. Ultimately, the Porte exacted a twelve and a half percent tax on all agricultural products throughout the Empire. The Icarians, however, never felt the full force of this onerous tax, because the bulk of their farming was on small terraced lots, not highly visible and therefore not on the tax register. There was no Ottoman corvée, but the Icarians willingly donated about four days a year to build and maintain the intervillage lanes that were the main means of communication until vehicular roads were built in the 1970s.[24]

One may ask what benefits the Icarians received for their tax payments. There was no investment in education, roads, or health, but the Ottomans made a significant contribution to the maintenance of law and order. The presence of gendarmes, and the threat of prison in Rhodes, was an important factor in preserving stability in the island. The greatest boon from the Ottoman Empire was access to Ottoman cities and markets. Icarians purchased timber concessions in Turkey, made charcoal, and sold the product in Alexandria. There was a demand for Icarian currants, a dry seedless grape, and other fruit in Alexandria, Egypt, and many other parts of the Ottoman realm. One successful trip to an Ottoman port could bring a bonanza. For instance, in the 1890s, a case of Icarian peaches brought over a hundred piasters (groschen) in Alexandria, enough money to support a family for one month in Icaria. Therma was beginning to acquire a reputation as a health spa, and a trickle of invalids came from Asia Minor to take the cure in the thermal baths. Finally, many Icarians secured seasonal work in the booming city of Izmir. The access to economic opportunities in the Ottoman Empire was ample recompense for taxes paid.[25]

In 1866, acknowledging the new development, the Ottoman government made Aghios Kyrikos the administrative center of the island. By the end of the 18th century there were five houses in Aghios Kyrikos. The inhabitants began the construction of the church Aghios Nikolaos around 1820. In a document of 1836, there is a reference to two stores, and a few years later Ross noted twenty houses. A growing village, which would have a hundred twenty houses by 1890, it seemed a curious choice because Evdilos had better port facilities. Evdilos, however, was in decline. The two hundred houses Ross noted in Evdilos in 1840, possibly an overestimate, had decreased to about one hundred in 1890. The development of Aghios Kyrikos, a departure point to Izmir, was related to the growing dependence of Icaria on Asia Minor where so many Icarians went to earn a living. Furthermore, neighboring Therma was burgeoning into a village of a dozen or so houses because of the hot springs. The small administrative force did not arrive in Aghios Kyrikos, however, until 1879, having been delayed by a rebellion in Crete, which absorbed the attention of the Porte. Icaria's northerner inhabitants always resented the loss of the capital, and in 1912 nearly went to war with the southerners to regain it. By the end of the 19th century, the most expensive land was in Aghios Kyrikos. A plot for a house, a *spitotopos,* went for fourteen Ottoman pounds. The most important merchants settled in Aghios Kyrikos, and they were responsible by and large for the relative prosperity sweeping over the island.[26]

Currants, Charcoal and Sailing Ships

In 1837, the British sent a commercial steamship, the *Levant,* to the Aegean. This 64-ton vessel was the first commercial steamship to ply Aegean waters. The new technology not only stimulated trade but also opened up the Aegean to the outside world. In 1840, Thomas Arnold of Rugby was quick to note the potential of these developments, writing that steam power was making it possible for scholars to visit what was once an obscure area. In 1841, Ross proved Arnold's hypothesis about steamships opening up the Aegean by touring the islands in such a vessel and visiting Icaria. His voyage foreshadowed an Aegean Pax Turcica based on steam vessels and an ironclad navy developed by the sultan Abdulaziz (reigned 1861–1876).[27]

While a sailship might take weeks, a vessel powered by steam made the voyage from Izmir to Istanbul in a day and a half, and reached Alexandria, Egypt, in about three days. But these early steam engines were untrustworthy and burned too much fuel, thus rendering travel by steam expensive and unreliable. Thus sail power in the Aegean for certain types of commercial ventures proved tenacious, and in fact enjoyed a "second wind." New and larger sailships emerged which were specifically designed for carrying the nonperishable types of cargo that the Icarians traded. Icarian wind-driven vessels coexisted with the new technology, indeed prospering by trading in zones that were being revitalized by steam power. The Ottoman Steam Ship Company began calling on Samos in 1844, and the Hellenic Steam Ship Company soon thereafter began making regular runs to Syros. By the end of the 19th century, twenty-seven Greek steamships serviced Aegean ports.[28]

By the mid-19th century, Icarian sailships specialized in conveying charcoal, the island's main export product. Charcoal fetches an especially high price in Egypt and it was lighter to transport than wood. Icarian charcoal producers, however, were creating an environmental disaster by depleting their forest. Despite the warning of Turkish officials that the Icarians were "killing" their mountains by cutting their trees, the deforestation continued. Charcoal was a voracious consumer of Icarian timberland. It took 10 kilograms of wood to produce 1.67 kilograms of charcoal, and this amount of charcoal yielded less than one-fifth the heat of the original wood, but it was light and easier to transport than wood. By the 1880s, the Icarian carbonieri began to shift their operations outside of Icaria. Between Izmir and Bodrum, some 100 miles south, they obtained timber concessions for about two groschen an acre. They preferred working their concessions with Icarians and not locals and thus arrived with crews, each member carrying a Turkish work permit costing one groschen. The major Icarian charcoal dealers were Vassilaros, Pamphylis, Loukatsos, and Kratsas. These "captains," with faces and clothes covered with soot, sailed to the far reaches of the Ottoman Empire. Most were powerful men with barrel chests who had a bent for adventure. In a land where the bulk of the population did not know what was on the other side of their own island, the long-range movements of these captains gave them an exalted status. Returning home, they told stories of evading pirates, encountering huge snakes and wild animals in the timberlands of Asia Minor, of combating outlaws like the Christian brigands who in the 1880s near Izmir robbed migrant workers and even held some for ransom. An Icarian charcoal merchant acquired a timber concession in this very area. He recruited men from his village of Chrysostomos and cleared the area of thieves before he began to work it.[29]

The method of systematic viticulture came to Icaria from Chios and Asia Minor. The island produced an especially sweet grape, which the

Icarians converted into high-quality dry seedless grapes, currants. Thus currants replaced charcoal in the last quarter of the 19th century as the great Icarian cash crop. At that time, phylloxera was wiping out vineyards in other parts of Greece and the Ottoman Empire, but this plant disease only reached Icaria around 1910. In the 1890s Icaria averaged an annual yield of 392,000 kilos of currants. Nearly every family on the island benefited. The Icarians exported the bulk of their currant production to Ottoman ports, particularly the Black Sea ports of Romania. The inhabitants of Izmir purchased Icarian lemons, peaches, oranges, and potatoes.[30]

In such preindustrial societies, economic growth was not reflected in the increase in personal wealth but rather in a surge in population, and the Icarians multiplied. According to Ross's unofficial estimate in 1841 there were nine hundred houses on the island sheltering seventy-five hundred inhabitants, a little more than eight people per house. The shortage in housing created crammed conditions, for these dwellings were approximately thirty by twenty-five feet. Such an arrangement allowed the married son to live in his father's home and thus dodge the head tax that was, in effect, a hearth tax. The Icarians disputed Ross's figure and in 1888 reported to the governor of the eastern Sporades, I. Kolettas, a population of 3,110—2,992 being too poor to pay taxes—squeezed into 636 houses. This self-serving undercount was not taken seriously, and the number of inhabitants in Icaria was probably in the range Ross reported until the reign of Adbul Hamid II (born 1842; reigned 1876–1909) when the population of the Ottoman Empire expanded from twenty to twenty-seven million, an increase of over thirty-seven percent. In Icaria, the census of 1893 reveals that the Icarian population nearly doubled from the seventy-five hundred of 1841 to twelve thousand eight hundred. The census figures also revealed twelve hundred goats, fifteen hundred sheep, four hundred cows, and five hundred pigs. Nearly everyone practiced animal husbandry and tilled a plot of land.[31]

The Icarian Diaspora

In the 18th century, Icarians found work in Chios and Samos. In the 19th century, Izmir offered many economic opportunities. In 1830, Izmir had twenty thousand inhabitants. Thirty years later, the population had risen to seventy-five thousand, and by 1890 to one hundred thousand. The Islamic inhabitants, who had military responsibilities and lacked the entrepreneurial skills of the Greeks, maintained smaller families than the

Greeks and were in the minority. Here Icarian charcoal manufacturers or currant traders had their first glimpse of urban life. They bargained with merchants from Western Europe who dealt not only in dried fruits, but also in cotton, wool, and mohair. The streets teemed with dockworkers, confectioners who sold sugared fruit, sellers of lemonade in tall glasses, and men who sharpened knives. For the most part people spoke Greek but Icarians in Izmir heard Turkish, English, and French as well. They not only sold their wares, but also stayed and worked. Women found employment as domestics.[32]

During the 1880s, Icarians discovered that the best prices for their charcoal and currants were to be found in Alexandria. Leaving Icaria in July and August, with the *meltimi* at their backs, Icarian captains reached Egypt in less that a week. They sold their products, and returned in September when the winds were favorable. Some stayed in Alexandria and brought their families. By 1890, there were about six hundred Icarians within the Greek community of a hundred thousand permanently settled in Alexandria. They prospered, and the women, many employed as domestics in Alexandria, when returning to Icaria hired village girls to serve them. The Icarians of Alexandria published a newspaper, *Ikaros*. Many learned French, Italian, and Arabic. The children enrolled in any of the nine Greek primary schools, or either of the two secondary schools. Well-qualified teachers, some of whom were trained in the Sorbonne, staffed the schools. The first adequately educated generation of Icarians sprang from this school system.[33]

At the end of the 19th century, European fashions and tastes were sweeping through Greece, the Ottoman Empire, and its Aegean islands. Icarians, however, were maverick cattle, not part of the herd. Styles and trends scarcely made any inroads into Icaria. They went to Izmir and Alexandria, saw Greek men wearing white collars, ties, and bowler hats, flannels, linen shirts, handkerchiefs, and women in silk dresses. Icarian maids worked in houses with fine furniture and glass windows. In Samos, a few wealthy men were turning from the *nargileh*, a smoking pipe designed with a long tube passing through an urn of water, and instead started smoking cigars, and in high society there were balls where well-dressed Samians danced the waltz and polka. But in Icaria there was no blossoming bourgeoisie craving for European goods and customs. In 1887, a Jewish merchant named Baruch established a business in Aghios Kyrikos selling fancy goods and European clothing. The Icarians burnt down his store. The sultan dispatched a military vessel to punish the

Icarians. They took collective responsibility for the act, indemnifying the merchant with three hundred Turkish pounds. The Icarians remained attached to a simple lifestyle. Not even on Sunday did they wear special clothes and shoes, and they took offense at anyone who possessed such attire or furniture. For instance, on one occasion an Icarian, who fancied himself *Salonfähig,* returned from Izmir with a four-post bed. The people saw him unload it from the ship. That night, his fellow villagers broke into his house, interrupted his dandified repose, threw him out of the luxurious contraption, and burned it in the public square. No elite would emerge on this island to engage in conspicuous consumption for another century.[34]

Education

By the end of the 19th century, there were 437 students enrolled in village schools in Icaria. The *demogerontia* supervised the teachers and arranged for their salary. For example, in 1851 the *demogerontia* of Fanari hired Demetrios Katsimidis, a Samian, to teach the youth of Tsouredos. Katsimidis was probably happy to leave Samos which was experiencing a serious economic depression resulting from the cold winter of 1849/1850. With a salary of two hundred groschen a year, one suit of woolen clothing consisting of a coat, a shirt, a belt, and shoes, Katsimidis was content to stay in Tsouredos for some fifteen years.[35]

He taught in a remote section of the village selected clearly for secrecy, but this was not one of the so-called *krypha scholia,* secret schools, which in popular lore served to educate Greek children who were allegedly denied access to education by the sultan's law. Such schools never existed in Greece. The enlightened sultans of the 19th century permitted the construction of schools and the repairs of churches, but many non-Muslim communities, to evade taxes, underreported their population figures, and were reluctant to undertake school construction, and thus provide the Porte with an indication of a growing population. The Icarians took measures to prevent the Ottoman authorities from discovering the school in Tsouredos and ascertaining the number of students enrolled, and the local Turkish authorities were not much interested in gathering such statistics. The Tsourediotes founded their school shortly before 1857 when the reforms known as the Hatti-i-Humayum, which aimed at establishing more accurate population figures, a more efficient bureaucracy and tax collecting system, were in effect. Eventually, the Icarians would provide accurate statistics about their population and there was no need for hiding their village schools.[36]

It was impossible for a backwater like Icaria to attract trained teachers, and one may assume that Katsimidis had few qualifications. His salary by mid-19th-century standards was meager. A regular teacher in Mytilene at that time received the annual salary of 4,500 groschen. In 1858, women workers made over 3 groschen a day in cotton factories in Asia Minor, and agricultural workers made 4 to 7 groschen a day during harvest. Thus teachers in prosperous communities made one hundred times Katsimidis' salary, and Greek rural and industrial workers in Asia Minor earned fourfold the wages of an Icarian teacher.[37]

By the 1870s the situation had changed. Icarians were building schools openly in nearly every village, and teachers of the Katzimidis type were replaced by young men trained in a Samian high school which also served as a teacher's college, or in the Evangeliki school in Izmir, which prepared Christodoulos Chagranis (1840–1914), one of the best educators ever to practice on the island. In the Indian summer of Ottoman Icaria, literacy was widespread. Even orphans received four years of schooling, and were provided books from charitable organizations in Izmir. In 1891, girls were admitted to the school in Evdilos, and by the end of the 19th century most girls were enrolled in primary school. Around 1895, J. Lombardas established a *scholarchion* in Aghios Kyrikos, a school for those, usually from the ages twelve to fourteen, who had finished the first six years of primary school. In the academic year 1897–1898, there were sixty-seven students enrolled in the school. Only a few wealthy merchants, shipowners, and farmers could afford such an education for their children, mainly sons, for only two girls were registered. Lombardas' *scholarchion* represented the highest educational level in Icaria, and only a few continued their studies beyond that point. Despite the educational improvements of the 1870s, Icaria in the area of education remained behind its wealthier neighbors. For instance, in Icaria there was no equivalent to the young men of affluent families in Mytilene, who lived off rentals from their land, and had leisure to read books, and earned diplomas from high schools in Chios, Izmir, or from the commercial school at Halki which required an annual tuition of three thousand groschen. Such diplomas brought huge dowries in the form of olive groves, mechanized olive presses, large sums of money, valuable clothing and houses worth as much as a hundred thousand groschen. In Icaria, there were no such rich pickings for dowry hunters. An education beyond the rudiments was of little use. Too much book learning was considered deleterious to the mind. The exceptions were teachers, doctors, and lawyers. By the end of the 19th century, Icaria could boast of about four medical men, and perhaps two lawyers. Whether all doctors had certified medical degrees is uncertain. Many people continued to resort to quack methods for therapy. For instance, it was widely believed that smoke from the water pipe, nargileh, purified the lungs.[38]

The half dozen men who made up the doctors and lawyers were the scions of successful ship captains, men who owned a sail ship and dealt in currants and charcoal. A ship captain earned more in one short trip to Chios than a farmer earned in an entire year. These were practically the only men on the island who accumulated any capital. Among the leading families were the Pamphylis, Malachias, Kratsas, and Spanos clans. While they all produced doctors, they did not spawn the type of capitalists that emerged in Chios, Samos, and Mytilene—islands that could brag of harbors, regular steamship service, and agricultural wealth. In Mytilene, men owned estates that produced great volumes of olive oil, deposited money in the *Trapeza tes Mytilenes,* the largest bank in the Aegean. Mytilenean businessmen earned 4% interest on their deposits, and were able to secure loans for machinery and ships, and to cover their enterprises with insurance. Icarian entrepreneurs, however, who did not deposit but buried their money, were unable to borrow funds to build ships. Furthermore, they could not afford to insure their cargoes transported by sail, which required higher insurance rates than cargo on steamships. Icarian businessmen thus never became prominent in the Ottoman Empire or later in Greece when Icaria joined the mother country.[39]

The Pamphylis family was among the most notable Icarian charcoal manufacturers. In the 1880s, Anagnostis Pamphylis prospered with several timber concessions in various parts of the Ottoman Empire. In partnership with his brother Konstantinos, they transported their charcoal by sail, and on one occasion, apparently conveying currants, sailed through the straits of Gibraltar and reached England where they made a huge profit on their cargo. The son of Anagnostis, Ioannes (1862–1902) studied in Athens where in the late 1870s he acquired the reputation of a spendthrift living in good lodgings. Allegedly he was the first Icarian to dine routinely in restaurants. He studied medicine in Western Europe and served as one of the first doctors on the island. The Malachias clan, which immigrated from Chrysostomos to Xyloserti, also made its money from charcoal and shipping. The newly arrived Spanos family excelled in agriculture and the retail business.[40]

By the end of the 19th century, despite progress and contacts with Ottoman cities, the island remained one of the most isolated parts of the Ottoman Empire. The Icarians did not keep pace with changing conditions in the Aegean. Their fellow Greeks had always considered them poor and ignorant, and now the Icarians themselves were no longer bragging about their Byzantine ancestors but were beginning to accept their humble status. Visitors encountered a shy people, self-conscious about their provincial dialect. The Icarian proverb, "Unfortunate Icaria, with your high mountains, diminutive houses, and humble people," revealed their inferiority complex. They no longer aggressively claimed they were *porphyrogenetoi* and their neighbor's *choriates*. In 1890, the Porte corroborated their lowly status by establishing a leprosarium outside Aghios Kyrikos. The cruelest blow to Icarian pride, however, was the work of Epaminondas Stamatiades, the principal of the Samian high school. He had trained many of the teachers who found positions in Icarian villages in the 1860s and 1870s. Stamatiades made his first visit to Icaria in 1864, when illiteracy was prevalent, and shortly thereafter described the Icarians in two magazine articles, *Chrysallis,* vol. 2 and *Ilissou,* vol. 3, as the poorest and crudest denizens of the Aegean. But in his book on Icaria published in 1893, he moderated his views, apparently impressed by the progress that had taken place during the thirty years from his first visit. Stamatiades obtained much information from his students who wrote to him from the various villages disparaging their crude charges and their loutish parents. Stamatiades' history became a collector's item because the Icarians, incensed by the author's negative remarks, assiduously accumulated copies and brought them to Aghios Kyrikos where they were ceremoniously burned in the public square.[41]

In 1892, Professor Hatzidakis, the founder of linguistic studies at the University of Athens, made a field trip to Icaria to study the Icarian dialect. He concluded that the idiom in the western part of the island contained more classical expressions than any other of the vernaculars in modern Greece. Furthermore, he judged that the surnames of many Icarians revealed an origin from Peloponnesians who arrived in the 17th century. Some Icarians rejected the professor's conclusion because it minimized the alleged connections the people had with the Byzantine aristocracy, and expressed reservations about the value of a study based on fifteen days of fieldwork. Hatzidakis, however, drew a positive portrait of Icarians. He saw them as simple, honest, industrious people, capable of generosity and exceptional hospitality.[42]

In the following year, Ludwig Bürchner, a professor of ancient history in Germany, visited Icaria to collect material for a historical study of the island. After hearing negative things about Icarians from their neighbors, he was surprised to encounter honest, hardworking, sociable, and hospitable people. Bürchner saw two Icarias—the eastern section where people, influenced by the outside world, slept in beds and behaved in a civilized way, and the western part where the inhabitants reposed on hard surfaces, ate without cutlery, and lived in one-room houses with earthen floors.[43]

Although in the more developed section of Icaria there was no demand for sophisticated goods, people purchased coffee, sugar, rice, tobacco, pasta, textiles, and clothes. The import of such merchandise led to the establishment of large general stores in Aghios Kyrikos and Evdilos. There were still a few pirates in the area. They did not generally assault stores, but raided people living in isolated areas near the shore taking from them store-bought goods, particularly clothing. The most notorious was a certain Emmanuel Mitakas who operated alone and specialized in robbing and killing Icarian fishermen. In 1860, Turkish authorities, with the help of his family, apprehended him in Fourni, his residence, and had him publicly beheaded in Samos. He told the executioner "if you are a *pallikari* (a manly and brave person) take my head with one blow." The execution of Mitakas more or less put an end to this type of marauding, but there was one final pirate raid in December 1886. Twelve men, armed with agricultural tools, arriving by caïque descended on Evdilos. They probably were rural workers from Asia Minor who had lost their jobs to the recent introduction of agricultural machinery and were driven to desperation. From a farmer coming back from his vineyard, they extracted the name of Rambetta, the wealthiest man in town and the proprietor of the biggest general store. When they arrived at his establishment, the merchant thought they were going to abduct his wife. The ransom price for a young woman was seventeen Turkish lira, a half year's wages, but bandits showed no interest in Aphrodite, a local beauty, but took instead the merchant's groschen and valuable items from his stock, mainly copper vessels. They proceeded to the customhouse where they relieved Arsan Efendis of his watch and clothes. While they were harassing other Evdilotes and threatening to burn houses, two gendarmes appeared with rifles. They pumped bullets into the pirate vessel forcing the miscreants to flee on foot about ten kilometers north to Galiskari where they were apprehended, bound with ropes, and delivered to authorities in Chios.

They probably suffered the fate of Mitakas. After this episode, no marauder ventured again to step on Icarian shores.[44]

Icaria lagged behind its neighbors, but by 1890 the people who lived in or near Aghios Kyrikos and Evdilos had become part of the modern world. The communities of Icarians living in Izmir, Alexandria, Athens, and America were by and large responsible for the changes. Dwelling among Greeks of the Diaspora, they were exposed to new ideas, and especially to the question of joining Greek territories in the Ottoman Empire with the Greek mother country. This would become the critical issue for Icarians in the beginning of the 20th century.[45]

1. J. Melas, *Istoria tes Nesos Ikarias* (Athens, 1957), pp. 166–167 notes the name of the Greek official, Zacharias Papagiannakis, but was unable to find any Icarian documents relative to his tenure.

2. Carter V. Findley, *Ottoman Civil Officialdom: A Social History* (Princeton, 1989), pp. 264–266, 270–271.

3. On July 17, 1832, Georgios Vassilaros was made customs official and authorized passports for ten paras; he held passengers from Turkey in quarantine for ten days, see L. Spanos, *Ikariaka Chronika* (Syros, Greece, 1925), pp. 98–99. The meagerness of the one hundred groschen salary: A generation later, a rural worker earned 6 to 10 groschen a day in Mytilene. Even with some inflationary developments over a thirty-year period, the difference in the wages between a civil servant in Icaria and a worker in Mytilene is significant; for wages in Mytilene, see Eurydice Siphnaios, *Lesvos: Oikonomike kai Koinonike Istoria, 1840–1912* (Athens, 1996), p. 177. Plague: Melas, *Ikarias*, p. 59, in 1950 interviewed a man in his late 80s who had heard of a smallpox plague from his grandmother. This seems to be connected with the plague of 1832 when people from Mytilene fled to Asia Minor to avoid the pestilence; see Siphnaios, *Lesvos,* p. 255. For the routes that diseases traveled, see Daniel Panzac, *La peste dans L'empire ottoman, 1700–1850* (Paris, 1985), pp. 134–146.

4. Melas, *Ikarias,* pp. 177–179. For the Turkish navy in Samos, see, J. S. Shaw, "Salem III and the Ottoman Navy," *Turcica: Revue d'études turques,* 1 (1969), p. 213.

5. See P. Savorinakis, *Nesiotikes Koinonies Sto Aigaio: E Periptose ton Ellenon tes Rhodou kai tes Ko, 18os–19os Aionas (Athens,* n.d.), p. 112, for 1834 delegation. For this tax, see Melas, *Ikaria,* pp. 179–180, and T. Binekos, *Atheras,* 1985.

6. Melas, *Ikarias,* pp. 179–180. For the full text of Mahmud's 1835 firman, see G. Lombardas, *Ikarias: Etoi Geographike tes Nesou Perigraphe* (Syros, Greece, 1903), pp. 41–42, or Melas, *Ikaria,* pp. 183–184. Later in the century, the Porte exacted a tithe. For the tithe see, S. Pamuk, "Commodity Production for World Markets and Relations of Production," in *Ottoman Agriculture in the Ottoman Empire and the World Economy* (Paris, 1987), pp. 178–202. L. Ross, *Inselreisen* (Halle, 1913), pp. 135–136, notes nineteen thousand (groschen).

7. Melas, *Ikarias,* pp. 183–187.

8. Melas, *Ikarias,* pp. 188–189.

9. Mytilene 150,000 groschen. Siphnaiou, *Lesbos,* p. 73. Tanzimat: E. J. Zürchner, *Turkey: A Modern History* (New York, 1997), pp. 52–54.

10. Taxes: Melas, *Ikarias,* pp. 188–189, L. Bürchner, "Ikaros-Nicaria, eine vergessene Insel des griechischen Archipels," *Petermans Mitteilungen* 40 (1894), 258. A. Plakidas, *It Could Happen Only in America* (Athens, 1966), p. 19 equates a groschen to 3 cents. Plakidas must be mistaken at putting his father's annual tax in the last years of Ottoman rule at 6 groschen. Plakidas' book is titled in English but the text is Greek.

11. Melas, *Ikarias,* pp. 178–179.

12. Forest laws for 1838 and 1864: The Ph.D. thesis of D. Koumparos, *The Communal Management of the Radi Forest on Icaria Island, Greece.* Published by the Department of Environmental Studies, University of the Aegean (Mytilene, 2001), pp. 6–7, 138–140. Document of 1842 law published in *Ikarike Phoné,* June 30, 1968. Icarians secure possession of their forests: J. Tsarnas, "Charalambos Pamphylis," *Atheras,* Nov./Dec. 1993.

13. Ross, *Inselreisen,* pp. 134–136.

14. Ross, *Inselreisen,* p. 137, refers to the aristocratic party "s'il y en a." See remarks of Gerasimos Augustinos, *The Greeks of Asia Minor: Confession, Community, and Ethnicity in the Nineteenth Century* (Kent, Ohio, 1992), p. 68. The first Ottoman government census took place a decade before Ross' visit, 1831, and was based on a count of households; see K. Karpat, "Ottoman Population Records and the Census of 1881/1882–1893," *International Journal of Middle East Studies* 9 (1978), 244.

15. Unfettered animals: Melas, *Ikarias,* p. 189. Reform: Carter Findley, *Bureaucratic Reform in the Ottoman Empire: The Sublime Porte, 1789–1922* (Princeton, 1980), pp. 157–158, discusses the difficulties the Ottoman state had in carrying out such reforms because of the small size of the bureaucracy. An example of the inept bureaucracy that Findley discuss-

es is found in a letter from the governor of Rhodes to the *demogerontia,* March 11th, 1843, threatening to release thieves if taxes are not paid. This document suggests that the "farmers" had recently gained control of the *demogerontia* through the aid of the Turkish authorities who had arrested their main opponents. The new *demogerontia,* however, was not raising the expected taxes. This document is in the papers of Argiris Koutsounamendos, Aghios Kyrikos, Icaria. Ottoman economic crisis of the 1840s, and attempts to raise revenues, see Pamuk, *Monetary History,* pp. 207–208. A food crisis in 1845: C. Issawi, *The Economic History of Turkey 1800–1914* (Chicago, 1980), pp. 199–200. L. Bürchner, "Ikaros-Nicaria, eine vergessene Insel des griechischen Archipels," *Petermans Mitteilungen* 40 (1894), 258, notes that a certain A. Glaros was kidnapped by Algerian pirates about 1820. During his captivity, he learned about the cultivation of the potato, and introduced this product to the island around 1840. In the 1820s, when Icaria was temporarily under the rule of the New Greek government, a Greek official tried to introduce the potato to Icaria, but failed; see Melas, *Ikaria,* p. 167.

16. Founder of the Spanos clan: Interviews with Christos Spanos, May 23, 1994, Raches, Icaria; Daniel Spanos, Raches Icaria, June 3, 1996, and George Spanos, Piraeus, March 17, 2002, who maintains a personal archive on the history of the Spanos family. Ross, who was unable to reach the northern side of the island, did not know about the agricultural developments at Campos. For the proverb about the Spanos clan, interview Isidoros Spanos, Raches, Icaria, June 29, 2004. He also cites another one: "Lord, I beseech you to protect me from plague, fire, and the Spanos clan." In the 1960s, it was widely believed in Raches that the orphan Spanos boy brought to Icaria was the offspring of Jewish parents massacred in Chios by the Turks in 1822. Such a belief was based not only on their efficient business methods but also on a physical appearance that, in many cases, is distinctly non-Icarian; interview Socrates Fakaros, Raches, Icaria, June 12, 1961. The Spanos family rejects their purported Jewish roots; interview Christos Spanos, Raches, Icaria, June 20, 1961.

17. Agricultural conditions: G. Lombardas, *Ikarias* pp. 37–38, who referred to friction between shepherds and farmers in 1903. Interviews about other coastal developments, George Manolis Lincoln Park, Michigan, July 1995; Steve Fakaros, Aghios Kyrikos, July 1995, who each passed on oral traditions—the former from Manganitis and the latter from Xyloserti.

18. A certain Papas Leodakis on July 20, 1868, purchased a plot of land in Tsouredos worth 70 groschen. Elias Moraitis sold this plot to a son on Jan 20, 1904, for 1,000 groschen. Document in the collection of Ioannes Papalas. The Icarians generally did not sell small plots like vineyards separately, as the Samians did; see A. Sevastakes, *Istoria Neou Karlovasou Samou, 1768–1840* (Athens, 1995), p. 48. H. Hauttecoeur, "L'île d'Ikaria," *Bulletin de la Société Geographique de Anvers,* 25 (1900), 363, notes that

the Ottoman authorities decapitated Manuel Mitakas in Samos for piracy in 1861. His descendant, N. Mitikas, recounted the family tradition that his pirate ancestor deploying Fourni as a base regularly raided Icaria; interview June 28, 2004, Aghios Kyrikos, Icaria.

19. Cold Wave: D. Thrasyboulos, "Agrotike Krese kai Koinonikoi Mechanismoi: Penia tou 1854," in *E Samos apo ta Byzantina Chronia mechri Semera* (Athens, 1998), II, 152–154, and Siphnaios, *Lesvos,* p. 112. Samian piracy, which developed as a result of the famine conditions, was mainly directed at the coast of Asia Minor and not at Samians: Christos Landros, "E Lestroperateia sten Samo peri ta Mesa tou 19[ou] Aiona," in *E Samos apo to Byzantina Chronia mechri Semera* (Athens, 1998), pp. 200–202.

20. Refugees: Tsarnas, *Ikariaka,* 2 (1975), 9–10. Interview Angelos Kalokairinos, Aghios Kyrikos, May 19, 2002, reported a tradition, heard by his father, a native of Armenistis, that several of these "settlers," drowned off the coast of Armenisitis. Two million people: Karpat, "Ottoman Population Records," 240–241. Also see Augustinos, *Greeks in Asia Minor,* pp. 28–29. Starvation in Samos: D. Thrasyboulos, "Agrotike Krese kai Koinonikoi Mechanismoi: E Penia tou 1854," 185.

21. Symi: C. D. Booth, I. B. Booth, *Italy's Aegean Possessions* (London, 1928), pp. 218–219. Popular *Kaimakames:* Plakidas, *Only in America,* pp. 20–21. Also see E. Stamatiades, *Ikariaka* (Samos, 1893), pp. 67–68.

22. For the working of this council, see Melas, *Ikarias,* pp. 190–191 and Hauttecoeur, "L'île d'Ikaria," 343–344. A good example of the *demogerontia*'s efficiency may be seen in the personal papers of Ioannes A. Papalas II: On April 1st, 1878, a certain George Tsouris claimed a portion of land owned by Ioannes B. Papalas in Tsouredo, and trespassed into the disputed property causing damage. On April 2nd, Papalas sent a complaint to the headman who acknowledged it on April 4th, and called a meeting of the demogerontia who assumed the function of a judicial body. On April 5th these magistrates notified Tsouris that if he were again to trespass he would be fined. Letters from the governor of Rhodes to the *demogerontia,* March 11th, 1843, threatening to release thieves: Personal archives of Argiris Koutsounamendos, Aghios Kyrikos.

23. Customs Officials: A. Plakidas, *Ikariaka,* 37 (1966), pp. 44–47. Fez: Augustinos, *Greeks of Asia Minor,* p. 67. There are several extant photographs from the end of the 19th century depicting Icarian members of the *demogerontia* sporting a fez.

24. Tax to bishop: Ross, *Inselreisen,* p. 137. Wages in Mytilene: Siphnaios, *Lesbos,* p. 177. Tax categories: Augustinos, *The Greeks of Asia Minor,* p. 170. Shortchanging tax collector: March 18, 1848, document in the collec-

tion of Argiris Koutsounamendos. Population: Melas, *Ikarias,* pp. 199–200. For the tithe, see S. Pamuk, "Commodity Production," pp. 178–202. G. Lombardas, *Ikarias: Etoi Geographike tes Nesou Perigraphe* (Syros, Greece, 1903), p. 38, notes the payment of 6,500 groschen to the bishop in Samos, and pp. 41–42, cites the sultan's 1835 firman noting the nonviolent record of the people inhabiting the islands of the White Sea—Icaria, Patmos, Leros, and Kalymnos—during the war.

25. Savorinakes, *Nesiotikes Koinones,* p. 102, discusses the prosperity created in these islands through commercial contacts in Asia Minor and Egypt. Spa: G. Lombardas, *Ikarias,* p. 21. A. Andréades, "The Currant Crisis in Greece," *Economic Journal* 16 (1906), pp. 43–44. Peaches and the value of 100 piasters (groschen): Hauttecoeur, "L'île d'Ikaria," 336, 350.

26. For 19th century taxes see Melas, *Ikarias,* pp. 201–203, and early 20th-century taxes and population of Aghios Kyrikos and Evdilos; see G. Lombardas, *Ikarias,* pp. 16–17, 23–24, 40–41. Value of a *spitotopon* in Aghios Kyrikos in 1888: Document in Ioannes Papalas' collection. The 19th-century population of Aghios Kyrikos and Evdilos: Bürchner, "Ikaros," 261. For the early houses in Aghios Kyrikos, see T. Katsaros, "Aghios Kyrikos Ikarias," *Ikariaka,* 42 (2001), 20–22.

27. Icarians enjoyed the reputation for building fine boats as early as the 17th century; see J. Georgirenes, *A Description of the Present State of Samos, Nicaria, Patmos and Mount Athos* (London, 1677), p. 60, who wrote "they are very expert in making boats and small vessels, which are in such esteem they are bought up by all their neighbors." More on Icarian ships: Melas, *Ikarias,* p. 195; Stamatiades, *Ikariaka,* p. 104. The first Ottoman newspaper, *Le Moniteur Ottoman,* established in 1831, provides information about sail and steam navigation; see *Le Moniteur Ottoman,* Sept. 17, 1836. For schedules: October 24, 1837, *Le Moniteur Ottoman.* Thomas Arnold, *The History of the Peloponnesian War by Thucydides* (Oxford, 1840), I, iii–iv.

28. Greek steamships: Konstantinos Papathanasopoulos, "Greek Shipping in Its Historical Context," *Greece and the Sea* (Amsterdam, 1987), p. 106. Mytilene service, soap, and leather: Siphnaios, *Lesvos,* pp. 233–236, 254. The Levant and Steamship service from Salonica to Istanbul: Mark Mazower, "Salonica between East and West," pp. 106–108. Revival of sailships: Gerald S. Graham, "The Ascendancy of Sailing Ships 1850–1885," *Economic History Review* 9 (1956), 74–78. The last will and testament of a shipowner and captain, Ioannis B. Papalas, May 7, 1934, states that in 1890 off Egypt, "I lost my sail ship and its cargo valued at more than 350 English pounds." Because sail rather than steam power transported his cargo, he could not afford to insure it. For the rise in rates for sail ships, see S. Palmer, "The indemnity in the London Marine Insurance Market," in *The Historian and the Business of Insurance,* edited by O. M. Westal (Manchester, England, and Dover, New Hampshire, 1984), pp. 74–94. As a result of his

A 17th century house from Pezi, on a mountain plateau above Raches. The area is now uninhabited. (Ch. Malachias' collection)

The interior of a house in Christos, Raches. The bishop Georgirenes stayed in it around 1650. (Ch. Malachias' collection)

Theoskepasti a 17th century chapel near Frantato. This chapel was dedicated to the remains of Saint Theokteste from Lesbos. (Ch. Malachias' collection)

A view of Kako Katavasi, a passage that the unfortunate cadi failed to negotiate in the early 17th century. (Ch. Malachias' collection)

The figures are walking at the point where the Icarians cast the
cadi to his death from Kako Katavasidi down into a valley below.
There are now stairs carved into the rocks, but this was a slippery
and treacherous crossing at the time the cadi was murdered.
(Ch. Malachias' collection)

The Yiemelia bridge on the upper reaches of the river Chalaris. The demogerontia supervised the construction of the bridge around 1880 and it was part of a larger project to connect the various Icarian villages with inter-village lanes. The bridge was a gateway to Vrakades and the isolated western region of the island. (Ch. Malachias' collection)

A member of the demogerontia around 1900. (author's collection)

A widowed Egyptian official, pictured in the front
row with his family, hired an Icarian girl to manage
his household and take care of his children. The
Icarian girl is in the upper left hand corner. The picture was taken in Cairo around 1910. (G. Charnas'
collection)

School children in Aghios Kyrikos around 1907. Despite the shoeless boy in the front row the children are well dressed. (Ch. Malachias' collection)

School children in Christos, Raches around 1912. (Ch. Malachias' collection)

School children in Christos, Raches around 1925. They seem somewhat less well dressed than their counterparts in the previous pictures. Perhaps this is an indication of the economic decline from the time of the Ottoman period. (Ch. Malachias' collection)

Dr. Malachias (upper left) and Papa
Kouloulias (upper right). This photo was
taken in 1912 when these men led the
movement to expel the Turks from Icaria.
(Ch. Malachias' collection)

Evdilotes celebrating the raising of the Icarian flag in August, 1912. (Ch. Malachias' collection)

Icarian force, 1912. (Ch. Malachias' collection)

Icarians occupying Fanari after the defeat of the Turks in 1912.
(Ch. Malachias' collection)

A veteran of the 1912 uprising, Papa Kyprios, before he became a priest. In 1948 he defied gendarmes and gave a proper burial to a guerrilla. (I. Kyrprios' collection)

The steamer *Frinton* around 1947. The government had taken it out of mothballs to convey prisoners to Icaria. (Ch. Malachias' collection)

The steamer *Aegeon* in the mid-1920s. (Ch. Malachias' collection)

Passengers being taken to a boat waiting safely off the shores of Aghios
Kyrikos before the mole was built. (author's collection)

Two Icarian shepherds about 1920. (Ch. Malachias'
collection)

loss, this man made arrangements to compensate his debtors by sending his sons to America to earn money. They were experts at using a naval "kandilitsa," a board tied to ropes and connected to a pulley that they later set up in steel mills to work at elevated sites. Document in author's private collection.

29. Charcoal: R. Bechmann, *Trees and Man: The Forest in the Middle Ages* (New York, 1990), pp. 151–154. Attempts to preserve Icarian forest: D. Koumparos, *The Communal Management of the Radi Forest*, p. 6. Greeks were selling timber products in Egypt as early as the fifth century B.C.; see B. Porten and A. Yardeni, eds. and trans., *Textbook of Aramaic Documents from Ancient Egypt* (Jerusalem, 1993), pp. 55–92. Passport: Plakidas, *Ikariaka*, 37 (1966), p. 17. Christian bandits: Henry Field, *The Greek Islands and Turkey after the War* (New York, 1885), pp. 162–163. Bodrum concession: interview Nick Achidafty, July 27, 1995, who heard such tales from his grandfather who worked this type of concession. Sarantos Ploutis cleared out bandits: J. Tsarnas, *Ikariake Phoné*, Nov. 1976. M. W. Helms, *Ulysses' Sail: An Ethnographic Odyssey of Power, Knowledge, and Geographical Distance* (Princeton, 1988), pp. 78–81, explains how men like the Icarian captains, who engaged in risky voyages to gain wealth and knowledge, achieved great status when they returned to their out-of-the-way communities.

30. Kilos of currants and other export fruits: Bürchner, "Ikaros," 257. Plakidas, *Only in America,* pp. 18–19; A. Andréades, "The Currant Crisis," 43–44. Ships: Stamatiades, *Ikariaka,* p. 104. Phylloxera: G. Ordish, *The Great Wine Blight* (London, 1972), pp. 177–178. Phylloxera in Icaria and high quality grape: G. Giagourtas, *E Oikonomike Zoe tes Ikarias apo ta mesa tou 19ou os ta mesa tou 20ou Aiona. E Paragoge kai Emporia tes Staphidas* (Athens, 2004), pp. 27–35, 86.

31. The population also doubled in Mytilene; see Siphnaios, *Lesvos* p. 245. Some of the surplus population from the islands settled in Izmir; see Karpat, *Ottoman Population,* p. 47. There were many migrant workers who left the Aegean islands for Asia Minor from May to October; see, Siphnaios, *Lesvos,* 253.

32. For population, see Kemal H. Karpat, *Ottoman Population 1830–1914. Demographic and Social Characteristics* (Madison, 1985), p. 47. K. Karpat, "Ottoman Population Records and the Census of 1881/82–1893," *International Journal of Middle East Studies* 9 (1978), 249–251. Work in Chios and Izmir: G. Hatzidakis, "Peri tes Ikarias Dialectou," *Messaionika kai Nea Ellinika* (Amsterdam, 1910), II, 397–460. Kolettas' figures: Hauttecoeur, "L'île d'Ikaria," 339.

33. An anonymous pamphlet entitled *E Ikariake Epanastases* (published by the Menikidou Brothers, presumably in Alexandria, Egypt, 1912), lists 57 male

members of the Icarian brotherhood in Egypt. Many of them had wives and children. Thus in 1912 the permanent Icarian settlement would be around 300. There were perhaps an additional 300 who were transitory.

34. Manners in Samos: Georgeta Penelea Filitti, "Une visite chez les prince de Samos 1848," *E Samos apo ta Byzantina Chronia mechri Semera* 2, 469–471. Jewish merchant: J. Tsarnas, "O Patsifikos tes Ikarias," *Ikariaka,* 6 (1972), pp. 4–5, and Hauttecoeur, "L'île d'Ikaria," 349. Four-post bed: Charles Newton, *Travels and Discoveries in the Levant* (London, 1858), 2, 234–235.

35. Katsimidis: Tsarnas, *Ikariaka,* 7 (1976), p. 11. For a denial of the existence of the *krypha scholia,* see P. Boukalas, *Kathemerine* (Sunday Supplement), March 25, 1998. Right to construct schools and repair churches: Siphnaios, *Lesvos,* p. 69, and Augustinos, *The Greeks of Asia Minor,* p. 146. Fraudulent population figures: Karpat, *Ottoman Population,* pp. 241–242. Also see the comments of Karpat, "Ottoman Population Records and the Census of 1881/82–1893," *International Journal of Middle East Studies* 9 (1978), 241.

36. For salaries, see Augustinos, *Greeks of Asia Minor,* p. 228, n. 53. Mytilene salary: Siphnaios, *Lesvos,* p. 147.

37. J. Tsarnas, *Ikariaka,* 7 (1976), p. 11. L. Spanos, *Ikariaka Chronika* (Syros, Greece, 1925), p. 80. George Poulianos' private school accepted girls: Citations from G. Poulianos' unpublished memoirs, see Baletas, *Ikariaka,* 1993, 14. School in Chalcis: Augustinos, *Greeks in Asia Minor,* pp. 151, 157. Chagranis and the Evangeliki school: N. Diamantides, "Aristides E. Phoutrides: Harvard's Schizocardiac Scholar," *Modern Greek Studies Yearbook* 8 (1992), 77.

38. Number of doctors, Bürchner, "Ikaros," 260. Banking: Siphnaios, *Lesvos,* p. 250. Shipping by rail: Ibid., p. 254.

39. Prominent Icarian families: Melas, *Ikarias,* pp. 202–203. J. Tsarnas, *Ikariake Phoné,* July 1976. Large landowners: Ibid. pp. 170–172. From 1880 to 1912 there was a great economic expansion in the Aegean area. In Mytilene banks were established and steam power and machinery appeared. Modern mechanized presses produced record olive yields. There were 269 olive presses, 10 powered by steam, 13 tanneries, and 164 flour mills. In 1891, a female worker could earn 3 groschen a day; see Siphnaiou, *Lesvos,* pp. 197–199. It seems that the introduction of machinery depressed wages. Buried money: interview Christos Spanos, Raches, Icaria, July 5, 1974. Value of a Mytilene house: Siphnaiou, *Lesvos,* pp. 159–163. In Icaria a good house was worth one thousand five hundred groschen; see Elias Moraitis' sale of house to son on Jan. 20, 1904. A generous dowry in Icaria: July 20, 1868, Papas Leonidas left earthen vessels, the Frankish plot of

land, and a pear tree. On January 30, 1871, Pantelis Karaphas, considered a man of property, gave a dowry to his daughter, who was about to marry Ioannes A. Choriates. It consisted of a vineyard, some beehives, a cow, and two goats, in the collection of documents of J. Papalas. Siphnaiou, *Lesvos,* pp. 145, 170–172, investigates the class of Mytileneans who produced 50 or more measures of olive oil without working themselves and who lived in luxury. Profits for ship captains: Giagourtas, *E Oikonomike Zoe tes Ikarias,* pp. 57–59.

40. Melas, *Ikaria,* pp. 202–203. J. Tsarnas, *Ikariake Phoné,* July 1976.

41. Leprosarium: G. Lombardas, *Ikarias: Etoi Geographike,* pp. 21–22. In the 1879 novel *Loukis Laras,* the author Demetrios Bikelas (Athens, 1988 reprint), pp. 131–141, introduces a character from Icaria to depict ignorance and poverty. On p. 134, the protagonist asks a man "Where do you come from?" He answers, "Icaria." "No wonder you are so stupid *'koutos.'* " Such is the view of Icarians implied in the work of E. Stamatiades, *Ikariaka* (Samos, 1893), passim. N. Poulianos, who hailed from Evdilos, Icaria, published a critical review of Stamatiades' book in *Amaltheia,* a Greek newspaper published in Izmir; see Baletas, *Ikariaka,* (1993), 12. Although Stamatiades' work is relatively accurate, and drew the praise of the great epigraphist L. Robert, Icarians still condemn the book for its "exaggerations and inaccuracies," see J. Tsarnas, "E Paidia sten Ikaria Sta Chronia tes Tourkokratias," *Praktika Aegeou Symposiou 1980* (Athens, 1993), p. 41. "They gathered copies of Stamatiades' books and burned them on the beach at Aghios Kyrikos"; see G. Karoutsos, *Ikariake Phoné,* August 23, 1958. For Stamatiades' students as village schoolteachers, see J. Tsarnas, ibid., p. 41. In 1910 a Samian teacher slapped one of his charges in Tsouredo. The uncle of the punished boy threatened the teacher with a beating; interview, L. Papalas Tsouredos, Icaria, June 17, 1990.

42. G. Hatzidakis, "Peri tes Ikarias Dialectou," II, 397–460. Autochthonous theory about Icarian origins: G. Karoutsos, *Ikariake Phoné,* August 23, 1958.

43. L. Bürchner, "Ikaros" 257–258.

44. Execution of Mitakas: Hauttecoeur, "L'île d'Ikaria," 361. Mitakas' modus operandi and last words are part of the family tradition; interview Nikolas Mitakas, direct descendant, Aghios Kyrikos, May 29, 2004. Raid: L. Spanos, *Ikariaka,* pp. 88–89. George Horton, *Home of Nymphs and Vampires: The Isles of Greece* (New York, 1929), pp. 218–220, translates a folk song dealing with the event. The men who raided Evdilos were apparently among those who had not shared in the economic prosperity of the late 19th century. As we have seen, above note 36, machinery was displacing some rural workers. Laborsaving machinery in Asia Minor: A. Andréades, "The Currant Crisis in Greece," *Economic Journal* 16 (1906), pp. 43–44. Plakidas, *Only in America,* pp. 18–19, discusses economic conditions.

Field, *The Greek Islands,* pp. 162–163, notes Christian bandits in Asia Minor, probably uprooted rural workers. They were similar to the Samian pirates of about 1850; see Christos Landros, "E Lestroperateia sten Samo peri ta Mesa tou 19[ou] Aiona," *E Samos apo ta Byzantina Chronia mechri Semera* (Athens, 1998), II, who notes, 201, a ransom of 17 Turkish lira for women captives, and, 205, cites execution as standard punishment for pirates. Bürchner, *Ikaros,* p. 979, who visited Icaria in 1893, noted that the Icarians had blocked the Chalares River perhaps in the previous century, to prevent corsairs from sailing deep into the northern interior and attacking the people of Raches.

45. Ottoman Greeks in the Aegean could emigrate to Greece and in three years obtain Greek citizenship and return to the islands, but the Porte, until 1908, pressed these new Greek citizens for taxes; see Siphnaios, *Lesvos,* pp. 83–84. Because of the limited economic opportunities in Greece, few Icarians chose this option.

CHAPTER 3

Unification
with Greece

ICARIANS who lived in the twilight years of the Ottoman Empire had fond recollections of life on the island under the Turks. There was peace, freedom from pirate attacks, much local autonomy, and low taxes. No one much cared that the island remained an economic backwater. Many of the men were engaged in sea-borne occupations, some settled in Alexandria, Egypt, and others went to America. By 1910, about ten percent of the adult males worked in United States factories, mainly steel mills in the Pittsburgh area of southwest Pennsylvania. They sent dollars to Icaria to support their families. As money flowed in from abroad, most people enjoyed a comfortable life, and were relatively happy under the Sultan's lethargic rule.[1]

Such an attitude prevented incidents from escalating into violence. Around 1890, a man killed two Turkish officials on the island. His motives were over either a personal matter or a tax payment. The man fled to America, and the community—taking collective responsibility for the act—amassed funds to pay a fine for the crime.[2] The Porte, with pressing problems in the Balkans, difficulties with the Armenians, and escalating public debt, was careful not to let such episodes poison relations between ruler and subject in frontier outposts. Furthermore, Ottoman authorities had no anxieties in Icaria, as they did in Crete, about Greeks with a warlike character living amidst a strong Muslim minority. They, therefore, ignored such occurrences as aberrations from the normal pattern, and did not maintain a costly number of gendarmes on the island.

In 1889, the Sultan Abdulhamid II (ruled 1876–1909) dispatched a huge force to Crete, and within weeks Ottoman forces suppressed a Greek uprising there, and displayed an impressive military prowess. In 1896, the Cretans rebelled again, and this time Greece stepped into the conflict despite its inadequate naval force. Athens sent several *agents provocateurs* to Icaria hoping to instigate an uprising against Turkey, but they made little impact, for the bulk of the people considered Turkey a stronger military power than Greece, enjoyed their condition in the Ottoman Empire, and thus professed loyalty to the Porte. The Icarians' assessment of the military situation was correct. From the start, the war did not go well for Greece. The Greek government actually had to hire commercial ships to transport its troops to Crete because it lacked an adequate navy, and then had difficulties supplying its forces.[3] The "Sick Man of Europe," as Turkey was called in European diplomatic circles, withstood the assault and seemed to be regaining some of its former health. As the war progressed, Greece, rather than acquiring new territories, faced the prospect of losing regions under its control. But the European powers intervened, imposing a peace that required Greece to pay an indemnity to Turkey but keep all its prewar territory. The Greeks, however, received a major concession. The great powers arranged for Crete to be autonomous, but under the nominal suzerainty of the Sultan.[4]

By the end of the first decade of the 20th century, Sultan Abdulhamid II had been deposed, Icarian sentiments regarding the Ottoman Empire were changing, and the people were being swept up into irredentist politics. The desire for reunification with Greece is reflected in an Icarian folk song, or rather a Greek one that became popular in Icaria at this time, about the boy born in the morning high in the mountains, who by the afternoon took up arms to resist the Turks, and in the evening vanquished the Sultan's army. Boys were motivated by such folklore. On one occasion, youngsters from Kountoumas, the village above Aghios Kyrikos, became too enthusiastic in a game entitled *Tourkos.* Besieging a high point outside the village, they raised the Greek flag. The *kaimakames,* a Greek from Asia Minor named Zapheiropoulos, detected the forbidden standard, dashed from Aghios Kyrikos to Kountoumas, had the emblem taken down, and threatened to punish the pranksters.[5]

A more serious affair followed. A man whose father had come from Crete in 1843 and settled in Glaredo, a village just above Aghios Kyrikos, had one of those stentorian voices so admired by Georgirenes and thus earned the post of herald. One evening at a well-attended festival, the herald decided to issue a proclamation on his own authority. "Hear ye, hear ye ladies and gentlemen, the decree of the Turkish cuckolds and faggots." Then he raised his leg mimicking a breaking of wind sound and said, "this is our reply to the decree of the faggots and cuckolds." A Turkish gendarme, who was attending the event, arrested him on the spot. Interrogated by the *kaimakames,* the herald explained that he suffered from chronic enteritis, and during the festival had an especially serious attack. Zapheiropoulos expressed sympathy but dismissed him from the position of herald because this medical condition rendered him unfit to execute his responsibilities in a manner befitting the majesty of the Ottoman Empire.[6]

The above episodes were trivial and handled in an appropriate nonchalant fashion. But organized resistance began to develop, and such defiance had to be met with harsher measures. One Icarian priest began to speak openly in church about union with Greece. In 1905, he was accused of inciting Icarians to civic disobedience and was imprisoned in Rhodes by the Turks. An Icarian charcoal merchant making a call in Rhodes heard that the priest faced a long prison term, and on his return to Icaria reported this to Charalambos Pamphylis, a lawyer in Aghios Kyrikos. Pamphylis dashed off to Istanbul where he had contacts with Ottoman authorities, and was able to obtain the release of the clergyman. The priest ceased to make political comments in church, but continued to urge union to receptive audiences in private meetings.[7]

By now the majority of the Icarians had changed their views and had become anti-Ottoman. There were many reasons why the Icarians desired unification with Greece. Religion, culture and language were primary factors, but financial considerations were also motives. The Icarians believed—and were to be disappointed in this matter—that they would immediately prosper as part of Greece. Furthermore, the Icarians feared that the Golden Age of the Ottoman Empire was coming to an end. The improving efficiency of the Turkish bureaucracy was eliminating *rousfeti,* a combination of personal relationships with officials, and bribes to higher authorities that settled matters before they entered the judicial labyrinth of the government. The Icarians had been very skillful at exploiting the informal and unofficial *rousfeti* system, obtaining privileges, and circumventing the strict application of the law. A new businesslike procedure for collecting taxes was being established throughout the Ottoman Empire, and the Icarians were not disposed to yield their fair share. One very conspicuous untapped revenue source was the radioactive spa at Therma, which had been known in antiquity as a healing center. By the end of the 19th century, the baths at Therma had acquired a reputation in Anatolia for their curative powers, and were attracting a handful of invalids from Izmir and other Anatolian cities. The Icarians never paid a duty on the fees they charged those using the public baths at Therma, though spas in other parts of the Ottoman Empire provided revenue for the Ottoman coffers. In 1910, the Porte instructed the *kaimakames* to collect taxes on the baths.[8]

The Icarians submitted to this tax, but fiercely resisted Ottoman efforts to suppress tobacco production on the island. Tobacco, introduced to the island around 1870, was a bad bet in Icaria.[9] The Icarian yield was restricted by the dry climate and limited land. The Icarian product was not comparable in aroma, taste, and combustibility to good Anatolian tobacco, and was mainly used locally, though small amounts of this contraband was sneaked out of Armenistis to other islands. This was an ideal port for smugglers who set off at night sailing with the aid of a breeze that came down from the mountains behind the small harbor.

Shortly after Icarians began to grow tobacco, the Ottoman government, as part of a policy to limit the cultivation of tobacco in areas where it would not yield sufficient tax revenues, prohibited it in Icaria, but did nothing to enforce the ban. But that situation was about to change. In 1887, the Porte defaulted on an international debt, and as a result the possessors of Ottoman government bonds in Europe were allowed to reorganize certain sections of the Ottoman economy. The Sultan permitted these creditors to form a public debt administration, the PDA. The main purpose of this council of seven European financial experts was to improve the efficiency of Ottoman tax collecting and thus amass funds to pay off the nation's external debt. The PDA assumed control of the sale of salt, postage stamps, spirits, fish, silk, and tobacco. For the latter item, they created the *Régie des Tabacs,* a bureau to administer the production and sale of tobacco.[10]

Tobacco producers were required to apply annually to the *Régie* for a license. At first, the small Icarian yield was not controlled, for the *Régie* was interested in the large tobacco producers of Anatolia such as the Greek farmers in the city of Samsum. Here in one of the great tobacco-growing regions of Turkey along the south coast of the Black Sea, Greek tobacco producers did not obtain a license or pay their tax. In 1887, the year the farmers defied the new regulations, they stoned and injured some representatives of the *Régie* when they arrived to collect the tobacco tax, but the Sultan could not retreat on this issue, and forced the farmers to settle accounts. Then the *Régie* turned its attention to minor tobacco growers, prohibiting cultivation behind stone walls, specifically on the type of modest, terraced plots that were typical in Icaria and other Aegean islands. The authorities regarded such production as an effort to circumvent taxes.[11]

All Icarian tobacco cultivation was illegal because it was behind stone walls on terraced plots, and about 1890 the *kaimakames* notified growers to stop cultivating the plant. No attempt, however, was actually made to curb production because the growers were providing a generous bribe, *peskes,* in the form of a good supply of the forbidden item to the gendarmes and the *kaimakames.* Eventually the *Régie* cracked down on the small producers, and eliminated them virtually everywhere—except in Icaria. Apparently, the *Régie* had informants in Icaria who reported illegal production. In 1904, this agency threatened to send representatives to Icaria if production was not terminated. The *demogerontia*, council of elders, of Fanari appealed to the fledgling Pan-Icarian Brotherhood of America for support.[12] There is no record of the Icarian-American response. We may assume that it impressed Turkish authorities, for it was widely believed in Icaria that the Icarians in America had support in high places, and apparently the Porte suspected as much. In 1907, the *Régie* rescinded the prohibition against planting tobacco in Icaria, and granted the Icarians a special exemption in this matter. An ecstatic council of elders expressed its gratitude in a letter to the Sultan describing how the inhabitants of the thirty-six villages of Icaria rang church bells and "praised the Lord praying for a long life to our master, the Sultan Abdulhamid."[13]

The jubilant mood was short-lived. In 1908, Turkish military officers from the Macedonian army forced Abdulhamid to restore the constitution, and in 1909 to abdicate in favor of his brother, who became Sultan on April 27. The new government, the so-called "Young Turks," put through sweeping reforms that were intended to improve the operations of the Ottoman Empire, limit corruption, bring the minorities of the empire together by assuring equality before the law, and finally to establish the efficient collection of taxes. Such an efficient and impartial government was not to the liking of the Icarians. Bribes to the *kaimakames* and his officials in the form of walnuts, wine, honey, goats, and such things guaranteed almost total autonomy. Corruption in small doses was an effective remedy against intrusive government.[14] For the Icarians, the reforms seemed to herald an end to the recent progress. They did not desire equal treatment before the law. Such reforms, in their opinion, simply meant that the Icarians would pay their fair share of taxes. The placing of an office of the *Régie* on the island heralded the end of the *rousfeti* system and its period of benign neglect. In 1909, Turkish officials, with authorization to search homes, a right the previous government had not granted their gendarmes, came from Chios to terminate the production of tobacco and register all taxable items including agricultural production and animals. A military vessel now patrolled the island to prevent smuggling. The *demogerontia* of Mesaria, the center of the "behind the stone wall" tobacco production, resisted, and the *kaimakames* Zapheiropoulos was obliged to dissolve the council, but was unable to find compliant men to form another.[15]

It is odd that the Icarians saw tobacco production, a minor business, as a major issue. Apparently, they felt that if they gave in on this, the *rousfeti* system would collapse, and they would fall under the yoke of tyranny. The threat of fresh taxes came as Icaria was passing through an economic crisis. Phylloxera had devastated the vineyards; the international currant market was beginning to collapse, and charcoal manufactures were facing higher fees for Anatolian timber concessions. At this point Dr. John Malachias emerged as a leading figure on the island. Born in Xyloserti in 1876, he studied medicine in Athens and Paris, and returned to Icaria in 1906. He quickly became a popular figure displaying more interest in helping his patients than collecting fees. Despite his youth he was elected to the *demogerontia* of Fanari and appointed *mouchtardemogeron*, head of *demogerontia* and chief Icarian official of the island. Dr. Malachias was ready to fight to the finish on the issue of tobacco. Since 1860, when the Levant Co. had laid a cable connecting the Dardanelles to Chios, the telegraph became an effective way of petitioning the Sultan, and appealing over the head of local authorities. Dr. Malachias rushed to Chios and sent a telegram to the Sultan pleading for the suspension of the tobacco restriction.[16]

Although the Porte rejected the plea, it invited the Icarians to participate in a discussion on the problems of the eastern Sporades at a colloquium in Symi, a small island some one-hundred miles southeast of Icaria. In October 1909, just half a year after Abdulhamid II was forced from office, the Icarian representative, who on other occasions could wax eloquent about the beauty and productivity of the island, maintained that Icarians were malnourished people struggling to survive on a barren rock. In 1840, Mahmut II had accepted such a characterization of Icaria and placed it with Patmos, Leros, and Kalymnos, the so-called *Tetranesa,* the "Four Islands," in a special low-tax category. In July 1909, the reform government abolished certain advantages enjoyed by the *Tetranesa,* but at the conference in Symi the Porte renewed certain entitlements to these four islands, which were rated as the poorest Ottoman possessions in the Aegean. The Ottoman government was not, however, prepared to make Icaria the most privileged of the four.[17]

The Icarians wanted to eat their cake and have it too. Benefiting from remittances from America, they were far better off than the inhabitants of the other *Tetranesa,* who did not have the bulk of their young men in America. They, nonetheless, wished to be regarded as the most destitute. While their neighbors accepted the ban on tobacco, they resisted the prohibition, and continued to cultivate the plant. Zapheiropoulos directed the *demogerontia* to put an end to planting it, and when this did not happen, the *kaimakames* arrested Dr. Malachias and several members of the council and dispatched them to Chios to stand trial. Long prison sentences were looming for these men when a telegram from the Porte arrived by boat to Icaria from Chios, granting the Icarians permission to cultivate tobacco for local consumption, and closing the *Régie's* office in Icaria. A relieved Dr. Malachias sent a telegram to the Sultan, Mohammed V, the brother of the deposed Abdulhamid, expressing the gratitude of the Icarian people.[18]

The tobacco issue was a tempest in a teapot. The Turkish losses of revenues from Icarian tobacco were so negligible that they did not cover the cost of collecting it, and granting the Icarians the right to produce it was in the spirit of the privileges granted to the *Tetranesa.* But military service, a new concern, was entirely a different matter, and here the Young Turks were not prepared to make any concessions. Previously, the Ottoman authorities had accepted a tax, the *bedel,* in lieu of military service from the non-Muslim population of the Empire. In the 17th and 18th centuries, the Turks, apparently, impressed some Icarians into the Turkish navy, but in the 19th century no Icarian had been officially conscripted into the Turkish military forces, although some men volunteered for naval service. Matters were about to change. In 1909, a Turkish steamer arrived off the shores of Aghios Kyrikos with three officers to collect the names of all young men eligible for military service.[19]

The council of elders, while providing the names and ages of the male population of the island, argued that most young men were working in America, and the few who remained were essential to maintain the local economy. If the island were deprived of its paltry manpower, the Icarians, loyal subjects that they were, would perish from starvation on their barren rock, and of course would be unable to pay their taxes. In any event, the "Young Turks" were not deterred from their aim. On April 10, 1910, the conscription office in Smyrna selected eight names from the register for military service, and presented the list to Dr. Malachias. In due course, he apprized Turkish authorities that none of these men were available. Some were in America, others could not be found, and one suffered from a disabling epileptic condition. Indeed some men were in America, and others left for America when their name appeared on the list, and still others slipped off to Athens, or retired to remote mountain villages.[20]

Zapheiropoulos did not believe Dr Malachias, and dispatched gendarmes to ferret out the suspected draft dodgers, but with no luck. Indeed no Turkish official could have unearthed men of military age in Icaria, for they were either gone or well-hidden. But the Porte held the unfortunate Zapheiropoulos responsible for the situation, and in 1911, after a decade of service in Icaria, replaced him with Thucydides Demetriades. Thucydides Efendis, as the Icarian respectfully called him, like his predecessor, was a Greek in the Ottoman civil service employed in Greek-speaking areas.[21] The Icarians seemed to take an instant aversion to the new *kaimakames*. Charalambos Pamphylis, the lawyer and future historian of Icaria, did not like his looks. Thucydides' facial features allegedly revealed anti-Hellenic sentiments and moral flaws. He was considered a tyrant, and rumors circulated in the Icarian communities of Alexandria and America that he was imprisoning and torturing people. Thucydides Efendis arrived with a lady, allegedly his sister, but it was widely believed that she was the *kaimakames'* mistress. Such a liaison scandalized the people. Unaware of the prejudices against him, Thucydides Efendis set out to win the approval of the Icarians, making a number of good-will gestures. He was exceedingly polite, traveled throughout the island, conferred with the people about individual problems, and offered suggestions for improvements in Icaria. The Icarians were unresponsive to his gestures. For instance, on a visit to Raches his "sister" had swings built for the children of the village but no youngster ventured to enjoy them.[22]

The new *kaimakames* incorrectly saw Dr. Malachias as the main opponent to the new conscription policy, and therefore decided to weaken his position by courting his rivals, the powerful Spanos and Poulianos clans in the north. To gain their favor he proclaimed Evdilos as the new capital, and divested Dr. Malachias of his office of *proestos,* headman, and of his seal of authority, and placed him under house arrest. In early March, Dr. Malachias escaped from his confinement and went to Chios where he persuaded a friend, a high Turkish official, to reinstate him as *proestos,* retain Aghios Kyrikos as the capital, and exclude Icarians from military service. The practice of *rousfeti* had not entirely disappeared, and Dr. Malachias was granted the bulk of his plea, but the appeal for concessions on conscription was forwarded to Istanbul and rejected by the Porte. On March 13, 1911, the council, using the standard Icarian arguments, appealed to the Sultan: "We have a deep sense of obligation to serve our fatherland as soldiers and are ready to spill blood on behalf of its grandeur and glory but we live on a barren rock with arid land and our only means of survival is through emigration. Our young men are all in America."[23]

Dr. Malachias had foreseen that conscription into the Sultan's army would be inevitable, and thus began pressing the Greek government for union in 1908, but the prime minister, Georgios Theotokis, and his successor, Demetrios Rallis, were preoccupied with events in Crete and did not offer the Icarians any encouragement. All this changed in October 1910 when Eleutherios Venizelos became prime minister. Dr. Malachias had met Venizelos in Athens earlier that year when Venizelos had left his native Crete to become a member of the Greek parliament. Both men shared irredentist politics. Venizelos' political career in Greece was meteoric. Within months of becoming a member of parliament, he emerged as prime minister, and now Dr. Malachias urged him to take action on the Icarian issue. Venizelos' irredentist fervor was tempered by the memory of the war of 1897. Greece then went to war with Turkey with an inadequate navy, outmoded weapons, and a generally unsatisfactory armed force. Venizelos would not again risk war by annexing Icaria or for that matter his native Crete before modernizing the Greek army. At that very moment, the new prime minister was negotiating a loan from France for that purpose.[24]

Konstantinos Myrianthopoulos, born in Cyprus in 1874, became an important figure in the drive for Icarian *enosis* with the mother country. Myrianthopoulos had received scholarships to study in various schools in the Middle East where he acquired fluency in Turkish and Arabic. In 1892 he prepared for the priesthood at the Theological School in Halki, outside Istanbul. He lost interest in the clergy and went to Athens around 1900 to study law.[25]

While in Athens he met Professor Hatzidakis who persuaded him to go to Icaria to examine the local culture. Arriving in Aghios Kyrikos in the summer of 1908, Myrianthopoulos made friends with Dr. Malachias and then proceeded to make a tour of the various villages, gathering material for an anthropological and philological study. His work, *The Life and Language of the Icarians,* was published in Cyprus in 1932. His main aim, however, was to prepare a report on the political conditions in Icaria for Stephanos Dragoumis, who had served as foreign minister of Greece (1886–1889, 1892–1893) and was dedicated to the liberation of Greek territories that were still within the Ottoman Empire. In 1897, when the Greek government had sent *agents provocateurs* to Icaria, the Icarians had shown no interest in revolutionary activity. Dragoumis hoped to instill irredentist fervor in the Icarians and provided Myrianthopoulos with anti-Ottoman material to disseminate throughout the island. One evening he arrived at the remote village of Proespera, on the northwest corner of the island. A young man, who was beginning a teaching career in Icaria that would extend over forty years, was visiting his family when he heard a knock on the door. Strangers rarely came to Icaria and never to this obscure village of about six houses. The teacher was astonished to see an extremely well dressed man with an elegant walking cane who introduced himself as Konstantinos Myrianthopoulos from Cyprus, a friend of Dr. Malachias, and a student of Icarian folklore. He was invited to spend the night. The next day he addressed the entire village consisting of about twenty people. Far from any Turkish official, he informed his audience that his real aim in visiting Icaria was to prepare Icaria for union with Greece. He spoke of events then taking place in Macedonia where Greeks were rebelling against Turkish rule, and fired their patriotism with stories about the heroes of the revolutionary war of 1821, some ninety years previous. The teacher escorted Myrianthopoulos to other villages and witnessed his inflammatory oration before hundreds of Icarians at the monastery of Evangelesmos at Monte. In the fall of 1908, the teacher found a position in Aghios Kyrikos where Myrianthopoulos had established a temporary residence. The Cypriot gave the educator a book on the Greek War of Independence, and recommended that he teach the subject secretly to his students.[26] Myrianthopoulos returned to Athens in 1909, reporting to the Rallis government that Icarians were ready to oust the Turks from the island. Apparently, Rallis, who was backing away from any clash with Turkey, was not interested in the report. It does not seem that anyone in the government consulted Myrianthopoulos on Icaria until 1912 when Turkey and Italy were at war.[27]

This conflict broke out in 1911 when Libyan nationalists, aspiring to drive the Turks out of Libya, inadvertently injured a few Italians. Italy accused the Porte of not taking adequate measures to protect the Italian population in the area and demanded territorial concessions. While Turkey was pondering the ultimatum, Italy declared war, but not before securing the neutrality of Britain, France, and Russia. The Turkish armed forces proved to be utterly ineffective. In the fall and winter of 1911, Italy occupied most of Libya and in the spring of 1912 took possession of Rhodes. In April 1912, an Italian fleet under admiral Leone Viale began to occupy the Dodecanese for the purpose of preventing a Turkish fleet from sailing through the Aegean to reinforce Turkish positions in Libya. On May 4th, the Italians defeated a Turkish fleet outside Rhodes, and thus ended any further military action by Turkey.[28]

Italy took the Dodecanese for strategic purposes, to further its long-range imperial policy. Leros and Patmos became Italian naval bases. Icarians often observed Italian battleships near their shores. Rhodes, however, became the jewel of the new Italian Aegean Empire. Mussolini later claimed that Rhodes had merely returned to its ancestral home, for the island had been an important part of the Roman Republic and Empire. In the 1930s Il Duce established an archeological office on the island to unearth Roman antiquities to strengthen Italian claims to these regions.[29]

The Italo-Turkish war had radically altered the political equation in Icaria. The Italian navy had virtually driven the Turkish fleet from the Aegean, but now the Italians were proving to be a menace. In the summer of 1912 Italian marines were prepared to land on Icaria. Had they done so, Thucydides Efendis would have immediately surrendered. Possession is nine-tenths of the law, and Icaria would have become part of the Italian Dodecanese. This did not happen, however, because of the growing international pressure against further Italian expansion in the Aegean. Austria feared that an enlarged Italian empire in the Aegean, particularly the addition of Chios and Mytilene, would alter the balance of power in the Mediterranean. The British had concerns of their own and worried about losing control over the routes to the Levant and the Black Sea. Such apprehensions were reflected in a memorandum of the English admiralty presented to the cabinet after the Italians seized Patmos. The admiralty maintained that the Italian occupation of the Aegean should be curbed, and even the "most useless islands," should be kept out of Italian hands. Icaria, mountainous and harborless, was probably rated among "the useless." [30]

The stream of Icarians, self-appointed ambassadors, who had been knocking on the doors of ministers in Athens now were appearing before the Italian admiral in Patmos. They promised to rise up against the Turks the moment Italian battleships established a permanent patrol off Icarian shores that would prevent Turkish reinforcements from coming to Icarian. Unbeknown to the Icarians the Porte had no intention of supporting its garrison in Icaria. The Italians presumed these conversations were offers to hoist the Italian flag in return for Italian help. Dragoumis saw that Icaria was about to be absorbed into the Italian Dodecanese Empire and thus recommended to the Venizelos government that it dispatch Myrianthopoulos to Icaria. It is not clear how much confidence Myrianthopoulos enjoyed with Venizelos, but the prime minister needed an expert on the area and an unofficial representative on the island to defend the interest of Greece. Myrianthopoulos, who had stirred up Icarian sentiments against the Turks in 1908, was instructed to cool the situation down in 1912.[31] A premature union of Icaria with Greece might provoke war with both Turkey and Italy. In Icaria these Fabian tactics were not well received, and a stream of ill-clad Icarians unfamiliar with international politics began again the trek to Athens going to the home of Venizelos or that of various ministers urging support for an uprising against the Turks. Their unsophisticated deportment made a negative impact on the ministers who generally turned them away without an audience. After seeing these "ambassadors," some of the ministers felt that if these men represented the leadership of the island the incorporation of Icaria into Greece would be a liability for the nation.[32]

Myrianthopoulos rushed back to Athens and informed Venizelos that the Icarians were playing into the hands of the Italians, and that it was imperative to give the Icarians assurances that union with Greece was imminent. Venizelos, who had just entered into secret agreements with Serbia, Montenegro, and Bulgaria to go to war with Turkey, could not do so, for an incident in the Aegean might undermine these arrangements. Venizelos was not disposed to provoke Italy by annexing Icaria while he was preparing for war with Turkey.[33]

Pamphylis, who never trusted Myrianthopoulos, accused him of aspiring to some high office in the Greek government through his service in Icaria. Accusing him of stalling on *enosis* for private reasons, he dashed to Athens to persuade Venizelos to take immediate steps toward unification. Pamphylis was a lawyer, distinguished in appearance, and had a political base in Icaria. He was well qualified to represent Icaria in Athens, but the stream of uncouth, unofficial Icarian ambassadors who had preceded him had rendered his diplomatic task impossible. While Venizelos had confided to Myrianthopoulos about his secret treaties, he was not disposed to tell every Icarian who knocked on his door why Greece could not immediately accept Icaria into the Greek nation, and simply refused to see Pamphylis, who then tried unsuccessfully to obtain appointments with other ministers. Disgruntled, he returned to Icaria and urged immediate collaboration with the Italians.[34]

By June, many Icarians felt like Pamphylis and regarded Italy rather than Greece as their potential deliverer from the Turks, not realizing the consequences. Myrianthopoulos perceived that an uprising against the Turkish garrison would take place any day, and so did the Turkish governor who had his Icarian informants, some of whom had business in Piraeus. These people reported arms shipments from there to Icaria. On the evening of June 21st, 1912, Thucydides Efendis and Myrianthopoulos discussed the crisis as they walked along the coast of Aghios Kyrikos. In view of Italian battleships maneuvering near Patmos, Myrianthopoulos intimated that an uprising against the Turkish garrison was imminent, and resistance to it would be pointless. The *kaimakames,* knowing that Myrianthopoulos would convey his response to the Icarians and Venizelos, replied that the Turkish garrison, which had grown to twenty-nine, would shed its last drop of blood to put a rebellion down. On June 23rd, Myrianthopoulos went to Chios and telegraphed Athens, presumably in code, that the die was cast, and the Turks would fight. Having lost control of events in Icaria, Venizelos made arrangements for the Italian fleet to evacuate the women and children to Astypalaea, an island some fifty miles south of Icaria, when the uprising commenced, an eventuality that proved unnecessary.[35] The *kaimakames* put his gendarmes on alert, arrested suspected insurgents, and encouraged others to flee to Athens.[36]

The Icarians were armed to the teeth. Some had hunting weapons, 19th century muskets, and those who could afford two gold sovereigns purchased modern rifles smuggled from Syros to Karkinagri. One of the few Icarians who had military experience was Georgios Fountoulis who had enlisted in the Greek army to fight against Turkey in the war of 1897. Condemned to death as a traitor to the Ottoman government, he resided in Greece. Fountoulis, apart from his military valor, was a self-taught architect whose talents had been much appreciated by the Ottoman authorities in Icaria. Needing his services for some building projects, the *kaimakames* arranged for a full pardon. Thus in 1912 he was in Icaria and available to lead the Icarian armed forces.[37]

Dr. Malachias prepared the military operation that would expel the Turks while he was under house arrest. He plotted to have armed men assemble in a village above Aghios Kyrikos, descend on the capital, take the garrison by surprise, and thus isolate the Ottoman troops in Raches and Evdilos, forcing them to surrender.[38] During this period Dr. Malachias received patients, many of whom were fellow conspirators, and by July he had all details in place. On July 14th, the doctor/general obtained permission from Thucydides Efendis to go partridge hunting. He rendezvoused with fifty armed men at Oxe, a village above Aghios Kyrikos.[39] As they began their march on Aghios Kyrikos, they startled a man working in his fields. Taking them for brigands, as he later claimed, he dashed to Aghios Kyrikos where he informed Thucydides Efendis that a group of bandits were roaming in the area. Whether this man believed they were desperadoes, similar to those who had descended some twenty years before on Evdilos, or whether he was a Turkish sympathizer is unclear. Thucydides Efendis immediately put his garrison on military alert, and when Dr. Malachias saw that Aghios could not be taken by a swift assault, he retreated to Arethousa where on the following day he joined forces led by J. Poulianos. They slipped out of Arethousa during the festival of Aghia Marina, and merged with a band led by Georgios Fountoulis, who now took over the military operations. On the morning of July 16th, they took the surprised garrison at Evdilos, for Thucydides had been unable to communicate with them from Aghios Kyrikos.[40]

A fourteen-year-old boy awoke on the morning of July 17th to hear the peal of church bells in Raches, and the news that Icaria was free, and the Turks in Raches under custody. He observed captive Turks, fearful and sweating in their heavy wool uniforms, being marched to a place of confinement. The Icarians provided the incarcerated soldiers with coffee, and food, and assurances that they would not be harmed.[41]

Two Turkish soldiers, however, had managed to flee from Evdilos before the garrison had surrendered, and informed Thucydides of the revolt. He dispatched nine soldiers to Evdilos to retake the village. These soldiers encountered an Icarian force of about fifty men outside of Chrysostomos, and here the two forces joined battle. The nine Turkish soldiers exchanged several rounds of fire with the Icarians, but at such a great distance that no one was endangered. They surrendered when they were outflanked, and were imprisoned in houses in Mavratos. During the volley, Georgios Spanos, one of the reinforcements from Evdilos, somehow detached from the Icarian force, was killed. Spanos, the only casualty of the uprising, perhaps died from friendly fire. According to one version of this event, Spanos' wife Marigo dreamed that disaster would befall her husband and did not awake him in the early hours of the morning when the detachment left for Aghios Kyrikos. In another version Spanos' horse refused to leave the stable for several hours, as if it had a premonition that this was not a propitious day. Whatever the explanation he did not depart with his comrades, and was obliged to rush to join them. He arrived on his "reluctant" horse when the battle was in progress, and his own men, apparently, thinking he was a Turk, shot him.[42]

Thucydides Efendis obviously was no military genius. He made the classic blunder of dividing his forces without establishing a link of communication.[43] He thus weakened his base in Aghios, and exposed the other half of his force to certain defeat. But such strategic criticisms are useless. Had he kept his entire detachment in Aghios Kyrikos, put on a better fight, and killed a few of the rebels, the small Turkish garrison would still have lost the battle and probably have been annihilated in the process.

Victorious in Evdilos and Raches, Dr. Malachias dashed back to Aghios Kyrikos to besiege Thucydides' reduced garrison. The original fifty armed Icarian rebels had now grown into a motley force of over two hundred. People were flocking from various parts of the island to enlist in the Icarian armed force. One of the most interesting new recruits was Manolis Koutsouphlakes, who in 1908 escaped an Ottoman jail in Icaria where he had been confined for resisting the reforms of the Young Turks. A precursor to the *andartes*, guerrillas of the 1940s, he hid in the mountains for four years, and now enrolled in the Icarian force.[44]

The Turks barricaded themselves in their administrative building, which had been designed by Fountoules who was now leading the assault against them. Throughout the night both parties exchanged fire. A merchant from Aghios Kyrikos lobbed several sticks of dynamite at the Turkish stronghold. While the explosives did no damage, the sound of the blast demoralized the Turks. On the morning of the 18th, the Turkish customs official, who somehow had slept throughout the commotion, stepped out of his house to go to his customs office and was arrested. Thucydides, who had used all his ammunition and was running low on food, surrendered. Dr. Malachias incarcerated the Turkish soldiers in his pharmacy for a day and then allowed them to return to their residences where they were kept under house arrest until a means of sending them back to Turkey was found. The Turkish gendarmes displayed a hearty appetite and ran up a maintenance bill of 2,758 grosia, a sum which was draining the Icarian treasury.[45]

Thucydides Efendis had proved true to his promise to fight, but he may have also made a secret pledge to Myrianthopoulos not to shed blood while he was squandering all his ammunition. Thucydides' resistance seems to have been no more than a *coup de theâtre*. How his forces could have expended so much ammunition without inflicting one casualty is a tribute to his ability rather than to any incompetence. The Icarians, too, were remarkable in their failure to shoot anyone except their own Georgios Spanos. It almost seems as if both sides had rehearsed the event to display great sound and fury without violence. Within a week of the uprising, Thucydides returned to Turkey.[46] The Porte did not hold him accountable for the loss of Icaria because his men had fought, used up all their ammunition, allegedly killed one Icarian, and held out for a short time against a superior force. Thucydides continued his career in the Turkish civil service until 1922 when he was expelled from Turkey with the bulk of the Ottoman Greeks. He immediately found employment in Athens in the Greek foreign ministry. The well-paying civil service position was perhaps a reward for his role in averting bloodshed in 1912.[47]

The scant casualties of July 17th may be also attributed to the Icarians' moderate temperament, and fear of reprisals from the Turkish garrison in Chios which consisted of twenty-five hundred men.[48] Furthermore, the Icarians were concerned that any Turkish casualty in Icaria would lead to retaliation against Icarians in Asia Minor, especially in Izmir where there was a large Icarian colony.

When the Icarians presented Venizelos with a fait accompli, the prime minister was not pleased. He not only rejected a request for unification with Greece, but also a petition for six hundred rifles and ammunition. Thus Icaria became the *Eleuthera Politeia Ikarias,* the Free State of Icaria, and for the next four months hovered on the brink of annexation to Greece. It was never a state in the sense that it had a government, bureaucracy, currency, and legitimate diplomatic relations. As a result of an international crisis, the island was in a state of limbo and more cut off from the world than ever. In early August Icarians from Alexandria chartered the *Aegeon*, a steamer that normally serviced the Piraeus–Syros route, and dispatched eighty-five rifles and five thousand rounds of ammunition. Other steamers did not venture through these troubled waters, and Icarians were running out of supplies. Dr. Malachias, who had relied on Myrianthopoulos to arrange *enosis,* dispatched his own representative to

Athens. The envoy obtained an interview not with Venizelos, but with Lambros Koromelas, minister of finance. Koromelas belonged to a prominent Athenian publishing family, and was himself a journalist, novelist, and playwright. This urbane minister held the Icarians in a disdain similar to that expressed by Georgirenes centuries before. After a humiliating wait of several days, the minister notified the Icarian delegate that the Greek government did not support the uprising, criticized the Icarians for being armed to the teeth, and warned that the island would fall into anarchy.[49]

It was unnecessary for the Icarians to be in a state of military preparedness. The Porte had no intention of assaulting Icaria, for the Ottoman navy lacked adequate armored cruisers to stand up to the Italian naval forces in the vicinity. The best ships in the Porte's navy, two 1891 vintage battle cruisers acquired from Germany in 1910, were obsolete, a fact made clear in May 1911 when the Italian battleship *Emmanuel Filberto* sank a Turkish warship in the harbor of Vathi. After this loss, the Turks withdrew their navy into the Sea of Marmara, and did not have a means of conveying the twenty-five hundred troops from Chios to Icaria, or reinforcing any of their Aegean positions. In June Venizelos dispatched the *Georgios Averof,* Greece's premier military vessel, and several other cruisers, to impose a blockade on the Turkish navy in the Dardanelles. Furthermore, the war with Italy had brought about the industrial collapse of Turkey, and its fleet was short of coal and ammunition. Thus Venizelos' reluctance to annex Icaria in August 1912 was not based on fear of Turkey but rather apprehensions about a confrontation with the Italian navy, for Venizelos suspected that the Italians aimed at adding to their Dodecanese possessions.[50] The Greek prime minister was encouraged by Sir Edward Grey who on August 6, 1912, informed the Italian ambassador that his Majesty's government opposed further Italian expansion in the Aegean. Venizelos, however, waited for other powers to take this position before he acted on *enosis.*[51]

In the meantime, the Icarians were left to their own devices. The body of Spanos, which had begun to decompose, was brought to Evdilos on July 20th. He was given a hero's burial. The funeral unleashed passions that had been long suppressed during the centuries of Turkish occupation. Spanos was seen as a martyr who gave his life for the liberation of Icaria. As the funeral cortege passed through Evdilos, hundreds of voices chanted "Athanatos, Athanatos." The Spanos clan and the residents of the northern side of the island hoped to use the funeral, and the prestige of the martyr, to make Evdilos the new capital. A provisional committee, now in charge of Icaria, granted a tremendous pension to his widow from the empty public treasury.[52]

On July 27th, Greater Fourni, consisting of Fourni itself, Thymaina, and several minuscule, uninhabited islands, declared its independence from Turkey. The Sultan had leased these islands just east of Icaria for the annual sum of five hundred Turkish pounds to an entrepreneur. The overlord of this feudal dependency recouped his outlay by smuggling, and harboring refugees. There were about 250 families in these islands, about 230 on Fourni and 20 on Thymaina. The Icarians tended to look down on the Fourniotes as people poorer than themselves. In the 19th century, they were even more isolated than the Icarians, but now the Fourniotes were encouraged to join Icaria in rebellion because of an event that had taken place the previous year. In December 1911, two smugglers from the Cyclades arrived in Fourni with contraband. In the past, Ottoman authorities on Fourni turned a blind eye to such activities, but now with the reforms of the "Young Turks" in place, smuggled goods in Fourni were no longer sanctioned. When the five Turkish gendarmes on the island attempted to arrest the smugglers, a brawl ensued leaving two gendarmes dead and two wounded. The lone survivor managed to escape. By the time Turkish reinforcements arrived on the island, the perpetrators of the deed had fled. The Ottoman authorities held local officials responsible for the violence, arrested leading Fourniotes and sent them to Aghios Kyrikos for detention. When the Fourniotes declared their independence and joined Icaria, the Icarians released the detainees, and eventually allotted to Fourni four of the fourteen seats of the executive committee.[53]

For the next four months, this executive committee of fourteen headed by Dr. Malachias administered Icaria. The council appointed a local militia, customs officials, postmaster, and gendarmes. It was one matter to commission officials and another to pay them. On July 20th, the council made an inventory of Turkish property which consisted of 41 Turkish pounds, 1 English pound, 47 blank passports, 9 blank power-of-attorney forms, registry forms for animals, and a seal. Though the cash would have come in handy, the Icarians in a princely fashion befitting their *porphyrogenitoi* roots dispatched it to Turkish authorities in Samos. They also returned all Ottoman documents, the garrison, and Thucydides Efendis.[54]

On July 31st, Dr. Malachias reported to the Icarians in Alexandria, Egypt, that they were expecting a Turkish offensive, and thus had mobilized two hundred soldiers. They needed, however, one thousand armed men, and were waiting for their kinsmen in America to supply them with guns and a second-hand torpedo boat. Myrianthopoulos, who had returned to Icaria as the official representative of the Greek government, would not give consent to the raising of the Greek flag. In early September, Dr. Malachias went to Athens to pressure Venizelos to annex Icaria to Greece, but the prime minister responded, "Be patient and have confidence in my policies." Venizelos, a great believer in secret diplomacy, was putting the final touches on a pact with Bulgaria, Serbia, and Montenegro to declare war on Turkey. In the agreement, there was a clause releasing Bulgaria from its commitment to support Greece in the event of a Greco-Turkish war prematurely unleashed by an incident in the Aegean.[55] Thus discussion about the unification of Icaria with Greece would have to wait until the conclusion of what would be known as the First Balkan War. In the meantime, there was no sign of the torpedo boat from the Pan-Icarian Brotherhood of America.

The Icarians had exhausted their resources. It mattered little that the shelves in stores were empty, for there was no money to buy goods. Remittances from America, Icaria's main source of capital, were being detained in Chios, the transit point for mail to Icaria. Ottoman steamship companies cut service to Icaria, and few Greek steamers were willing to venture into such troubled waters. Icaria was literally cut off from the world. The executive committee leased the *Cleopatra,* a broken-down steamer from Nearchus Psychoures, a resident of a neighboring island. The Icarians deployed the battered steamer as their navy and link to the outside world. Koutsouflakes, a hero in the recent fracas with the Turks, was in command of the ship. For passage, men paid ten groschen and women and children went gratis. She made several trips to neighboring islands, and sailed to Piraeus, apparently, on one occasion. There was, however, a shortage of funds to pay the eight sailors and buy coal for the steam engine.[56] Unbeknownst to the Icarians, the commanding officer of the Italian cruiser at Patmos had declared the *Cleopatra* an outlaw ship because Nearchus had previously deployed the vessel to smuggle goods through the Italian zone. Spotting the *Cleopatra* while it was patrolling Icarian shores, the Italians attempted to sink her. Koutsouflakes, who had earned his spurs in the infantry, showed some skill in naval matters by taking evasive action to save the vessel. Fearing for the safety of his ship and not willing to extend further credit to the Icarians, Nearchus withdrew the *Cleopatra* from Icarian service.[57] The Icarians thereafter relied exclusively on their caïques, sailing to Syros, where they had the option of either steam or sail navigation.

In early September, the executive committee appealed again to the émigré community, this time to raise 2,734 groschen to pay the September salary of teachers. The 57 men registered in the Icarian association in Alexandria, Egypt, immediately dispatched 300 English pounds and then an additional 200. The Pan-Icarian Brotherhood in America ignoring the request for a torpedo boat offered both money and men. By the end of September, fifty armed men arrived from America with funds to pay the teachers, but were disappointed that the fighting was over.[58]

Despite international pressures against further Italian expansion in the Aegean, Italy aspired to consolidate Icaria with its Dodecanese Empire. The battleship *Emmannuel Filberto* moored at Patmos, made regular jaunts from Patmos to Icaria. As she sailed along the Icarian shore, the people waved banners inscribed, "E Viva L'Italia," and on several occasions rowed to the cruiser with small boats to deliver supplies of grapes and potatoes. The officers accepted the offerings believing they were indications of a willingness to unite with Italy, but these were rather expressions of gratitude for keeping the Turkish navy out of the Aegean.[59] On another occasion, officers from the *Emmanuel Filberto* went to shore to inform the Icarians that they were descendants of Venetians, and urged them to raise the Italian flag.[60] There was never any sentiment on the island to take such action, and Dr. Malachias dispatched a delegation to the Italian embassy in Athens thanking Italy for its support, but making it clear that the Icarians did not wish to be incorporated into Italy's Aegean Empire.[61]

Italy regarded Icaria chiefly as a staging point to Chios, but by late September the Italians acquiesced to international pressure against further expansion in the Aegean. By then the officers of the *Emmanuel Filberto* had assessed the value of Icaria. Without ports, roads, and with little arable land, the island was of little value to the Italians.[62] Thus by October 2, 1912, when the First Balkan War broke out, Italian ships ceased to appear off the coast of Icaria. The Icarians were no longer obsessed with Turkish reprisals, for it was clear that Turkey was unable to deploy ships in the Aegean. As a result of Turkey's total naval collapse, the Porte came to terms with Italy. According to the treaty signed on October 16th, Italy retained Libya, but agreed to return the Dodecanese when all resistance to Italian occupation in Libya ended. The Turks, however, had no control over native insurgents who now opposed the Italian occupation of Libya. Thus Italy had an excuse for retaining its Dodecanese Empire.[63]

Venizelos was quick to exploit the Porte's predicament. On October 17th, 1912, he pushed a decree of union of Greece with Crete through the Greek parliament. But Venizelos did not take a similar step for Icaria because he was unsure of the Italian position.[64] In the meantime, economic matters in Icaria were going from bad to worse. Funds from Alexandria and America were exhausted, and the island continued to be isolated. The council decided to raise money by issuing a series of postage stamps for philatelists, allocating 1,903 grosia for the services of a lithographer and printing expenses. Though Icaria never received recognition as an independent state and did not have permission to issue stamps from the appropriate philatelic agency, the executive committee commissioned an Athenian lithographer to produce a limited edition of 56,000 stamps ranging from 2, 5, 10, 25, and 50 lefta and 1, 2, and 5 drachmas. The stamps were cast in the Greek blue and bore the inscription *Eleuthera Politeia Ikarias* (the free state of Icaria).[65] For their own postal needs, the Icarians continued to use Turkish and Greek postage stamps, and there is no record that an Icarian stamp was ever used to dispatch mail. But Icarian cancellation marks were employed. For example, in September 1912, the merchant Elias M. Zizes, wrote a letter to a French merchant in Vathi, Samos, using a Turkish stamp that bore the cancellation "Free State of Icaria." After Icaria was united with Greece in November 1912, the postmaster at Aghios Kyrikos, Kapnistos, "authenticated" Icarian stamps on a special envelope with an Icarian cancellation mark.[66] Collectors were eager to acquire the stamps. As prices soared, forgers issued fakes. The value of the stamp plunged when philatelists discovered that the lithographer had not destroyed the plates and was flooding the market with a massive unauthorized second issue. Ultimately the fake Icarian stamp acquired more philatelic value than the original, though it too was virtually worthless.[67]

Not only was the philatelic enterprise a financial disaster, but also everything else was going badly. Ottoman ports were closed to Icarian ships. Caïques delivered supplies from Syros, but goods from Greece were more expensive than Turkish commodities. The Icarians possessed mainly Turkish currency that had little value in Greece. In Icaria the worth of Turkish money fluctuated widely because its value was based on the wavering expectation of union with Greece. Furthermore, the exchange rate varied from Aghios Kyrikos to Evdilos.[68] Black market conditions prevailed resembling those that emerged later in the Second World War.

People resorted to barter and criticized the cupidity of merchants who demanded exorbitant prices for goods. Some retailers, however, lost money on merchandise paid for but never delivered from Chios, Samos and other Ottoman markets. One Icarian businessman did not receive payment for a shipment of 1,000 kantars of currants dispatched to Romania.[69] Other merchants risked their lives going to Turkey to purchase supplies and grain.[70]

Hard times engendered crime. To maintain law and order the executive committee appointed two judges and commissioned Myrianthopoulos as prosecuting attorney with great powers.[71] Myrianthopoulos and his fellow magistrates, however, were unable to cope with the heavy case load of the new litigation, and unresolved cases which had accumulated during the last year of Ottoman rule. Some new litigation involved tax evasion; for the executive committee imposed a levy on meat, fish, and all produce, especially grapes, figs, potatoes, and almonds. Icarian authorities heavily taxed the few imported goods that made their way to the island.[72] Icarians, who had developed tremendous skills at evading taxes during the Turkish period, were using the same techniques to dodge assessments from their own government.

With shortages and unresolved legal disputes, the large force of armed Icarians posed a threat to the stability of the island, an eventuality foreseen by Koromelas and other members of the Venizelos government who had advised against premature revolt. The threat of civil disturbance was eased in September when volunteers went to Samos and Chios to assist forces fighting the Turks. These two islands soon gained their freedom, and the armed men returned.[73] Their presence put an edge on the long-standing antagonism between the southern region, *staventi,* and northern, *sophrano.* These two distinct geographical entities were in the classical period autonomous political units. Oenoe, the area around Evdilos, and Therma, the present-day spa, paid separate taxes to the Delian League.[74] The sharp regional differences remained well into the 20th century, and it was only in the mid 1960s when a road was cut through Mount Atheras that the two sections were finally physically and emotionally united.

Campos and Evdilos had been the hub of the island from the classical to the Byzantine period while Aghios Kyrikos was settled only early in the 19th century. It is, therefore, not clear why in the 19th century the Ottoman authorities selected Aghios Kyrikos as the capital. Perhaps they considered Aghios more accessible from Asia Minor than Evdilos. Now that Icaria was free of Turkish rule, the *sophranoi* alleged that Evdilos and not the upstart Aghios Kyrikos should serve as the capital.[75] But the *staventoi* controlled the executive council receiving support of the Fourni delegates who were indebted to the people of Aghios Kyrikos for protecting and providing hospitality to their imprisoned relatives in December 1911.

The issue about the location of the capital became the main question in the council, and scarcely any other business could be conducted. Dr. Malachias passed a resolution that the issue could no longer be discussed, but the two leading *sophranoi* families, the Poulianos and Spanos clans, would not abide by this decision. Pamphylis, a native of Aghios Kyrikos and member of the council, unfairly blamed Dr. Malachias for the chaos. Rumors reached Aghios Kyrikos that the northerners were preparing an armed onslaught. On September 18th, the secretary of the council in Aghios Kyrikos sent a letter addressed to the "Law-abiding and peace-loving people of Evdilos," urging them to remain calm, and saying that the "demagogues of the street corners and cafés should cease their inflammatory rhetoric." But on October 30th, Papas Kouloulias, an impetuous priest who would later become a strong supporter of the Greek dictator Metaxas and a ferocious anti-Communist, took matters into his own hands. Under the influence of John Poulianos, he gathered an armed force of about two hundred men, some of whom had recently returned from Samos and Chios and prepared his men for a march on Aghios Kyrikos. On November 10th, Papas Kouloulias sent an ultimatum to Dr. Malachias decreeing Evdilos the capital and warning Dr. Malachias that if he valued his life he would offer no resistance. The people of Evdilos argued that the bulk of the island's population lived in the surrounding villages, that most of the Icarian shipping went through Evdilos and that a mole could easily be built there creating an artificial harbor.[76]

While the northerners were preparing to descend on Aghios Kyrikos, John Poulianos encouraged the Evdilotes to raise the Greek flag. Dr. Malachias feared such a display might provoke Italian intervention, and instructed the gendarme in Evdilos, his appointee, to block any actions along these lines, but the gendarme caught up in the enthusiasm of the moment participated in the ceremony.[77] During this time, Myrianthopoulos was in Athens apprising Venizelos of the critical situation, and urging him to proceed with union. Admiral Pavlos Kountouriotes was maintaining a blockade of the Ottoman fleet at the straits, and some European powers were encouraging Venizelos to seize the opportunity and claim all former Turkish possessions in the Aegean except Tenedos, Imbros, and the Italian-occupied Dodecanese.[78] Thus on November 1st,

Kountouriotes dispatched the cruiser *Thyella* under vice-admiral Vlachopoulos with instructions to incorporate Icaria into the Greek nation. Kountouriotes, who was preparing a naval battle against the Ottomans, the Battle of Helle which would take place December 12th, gave Vlachopoulos instructions to return to the straits immediately. Vlachopoulos arrived in Evdilos where he was surprised to learn that the Greek flag had been displayed for the past several days. Members of the Spanos clan went on board to finalize the unification arrangements and to secure for Evdilos the honor of capital of Icaria. They argued that not only did Evdilos have the potential to develop port facilities, but also the people were more loyal to Greece than the southerners who had not yet raised the Greek flag. Vlachopoulos declared that Icaria with all its cities and villages was incorporated into Greece, that local officials would manage affairs until Greece could install its administrative machinery, and that Evdilos was the new capital. Pamphylis, who was the official representative of the executive council, protested in angry terms that the issue of the capital had already been decided. The vice-admiral, who had no time to become embroiled in local politics and had no need for a lecture from the son of a charcoal maker, threatened to punish Pamphylis for insubordination. Pamphylis left Evdilos, smarting from the threat, and declaring that the Greek flag would not be unfurled in Aghios Kyrikos unless the question of the capital was settled in a satisfactory manner.[79] In the afternoon of November 4th, the *Thyella* reached Aghios Kyrikos. While an enthusiastic crowd greeted the Greek ship, officials in Aghios Kyrikos did not raise the flag, an indication of their dissatisfaction about the decision on the capital. Indignant officers from the cruiser accused the people of harboring pro-Turkish sentiments and threatened to hang the traitors.[80] At 8:30 p.m., Dr. Malachias ordered the Greek flag to be raised to a twenty-one gun salute. People from the villages on the southern side of the island streamed to Aghios Kyrikos, and celebrated through the night, dancing and weeping while lights from the battleship illuminated the public square. On the following morning, November 5th, Dr. Malachias addressed the Icarians in simple Greek, commencing with the words, "this is a day of joy and a day of freedom."[81]

In the next few months the question of the capital was quietly resolved. Dr. Malachias, using his influence with Venizelos, regained Aghios Kyrikos as the administrative seat. By this time, there were Greek gendarmes on the islands, and the frustrated Spanos-Poulianos clans did not consider resorting to arms. It was remarkable that in 1912, a year of international crisis and violence, Icaria succeeded in joining Greece with almost no bloodshed, and internal tensions were resolved without carnage. Although in fact Dr. Malachias deserves much credit for this, Pamphylis blamed him for all the turmoil and chaos of the 1910–1912 period. He believed that the doctor relied too much on sycophants, gave Myrianthopoulos too much power, did not take effective action in preventing the formation of the Spanos-Poulianos faction, was poor at evaluating men, and took decisions without consulting the executive committee.[82]

Pamphylis, an intelligent and decent man, was obviously piqued about the secondary role he played in the political and military events of 1910–1912. A decade later, as he wrote his history of the period, he remembered bitterly how Myrianthopoulos had ignored him, how various high officials in Athens kept him waiting in their antechambers, and the rude reception of vice-admiral Vlachopoulos. Melas, on the other hand, is more reliable in this matter. While the inhabitants from the north felt that Melas was too focused on the southern section, and gave too much credit to the people of Aghios Kyrikos for the revolt against Turkey, he did provide a relatively objective account of the events of 1912. He praised Dr. Malachias for performing ably under difficult circumstances. Though trained as a doctor, Dr. Malachias possessed the talents of a military leader and politician. Under the guidance of a less competent man, Icaria could have either fallen into Italian hands or been torn apart by civil strife. He would continue to play an important role in Icaria for the next forty years. Dr. Malachias, a liberal in the early part of the century, was regarded as a conservative in his later years. As the people turned to radical politics in the 1940s and 1950s, his great contribution to the island was disregarded.[83]

In 1912 there were a few men in their nineties who had childhood memories of Icaria gaining its freedom in the 1820s, joining Greece, and then within a few years reverting to the Ottoman Empire. There was some uneasiness on the island in late 1912 that the European Powers would again allocate Icaria to Turkey. But the Venizelos government was determined not to allow this to happen and sought international recognition for its unification with Icaria. The issue of the Aegean islands was addressed at the London conference of December 18, 1912. The Russian ambassador had misgivings about the new order of affairs, and specified that at least Tenedos, Imbros, and Samothrace should remain in the hands of Turkey. Germany and Italy opposed Greek claims in the Aegean, arguing that Chios, Samos, Mytilene, and Icaria be returned to the Turks. Lord Grey demurred, maintaining that the inhabitants of these islands were Greeks who wanted to be part of the Greek nation, and that any other arrangement would destabilize the region. The British position prevailed, and Greece was allowed to keep the islands on condition that the area be demilitarized. Icaria's status as a Greek province was included in Article five of the Treaty of London signed May 30, 1913, and ratified by the signatories on February 22, 1914, but Italy's claim on the Dodecanese remained in limbo.[84]

Icaria became part of the Greek nation just when Greece was engrossed in warfare, and insecure about its national boundaries. Greece had just completed the First Balkan War, about to engage in the Second Balkan War, and then in the ensuing First World War. Under Ottoman rule, few Icarians served in the armed forces, but now Greece conscripted men from the island. The First World War also raised the issue of the extent and permanence of the Italian Dodecanese, whether Italy's Aegean empire would endure, and other islands be annexed. According to the 1915 secret treaty of London, Italy was to retain its Aegean possessions after the war, but in 1917 the United States entered war on the understanding that no secret treaties were to be honored. At the peace conference at Versailles, Italy agreed to return the Dodecanese to Greece except for Rhodes, but was still in possession of the islands in 1921 when Greece went to war with Turkey. Greek armies marched into Asia Minor but were repulsed by Turkish forces. As a result of the war, 1.2 million Greeks were forced to leave Turkey. Icaria had to absorb about two thousand refugees at a time when America finally closed its doors on Greek immigration. Greece was in no position to request the return of the Dodecanese. Indeed, the Hellenic Nation stood in danger of losing Icaria and other islands to the Turks, but the European fleet prevented a Turkish incursion into the Aegean. According to Articles 6, 9, 12, and 13 of the treaty of Lausanne, signed July 24, 1923, Turkey retained Imbros and Tenedos, Greece kept Icaria and the other islands that had joined Greece in 1912, and the Dodecanese remained Italian possessions.[85]

1. Fond memories: L. Spanos, *Ikariaka Chronika* (Syros, Greece, 1925), pp. 41–42, notes that in 1910 one purchased an oka, 2.82 pounds, of grain for one groschen, a fraction of the price paid in 1925, and concludes, "the Turks never oppressed us." Similar views expressed by A. Plakidas, *It Could Only Happen in America* (Athens, 1966), pp. 19–21; J. A. Papalas, born in Icaria

in 1895, left for America in 1911, and recalled Turkish gendarmes giving him copper coins. Interview, June 17, 1974, Lincoln Park, Michigan. But Christos Kratsas, *E Seghronos Exelixis ton Loutron tes Ikarias* (Athens, 1958), p. 5, accused Ottoman authorities of preventing the development of the spas at Therma and of generally opposing progress in Icaria.

2. The man's name apparently was Apostolos; see L. Spanos. *Ikariaka Chronika,* pp. 12–13. H. Hauttecoeur, "L'île d'Ikaria," *Bulletin de la Société Geographique d'Anvers,* 25 (1900), 340, notes that the Icarians committed the murders because the Turkish gendarmes had made immoral propositions, and notes that while the perpetrators were never apprehended, the Icarians paid a fine.

3. Theodore G. Tatsios, *The Megali Idea and the Greek-Turkish War of 1897: The Impact of the Cretan Problem of Greek Irredentism 1866–1897* (New York, 1984), pp. 66–104, especially pp. 95–96.

4. Robust health: Erik K. Zürchner, *Turkey: A Modern History* (London 1993), p. 88. Treaty: Tatsios, *The Megali Idea,* pp. 115–120.

5. Folksong: Remembered by Sophia Plakas, *Ikariaka* 37 (1966), 15. Game of *Tourkos:* J. Tsarnas, *Ikariaka,* July 1976, no. 3.

6. The herald was Pericles Papadakis; see Stephen Glaros, *Ikariake Phoné,* July 1976. Such insignificant incidents in the context of two different cultures, Christianity and Islam, were potential flash points. The role of a Greek *kaimakames* kept such incidents from escalating into a conflict with loss of lives. A similar episode led to carnage in Jerusalem in A.D. 68 during the feast of unleavened bread. A Roman soldier "pulled up his garment and bent over indecently; turning his backside towards the Jews he made a noise as indecent as his posture." A riot ensued and thirty thousand Jews were massacred; see Josephus, *The Jewish War,* 2. 23.

7. The priest: Papahatzes. The captain: Christodoulos Mougiannis; see I. Tsarnas, *Ikariake Phoné,* July 1976.

8. Tax: J. Melas, *Istoria tes Nesou Ikarias* (Athens 1959), p. 223. Spa: A. J. Papalas, *Ancient Icaria* (Wauconda, Illinois, 1992), pp. 58–68. L. Ross, *Inselreisen,* (Halle, 1913 reprint of the 1863 Berlin edition), vol. 3, p. 136.

9. A. Vassilaros introduced tobacco; see Melas, *Ikaria,* pp. 217–218.

10. D. Quataert, *Social Disintegration and Popular Resistance in the Ottoman Empire, 1881–1908: Reactions to European Economic Penetration* (New York 1983), pp. 13–14, 18–19.

11. Quataert, *Social Disintegration,* pp. 20–24.

12. Melas, *Ikaria,* p. 209. There is no record of this correspondence in the archives of the Pan-Icarian Brotherhood of America in Verona, Pennsylvania. In 1912, as a result of a dispute between the Icarians who wanted Evdilos as capital and those who supported Aghios Kyrikos, many of the records were either lost or destroyed.

13. Melas, *Ikaria,* pp. 204–207, 217–218. In 1935, the Icarian-Americans invited President Franklin Delano Roosevelt to join them at the banquet of their annual meeting. His secretary, William D. Hasset, wrote on behalf of President Roosevelt thanking the Icarians for the invitation, and sending the president's best wishes, but pressing duties kept the chief executive in Washington. Hasset enclosed a picture of Roosevelt for the commemorative album of the *Pan-Icarian Convention Book,* Pittsburgh, 1935.

14. See A. Macfie, *The End of the Ottoman Empire 1908–1923* (London and New York, 1998), pp. 29–30, 39–40; M. Ş. Hanioğlu, *The Young Turks in Opposition* (Oxford, 1995), pp. 24, 76.

15. Melas, *Ikaria,* pp. 216–217.

16. Melas, *Ikaria,* pp. 210–211. Malachias' biography in his obituary, *Ikariake Phoné,* Aug. 23, 1958. H. Davison, "Advent of the Electric Telegraph in the Ottoman Empire," in his *Essays in Ottoman and Turkish History, 1774–1923: The Impact on the West* (Austin, Texas), 1990, pp. 137–148.

17. Melas, *Ikaria,* pp. 212. In October 1909, the Icarian representative, Zacharias Moraitis, put forth the Icarian position.

18. Melas, *Ikaria,* pp. 220–221.

19. Melas, *Ikaria,* pp. 216–218.

20. Melas, *Ikaria,* p. 218.

21. Thucydides: Charalambos Pamphylis, *Istoria tes Nesou Ikarias* (Athens, 1980 reprint of 1921 edition), pp. 207–209. C. V. Findley, *Bureaucratic Reform in the Ottoman Empire: The Sublime Porte, 1789–1922* (Princeton,

1980), p. 209, argues that officials like Thucydides were not totally loyal to the Ottoman Empire.

22. Pamphylis, *Istoria Ikarias,* pp. 207–209, and A. Karoutsas, reprint of a 1962 interview, Atheras, June–July, 1994. Torture: N. P. Ioannou, *H Ikariake Epanastasis kata to 1912* (Alexandria, Egypt, 1912), pp. 12–13.

23. Melas, *Ikaria,* pp. 217–224.

24. G. B. Leon, "Greece and the Central Powers, 1913–1914: The Origins of the National Schism," *Südost-Forschungen* 39 (1985), 123–125.

25. V. Englezake, To Antiochikon Zetema kata ta ete 1897–1899—Anekdotou Emerologion K. I. Miranthopoulou, *Kypriakai Spoudai* 47 (1983) 109–112. A. Benikos, *Atheras,* January–March 1994.

26. Memoirs of the teacher Karoutsos: *Atheras,* June, 1962. Cypriot newspaper, *E Semirine,* Dec. 29, 1986. I was unable to obtain a copy of Myrianthopoulos' work on Icaria; it is mentioned in "Myrianthopoulos, Konstantinos," in *Cyprus Who's Who* (Nicosia, 1968). I acquired much information about Myrianthopoulos from his grandson Leon Myrianthopoulos, interview Chicago, Sept. 1, 2004.

27. Cypriot newspaper, E Semirine, Dec. 29, 1986 "Myrianthopoulos, Konstantinos," in *Cyprus Who's Who* (Nicosia, 1968); interview Leon Myrianthopoulos, grandson of Konstantinos, Chicago, Sept. 1, 2004

28. R. Bosworth, "Britain and Italy's Acquisition of the Dodecanese, 1912–1915," *The Historical Journal* 13 (4), 1970, 685–686.

29. See A. Legnani, *Il Dodecaneso e la sua base navale* (Taranto, 1923), pp. 1–37, for the strategic value of the Dodecanese, and the Italian interest in islands with a good agricultural base, roads, and especially port facilities. Roman archeological work: G. Konstantinopoulos, "Dodekanesa: Italokratia-Ensomatose," *Ephemerida E Kathermerine/Epta Emera,* 30, Nov., 1997; S. Jacopi, "Scavi e richerchi di Nisiro," *Clara Rhodos,* 6–7, 2, 469–552.

30. Foreign powers against further expansion: W. Miller, *A History of the Greek People, 1821–1921* (London, 1922), p. 133. Christopher Seton-Watson, *Italy from Liberalism to Fascism: 1870–1925* (London and New York, 1967), pp. 313–314. R. Bosworth, "Britain and Italy's Acquisition of the Dodecanese", 685–686.

31. Benikos, *Atheras,* January–March 1994; Karoutsos, *Atheras,* January–March 1962. For Myrianthopoulos' report on the Icarian situation to I. Dragoumis, see *Atheras,* October/December 1994, and also Benikos' comments in *Atheras,* March/April, 1995.

32. The views of these ministers were summarized in an editorial in the Athenian newspaper *Neon Asty* on July 21, 1912, which asserted that it would be best for all concerned if Icaria became part of the Italian Dodecanese Empire.

33. J. Melas, *Ikaria,* pp. 228–229, 233, *Atheras,* June–July, 1995.

34. H. Pamphylis, *Ikaria,* pp. 209–213.

35. H. Pamphylis, *Ikaria,* pp. 209–213.

36. A. Benikos, *Atheras* Oct. Nov. 1994.

37. Pamphylis, *Ikaria,* pp. 208–209; A. Karoutsos, interview Raches, Icaria, June 14, 1962, and in *Atheras* July 94; *Atheras,* March–April 1995. Fountoulis: Interview with his daughter-in-law, Anna Fountoulis, Aghios Kyrikos, May 28, 2002. She showed the author a number of documents connected to Fountoulis, including his discharge papers from the Greek army of December 12, 1897.

38. Melas, *Ikaria,* p. 231 Benikos, *Atheras,* Jan.–Feb. 1995.

39. Pamphylis, *Ikaria,* pp. 213–214.

40. Melas, *Ikaria,* p. 233; J. Tsantes, *Ikariaka* 2 (1975), 11–12.

41. Fourteen-year-old boy: Lombardas, *Ikariake Phoné,* July 1975. For further reminiscences of 1912, see, Angeliki Antoniou Ploutis, Sept. 4, 1958, *Ikariaka;* Pamphylis, *Ikaria,* pp. 212–214; I. Th. Tsantes, "E Giorte tes Aghias Marinas sten Arethousa," *Ikariaka* 2 (1975), 11–12.

42. N. P. Ioannou, *H Ikariake Epanastasis kata to 1912* (Alexandria, Egypt, 1912) wrote a play about the uprising and staged it in Alexandria. In this play, Spanos' wife dreams that harm will come to her husband, and thus does not awaken him to join his comrades. Georgios Plakidas, a relative of Spanos, supports this version; interview Aghios Kyrikos, May 27, 2002. Despina Spanos Ikaris heard from her father Dr. Chrisots Spanos, the brother of man shot, the story about the reluctant horse. I obtained this information in a letter December 8, 2004 from Mrs. Ikaris. Georgios Spanos, grand-

son of the 1912 warrior, in 1957 interviewed a lady in Chrysostomos who witnessed the battle. She claimed that Spanos was killed by Turkish fire. The grandson rejects the story that Spanos' wife was responsible for Spanos' delayed departure and subsequent isolated position. L. Papalas, interview May 21, 1994, Tsouredo, Icaria, heard from Dimitri Poulianos that as the detachment passed through Arethousa Spanos decided to have supper with a friend, and rejoined the detachment near Chrysostomos. One version explains the delay resulting from a visit to a lady friend. Photene Gemelos, who participated in the revolution loading cartridge belts for the Icarian forces and carrying the Icarian flag in the independence celebration of 1912, had a different version of the event. From California, where she settled, she sent a letter in 1990 to the Georgios Spanos chapter of the Icarian Brotherhood in Lincoln Park, Michigan, accusing Spanos of unsubstantiated charges. She offered the chapter a generous donation if it would change its name. This letter is in possession of Nicholas Achidafty, Clearwater, Florida.

43. Melas, *Ikaria,* pp. 233–234. Pamphylis, *Ikaria,* pp. 216–217.

44. *Ikariaka* 14, 1957.

45. Pamphylis, Ikaria, pp. 218–219. Budget document from July 18th to September 14th in *Elethera Politeai Ikarias* (Aghios Kyrikos, n.d.)

46. N. Binekos, *Atheras* Jan./Feb. 1995.

47. Melas, *Ikariaka,* pp. 233–234. Melas, who was a member of parliament and served as a minister in the government of Georgios Papandreou, heard in government circles that the Greek state a decade later rewarded Thucydides for his conduct in the 1912 episode by providing him with a good civil-service position; interview May 22, 1998, Aghios Kyrikos, Icaria.

48. Fear of Turkish reinforcements: Pamphylis, *Ikaria,* pp. 235–238. Chios garrison: Philip Pandely Argenti, *Chius Liberata: Or the Occupation of Chios by the Greeks in 1912, as Described in Contemporary Documents; and Chios during the Great War* (London, 1933), pp. xviii–xx, notes that the dearth of casualties in Chios was "most unusual in the annals of warfare."

49. Ch. Pamphylis, *Ikaria,* pp. 209–213. Dragoumis, however, recommended to one of the unofficial Icarian delegations the expulsion of the Turks; see T. Binekos, *Atheras,* Jan. Feb. 1995.

50. For an analysis of Ottoman sea power in 1912–1913, see Bernard Langensiepen and Ahmet Güleryüz, edited and translated by J. Cooper, *The*

Ottoman Steam Navy 1828–1923 (Annapolis 1995), pp. 16–19. Dardanelles: Argenti, *Chius Liberata,* p. xlvii.

51. Grey: R. Bosworth, "Britain and Italy's Acquisition" 686–689.

52. Pamphylis, *Ikaria,* pp. 247–249); Christos Spanos, interview May 27, 1996, Raches, Icaria.

53. Pamphylis, *Ikaria,* pp. 272–274. Fourni: http://www.geocities.com/fournoi2001/greek.htm

54. Pamphylis, *Ikaria,* pp. 245–247; Melas, *Ikaria,* pp. 235–236. For the next four months, an executive committee consisting of Dr. Malachias, H. Pamphylis, A. Tsantes, J. Poulianos, K. Poulianos, N. Malachias, K. Kouloulias, L. Spanos, Th. Spanos, Ch. Spanos, and four Fourniotes governed Icaria.

55. Malachias' letter: N. P. Ioannou, *E Ikariake Epanastasis kata to 1912* (Alexandria, Egypt, 1912), pp. 5–6. Pamphylis, *Ikaria,* pp. 239–242. Melas, *Ikaria,* pp. 233–240. Venizelos' policy: D. Alastos, *Venizelos: Patriot, Statesman, Revolutionary* (Gulf Breeze, Florida 1978), pp. 97–103. Torpedo boats figured prominently in Greek military circles at the time; see Leon, "Greece and the Central Powers," 123–124.

56. Pamphylis, *Ikaria,* p. 281; also see reminiscences of M. Koutsouflakes in *Ikariaka* 2, 1975.

57. Pamphylis, *Ikaria,* p. 281.

58. Pamphylis, *Ikaria,* pp. 283–285. The Icarians in Alexandria contributed 500 pounds sterling, while those in Pittsburgh sent the equivalent of 400; see N. P. Ioannou, *E Ikariake Epanastasis,* p. 48. While this work is a dramatization of the events of July 1912, the author includes documents and data. Ioannou lists 57 men registered in an Icarian club in Alexandria. By 1920, there were approximately 1,000 Icarians in Egypt; see Spanos, *Ikariaka,* pp. 66–67. Teachers' pay: Budget document for Nov. 4, 1912, in *Eleuthera Politeia Ikarias* (Aghios Kyrikos, n.d.)

59. Pamphylis, *Ikaria,* p. 260.

60. Pamphylis, *Ikaria,* pp. 260–261.

61. Pamphylis, *Ikaria,* pp. 263–264.

62. Bosworth, "Acquisition of the Dodecanese," 690–701.

63. Langensiepen, *Ottoman Navy,* p. 19.

64. Alastos, *Venizelos,* pp. 103–104.

65. Pamphylis, *Ikaria,* pp. 275–280.

66. Aeneas Constantine collection, Harrisville, Michigan.

67. Pamphylis, *Ikaria,* pp. 298–299. Value of fakes: Phone interview, Elias Pardos, a stamp dealer, Akron, Ohio, Feb. 26, 2002.

68. Pamphylis, *Ikaria,* pp. 281–298.

69. Pamphylis, *Ikaria,* p. 299.

70. Pamphylis, *Ikaria,* p. 299, states that I. Klikos and S. Lakios risked their lives by going to Asia Minor to buy grain.

71. Pamphylis, *Ikaria,* p. 283.

72. Pamphylis, *Ikaria,* p. 272.

73. Icarian volunteers slipped in and out of Samos and Chios during the summer and fall of 1912. M. Kastanias took a small force to Karlovasi, Samos: Melas, *Ikaria,* p. 171. Manolis Koutsouflakes went to Chios, Dec. 12–25, 1912: *Ikariaka* 2, 1975. In November, after independence, E. Koukoudeas took a force to Chios: Lombardas. *Ikariake Phoné,* July, 1975. p. 7.

74. Papalas, *Ancient Icaria,* pp. 45–75.

75. Pamphylis, *Ikaria,* p. 304.

76. Letter written by G. S. Lombardas, Secretary of Committee; see document in *Eleuthera Politeia Ikarias.* Kouloulias: Pamphylis, *Ikaria* pp. 304–315. Christos Spanos, in a letter written to the Greek foreign minister, Oct. 28, 1912, argued the case for Evdilos to become the new capital. The letter is in possession of his daughter Despina Spanos Icaris, New York, N.Y.

77. Pamphylis, *Ikaria,* pp. 311–313.

78. Leon, "Greece and the Central Powers," pp. 136–142.

79. Pamphylis, *Ikaria,* pp. 314–315.

80. Pamphylis, *Ikaria,* pp. 311–313.

81. Pamphylis, *Ikaria,* pp. 291–294, 304–307, 318–319.

82. Pamphylis, *Ikaria,* pp. 306–307.

83. In a review of Melas' book, Dr. Christos Spanos, *Ikariake Phoné,* May 3, 1958, argued that Melas minimized the role of northern Icaria, particularly the Evdilotes, and gave Dr. Malachias too much credit. He asserted that the book is biased, and that Melas, who was not a native Icarian but had married a woman from Aghios Kyrikos, wrote a pseudohistory of the island aiming at flattering the Icarians for the purpose of furthering his political career. Dr. Spanos recommended that the Icarians should stick with the history of Icaria written by K. Tsapaliares, *E Nesos Ikaria* (Athens, 1927), a native of Arethousa, the northern section. Spanos' charges were unfair and reflect the regional animosities that existed in Icaria in the 1950s. Melas represented the district of Piraeus in Attica and served as a member of parliament and a minister of commerce in the government of Georgios Papandreou. In 1962, while representing Piraeus, Melas spoke in favor of a government subsidy for the baths at Therma; see *Ikariake Phoné,* April 30, 1962. He ran the risk of alienating his constituents in Piraeus and did not expect any political advantage for his position.

84. *Origin of the War* edited by G. P. Gooch and Harold Temperley, *The Balkan Wars,* II (London, 1934), 9, part 2, doc. 437, 474, 1019. *British Documents,* x, part 1. *The Near and Middle East on the Eve of the War* (London 1936), Doc. 252.

85. Chios with a greater capacity to absorb refugees saw 60,000 pass through the island, and allowed 18,000 to remain; see Argenti, *Chius Liberata,* p. lix. Despite the war, Greece soon repaired its relations with Turkey and the late 1920s and 1930s marked good relations; see A. Alexandris, "Turkish Policy towards Greece during the Second World War and Its Import on Greek–Turkish Detente," *Balkan Studies* 23 (1982), 157–197.

CHAPTER 4

Between Pittsburgh and Athens

L OCAL LORE has it that the first Icarian to go to America was a man named Loukatsos who left Icaria around 1850. His voyage had no impact on his native land. He disappeared in the New World. But a generation later, men went and returned, and their voyages had great repercussions on the island. In an Icarian village around 1895, a man emerged from his shack with a box full of money. His son had conveyed the fortune from America. He gleefully showed it to his neighbors. The poorest man in the village was now the wealthiest. Until then Icarians sought for riches that Byzantine refugees had allegedly buried on their island, but now word spread through all the villages that the real treasures were in a distant land called America where the streets were paved with gold.[1]

The first Greeks in America worked there mainly as bootblacks, fruit vendors, candy makers, waiters, and owners of small restaurants. At first the Icarians followed this path. In 1896, an Icarian sailor settled in Wilmington, North Carolina, and others followed him. About the same time, an Icarian arrived in San Francisco. In seaport communities, they undertook traditional immigrant jobs. In Wilmington, they became fruit vendors, established candy stores, ice-cream parlors, and small restaurants. At first they did business in the poorer sections of town, and the newspaper records of those days reveal a number of clashes with their black customers. In Sherwood, California, several Icarians purchased a forest and went into the timber business.[2]

The bulk of the Icarian immigrants, however, were employed in steel mills in America's industrial belt. Unlike many of the other Greeks who came from the Ottoman Empire as shoemakers, blacksmiths, tailors, tanners, pastry makers, the Icarians were peasants and sailors. Most of them, however, knew how to make charcoal. When they arrived in New York in the late 1890s, they met other Greeks and identified themselves as manufacturers of *karvouna,* charcoal. Their compatriots innocently mistranslated *karvouna* for coal, and dispatched them to the coalfields of Pennsylvania, a good occupation for unskilled immigrants of that era. The Icarians, however, loathed toiling in coal mines, and soon found jobs in the nearby steel mills of Pittsburgh, and its suburb Verona. In the summer of 1892, before the fist wave of Icarians arrived, a violent strike had broken out at the Homestead Works, Carnegie Steel Company's huge mill on the banks of the Monongahela River. The Carnegie Steel Company smashed the Amalgamated Association of Iron and Steel Workers, and began hiring immigrant workers who had no interest in joining unions or demanding union wages. Icarians, like other immigrants, were content with a wage of 15 to 16 cents an hour and a 10-hour day. Unlike many of the other foreign-born workers, the Icarians had no intention of staying in America, and were eager to work hard, save money, and return to their island. They were industrious, tolerated precarious altitudes in steel mills, did not binge on alcohol, and were dependable in adhering to their work schedule. Their foremen inquired about brothers or cousins back home who wanted a job. They informed relatives in Icaria that a man in America in one day earned the equivalent of 150 groschen, enough to support a family in Icaria for one month. So many went to Pittsburgh that it became the center for Icarians in America. Thus they followed the pattern of Aegean Greeks who left specific islands to trail their people to a certain American city and specialize in particular occupations.[3]

These Icarian men at first were engaged in the operations of making steel, but gradually found work in the maintenance of steel mills. Around 1900, Anastasios Tiniakos and Angelo Tsantes formed an industrial roofing and painting company in Pittsburgh and obtained contracts to paint ore bridges and maintain corrugated metal sheets in steel mills. Like the captains-cum-charcoal-merchants of Icaria who exerted so much influence on the island, they became the leaders in the Icarian-American community. Following naval scaffolding methods from Icarian sail ships, they fastened boards to ropes and linked them to a pulley, and deployed a type of swing "kandelitsia," to pull them to what had been previously virtually inaccessible areas in the mill. With such an inexpensive contraption, they easily outbid their American rivals who used standard scaffolding to reach towering sites. The Icarian method was a bargain for management that then assumed no liability for workers, many of whom perished on the job. At first, Tiniakos imported men from Fourni who were willing to do the most dangerous jobs for even less pay than Icarians. The social pecking order established centuries ago in the Aegean was now observed in Pittsburgh. Tiniakos not only became the pillar of the Icarian community in America, he was also revered in Icaria and even in Fourni where the women sang his praise for employing their men. "Ton Ankeli agapo, ton Tianiako doxazo, pou eche ton andro mou doulia, kai den anastechazo," (I love Angelo, but worship Tianiakos who has found work for my spouse and has lifted worries from my house). Soon, other Icarian entrepreneurs established similar ventures and needed men who could work on the Icarian scaffolding system. Icarians arrived in New York with a sign "Verona, Penna." affixed to their clothing. Helpful people guided them to the appropriate railroad depot. The train station in Verona was across the street from the Icaros Club, and upon arriving these newcomers were spotted by Icarians who rushed them to jobs. In Icaria it was presumed that every young man would go to America, stay several years, return with his dollars and marry the girl of his choice. The flow from the island to the New World increased every year until 1921 when the United States restricted immigration from Mediterranean countries and practically stopped it in 1924 with the Reed-Johnson bill.[4]

Pittsburgh at the turn of the century was a growing industrial city with one quarter of the population foreign-born. Icarians wrote home describing things they had never seen in Izmir, Alexandria, Istanbul, and Athens. At night, the mills lighted up the heavens, and in the day the city belched smoke and fire. Clouds of black soot shut out the sunshine for most of the summer. There was no *meltimi* to dissipate the industrial miasma. Some of the newcomers ventured out of Pittsburgh to small mill towns strung along the Monongahela, Allegheny, and Ohio Rivers. By 1910, there were over two hundred Icarian men in Allegheny county chiefly employed in steel mills, and approximately another three hundred fifty in various parts of America. A decade later there would be nearly three thousand Icarians, mainly men, scattered throughout the industrial cities in the Midwest. The Ottoman government encouraged emigration to the United States valuing remittances sent from America to backward regions of their empire like Icaria.[5]

It Could Happen Only in America is the only extensive account of this emigration experience. Antonios Plakidas describes his flight from difficult conditions in Icaria where at the age of 10 every morning at five o'clock he was tending animals and doing rural chores. After school he was again working in small terraced plots helping his father. When he reached his teen years, people would routinely ask him, "When are you leaving for America?" Few of these boys and young men really wanted to depart. At that time a poem circulated in Icaria entitled "Anathema sou Ameriki, (Damn you, America)." The inevitable decision was thrust upon him when phylloxera appeared in 1908 and ravaged the vineyards in his village. Friends and family wept the entire month before his departure. Plakidas left at the age of 14. His aim was to obtain a degree in some area of agriculture or botany and return to help improve agricultural production in Icaria. To pay the deck-passage fare, he borrowed 100 drachmas from his father, a sum earned in three months by an Icarian peasant. It was a difficult 17-day voyage. In New York, he worked as a shoeshine boy, shared tips with his boss, and then he made his way to Youngstown and Akron, Ohio, where he worked in heavy industry. At night, covered with soot he returned to a room shared with other Icarians. Eventually, he found a job at a bakery for $20 a week plus all the baked goods he could eat. With his surplus funds, he rented a room in the house of a Jewish family, and for the first time in his life he had a good bed and access to hot water. Then his story becomes the atypical Icarian experience, for he goes to Boston, works his way through high school, is chosen valedictorian, and goes on eventually to become a Ph.D. in botany.[6]

The first Icarians in America arrived at a time when accepted scientific theories placed Greeks very low in the scale of races. Scholars rated them below WASPs and native-born minorities. It was expected that Greeks would do dangerous and difficult jobs and live in degraded conditions. In Pittsburgh, most of the Icarians resided on south side, near the National Tube works, in two-room tenement apartments without plumbing. As many as six men often dwelled in one room, slept in eight-hour shifts, and had access only to untreated river water from hydrants near their apartments. These inadequate sanitary conditions resulted in typhoid epidemics and other diseases that discouraged Icarians from bringing wives and children to America.

These men worked sixty hours a week. Their leisure hours were passed in an Icarian *kafenion,* a coffeehouse, playing cards and billiards. They occasionally ventured to nickelodeons to enjoy Charlie Chaplin films or to baseball games at Forbes Field to see the bow-legged, barrel-chested Honus Wagner, the great shortstop for the Pittsburgh Pirates who bore a physical resemblance to the Icarian captains who traded in charcoal. While this first generation of Icarian men did not assimilate, they had a fondness for America's national game, and when they returned to Icaria some packed a baseball, a baseball glove, and tobacco baseball cards in their trunks.

Icarians who arrived at the turn of the century barely eked out a living, and it would take them several years to build up a surplus and start making substantial contributions to Icaria. Thus in 1902, when the *demogerontia* of Fanari appealed to the Pittsburgh Icarians to subsidize a Samian steamship company, the Pittsburgh workers were unable to help. By the end of that decade, however, they were managing to save half their income. A few were married to women who stayed on Icaria and went back every two years to father a child, and then returned to work in America. But those who managed an uninterrupted five-year stint in the factories in the Monongahela Valley earned enough money to build a house in Icaria, buy a fishing boat, invest in some business, secure a dowry for a sister, and return permanently to Icaria.[7]

The first Icarians in America not only lacked means for their own burial, but also had no resources to survive an illness. Several had died in industrial accidents and others from typhoid. In the state of Pennsylvania, employers until 1912 were only accountable for compensation to widows or children who lived in the state. Injured workers received minimal benefits. For instance, there was no compensation for an Icarian man who lost his sight in a Pittsburgh mill. He became a baker to raise his nine children. A less fortunate man died of appendicitis in Pittsburgh. Possessing only work apparel, and without money for a funeral, his fellow Icarians contributed articles of clothing for his burial, made a coffin, purchased a lot, and dug the grave. Mindful that they were all subject to such a misfortune, eleven Icarians met on January 26, 1903, in Verona and chartered the Pan-Icarian Brotherhood of America. Dues, which were 50 cents a month, went for burial expenses, a modest life insurance, and a fund to aid sick and disabled members.[8]

Gradually the Pan-Icarian Brotherhood of America expanded its goals. In 1910, it sent telegrams from Pittsburgh to the Sultan supporting Icarian tobacco producers.[9] As membership grew, funds were accumulated to finance public works in Icaria. Members who had emigrated from the southern section of Icaria collected money to build a high school in

Aghios Kyrikos, while the northerners sought funds for constructing an artificial harbor in Evdilos. In 1910, Icarians in Allegheny, Pennsylvania, chartered the Pan-Icarian Beneficial Society of Artemis. The people from the northern section of Icaria believed that the famous temple of Artemis lay beneath the soil somewhere in their territory, and indeed in 1939 the archeologist Kontoleon discovered it at what was then the deserted sea-side village of Nas. Establishing separate headquarters, the "Northerners" began collecting money for a harbor in Evdilos.[10] In 1912, the main organization succored the Icarians with funds and equipment in their uprising against the Ottoman Empire. While the Icarian-Americans lacked funds to provide a requested torpedo boat, in early August they dispatched a representative to Greece with over $1,000. Upon reaching Piraeus, at the end of that month, he purchased 31 rifles, and then transmitted the arms to Icaria through Syros.[11]

The Icarians in America of this era generally did not consider the United States as their permanent home. In 1912 when Icaria became part of Greece there was an expectation that the men in America would soon be returning to Icaria. In 1913 a man from Kountoumas wrote to his brother, a carpenter living in Willets, California, urging him to come back. He foresaw an epoch of economic prosperity in which people would build modern homes while the Greek government would invest in public works. In such circumstances an enterprising craftsman would prosper. This, however, did not happen, and from 1912 to 1916 Icaria funneled about fifteen hundred more of its men to the United States. The movement peaked in 1916 with approximately 450 Icarians arriving at Ellis Island, known also as Castle Garden. Passing through "Kastigari" was one of the most vivid experiences of their lives. By 1920, there were about three thousand Icarians in the United States, approximately a thousand in the Pittsburgh-Verona area, nearly five hundred in the Youngstown-Warren locality, and the rest scattered throughout the country.[12]

The stream of Icarians to America virtually halted in 1924 with the passage of legislation limiting the number of emigrants from the Mediterranean region allowed into the United States. Realizing that if they departed they might not be able to return legally to America, Icarians began to seek citizenship and become permanent residents. About half remained industrial workers; others established businesses ranging from restaurants to enterprises connected to maintenance of steel mills. There was a type of competition among the Icarians on jobs to see who could work the hardest, and earn the most money. A man gained prestige in this community by the sweat of his brow. Sons were expected to join their fathers at work at an early age. Few had the means or inclination to acquire a high-school diploma let alone a college education. They discovered that in America people might discriminate against races but did not look down upon physical labor as much as they did in Greece, for in America a worker earned decent wages and could move up the economic ladder.[13]

By the mid-1920s, most of the Icarians still in America were now citizens of the United States and were transporting their families to America rather than returning to Icaria. They were buying houses, preferably on the outskirts of cities like Pittsburgh, Warren, and Youngstown where they could raise goats and sheep, and cultivate gardens. They endeavored to preserve their Icarian identity. The women stayed at home tending a vegetable garden, goats, and chickens and making bread, clothes, and even soap. They never learned English and to their children they spoke incessantly of a rural paradise in a specific Icarian village. But their offspring were more interested in America, and some influenced by strong assimilative forces, rejected their language and heritage. For a people who had been so isolated, who suspected outsiders, and who practiced endogamy for centuries, this was unacceptable. They established local Icarian clubs, and arranged to have their children learn Greek at the neighborhood Greek Orthodox church. A small percentage decided to return and relocate their families in Icaria. Wrested from America, these children found their new life difficult. On their remote island in the Aegean, they reminisced about snowy Christmases, Santa Claus, extravagant candy displays in confectioneries, buses and automobiles.[14]

After 1912, the Icarian-Americans from the northern part of the island were resentful that the Greek government established the administrative seat of Icaria at Aghios Kyrikos rather than Evdilos. In protest to this development, the northerners expelled the few southerners from the Pan-Icarian Beneficial Society of Artemis and for several years excluded Icarians from the Aghios Kyrikos area at their July 17th Icarian Independence day picnic. In 1916 the two societies made a truce. The Society of Artemis for a decade after its establishment was a successful social organization, but was ineffective at raising funds. It never amassed the requisite sum to build an artificial port at Evdilos. On the other hand, the Pan-Icarian Brotherhood of America collected $400 in 1917 for the high school to be built at Aghios Kyrikos, and had accumulated $48,000 by 1926.[15]

As the high school fund grew, the northerners realized that the high school would benefit the entire island and began to contribute to it, and by the mid-1920s most of the malcontents were brought back into the fold. The Society of Artemis vanished from the annals of Icarian history while the Pan-Icarian Brotherhood of America flourished, chartering regional chapters in various American cities. Gradually, the Icarian Americans began identifying themselves with the American city they had settled in, and not with their Icarian village. In the 1930s, the annual picnic evolved into a weekend convention in a fine hotel. It held business meetings, social events, and a ballroom dance. Eventually, the date for the annual meeting was shifted to the first weekend in September, to correspond with the Labor Day holiday. By 1935, there were five chapters in Ohio: Youngstown, Akron, Cleveland, Warren, and Steubenville. New York City and Pittsburgh boasted one each. By the 1940s, there were branches in Detroit, Chicago, and South Pasadena, California.[16]

At all Icarian gatherings, Eleutherios Venizelos was the center of discussions. He had played an important role in uniting Icaria with Greece, and was revered by Icarians in both America and Icaria. In America, they tended to equate Venizelos' liberal Party with the American Democratic Party, and by the 1930s they regarded Franklin Delano Roosevelt as another Venizelos. They generally subscribed to the pro-Venizelos *National Herald,* which was established in 1913, and scorned the *Atlantis,* the conservative and pro-royalist newspaper founded in 1894. Both dailies, published in Greek, were based in New York. For specific news about Icaria, the men went to Icarian cafés in Pittsburgh and Verona where they read *Pandeki,* which at $3 an issue was too expensive for individual subscriptions. Ch. Pamphylis, the publisher, mixed local news about Icaria with utopian theories that were attractive to a growing radical group among the Icarians who were turning away from Venizelos and seeking other political solutions. After 1918 the radical Icarian-Americans subscribed to a Communist paper published in America, *Phoné tou Erghatou* which in 1923 became *Embros.* The Icarians often clashed with fellow Greek immigrants, particularly from the Peloponnese, who were generally royalists, and backers of Constantine I (king 1913–1917 and 1920–1922), who opposed Venizelos' liberal policies. This hostility surfaced in several cities. For instance, in the mid-1920s in Warren, Ohio, Peloponnesian royalists controlled the Greek church. The Icarians broke away and established their church in a storefront. Oddly, this rivalry would resurface in Icaria after World War II when gendarmes, largely from the Peloponnese, displayed great hostility to the Icarians.[17]

Most men of this first generation in America remained workers, and identified with the proletariat. On the island, they had been mainly self-employed, but in America many worked for an all-powerful tycoon, a remote *efendi,* as it were, who took no interest in them. A woman who had lived in Icaria apart from her husband for many years arrived in Detroit to set up a household, and was surprised to learn that her spouse, who had worked at the Ford Motor Company for twenty years, was not a partner.[18]

Many worked in U.S. Steel, Republic Steel, Youngstown Sheet and Tube, and other such mills that were located between Pittsburgh, Pennsylvania, and Youngstown, Ohio. The bulk of these Icarian workers were not employed by the steel mills, but rather by private companies servicing the mills. Throughout the 1920s and 1930s, the Communist Party had agents operating in this area, and it recruited several Icarians.

Gus Hall (born Arvo Kusta Halberg, 1910–2000, son of Finnish immigrants), who in 1959 after his release from prison became general secretary of the Communist Party USA, arrived in the Ohio Mahoning Valley in 1937 to unionize the steel workers and workers in related industries. Despite his having been a Communist since 1926 and having studied at the Lenin Institute in Moscow from 1931 to 1933, he obtained a job in Youngstown Sheet and Tube, and immediately began to agitate for a contract for the workers. During this time, he made speeches in the Icarian clubs in Warren and Youngstown where he met E. Viores, P. Tsarnas, and S. Tsermengas. Apparently, they assisted Hall in organizing the Little Steel Strike of 1937 against Republic Steel Corporation in Warren.[19]

The walkout was a violent affair. The strikers, who had been replaced with scab labor, besieged the mill cutting off their replacements from supplies. The police, in trying to drive away the workers, killed ten strikers, and the workers responded by shooting down a company airplane that was supplying the scab workers with food. For his role in the strike, the government deported Tsermengas. He volunteered to fight in Spain and wrote a book in Greek about his experience in the Spanish Civil War. Compromised by his political ideology, he was obliged to seek refuge in Poland. Tsarnas, however, remained in America and proved useful to Hall.[20]

The 1930s were devastating years for the Icarian-Americans, as it was for the bulk of the working class. The men did not have steady work, and families relied on women tending gardens and animals, and boys selling newspapers and shining shoes. Conditions, however, were much worse in Icaria where agricultural production declined while farmers gained solvency in Samos, Mytilene, and Chios exporting wine and olive oil. The Icarian-Americans realized that Athens had no intention of giving Icaria a "New Deal." Thus the Pan-Icarian Brotherhood in 1933 raised dues from 50 cents to 75 cents a month, in part to build up a relief fund for Icaria. In 1934, the Pan-Icarian Brotherhood earmarked two hundred dollars to aid farmers in Icaria develop a cash crop. The investment had no effect. It was decided to transfer the bulk of the Brotherhood's resources to Athens to be more readily available for Icarian projects. The money was lost in the late 1930s in a bank failure.[21]

A Frontier Province

In the first four decades of the 20th century, the island became more and more dependent on the American community. Indeed Icaria fell into economic stagnation after it joined the Greek nation in 1912. For its first half-century under the Greek flag, Icaria did not obtain major public works from Athens, or any help in the economic development of the island. On the other hand, the Greek government dispatched tax collectors. When they arrived, men fled to the mountains to avoid paying a levy ranging from twenty to fifty drachmas per person. There were taxes on agricultural products, slabs of schist used as building material, charcoal, houses, animals, and fish.[22]

The negative economic impact of *enosis,* union with Greece, was not at first discerned. By 1913 Icarians reestablished commercial contacts with Turkish cities where there was still a vast Greek population, and they maintained a commercial exchange until 1917 when Venizelos forced King Constantine I to abdicate, overturned the king's pro-German neutrality, and had Greece join the Allies. Turkey thus became an enemy, but when the war ended in 1918, Icarian merchants and farmers resumed selling goods and purchasing products from Greek counterparts in Izmir. In 1920, however, this commerce came to an end when the Greek government, which had gained a base in Izmir as a result of its support of the Allies, launched an expeditionary force into the interior of Asia Minor. In 1922, the Turks managed to repel the incursion. The war with Turkey not only conclusively ruptured the economic link to Asia Minor, but also brought about a thousand refugees from Turkey, unfortunately about the time America was closing its doors to Greek immigrants. For several months, Aghios Kyrikos was packed with louse-ridden, starving people whose only possessions were the clothes on their backs and a few goats and sheep. Most of them moved on to Athens, but their temporary presence was a burden on the local people. As for the approximately one hundred and fifty refugee families that remained in Icaria, there was no work for the men. The economic significance of being cut off from Turkey was now comprehended, and men bemoaned the loss of Asia Minor "*E Kaimene Anatole,*" as if it were a deceased, beloved relative. Turkey no longer offered financial opportunities.[23]

As the economic orientation of the island shifted from Asia Minor to Athens, the economy of Icaria fell into a terminal decrepitude. By this time, Icaria claimed one export crop, currants. The chief market for this dry seedless grape was in the Ottoman Empire. After 1912, the Icarians were obliged to sell some of their currant crop in Peiraeus, but for less than they received in Izmir. In Greece, there had been a decline in currant prices since the beginning of the century even though the Greeks were shipping the product to Europe and America. But by the early 1920s, Greece had lost about half its market in currants because modern dehydration machinery in California and Australia produced a good and more hygienic fruit. Moreover, trade in such crops was limited by protectionist policies instituted throughout Europe during this period, and the decline in local currant production. Phylloxera began devastating the Icarian vineyards around 1908 and continued its destructive course throughout the 1920s. Icarians attempted to save their important currant industry by importing vines from America but they were never as productive as the old plants. Furthermore, with so many of the men in America, there simply were not enough farm laborers to replant all the ruined vineyards. Farmers in Chios, Samos, and Mytilene were not dependent on one crop and therefore not as vulnerable to the economic downturn as those in Icaria. On these islands, farmers grew various export fruits and developed the production of olive oil. In Samos, French businessmen invested in planting new vineyards after phylloxera swept through the island. Because of the available capital and work force, these fresh vineyards produced high quality wine. Furthermore, Samian farmers participated in the establishment of a flourishing leather industry in Karlovasi. In America, the Icarians realized that their island was in worse financial difficulties than many of the other Aegean islands. Thus in 1934 the Pan-Icarian Brotherhood of America dispatched a subsidy to help the farmers develop cash crops and businesses, but was too late to revive the agricultural base of the island. In the 1930s, Icaria was ranked as a rural economy without much agricultural production and only a few self-sufficient farmers. A rural worker's wages for a day's work was generally paid in bread.[24]

Icarian forestlands had been almost depleted by the end of the 19th century, and after 1912 the timberlands of Turkey were no longer available. Some charcoal manufacturers secured woodland concessions in Euboea, but these areas could not provide employment for all the men who sought this work. In 1927, the Icarians attempted to regenerate their forest, not with the magnificent oaks but with pine trees that were less valuable.[25]

Sail ships had transported Icarian products in the Ottoman Empire, but now they could not compete with the improved steam navigation of the 20th century. Merchants were unable to insure their cargoes on sailboats, and most of the large caïques disappeared. Sailors, charcoal makers, and farmers remained, by and large, unemployed in Icaria, and often sought employment in other parts of Greece.[26]

Mussolini's policies in the Italian Dodecanese created fears in Icaria that the island would fall into the hands of the Italians. Throughout the 1920s, reports of Italian repression in the Dodecanese, especially on Rhodes, reached Icaria, and on nearby Leros Mussolini was constructing military fortifications, and an airfield. With such naval bases, Mussolini decided not to build aircraft carriers. The Aegean islands served Italian strategic interests. It was widely believed that the Italians intended to enlarge their Aegean Empire, and deploy these islands as bases either to take more islands or to attack Turkey. The Italians made very detailed maps of Icaria, either clandestinely in the late 1930's, or during the war when they occupied the island.[27]

Now that the doors to America were practically closed, young Icarian men left for other parts of Greece where opportunities for success were not as abundant as they had been in America. By 1932, nearly half the working class in Greece was seeking jobs, and in Athens it was nearly impossible to find work. The Venizelos government did not establish a relief program for the unemployed and indeed persecuted workers who tried to improve conditions through labor unions. In Athens, Icarians lived in hopeless poverty and even those who found jobs were at the lowest end of the social and economic ladder, with no hopes of escaping their lot. In Samos "Icarian" was a synonym for "beggar." Icarians without funds from America barely eked out a living on agriculture, and rarely had surplus funds to educate their children beyond primary school. Poverty drove some to smuggling goods from the Italian Dodecanese. A thriving illicit trade in cigarettes, cigarette paper, ouzo, cognac, and other goods passed through Armenistis, a port with warehouses but few inhabitants. The Greek government imprisoned smugglers and confiscated their craft. With the head of the household in prison or without a boat, a family would suffer great hardships.[28]

The best prospect for escaping the economic depression was tourism, and the Icarians thought in these terms long before their neighbors did. In the early 1920s, officials from Icaria requested a subsidy from the Greek government to develop the spas at Therma. An agency dealing with tourism sent them a brochure, published in 1922 by the government's committee to develop summer resort areas and spas, advising the Icarians to build lawn-tennis courts and a golf course. While the Icarians were in no position to follow up on these recommendations they did enjoy some success in enticing tourists to Therma. The spas attracted around fifty visitors each summer, and Raches became a summer resort. In 1924, a Samian shipowner established service between Peiraeus and Armenistis. In the summer season, the *Frinton* left Peiraeus every Friday at 9 in the evening and reached Armenistis at 10 Saturday morning. After calling on Samos, it would return to Armenistis on Sunday and then return to Peiraeus. Tourists paid 25 drachmas to be transported by mule to Raches where they had a choice of three small hotels. The brochure published by the local tourist committee boasted of a cool summer village located high above the sea and surrounded by pine trees. The brochure claimed that the charm of this bucolic village in an Alpine setting made up for the lack of modern urban amenities such as cinemas. Compared with taking the limited railroad lines and using the inadequate roads of Greece at that time to go to a mainland resort, reaching remote Raches was relatively easy. Most of these tourists, an average of fifty each summer, were Athenian doctors and civil servants, though the names of several British and Dutch tourists appear on the Polits hotel registry. While Raches was not the little Switzerland its inhabitants alleged, it did provide an escape from a hot and dusty Athenian summer.[29]

Tourism brought about one hundred people to the island each summer. Outsiders paid more for local goods and services. But tourism was not significant enough to offset the general decline in agricultural and maritime activities. With so many of the young men in America, there were few left to farm, to make boats, or to fish. One of the greatest indications of the decline of the economic base of the island was the fact that the Icarians were no longer supplying the people with fish. Fourniotes and Chians trawled off the shores of Icaria, and sold their catches to people who had dollars. With declining opportunities for self-sufficiency, remittances from America were the main source of money for the people. About forty percent of the people received dollars, and purchased essential goods from stores. There was therefore a bizarre growth in consumer goods during a long stagnant economic period. Manufactured products were, however, more expensive in Icaria than in other parts of Greece because it was difficult to deliver merchandise to an island with no ports, and costly to transport goods on donkeys through inter-village lanes, for there were no vehicular roads.[30]

Male merchants tended not to stock items for feminine needs and exploited women receiving money from America by not giving full value in the exchange of dollars to drachmas. As a result, in Aghios Kyrikos many women preferred dealing with a lady merchant, Erato Patrinos who came from Chios and established a general store around 1910. Not only did she stock items not available elsewhere in Aghios, she seemed to give a fair exchange rate on the dollar. In a society where people thought in general and not precise terms it was easy for a conniving merchant to obfuscate accounts. In 1926, after accumulating many checks from America and owing a considerable balance to her clients, Erato surreptitiously closed her store, packed her goods on a caïque, and absconded to Chios owing her clients money. In Chios she declared bankruptcy justifying the action by claiming that Icarians would not pay their accounts. The local Icarian newspaper warned people about opening up such accounts with merchants, and urged that all transactions be made in cash. But credit was available to everyone, even to families who did not have access to a flow of dollars from America, and they continued to maintain such financial arrangements with merchants. In local folklore, a poor, semi-literate farmer became so indebted that he monthly gave a merchant all his earnings but could never pay off his debts. Finally he demanded an itemized account of his purchases. When he spotted a broom on the list, he declared "Now I know you are dishonest. I never have bought a broom in my life. I make brooms from rushes."[31]

Utopian Thinking

The local economy continued to decay despite the growing consumer society that was taking hold of the island. The people, however, were slow to turn to extreme politics for a solution. In the first two decades of the 20th century, union with Greece and fear of Turkey were the key political questions on the island, and the policies of Venizelos' liberal party seemed to be the most reliable on these questions. About sixty percent of the population supported Venizelos, and the leading Icarian Venizelists were Dr. Malachias and Charalambos Pamphylis. The Icarians sent them repeatedly to parliament while the Royalists, led by Dr. John Kratsas, Dr. Christos Spanos, and the lawyer Zacharias Moraites, remained a minority party on the island. The political atmosphere was friendly, and the leaders of both parties sat hours in cafés discussing their differences.[32]

By the middle of the 1920s, the political situation began to change. Many Icarians realized that union with Greece had not been an economic blessing. Furthermore, neither of the two major parities, Venizelists or Royalists, showed any interest in Icaria. Indeed, Venizelos was a great disappointment to his Icarian followers. His *Megali Idea,* "Great Idea," the aspiration for a Greater Greece, resulted in the disaster of 1922 which finally closed off Asia Minor from Icaria. This political blunder proved to be the coup de grâce to the already dwindling economy of the island. The diminutive Icarian middle class continued to support Venizelos, but the bulk of the people, peasants, were disenchanted. Thus Pamphylis, like many other Icarians, turned away from Venizelos and took the first steps toward radical politics. In the 1920s, Pamphylis expressed his views in a series of editorials and public speeches published in his newspaper *Pandeki.* Oddly, he wrote in the formal *katharevoussa* (a form of Classical Greek) though he was a strong supporter of the plain *demotike* (spoken language).

For Pamphylis, the Icarian willingness to take collective responsibility, *ouloi emeis efendi,* which was the motto of his newspaper, could be put to use in solving the difficulties of the island. In 1926, he delivered an inaugural address at the new high school in Aghios Kyrikos where he attacked the tyranny of capitalism and advocated a new system which would liberate the rural worker from poverty, provide for the sharing of communal wealth, and end the exploitation of the poor. He concluded that Greece should not take loans from "Shylock" nations, but find other means to meet its financial requirements. Addressing the lawyers' association in Samos, he attacked the inequities produced by capitalism. He warned, however, that Communism, which was taking its first steps in Icaria, was not the solution, for it would lead to a dictatorship. In a subsequent editorial, he proposed Icarian wine, currants, and figs be exchanged in Europe for gold. In a pamphlet, the *Republic of the Humble,* Pamphylis provided a comprehensive account of his political and economic ideas. He concluded that the Icarians should return to an earlier Golden Age when they lived in cooperative harmony untouched by feudalism and the first stages of capitalism. He concluded that this felicity and good order deteriorated when the island came into contact with the outside world.[33]

Pamphylis was a man searching for an ideology, and his unrealistic solutions for the problems of the island, riddled with inconsistencies, reflect the general frustration about decades of economic decay, and a strong desire for change without a practical program. But in the early 1920s, Pamphylis did not contemplate social upheaval. Icaria, as we have seen, still preserved some elements of Pamphylis' simple society without a conspicuous landowning class. The half dozen doctors, the fifty or so merchants, the families that derived incomes from America, the handful of prosperous farmers who had many scattered terraced plots of land, might be considered a privileged class, but they generally did not flaunt their advantages. The largest landowner in Raches never possessed a pair of shoes. Nearly everyone maintained a garden and tended a few goats and sheep. The community, though it might ridicule the unfortunate and disabled, provided charity for them. Most people enjoyed a measure of self-sufficiency, and scarcely anyone had to deal with a powerful employer. Thus people on the island did not acquire a sense of class.[34]

Icarians disliked anyone who became financially successful and made large investments in Icaria to bring about change. For instance, in 1909, an Icarian businessman from Alexandria, Egypt, E. Georgiadis, who had made a fortune employing Icarians to work on the Suez canal, returned to Icaria with a private yacht. The people from the villages around Arministis greeted him with great ceremony. He arranged to exploit huge tracts of land at Erifi, enclosed his holdings with a tremendous wall that still stands as one of the great architectural feats of Icaria, hired many men from the area and attempted large-scale agricultural operations. When one Icarian hired another, the word *efendi* was used in jest, and it was expected that the boss would protect his worker. But this man did not form personal relationships with his workers and required certain production levels. His Icarian employees complained that he exploited them, the inhabitants of

Kountoumas, his native village, removed his name from the village register, and there was a general uprising in the Perameria region against his efforts to establish a plantation.[35]

The most striking feature of Icaria in these decades was the prominence of women. Until the 20th century, we know very little of the Icarian female, and it is appropriate here to review what early evidence we have. In the 17th century, Georgirenes noted that pregnant women received a double portion of food. Such a concession is significant in the light of a practice on Ceos at that time where pregnant women worked as rural laborers to the day of their confinement, giving birth in the fields they cultivated.[36]

Another 17th century traveler, Lithgow, sailed past Icaria and was allegedly informed by Turks on board his ship that the Icarians were excellent divers, and once a year men and women swam to a point where a Turkish official cast an object into the sea. If they recovered the item, the Turks allegedly granted the Icarians immunity from taxes that year. Lithgow claimed that when his ship moored offshore, a man and two women hauling a basket of fruit, swam out to his boat, and, hawking their wares from the sea, sold them to the crew. Lithgow's account does not correspond to anything we know about 17th-century Icaria. Indeed, women kept away from the coast because they were highly prized as booty by pirates. Even in the following century, when men began to use the plains near the sea as grazing land, women stayed in their mountain villages. Such far-fetched stories about female divers, presumably scantily clad, were designed to titillate the nascent British reading public. This corresponds to the travel literature of the time which portrays women of the Aegean as wanton, promiscuous creatures.[37]

In 1688, a Chian artist depicted Maria Gardias, the mother of Papas Gardias, on the wall at the Theoktistes monastery. She is dressed like a nun, but in a very elegant fashion resembling the attire of the wealthy women who lived in the urban areas of the Byzantine Empire. These ladies, like nuns, were confined to their homes, and had little truck with the world outside.[38] Her son, the priest, was the great entrepreneur of the island, and presumably she had the means, unlike other Icarian women, to dress like a fashionable Byzantine lady.

Since the 16th century, women in Icaria inherited property and unlike their counterparts in Naxos could bequeath it to whomever they wished without creating special problems. It must be admitted that Naxos was considerably wealthier than Icaria, and conveying substantial property to heirs was more complicated than bequeathing goats and beehives. In most Greek rural areas, a bride left her parental home and transferred her loyalties to the house of her husband's family. In Icaria, the island that held to endogamy more than any other region in the Aegean, many fathers gave a house to a daughter to keep her nearby and to protect her from the arrogance of in-laws. These practices suggest that Icarian men thought more highly of their women than their neighbors did, idealizing them to some extent. For instance, they believed that each fountain had its beautiful Nereid, a protective force, while people on neighboring islands emphasized the presences of *kalomeres,* evil female creatures.[39]

In 1914, as the diaspora of the men was taking place, a teenage Icarian girl wrote an essay on Icaria which included a section on women. She noted that women had to dress modestly, eschew European millinery, and make their public appearances very scarce. Apart from festivals, baptisms, funerals, and marriages, men saw non-related women only at church or on their way to do a chore. Women of that era rarely left their native village.[40]

By 1920, most of the young men were in America, and women could no longer adhere to their traditional role. With their men gone, they became de facto head of the household. Not only did they have to raise their children and care for the elderly in their family, they had to make purchases, possibly run a small store, travel from village to village, and thus make themselves visible in ways that were previously considered unacceptable. With dollars from America, they hired Icarian girls to do their traditional chores, but providence dealt a particularly bad hand to women who lost their men in the diaspora.

By the late 1920s, women were going to America either to join their husbands or to find husbands in the Icarian community there. The Icarian women who stayed in Greece had difficulties finding husbands. Some of them turned to politics for a career. Olga Malachias represents the new radical women. Born in the first decade of the 20th century, she left Icaria in the 1930s to join the Communist Party in Athens. She returned to proselytize her people, and died fighting for her beliefs on mainland Greece. Perhaps the most radical Icarian female was Maria Saranta Batouyios. She was virtually a homeless person who wandered the island with a bag full of seeds planting trees and trying with modest success to regenerate the vanished Icarian forests. She urged the Icarians to build a reservoir to preserve the island's water, for the "sea does not need to be irrigated." She was a vegetarian, loved animals, and referred to wolves, as "my brothers."

Once she broke into a butcher's establishment and chased the proprietor, who was about to slaughter a cow, with a cane. She angered the priests by going into churches to put out candles because they were wasting the labor of bees.[41]

The Greek government did not confer the franchise on women until 1956, but in Icaria women voted in the local election of 1944. It was appropriate that Icarian women enjoyed the franchise at such an early date. During the war years it was the women, and not the men, who undertook the only open stand against the occupying forces. It was the women who ventured unprotected into rowboats and sailed with their starving children into the unknown hoping to find refuge camps in Anatolia. In the dark decades of the 1940s and 1950s, women emerged as the heroic fighters of the island.[42]

In the years between the wars, 1918 to 1939, there were two Icarias—one in America and the other on the island. One cannot be understood without the other. World War II separated them, and the postwar years were to reveal how different they had become.

1. L. Spanos, *Ikariaka Chronika* (Syros, Greece, 1925), p. 52.

2. For the pattern of emigration from the Aegean islands to America; see M. Logothetes, "E Ensomatose tes Dodekanesous," *Istorika, Eleutherotypia,* 8, March 2001, p. 26, and Logothetes, ibid., "Oikonomia kai Plethesmos," p. 31. Peter B. Saffos opened an ice-cream parlor in Wilmington, North Carolina, in 1896: Letter to author from Bebe Karnavas Saffos, March 17, 1980. The Icarians play a prominent role in the history of Greeks in Wilmington; see B. Reaves, *Wilmington's Greek Community: A Brief History* (unpublished, 1982), in the North Carolina room of the New Hanover Co. Public Library, Wilmington, North Carolina. Icarian community in California: letters of Gregory Xenakis, 1907–1913, in possession of his daughter, Toula Moraitis. Xenakis worked with N. Tsarnas and Co. All Kinds of Cord Wood, Willets, California, founded 1910.

3. Professions of Ottoman immigrants: K. H. Karpat, "The Ottoman Emigration to America, 1860–1914," *International Journal Middle East Studies* 17 (1985), 191. Labor conditions in Pittsburgh: Peter Roberts, *The Immigrant Wage Economy, Wage Earning in Pittsburgh* (New York, 1911), pp. 33–39. Homestead Strike: Jack Beatty, *Colossus: How the Corporation Changed America* (New York, 2001), pp. 169-176. H. Hauttecoeur, "Lîle d'Ikaria," *Bulletin de la Société Geographique d'Anvers*, 25 (1900), 350,

reported that around 1900 many families survived on less than 100 piasters (groschen) a month.

4. Tiniakos: N. Batouyios, "The Early Ikarians of the United States and the Pan-Icarian Brotherhood of America," *Ikaria* 24, (2002), pp. 11–14. Women of Fourni: Interview, John Pastis, 94 years old, July 29, 2002, Wilmington, North Carolina.

5. L. Spanos, *Ikariaka Chronika,* p. 55, converts American dollars into pound sterling and estimates that between 1900 and 1920 about 2,150,000 pounds came from America. Spanos: ibid., pp. 44–45, notes the letters detailing conditions in America. Ottoman emigration policy: Kemal H. Karpat, "The Ottoman Emigration to America 1860–1914," *International Journal of Middle East Studies* (1985), p. 185. A. Plakidas, *It Could Only Happen in America* (Athens, 1966), pp. 10–49. The book was translated into Greek by A. Poulianos, and there is no published English version. For a rather self-serving review of the book, see A. Poulianos, *Ikariaka* 37 (1966). "Damn you America": Spanos, *Ikariaka Chronika,* pp. 42–43.

6. Plakidas, *Only in America,* pp. 10–49. I. Melas, *Istoria tes Nesou Ikarias* (Athens, 1957), p. 208, dates the appearance of phylloxera in Campos, where Plakidas' native village was located, to 1908. Inferior Greeks: Henry P. Fairchild, *Greek Immigration to the United Statues* (Yale, 1911), p. 237. Racial theories: Michael Herzfeld, *Ours Once More: Folklore, Ideology, and the Making of Modern Greece* (Austin, Texas, 1982, and New York, 1986), pp. 75–79.

7. For general conditions, see Plakidas, *Only in America,* pp. 10–49. Nikolaos Seringas worked in a Pittsburgh steel mill from 1905 to 1910 and returned to his village, Maganitis, where he used his savings to build a house and buy a caïque for a family business; interview, Vankelis Seringas, July 11, 1995, Lincoln Park, Michigan. Manolis Magkoulakis went to America around 1905 to earn a dowry for his sister, sent the money to Icaria, and stayed in America; interview, Zacharias Magkoulakis, September 1, 1999.

8. Blind Man Petro Kratsas, interview, Basilis Kratsas, July 17, 1995, Pittsburgh. Nikitas J. Tripodes, *History of the Icarian Greeks of Southern California* (South Pasadena, California, 2001), pp. 7–9, deals with the foundation of the Brotherhood. When John Kefalos left for Icaria in the middle of April, 1906, he paid half his dues, 25 cents; see membership register, Verona, Pennsylvania. The author consulted the archives in July 1995. A sample from the records of the archives in Verona reveals that some of the members in 1910 were Vasilis Saffos, Constantine Caras, Christodoulos

Caras, Panagiotis Saffos, Antonios Papalas, Stephanis Papalas, Basilis Papalas, John Kefalos, and Diamantis Kotses.

9. Melas, *Ikaria,* p. 209, notes letter of *demogerontia* requesting the Pan-Icarian Brotherhood of America to intervene in the tobacco crisis of 1910. The records in Verona do not have a record of this.

10. N. Tripodes, *History of the Icarian Greeks of Southern California,* pp. 6–9, discusses the split.

11. Bill of sale from Theodoropoulos and Serigos, August 23, 1912, Arms Dealers, 30 Aristidou St., Peiraeus. Document in archives, Verona, Pennsylvania. Request for torpedo boat in letter of Dr. Malachias; see N. P. Ioannou, *E Ikariake Epanastasis kata to 1912* (Alexandria, Egypt, 1912), pp. 6–7.

12. August 31, 1913, letter to Gregory Xylas living in Willets, California, in possession of his daughter Toula Moraitis, Kountoumas, Icaria. Emigration figures: Spanos, *Ikariaka Chronia,* p. 55. America not permanent home: K. H. Karpat, "The Ottoman Emigration to America, 1860–1914," 185.

13. Physical work: Plakidas, *Only In America* (Athens, 1961), pp. 16–17, left Icaria in 1912 as a boy of 14. He worked in factories before obtaining a Ph.D. in botany; he became a professor at Louisiana State University and visited Icaria in 1932 where he described his experiences in a lecture to students. Phoutrides; N. Diamatides, "Aristides E. Phoutrides: Harvard's Schizocardiac Scholar," *Modern Greek Studies Yearbook* 8 (1992), 73–94. Plakidas, *Only in America,* p. 10. J. Magoulakis recalled that his father, who owned a meat market in Youngstown, had little regard for education, and expected his son to help in the family business after school; phone interview, Youngstown, Ohio, March 9, 2002. There were, however, a few who received university educations. Aristides Phoutrides received a Ph.D. in Classics at Harvard, and taught at Yale before his early death at the age of 37. Antonios Plakidas earned a Ph.D. in botany and taught at Louisiana State University. V. I. Chebithes became a successful attorney.

14. Such was the case of N. Dimantides, born in a small town in Ohio in 1917. His father, fearful that his son would not learn Greek, took the seven-year-old boy to Icaria where he remained until after the Second World War; interview, Atlanta, Georgia, Sept. 1, 1999, and "Memorial Tribute," in *Ikaria,* vol. 24, no. 100 (2002), 41.

15. Gregory Xenakis from Kountoumas in the southern section of Icaria, work-ing in Willits, California, in March 1921 donated $100, more than a third of his savings, for the high school; receipt in possession of his daughter, Toula Moraitis, Kountoumas, Icaria. In 1926, the Pan-Icarian Brotherhood dis-patched $48,307.05 to Icaria, for the high school in Aghios Kyrikos. See *Katastatikon tou Philekpaideutikou Syllogou Ikarias* (Cosmos Printing Company, New York, 1926), pp. 25–39, for a list of contributors. For the inaugural lecture, see T. Benikos, *Atheras,* Jan.–March, 94. N. Diamantides, who graduated from the high school in the mid 1930s, maintained that it provided a good education and prepared him for his three master's degrees earned in America; phone interview, Akron, Ohio, Aug. 16, 1993.

16. The first modern convention at a first-class hotel was held in Youngstown, Ohio; see the *Pan-Icarian Convention Book,* Youngstown, Ohio, November 28, 1935, in the Icarian archives at Verona, Pennsylvania. The Pittsburgh chapter hosted the convention. It seems that the New York chapter, Pandeki, pioneered the idea of a meeting in a first-class hotel, the Palm Garden, with a regional supper meeting followed by a ball, February 10, 1935. Georgirenes would have been astounded to see these descendants of his Icarians in formal attire; see photo in *Pan-Icarian Convention Book,* 1935.

17. Interview, Marino Papalas, Aug. 3, 1994, Lincoln Park, Michigan, reminisc-ing about Warren, Ohio, in the 1920s.

18. Interview, G. Mugianis, Lincoln Park, Michigan, July 17, 1994.

19. For Hall, see H. Klehr, "Gus Hall," *American National Biography,* ed. by P. Betz and M. Carnes (Oxford, 2002), pp. 255–256. For the minimal influ-ence of Marxism on Greek immigrants, see Theodore Saloutas, *The Greeks of the United States,* (Cambridge, Massachusetts 1964), p. 332.

20. An interview with Hall and a discussion of the strike of 1937 in *The Youngstown Vindicator* August 2, 1987, Dec. 3, 1987. Viores, Makkas, Tsermingas: *Nea Ikarias,* Jan. 1993. Tsarnas: Phone interview, Z. Magoulakis, Youngstown, Ohio, March 9, 2002. Hall claimed that the "Warren strike was unique because the community supported it . . . and the area has never been the same," *Warren Tribune,* Dec. 1987. Spanish Civil War: Stephanos Tsermengas, *No Passarn—Ellenes Ethelontes sten Ispania* (Athens, 1987).

21. Based on a 22 to 12 vote, send $200.00 for Icarian agriculture, minutes August 1934. Dr. Stephen Pamphylis, a dentist, proposed that the organiza-tion's money be kept in the United States, but his proposal was turned

down. In the previous year, the Brotherhood sent $100 to help earthquake victims in Chalcide.

22. Lack of olive-oil production and tax collectors: N. Makkas, *E Istoria tes Kommounistikes Organosis Ikarias* (Athens, 1989), pp. 19–21. Icarian Communists believed Ottoman rule was more enlightened in Icaria that that of the government of Greece; see editorial by anonymous writer, an "Icarian", *Nea Ikaria,* July 17, 1946. Emigration figures: Spanos, *Ikariaka Chronia,* p. 55. For the Icarian-American support of Icaria, see *Katastatikon tou Philekpaideutikou Syllogou Ikarion,* pp. 25–39. R. E. Kasperson, *The Dodecanese: Diversity and Unity in Island Politics* (Chicago, 1966), p. 114, discusses how remittances from America proved to be a disincentive for local development in Dodecanese islands.

23. For an estimate of the refugees in Icaria, see Emile Y. Kolodny, *La Population des îles de la Grèce: essai de géographie insulaire en Méditerranée orientale* (Aix-en-Provence, 1974), II, 488–489. Poverty of Greek refugees from Asia Minor: Stratis Haviaras, *Kathemrine,* English Edition, June 1, 2000. Also see R. Hirschon, *Heirs of the Greek Catastrophe: The Social Life of Asia Minor Refugees in Peiraeus* (Oxford, 1998)), pp. 49-55. Interview, John Pastis, 94 years old, July 29, 2002, Wilmington, North Carolina, who saw refugees with their sheep and goats living in tents around Aghios Kyrikos. Georgios Eleutherios spoke of how he arrived with his parents from Asia Minor. As the bulk of the refugees were leaving Icaria, his father decided to stay because he was afraid of another sea voyage; interview, Aghios Kyrikos, May 27, 2002. G. Papaseimakes recalled his grandfather referring to Turkey as "E Kaiemene Anatole," interview, Raches, May 23, 2002. Christodoulos Malachias was a very prosperous merchant in Raches between 1912 and 1920, importing grain and exporting wine and grapes to Izmir. He was ruined by the events of 1920 and 1921. He died of a stroke, and the family went into decline; note from Angelos Kalokairinos, May 27, 2002. For the importance of Anatolia to the economy of the islands of the eastern Aegean, see "Development of the Resources of the Island of Rhodes under Turkish Rule, 1522–1912," *Balkan Studies* 4 (1963), 45–46. On May 19, 1921, the United States put into law the immigration act, limiting immigrants from a given country to three percent of the number residing in the United States according to the census of 1910.

24. Lack of olive-oil production N. Makkas, *E Istoria tes Kommounistikes Organosis Ikarias* (Athens, 1989), pp. 19–21. Rural poverty: Antonis Kalambogias, *Ikaria: O Kokkinos Vrachos* (Athens, 1975), pp. 4–5. Currants: A. Andreades, "The Currant Crisis in Greece," *Economic Journal,* 16 (1906), pp. 43–44. and A. Plakidas, *It Could Only Happen in America* (Athens, 1966), pp. 18–19. For trade in currants, see the chart in Eliot

Grinnell Mears, *Greece Today: The Aftermath of the Refugee Impact* (Stanford, 1929), pp. 64–68. Landowner: Scirianos, the entrepreneur, was born ca. 1875, and made his fortune in the first decade of the twentieth century exporting currants to various parts of the Ottoman Empire. He continued, despite adverse conditions, to export his products in the 1920s and 1930s; interview with his nephew, Christos Spanos, May 23, 1994. Phylloxera and immigration to America: G. Giagourtas, *E Oekonomike Zoe tes Ikarias apo ta Mesa tou 19^{ou} os ta Mesa tou 20^{ou} Aiona. E Paragoge kai Emporia tes Staphidas* (Athens, 2004), pp. 85–86. Subsidy: Records of the Pan-Icarian Brotherhood of America, Verona, Pennsylvania, for the year 1934.

25. Replanting the forest: D. Koumparou, *The Communal Management of the Radi Forest on Icaria Island, Greece,* Department of Environmental Studies, University of the Aegean (Mytilene, 2002), p. 7. According to Spanos, *ibid.*, pp. 66–67, there were 500 Icarian charcoal manufacturers in 1920. Apparently, they plied their trade in Euboea, and Epirus. Being far removed from their source of timber, they had less profit margin than their predecessors.

26. By the end of the 19th century, the Icarian sail ship began to decline. The first stage in this process may be seen in the last will and testament of a shipowner and captain, Ioannis B. Papalas, May 7, 1934; it states that in 1890 near the shores of Egypt, "I lost my sail ship and its cargo valued at more than 350 English pounds." Because sail rather than steam power transported his cargo, he could not afford the expensive insurance policy for cargo transported by sail. For the rise in rates for sail ships, see S. Palmer, "The indemnity in the London Marine Insurance Market," in *The Historian and the Business of Insurance,* edited by Oliver M. Westall (Manchester, England, and Dover, New Hampshire: 1984), pp. 74–94. As a result of his loss, this man could not purchase another sail ship and thus he made arrangements to compensate his creditors by sending his sons to America to earn money to pay the family debt. They were experts at using a naval "kandilitsa," a board tied to ropes and connected to a pulley that they introduced in steel mills to work on elevated sites. Document in author's private collection.

27. Mussolini's policy in the Aegean: C. D. and I. B. Booth, *Italy's Aegean Possessions* (London, 1928), pp. 256–257, and for the use of Aegean islands as military bases, pp. 285–287. It was the policy of Mussolini to build airfields on islands such as Leros and thus not invest in costly aircraft carriers; see J. Greene and A. Massignani, *The Naval War in the Mediterranean 1940–1943* (London. 1998), pp. 109–111. Italian maps: The 1:25,000 maps of Icaria are in the Istituto Geografico Militare in Florence. For this information, I am grateful to Nicholas Purcell.

28. Unemployed: L. Apostolakou, "Greek Workers or Communist Others: The Contending Identities of Organized Labor in Greece, ca. 1914–1936," *Journal of Contemporary History* 32 (3), 422. Angelike Oeconomou, born in Samos, recalled that in the 1920s and 1930s the word Icarian was synonymous with beggar in her native village in Samos; interview, Aghios Kyrikos, May 25, 2002. Evangelia Sophoulis, born in Icaria but married to a Samian, heard the same usage from her husband; interview, Aghios Kyrikos, June 3, 1970, and so did Basili Kratsas from his Samian wife; interview, Aghios Kyrikos, June 22, 2004. A. Plakidas, *Only In America* (Athens, 1961), pp. 16–17, left Icaria in 1912 as a boy of 14 and worked in factories before obtaining a Ph.D. in botany. He visited Icaria in 1932 where he astonished students when he told them that Americans did not scorn manual workers and it was not unusual for someone to start in a factory and become prosperous.

29. Average number of tourists in Raches for the 1930s: *Nea Ikaria,* Dec. 3, 1946. Golf courses: *Topikai Epitropia eis Therinas Diamoneis kai Loutropoleis* (Athens, 1922), p. 9. Tourist Brochure: *Rachai tes Ikarias— Exochos topos Therines Diamones,* Committee for Tourism, Raches, 1931. The records of the Politis hotel in Raches reveal about 100 annual guests, not all tourists, in the early 1930s. The names of the three English guests from 1937 cannot be deciphered. The other non-Greek tourist was a certain Dutchman, E. F. De Jonsh. There were two other hotels, and some private homes accepted tourists.

30. In the 1920s, a man with a mule earned 10 drachmas a day conveying goods or people, when he found paying customers. This was too expensive for most people who preferred to carry loads on their backs. Business was rarely good for muleteers. In 1935, L. Tsouris sold his mule and joined the merchant marine; interview, L. Tsouris, Tsouredo, Icaria, June 2, 1997. In 1927 in Armenistis a boy with a mule, Kostas Kalokairinos, earned 25 drachmas a trip taking Athenian tourists to Raches. On the other hand, Kalokairinos earned only 10 drachmas for the same trip conveying locals; interview, Angelos Kalokairinos, May 27, 2002.

31. Chian fishermen: L. Tsouris, Lincoln Park, Michigan, March 18, 1994. Konstantinos Papadakis had the largest store in Aghios Kyrikos dealing in clothing and hardware while Zanos maintained the biggest grocery store. Erato Pratinos: *Ikariake Enosis*, December 1926, no. 7. Men believed that Erato was supplying her female customers with inappropriate merchandises, interviews, L. Tsouris, March 18, 1994, Lincoln Park; Christos Spanos, Raches, May 23, 1994; Argyrios Koutsounamendos, Aghios Kyrikos, May 27, 2002; John Pastes, Aghios Kyrikos, July 29, 2002. Number of stores in Aghios and Evdilos: G. Lombardas, *Ikarias—Etoi Geographike tes Nesou Perigraphe* (Syros, 1903), p. 17. Broom story: *Ikariake Phoné,* May 1977.

32. J. Tsarnas, "Charalambos G. Pamphylis," *Atheras*, November/December 1993.

33. D. Close, *The Origins of the Greek Civil War* (London, 1995), pp. 98, 209, argues that Icaria and several other islands which had joined Greece under Venizelos were loyal to the man who had achieved *enosis* and therefore disposed to be anti-Metaxas, and liberal. By the mid-1920s, Icarian liberal politics were driven by factors other than the Venizelos tradition. B. Birtles, *Exiles in the Aegean: A Personal Narrative of Greek Politics and Travel* (London, 1938), pp. 304–305, in the mid-1930s interviewed a number of Communists who had been former Venizelites. Pamphylis: *Pandeki* March 25, 1926; March 16, 1927; August, 1928; November 15, 1928. He argues that 17th-century Icaria was not a feudalistic society and thus was more liberal, orderly, and advanced than contemporary France; see *Pandeki*, December 15, 1928, issue 5. J. Tsarnas, "Charalambos G. Pamphylis," *Atheras*, November/December 1993, discusses Pamphylis' student days and commitment to the *demotike* language. Pamphylis' views about "Shylock" nations were similar to Greek Communist ideology of the period; see the interview of Sklavanas, leader of the Communist deputies in parliament in 1935, B. Birtles, *Exiles*, pp. 276–277.

34. Impossibility of using machinery in Icarian agriculture: Giakos Mauvrogeorges, *Atheras*, May/June 1989. *Nea Ikaria*, October 18, 1946, discusses how young sailors in Manganitis took care of old or disabled seamen. G. Katsas, *Etan O Dromos Sostos? Apo Ikaria, Athena, Intzedia, Aegina* (Athens, 1992), p. 29, notes villagers of Chrysostomos taking care of a handicapped boy.

35. G. Mylonas, the head of the Agricultural Party while in exile in Icaria in 1939, spoke in favor of the type of great agricultural operations launched by Em. Georgiadis as opposed to those that took place on small, scattered terraced plots, but his suggestions were opposed by the people; interview, I. Moulas, Aghios Kyrikos, June 20, 2004. In the 1909, Nov. 29 issue of *Ikaros*, the weekly newspaper of the Icarians in Alexandria, Egypt, two articles and one letter attacked Em. Georgiadis for his various investments. The people of Marathon, Frantato, Stavlos, and Lapsachades united in their protest against his efforts at enclosing large areas of land in Perameria. In a letter dated Nov. 9, 1909, Aristides Tseperkas criticized Georgiadis, who lured him with an offer of employment to Alexandria, Egypt, and did not provide a job. Tseperkas hoped to shame Georgiadis into reimbursing him for the expense of the trip.

36. J. Georgirenes, *A Description of the Present State of Samos, Nicaria, Patmos and Mount Athos* (London, 1677), p. 62. B. Randolph, *The Present State of the Islands of Candia and Rhodes* (Oxford, 1687), pp. 41–47.

37. For William Lithgow, *Travels and voyages through Europe, Asia and Africa, for nineteen years containing an account of the religion, government, policy, laws, customs, trade etc. of the several countries through which the author travelled and a description of Jerusalem and other remarkable places mentioned in sacred and profane history. Also a narrative of the torture he suffered in the Spanish Inquisition and his miraculous deliverance from those cruelties* (Leith, Scotland, 1814); see K. Simopoulous, *Xenoi Taxidiotes Sten Ellada, 333 B.C.–1700* (Athens, 1984), p. 688. In the Aegean about this time, women were more valuable than men, and they were a prime target for pirates; see P. Lock, *The Franks in the Aegean, 1204–1500* (London, 1995), 256. Wanton women: B. J. Slot, *Archipelagus Turbatus: Les Cyclades entre colonisation latine et occupation ottomane 1500–1717* (Istanbul, 1982), p. 22.

38. Byzantine dress: Ph. Koukoules, *Vyzantinon Vios kai Politismos* (Athens, 1948–1955), vol. 2. part 2, 166–168. Maria Gardias: Chrysoula Fradelou-Kokkore, "Gia ten Paradosiake Foresia tes Ikarias," *Ikariaka* 42 (2001), 208.

39. House and Nereids, G. K. Spyridakis, "Laographike Apostole eis Ikarian," *Epeteris tou Kentrou Erevnes Laographias,* 15–16 (1962–1963, pub. 1964), pp. 234–243. The Icarians did not fear Nereids as other Greeks did who saw them as intriguers who render handsome men impotent; see N. Polites, *Paradoseies* (Athens, 1965), I, 356. Also see the comments of Juliet Boulay, *Portrait of a Greek Mountainous Village* (Oxford, 1979), pp. 136–137, about the bride transferring her loyalties to her in-laws. Naxos: Aglaia E. Kasdagli, "Gender Differentiation and Social Practice in Post-Byzantine Naxos," in *The Byzantine Tradition after the Fall of Constantinople,* ed. by John James Yiannias, editor (Charlottesville, Virginia, 1991), p. 61. A Naxian woman in 1689 indeed did have the right to leave, as one woman did, all her property to a child from her first marriage, but the children of her second marriage contested the will. Wealth of Naxos, Slot, *Archipelagus Turbatus,* p. 312. Endogamy, Georgirenes, *Nicaria,* p. 66, wrote, "Of all the isles of the Archipelago this only admits of no mixture with strangers."

40. Athenas Ch. Pamphylis, *To Ikariakon Eidyllion tou 1912 kai Semeioseis peri tes Ikarias* (Athens, 1914), pp. 91–92. Conditions in 1914: Athenas Ch. Pamphylis, *To Ikaria Eidelon* pp. 92–93.

41. Olga Malachias: "Mnemosene," *Nea Ikaria,* November, December 1963. Maria Batouyios: D. Poulianos; *Ikariake Phoné,* 31, Oct/Nov. 1963, and *Ikariaka* 27/28, 1963. In the novel by Margarita Lemperake, *Ta Psathina Kapela* (Athens, 2001 reprint), p. 187, originally published in 1946, there is a reference to a mad woman in Icaria who had no other job but to plant trees

and flowers from dawn to dusk, and whatever she planted grew quickly and luxuriantly. Apparently, the author had Batouyios in mind.

42. Women uprising against Italians: Katsas, *Etan O Dromos Sostos,* pp. 34–39. Despina Pamphilys, who slapped a certain Rafael, struck the only blow landed by an Icarian against the enemy during the occupation. Toula Moraitis took part in the demonstration; interview, Dec. 29, 1994, Lincoln Park, Michigan. For the goals of the demonstrators, see S. Karemalis, *E Nikaria Sten Antistasi* (Athens, 1992) p. 33. House and Nereids, Spyridakis, "Laographike Apostole pp. 234–243. Right to vote: G. Lombardas, "Gia to EAM tes Ikarias," p. 51.

CHAPTER 5

Une Saison
en Enfer*

On the Eve of Axis Occupation

B Y THE END of the 1930s, Icaria had completed a quarter century under Greek rule. It remained the backwater it had been in the Ottoman Empire as indicated in the 1878 edition of *Murray's Guide* which gave hardly any information about the island but rather a summary of the myth of Icarus, and characterized the Icarians as "the rudest and most unpolished of all modern Greeks." Baedeker had only one line about Icaria in its 1911 issue, and in its subsequent editions, after Icaria joined Greece, omitted mention of the island entirely. Perhaps the guide books would have shed more light on Icaria if the daily ship service provided by several lines in 1927 connecting Icaria to Piraeus had lasted, but by 1930 there was only one boat that called twice a week. Thus the 1930s issues of the *Guide Bleu* deigned only a short sentence. By the late 1930s, it was not only difficult to obtain reliable information about Icaria but inconvenient to go there. Thus few non-Greeks came and indeed even Greeks thought Icaria was remote and the people odd.[1]

The arrival of foreigners in mid-August 1939 created a sensation. Alexander "Shan" Sedgwick, the Athenian correspondent of the New York *Times,* came to Icaria with his Greek wife, their Icarian maid, and the writer Dilys Powell who was, in the following decades, to write several

---

* "A Season in Hell," title of Arthur Rimabaud's autobiographical poem, 1873.

153

books on Greece. Their ship, apparently, anchored off Evdilos. They descended into a large rowboat that conveyed them along with shabbily dressed men, women in vast skirts, chickens tied in bundles, tin trunks, and seasick children—to shore.[2]

While they waited for the only motor vehicle in the area to take them to their quarters, the house of Sedgwick's maid, in a village several kilometers from the port, they ate fresh grilled fish. The café owner wore a faded blue shirt, and trousers patched at both knees. The next morning they discovered figs and grapes placed on their doorstep. The hospitable people, the special radiant quality of the parched landscape, the noiseless, shaded village perched over the sea, the utter isolation, suggested an unreal world that stood beyond time.[3]

There was, however, a recent scar on this bucolic scene otherwise untouched by the modern world. John Metaxas (dictator of Greece, 1936–1941) had exiled about two thousand radicals to various Greek islands, and some were kept in Icaria. Many were members of the KKE, the Greek Communist party. The bulk of the one hundred detainees in Icaria, however, were trade unionists, government officials who had lost their positions because of liberal but not necessarily Marxist political views. There was no reason to separate them from the civilian population as the government did with Communists by dispatching them to sparsely settled islands such as Anafi and Gavros. Sedgwick's purpose in coming to Icaria was to interview George Mylonas, the leader of the agrarian party, banished to the isolated village of Frantato. In May 1936, the Communist party had formed an alliance with Mylonas' faction in hopes of preventing Metaxas from taking over the Greek government. While Mylonas controlled only a few seats in parliament, by coming to an agreement with the Communists he emerged as a rather important adversary of the regime, and thus warranted internal exile to the remote and rural Greek island. The villagers respected Mylonas, a dignitary, *megalokarcharias,* because he led a political party which had a positive program for rural areas like Icaria. Each morning he walked across the village to report to the dictator's gendarmes. One afternoon the villagers were astonished to see a foreigner, with his Greek spouse, who introduced him as a journalist from New York. Sedgwick arrived in the middle of the afternoon, and thus had to wait in the shade of a tree for Mylonas to rouse from his afternoon siesta. Accompanied by his wife, Mylonas grudgingly admitted that he found his Icarian sojourn agreeable. The village was beautiful. Situated high above the sea, Frantato boasted the best climate in Icaria. Mylonas could walk as far as neighboring village, Marathon, a kilometer down the road. There were six hundred hospitable people in the two villages combined. Mylonas made many friends and even promised that when the political situation changed in Athens he would most likely become minister of agriculture and so be in a position to do something for Icaria. He suggested that the tiny plots of land be brought together for greater productivity. Although the people thought that the redistribution of the land into the hands of fewer people for greater agricultural productivity was impossible, Mylonas, they believed, would think of other ways to help them when he resumed his political career. But for the time being, he was helpless to do anything for the Icarians or for himself and confessed to the American journalist that his isolation was unbearable. He felt like one of those ancient Roman senators deported to an obscure but pleasant venue.[4]

The most exquisite summer days are during the stormy *meltimi* season, but when the *meltimi* gales are not blowing. People remembered August 23, 1939, as such a day when they heard reports from the wireless radio about the Hitler-Stalin pact. The news created a panic in Greece and temporarily disrupted the schedule of the steamer that called on Icaria twice a week. Sedgwick and his party immediately hired a caïque for Chios, and then took a cargo boat back to Piraeus. A few Icarian-Americans who were visiting their families and about fifty people taking the cure at the baths at Therma managed to leave in the following weeks. Those who hesitated were trapped for the duration of the war, and either died or suffered great hardship. The fortunate ones reached Piraeus to book passage on ships like the *Nea Hellas* for New York. Greek-Americans, however, were returning to the States in such great numbers that the price for passage had increased thirty to forty percent. The shipping lines were obliged to extend credit to many travelers.[5]

On September 1, 1939, Germany invaded Poland, claiming that it was acting in self-defense against Polish aggressors, and two days later Britain and France declared war on the Third Reich. Greece successfully remained neutral during the first year of the war, but her position as a non-combatant became increasingly more difficult. On June 10, 1940, Mussolini's Italy declared war on France and Britain. Mussolini's next step was to draw Greece into the war, and to this end he committed a series of aggressive acts, but Metaxas refused to be provoked. Il Duce's only real grievance—Greek ports remained open to British ships—was not a *casus belli* in terms of international law.

The Icarians heard the first portent of the coming calamity on August 15, 1940, when a radio bulletin announced that Italy had torpedoed the Greek cruiser *Helle,* a twenty-eight-year-old ship launched in 1912, modernized in 1927, but outdated by 1940. A submarine sank the *Helle* while she lay anchored in the harbor of Tenos, and a second torpedo shattered a section of the port's mole, resulting in the death or wounding of a score of pilgrims who had assembled there to celebrate the Feast of the Assumption, one of the most important religious holidays in Greece.[6] Mussolini, alarmed by the international outrage, denied responsibility for what the world press characterized as a barbaric and sacrilegious act. Fragments of the torpedoes, however, revealed their Italian origin.[7]

The sinking of the *Helle* did not start the war but it began the mobilization of the Greek forces and inflamed Greek patriotic feelings. Icarian men, many of whom were working in various parts of Greece, enlisted, returned to spend a short time with their families, and then left in caïques for Samos as their women supplied the men with biscuits and fruit, and waved farewell with banners displaying patriotic slogans. There was an irony in the departure to fight on a far-off front leaving the island undefended while Italian cruisers and planes were visible to the people in Patmos and Leros. From Samos they took passage to Piraeus and then were dispatched to the Albanian frontier where they served in the same unit. The note of patriotic optimism was somewhat undermined by a few religious people who quoted from the apocalyptic passages of St. John and saw the mobilization as a sign that the world was coming to an end.[8]

Within months after the sinking of the *Helle,* Mussolini resumed his bellicose posture, and on October 28th, 1940, demanded that Greece relinquish certain Greek bases to Italy. Before Metaxas could reject the ultimatum, Il Duce declared war, and the Italians were invading Greece from Albania, which Italy had annexed in 1939.[9] The Italian forces in the Aegean—the formidable cruiser *Tarquinia* at Leros, submarines, and airplanes in various Dodecanese islands—remained inactive because Mussolini did not want a war on two fronts. The Icarians believed it was only a matter of time before neighboring Italian forces would invade Icaria. But some Icarians, Samians, and Chians foresaw a Greek victory, a latter-day Battle of Salamis. Had Mussolini opened an Aegean front, there would have been no Greek triumph, for there was no latter-day Themistocles or new Greek fleet. Icaria and the adjacent islands would have fallen into Italian hands, but Italy did not have the manpower to occupy the islands while fighting on the Albanian front. It would have been difficult for Il Duce to supply a major Aegean operation while the British navy was stationed at Alexandria, Egypt. Finally, Mussolini did not wish to annex islands and thus offend Turkey, which coveted its former Aegean possessions and hoped to claim them during the war. Thus a sort of *drôle de guerre* settled into the Aegean, while Greece and Italy waged their real war in Albania.[10]

Churchill, aware of Mussolini's Aegean dilemma, called the area "the soft underbelly" of the Axis in his report on the war to the House of Commons, November 11, 1942, but the Allied command (that is, Roosevelt and the American generals) never accepted his view, nor gave the Aegean a high military priority. In the meantime, the Italians were waiting to terminate the war on the Albanian front before pouncing on the islands. But in Albania Il Duce had caught a Tartar, and he required additional men and war matériel. The stalemate in the Aegean, however, prevented Mussolini from transferring reinforcements to the Albanian front.[11]

Because most adult males were gone, the Metaxas youth organization, EON, undertook the defense of the island. They patrolled the coast at night, and took note of Italian reconnaissance planes. One night the patrol spotted lights coming from Patmos, and announced that an Italian flotilla was approaching. People fled to the mountains with supplies and blankets. The "invasion" was in fact several Greek fishermen trolling in the early hours of the morning.[12]

The Icarians followed the war, before it reached them, through radio bulletins and newspapers. The *Asyrmatos, Kathemerine,* and the satirical sheet *Aeras* arrived weekly from Piraeus on steamers that steamed past Italian warships moored at Patmos.[13] The vessels also brought letters from soldiers in Albania confirming newspaper and radio broadcasts that the Greeks were winning the war. But in April 1941 the good news ended. Germany invaded Greece from the inadequately protected northern frontier, forcing the Greeks to withdraw from Albania. Unable to stop the enemy, the Greek army retreated to Athens followed by the Germans who took the capital on April 24th, 1941, and secured the surrender of Greece. For several weeks the Axis powers postponed occupying the Aegean. Reluctant to tie up troops in islands like Samos and Icaria, Germany and Italy considered assigning these islands to Turkey for the duration of the war. Initially such an arrangement was acceptable to the Allies, and the Turks relished the idea of serving as custodians of their former possessions. They argued that under Turkish rule the islands would be spared from brutal Fascist subjugation. Indeed Turkish rule would have assured a flow of supplies from Asia Minor minimizing the suffering of the war years. But the Icarians and their neighbors preferred starvation to Turkish hegemony.[14]

German Occupation

The Germans and Italians finally decided to occupy Samos, Icaria, Chios, Mytilene, and other Aegean islands. At the beginning of May 1941, the Germans took possession of Samos and Chios, and on May 10th, two hundred and fifty German soldiers from the 18th division disembarked at Armenistis, the northwest port facing Chios.[15] From that point the Germans marched on footpaths to Aghios Kyrikos, the capital on the south side of the island. The efficient march of the Germans led people to recall the visit of several foreign hikers to Icaria in the summer of 1938 and wondered whether they had been sent to make maps of the inter-village lanes. As the Germans passed through villages, they confiscated victuals and animals. Word of their deeds preceded them, and people fled with provisions and livestock to less accessible mountain villages.[16] Unbeknown to the Germans, there were perhaps thirty British soldiers, who had evacuated the mainland with British forces but had fallen behind, and who were hiding in Icaria. The Icarians managed to convey all of them to Turkey. We have documents confirming the presence of four of these soldiers—two in Proespera and a second pair in Livadi—but for the rest we have only an oral record. While the Icarians were aiding and abetting these men, the Germans established their camp at Fleves, the neighborhood west of Aghios Kyrikos. They aimed to instill the inhabitants with fear. However, during swimming drills, they cut a funny image because many could not swim and were secured with ropes. An officer slapped a local boy for laughing at them. But during their morning military exercises in Aghios Kyrikos they were efficient and frightening. One day a student observed the spectacle with his professor of ancient Greek, who quietly recited Herodotus' account of Leonidas and the three hundred Spartans who resisted over a hundred thousand Persian troops at Thermopylae. Upon a later occasion, another teacher contrasted the Germans, monsters from the House of Hades, with the Greeks whose humanity was molded by their classical tradition. During the hard years of occupation the Icarians to some degree maintained their identity and spirit of courage by reflecting on their classical heritage. It was, however, the national holiday, March 25th, marking the start of the Greek War of

Independence in 1822, which kindled a spirit of resistance in Icaria in 1942 and 1943.[17]

General Tsolakoglou, head of the Greek quisling government, feared such developments on a national level, and understood how to play on Greek historical traditions. On March 25, 1942, Tsolakoglou urged the Greeks to be obedient to their German overlord reminding them that they were descendants of the men who had fought at Marathon, soldiers who had fought to preserve the status quo, and that it was the duty of every Greek citizen to do likewise. A year later, another quisling prime minister, Rallis, declared that as Heracles had to pick between virtue and vice, so the Greeks had to choose between Europe, the code word for the Germans, and Bolshevism.[18]

Several Icarians had studied at German universities. Before the war some Icarians, mainly those who had a high school education, respected German culture. Any illusions, however, about a humane occupation were soon shattered. The Icaria quickly discovered that, as in the rest of Greece, the *Wehrmacht* supplemented its limited food supplies from local sources. A teacher approached a German officer and complained about the confiscations that had taken place the previous day during the trek between Armenistis and Aghios Kyrikos. The officer, offended that his heroic infantrymen were libeled as chicken thieves, sharply replied that German soldiers appropriated but did not steal. All provisions, even fruit on the trees, were considered possessions of the Third Reich.[19]

As shortages developed, Icarians began to steal animals and crops. Any thought, however, of pilfering from German stores was swiftly quelled. Weighing a huge burlap bag in which sugar was shipped, Germans discovered a deficit, immediately arrested the culprit, an Icarian who had supervised the transportation of German supplies, and summarily led him away for his intended execution. The local agronomist, who had been trained in Germany, interceded, and saved his life.[20]

The Germans who stayed through May and June 1941, and returned in November 1943 to occupy Icaria until the end of August 1944, were not interested in a remote island without airstrips, ports, or roads. The chief aim of their first visit was to pave the way for the Italians whose military prowess was held in contempt by the Icarians. By late May, many of the Icarians who had fought in the same unit on the Albanian front had returned believing that they had defeated Mussolini's *makaronades*.[21] Such sentiments were widespread in Greece. For instance, in April 1941, the Germans forced the inhabitants of Cephalonia and Corfu to accept Italian occupation.[22] The show of German arms in Icaria was a clear message. If the Icarians resisted the Italians, they would have to deal with the Germans who were occupying nearby islands.

The Arrival of the Italians

The Italians took possession of Samos on May 8, 1941, a month before coming to Icaria, and combined Samos and Icaria into one administrative unit. A summary of their operations in Samos provides the background for the Italian occupation of Icaria. It was evident, as the small contingent of gendarmes and officials arrived at Vathi, that the Samians had little respect for soldiers who came with accordions and guitars. As the Italians lowered the Greek flag, a teenage boy insulted an Italian gendarme who slapped him and put him under guard for a few hours. Two months later the occupying force, with a strong contingent of Blackshirts, arrived. Surprised at the number of soldiers, the Samians suspected that the Axis was preparing an invasion of Turkey, but the bulk of these forces remained in Samos until the Italians withdrew from the war. The deployment of Fascist troops among the regular soldiers made the situation in Samos volatile, and had it not been for Irineos, the bishop of Samos and Icaria, the people would have felt the Italian yoke more keenly.[23]

Educated in France and installed as Greek Orthodox bishop of Samos and Icaria in 1926, Irineos soon earned the respect of the Italian command. Through his ability to speak French and understand Italian, he procured edibles, clothes, and medicine from the Italians for the local population. It was mainly through Irineos' prodding that the occupying forces established a lunch program in the high schools in Vathi and Pythagorion. Although students were not officially permitted to take any food home, Italian victuals from the school kitchen nonetheless trickled into households, and were an important source of nourishment. While maintaining working relations with the Italians, the bishop supported the resistance movement, developed contacts with British agents in Turkey, and helped many Samians escape to the Turkish coast by overseeing a fake identity-card operation. Perhaps his greatest contribution was administering an equitable distribution of Red Cross supplies in Samos.[24]

The Samians were able to harvest their crops and survive the summer of 1941, but the winter of 1942 in Samos was, as in Icaria, a catastrophe. It was marked by starvation, the emergence of the black market, the advent of collaborators, and the beginning of the guerrilla movement. Privations were especially felt in Pythagorion, Vathi, and Karlovassi. In the prewar days, the inhabitants of these coastal cities depended on commerce and industry. Many of the people in the seaboard cities did not cultivate land or keep animals. Without stocks of food and unable to produce it, they survived by bartering clothes, furniture, and jewelry. Villagers often demanded gold for olive oil and meat. The food shortages in the Aegean were partially a result of a British blockade and the Italian navy's difficulties in finding an adequate fuel supply. By the middle of 1942 the Italian government was experiencing difficulties in supplying its Aegean bases. Rather than providing rations to the civilian population, the Italian forces relied more and more on local production.[25]

The March 1942 decision of the Italians to tithe animals, agricultural products, control the production of olive oil, and limit the quantity of olive oil any family could possess spawned a legion of informers providing intelligence about hidden provisions. The Italians compensated these *roufianoi* with olive oil and Italian supplies. There was no mystery about their identity for most openly consorted with Italians. They were better fed and dressed than the average Samian. The activity of these informers brought about the guerrilla movement. For instance, in the village of Mytilene, two *roufianoi* guided three Italian soldiers to a flock of concealed sheep. As the party attempted to confiscate the animals, the shepherd killed the soldiers and the two informers as well, and fled to the mountains becoming the first guerrilla. The Italians did not retaliate, but during the funeral of the soldiers, maltreated people who happened to be in public places. By 1943, several hundred men had fled to the mountains, and periodically raided Italian outposts killing several soldiers. On at least two occasions, Italian forces, Blackshirts, entered villages surprising and killing suspected guerrillas. The Samians associated these reprisals with the Blackshirts, a devoted Fascist element, but not with the ordinary Italian soldier. "We got along with them. They gave food to the *piccola*."[26]

The Italians came from Patmos to Aghios Kyrikos in mid-June. The contingent consisted of merchant seamen, several officers of the Italian navy, and a doctor. These men were decidedly less exuberant than at the outbreak of the war when Italian soldiers marched into Albania singing:

> *Andermo nell' Egeo*
> *Prenderemo pure il Piero*
> *E—se tutto van bene—Prenderemo anche Atene*[27]

Dr. Malachias and a priest received the Italian delegation. The occupying forces took down the Greek flag, neatly folded it, and ran up the Italian standard. Within a week the main occupation force arrived. Disembarking, one of the soldiers dropped his weapon into the sea. A boy dived from the dock to retrieve it. Such acts contrasted sharply with the unconcealed animosity the Chians and Samians exhibited to arriving Italian soldiers, and did not go unnoticed by Icaria's neighbors.[28]

Unlike Samos, Chios, and Mytilene, Icaria depended on remittances from abroad. Over forty percent of the Icarians were receiving money regularly from America before the war began. At that time, the Icarians supplied one-third of their foodstuffs through fishing, farming, animal husbandry, and the other two-thirds through the purchase of victuals, importing seventy thousand pounds monthly. The war nearly ended all imports except for those of the occupying forces. Efforts to increase local food production were unsuccessful. As a result of the massive out-migration to America in the first two decades of the century, and the recent mobilization for the war, marginal lands consisting of small terraced plots had been abandoned, and even some of the fertile lowlands had recently passed out of cultivation because the owners were gone, or the families were relying on money from America.[29]

Times of Famine

At the beginning of the war, Icaria had approximately twelve thousand inhabitants. By September 1943 there were only eight thousand, about three thousand had left and one thousand had perished from famine, hardships, and natural causes.[30] When they had consumed their provisions, people slaughtered their animals. Goatherds transported the goats from the mountain range to enclosures connected to their houses, and slept near them to ward off thieves. Inhabitants of the more rural villages were generally better off than the citizens of Aghios Kyrikos, Karavostamos, and Evdilos, who possessed fewer animals, fruit bearing trees, or fields. On occasion, these "urban" folk ate the flesh of dead mules, but their staples were mountain greens *(khorta)*, dandelions, and wild onions so thoroughly harvested that the verdant valleys and mountain slopes of March and April became barren. In the summer, they devoured lupines, acorns, leaves of mulberry trees, and fruits and vegetables before they ripened. Women ground carobs or acorns into flour to bake the only type of bread most people ate during the war. Without per-

Icarians in Pittsburgh, 1905. Most of these men lived together in this small attic room. (author's collection)

A reconciliation meeting between the Pan-Icarian Brotherhood of America (Icaros Club) and the Pan-Icarian Beneficial Society of Artemis (Artemis Club) in Verona, Pennsylvania, in 1916. Papa Kouloulias, without his rifle and ammunition belt, who came to Pittsburgh after 1912 and stayed several years, is in the third row left center. He served as a priest in the Pittsburgh area and was very popular with Vlach immigrants, who admired his military career. Note the scarcity of women. (Angela Koutsoutis' collection, restored by N. Tripodis)

Apparently the reconciliation was not perfect. Here only men representing the Icaros club are celebrating the July 17th Icarian day of independence in Verona, Pennsylvania, around 1920. (Nikita Tripodes's collection)

At the same time only men from the Artemis club are celebrating the Icarian July 17th day of Independence. (George Achedafty's collection, restored by C. Frangos)

One of the earliest Icarian marriages in America. The event took place in 1919 in Verona, Pennsylvania. (Irene Mylonas's collection)

Icarian steel works around 1930 in Pittsburgh. They exhibit no discomfort working at high altitudes. (author's collection)

Icarian steel workers around 1930 in Pittsburgh. Walking on sharp-peaked steel mill roofs, which resembled the contours of Icaria, was just playing around compared to crossing Kako Katavasidi. (author's collection)

Two Icarian Steel workers with an American colleague
(left) in Detroit, Michigan, around 1940. (author's collection)

Henry Ford II, second from left, assigned an old employee, Nicholas Mavronicholas, white coat in center, to escort King Paul of Greece on a tour of Ford's factory around 1950. The king was charmed by the Icarians' disarming manner. Here Mavronicholas is asking about Queen Fredericka, who decided to stay in her hotel room. Mavronicholas has just asked the king "pos pae e kera sou?" (how is the missus doing?)

The architectural plan for the Hotel of the Icarian Radioactive Hot Spring Corporation of America around 1950. (author's collection.)

The architectural plan, around 1950, to transform Therma into a modern spa center. (author's collection)

John Manta, a prominent Icarian-American businessman and president of the Icarian Radioactive Hot Spring Corporation of America, conferring with prime-minister Karamanlis in 1955 about the spa at Therma and the Icarian road. (A. Kalokairinos' collection)

27. Icarian-Americans in Detroit, Michigan hosting the nomarchos (governor) of Samos-Icaria, around 1950. (author's collection)

mission to use hunting rifles, the omnipresent partridge multiplied but was unreachable and so they trapped the horned owl, and ingested this rancid-tasting fowl shunned in normal times.[31]

When the tattered nets of the fishermen became irreparable new nets were unavailable. Fishing villages such as Fanari practically disappeared because the Italians prohibited the harboring of vessels anywhere except in Aghios Kyrikos and Evdilos. Even the British, who were in Icaria from September to November 1943, imposed restrictions on fishing because they wished to control all boat traffic. On the beaches, the hulks of fishing boats rotted. Fish, a staple on an island once known as Icthyoessa, "abounding in fish" became an extravagance.[32]

In 1942, the Italians confiscated the contents of the pharmacies obliging the doctors on the island to practice almost without medicine. Dr. Malachias endeavored to preserve his six-bed clinic located in his home, but most Icarians tended to their own health. Chamomile, which generally grew in inaccessible crags, relieved upset stomach while pennyroyal cured toothaches and headaches. Ironically, only healthy people had the ability to harvest these plants. Ouzo made from the arbutus berry, *koumara*, had medicinal qualities and was so plentiful that in the fall of 1943 a quart was exchanged for a few packets of British army biscuits.[33] Despite the numerous deprivations and hardships and the availability of homemade ouzo there was practically no alcoholism, nor mental depression nor self-pity.

However, hard times altered many traditions. Hospitality was still observed, but at a much diminished level. At mealtimes, a member of the family stood on guard to warn diners of unexpected company, and thus enable the family to hide food and not share it with unwanted guests. Two British officers, who had landed in Icaria in 1941 as they fled the Germans, hid for two weeks with an Icarian family. In normal times Icarians would have been open-handed to men in such distress, but their host in September 1943, when the British briefly occupied the island, presented them with an itemized bill for the upkeep of the two men. Before the war, friends gathered at the home of a deceased friend, spent the night, attended the funeral, and then took a common meal. Now people were too weak to spend a night in mourning, and too poor to partake in a memorial meal. There was a dearth of strong people to carry the dead to graveyards, and even a scarcity of coffins. Malnourished priests were too feeble to make frequent trips to the cemetery. The bereaved dumped their dead wrapped in rags in trenches, for sheets and separate graves were extravagances. Minimal burial observances were, however, sustained, for the Icarians feared that the soul of the deceased would not find peace if a priest did not perform necessary rites.[34]

The first cases of starvation surfaced in January 1942 as the Italians were cutting back on rations. Initially, the old and the helpless died. The extremely cold winter of 1942 finished off many malnourished people. Those who survived were emaciated but surprisingly healthy and seemingly immune from headaches, common colds, or other ailments that had troubled them before the war. There were surprisingly few cases of dysentery, typhoid, typhus, or malaria, but a scarcity of soap led to an outbreak of scabies.[35] While all areas suffered privations, Karavostamos, a village of about fifteen hundred inhabitants, was hit the hardest. In the winter of 1941 about one hundred and thirty perished from hunger. The Karavostamiotes tended not to have livestock or farms because so many of the men were involved in sea-borne professions, particularly charcoal commerce. Indeed, there is little arable land around their village. In 1940, about two hundred Karavostamiotes had worked in various areas of Greece manufacturing charcoal, selling it in August, and returning to their village in September to enjoy the remainder of the year playing cards and dominoes. In the summer of 1941, they were unable to practice their trade, and the entire village suffered from want of necessities in the coming winter. People in the interior, who were more self-sufficient, had long felt that the inhabitants of Karavostamos were indolent because they did little farming and were thus responsible for their plight.[36]

In Karavostamos an old woman, whose husband had been dead for some time, appealed to men transporting a corpse to the burial ground to take along the putrefied remains of her husband. She provided the door of her house for conveying the decomposed cadaver and for paying for the service. A malnourished priest agreed to perform the burial rites, but insisted that it would be part of a mass burial, "Let them accumulate. I can't go every day. I'm too feeble." The woman lived in a doorless house for three days and then died herself. One young girl from the same village collapsed from hunger as she left the house to harvest mountain greens. Her mother took the *touloumi,* a leather bag, from the wall and boiled it to make broth.[37]

In some villages such as in Chrysostomos where olive oil was produced in abundance there was little starvation. In Maganitis some inhabitants cultivated grain on small terraced plots and made a type of pita bread on stoves rather than regular bread in ovens that would attract attention by its fragrance. There were about ten households in Ano Proespera and five in Kato Proespera that enjoyed a bumper wheat crop produced by freak local conditions in 1941 and 1942. A teacher in Raches resigned his position and moved back to his paternal house in Proespera to take advantage of the providential harvest.[38] The wheat crop, small quantities on tiny plots of terraced land, earned Proespera the title "Canada of Icaria" and people swollen with hunger came from seaboard villages, especially Karavostamos, to procure a crust of bread.[39] Apart from this random production, there was no wheat grown on the island, and for most children the word bread was an abstract notion. One man's most vivid recollection of the occupation was visiting relatives in Karkinagri in September 1942 where he ate his first morsel of bread in one year.[40]

Reports of starvation in Samos and Icaria reached the Red Cross early in 1942. From its base in Izmir it shipped supplies, mainly flour, on Italian transports to Samos. Bishop Irineos gave it directly to the people, rather than allowing it to be stored in warehouses for gradual dispersion and thus fall into the hands of speculators. Each family in Samos received about twenty-pounds of flour, but no shipment reached Icaria. On October 1942 the Red Cross expressed regrets that it did not have the facilities to aid Icaria while acknowledging conditions were worse there than in Samos.[41]

While the Samians celebrated by making pancakes and trading flour with the Italians for rice, pasta, and clothing, the Icarians endured their privations. Finally, in August 1942, the Italians provided a ship to convey forty-seven tons of Red Cross flour to Aghios Kyrikos. The Red Cross appointed Dr. Malachias to distribute to each Icarian approximately 10 pounds, but due to transportation obstacles some villages in the northern section did not receive a fair share.[42]

In the summer of 1943 Red Cross officials returned to Icaria and found some improvement in Aghios Kyrikos, but the northern coastal villages were still devastated. The officials noted the special needs of Karavostamos, and gave an eerie depiction of Evdilos. They described a treeless village of dilapidated houses. Children dressed in their Sunday best that did not conceal distended stomachs and bodies dried on bones greeted them with bouquets of wild flowers. They made a second distribution of food, the bulk of which fell into the hands of EAM (National Liberation Front) officials.[43]

New Morals and a New Economy

In the early 1920s, the teenage son of a schoolteacher in Aghios Kyrikos was apprehended in a store pilfering pencils and notebooks. The gendarmes sent him to Samos for trial. His disgraced father was too humiliated to appear before his students for several days. In the pre-war years such acts of petty theft would have disgraced any respectable family on the island. People adhered to a strict moral code. Charity alleviated poverty. In Chrysostomos there was a retarded, threadbare boy, Georgaki. While he was routinely ridiculed for his defects, he was the village pet and received food from every house. For a short period the Italians adopted Georgaki, giving him daily rations, clean clothes, and a wooden rifle, including him in all drills. Georgaki died in the winter of 1942 when food shortages became serious.[44]

The Red Cross report on Evdilos provides a detailed description of rampant starvation. The end of regular food shipments and the loss of men in Albania rendered many households unable to satisfy their daily needs. Thus the character of some people descended to the level of their economic circumstances. In a community where there had been almost no crime, where shepherds left their sheep and goats unattended, people were inclined to purloin anything edible. Families required male members to protect their food supply. One boy slept with sheep, and one night threw an ax to drive off an intruder coming to steal one.[45]

Despite the threat of capital punishment, theft of crops and livestock was rampant.[46] Even family members hid sustenance from one another. A father allegedly drank the milk from the breast of his wife depriving his infant son of nourishment.[47] But the old ethical standards did not completely vanish. There were starving priests who refused compensation for burying the dead, and others who gave what little they had to malnourished people. Most parents went hungry to feed their children.[48] In a society where blood ties connected most people, public shame dictated behavior. Acts of generosity and decency exceeded those of avarice and treachery. For every thief and informer, there were scores of upstanding Icarians who would not steal from or betray their neighbors for any reward.[49]

If there was one element that pushed the island toward a Hobbesian war of Icarian against Icarian, it was the new barter economy. Merchants, like everyone else, traded goods. There was an unofficial established price for the exchange of commodities, but shrewd negotiating gave an edge to those skilled in bargaining. To survive one needed *poniria*—cleverness, and cunning. In normal times this was an acceptable, indeed, an admirable quality if it were deployed in proper circumstances. Men made good reputations by getting the best of a merchant, or tax collector. It was gratifying to see someone get a good civil-service job through trickery. People were amused if the victim, *koroido,* was an unpopular person, a prosperous merchant, or a government agency. Such marginal figures in the community merited little consideration in any dealings. But in these times, the *koroido* was a neighbor, a friend, or even a relative.

In a black-market economy, however, *poniria* was the most essential quality for survival. Though the Italian military administration decreed that the black market and hoarding were a capital crime, and stipulated that merchants had to post the price of goods in front of their stores and sell them at listed rates, merchants never displayed goods or publicized prices. Indeed, there were no facilities in stores to display wares, for merchants had bartered their shelves along with their goods. A dentist, a prominent Communist in the local party, sought to purchase a high-grade bar of soap, but could not afford the asking price, about forty pounds of dried figs. Complaining that he did not have a fig plantation, he later received gratis four bars from a fellow Communist, who recently returned from Turkey, where he had obtained supplies at an Allied base. The dentist contrasted the unselfish behavior of his friend with the avidity of the merchant.[50]

Communists like the dentist, influenced by political ideology, believed that merchants created scarcity. They assumed they were shameless war profiteers withholding goods for speculative purposes. Such people existed in Athens and other big cities where factories produced cigarettes, spirits, and other commodities, and there were large stores of German goods. Some unethical men were able to hoard merchandise, sell it at illegal prices, and live in comfort. Most people participated on the black market but on a daily basis just to survive. For instance, young boys regularly obtained cigarettes and prophylactics, goods produced in Athens, and then bartered these items with Germans for bread.[51]

In Icaria there was precious little to be cornered and thus it was impossible for a black market to operate on a systematic basis. Occasionally quisling Greek merchants arrived in Icaria with rare shipments of spaghetti, soap, or tinned meat. A few merchants had pre-war inventories that they doled out. Likewise, people acquired through barter or service goods such as sugar, pasta, rice, flour, tinned meats, canned tomatoes, marmalade, coffee, salt, and biscuits from Italian stores. Olive oil, goat meat, and sex were the primariy Icarian commodities available on a regular basis for barter. Some women accepted invitations from Italian soldiers to attend parties, to enjoy food and music, and to sell themselves for a can of tinned goods or a small loaf of bread. The quantity of food and clothing dwindled during the war. Sewing needles became one of the most valuable items on the black market. Since there was not a regular flow of supplies, most exchanges were one-time transactions with one party getting the better of the other in what became a zero-sum improvised economic system.[52]

The Communists equated this economic pattern with capitalism, and spoke about *aphilokerdo* (nonexploitative) behavior in a new system where people did not succeed by taking advantage of others, a society where people did not need *poniria* to survive. But any assessment of Icarian merchants as swindlers, or certain women as harlots, ignores the circumstances that created the scarcity, and the fact that everyone had to drive a hard bargain to survive.[53]

There was a curious trade in luxury goods. In neighboring Vathi, Samos, a rich lady sold her piano for eighty pounds of flour. Although pianos were nonexistent in Icaria, people walked from village to village with fur coats, typewriters, top hats, eggbeaters, and other nonessential items mainly brought from America in the pre-war period, offering them for food. Even the classical artifacts excavated in 1939 at the temple of Artemis turned up on the black market.[54]

Adventurous men took their wares to sea. They were rarely successful. In the winter of 1943 two men loaded a large rowboat with wooden handles for picks, shovels, and axes and tried to navigate to Tenos to exchange their cargo for edibles, but were swept to Chios. Villagers in Pyrgi notified the occupying German forces that imprisoned them for six months.[55] Another man made a boat and sailed to Myconus where he peddled olive oil. Upon his return, a village *roufianos* informed the Italians who arrested him and sent him to jail in Samos. During his incarceration, his wife and six children nearly perished from hunger.[56]

EAM and Relations with the Italians

In September 1941, the KKE formed the National Liberation Front EAM, and sometime in October of that year a group of men met at Petropouli to organize the Icarian branch of EAM that provided the only real local government during the war. There are no records revealing how the Icarian EAM went about its business, and therefore few details about its operation. It made efforts to suppress the so-called black market, produce food in Icaria, import provisions from Turkey, and provide for the needy. It helped some starving families flee from Icaria, arrested informers, and punished them by parading them and their stolen goods through the village of their crime. They permitted a victim, who had lost much of his crop to a thief, to kill the culprit. On one occasion they carried out a mock execution to gain information. A British civilian affair's officer, who arrived in September 1943, complained that EAM judicial procedures lacked due process, and feared that its decisions were influenced by politics. The British vainly attempted to transfer some criminal cases to a Greek tribunal in Samos.[57]

On several occasions, EAM negotiated with Italians to distribute more supplies, and circulated throughout the island a mimeographed newspaper, based on reports from a wireless in Raches. In the first two years of the war, EAM provided people with a sense of hope for the future. The majority of the men joined, though some merchants and strong royalists did not enroll. The small medical community, which had provided Icaria with critical leadership in the past, was split on the matter of EAM. Dr. Malachias enlisted after considerable pressure, but was never trusted by EAM officials. Dr. Tsantiris, after agreeing to join, withdrew because EAM, in his view, had fallen under control of the KKE. Dr. Amaxis was absolutely opposed to EAM. Dr. Stavrinades, however, became one of the leaders of the organization.[58]

The Icarian EPON, the youth organization of EAM, was established on February 23, 1943. The death of Greece's great poet Palamas on that very day, according to EPON, symbolized the patriotic character of the movement. With the exception of a few young people from conservative families, most young people joined. Members were not necessarily Communists, but the leadership was militant. Members were highly idealistic and strongly opposed to the occupation. They wished to do something constructive for the island, and some even sacrificed their lives for it. Young people who did not enroll, mainly from merchant families, suffered a degree of social ostracism in a community that was becoming politically radical.[59]

At the start of the Italian occupation there were over five hundred Italian soldiers in Icaria, and in the summer of 1943 the figure reached a thousand. The original garrison consisted of either older or wounded vet-

erans placed in Evdilos and Aghios Kyrikos with small detachments at
Cape Papas and Fanari. The Icarians generally saw Italians as individuals
and enjoyed good personal relations with them even when military rule
became oppressive. On September 10, 1943, Soldarelli, governor-general
of Samos, who had accepted terms for an armistice, reinforced this easy-
going contingent with fifty militant Blackshirts. For a short period, there
was great tension between civilians and soldiers. As we shall see,
Soldarelli's aim was to isolate these hard-core Fascists on Icaria, a secluded island, while he made arrangements for his forces on Samos to cooperate with the Allies.[60]

While there was a general contempt for the military prowess of the
makaronades, nearly everyone on the island preferred them to the
Germans. Unlike the Germans, the Italians did not enter Greece without
sufficient provisions. In the first year of the war, the Italian warehouses in
Samos were laden with supplies that were regularly shipped to Icaria. At
the start of the occupation, the Italians allocated each family about five
pounds of flour a month. The soldiers tended to learn some Greek, shared
rations with children, were on a first-name basis with the people, and routinely showed Icarians pictures of their mothers or children. They volunteered to bring their musical instruments and participate in local festivals.
"It was the first time I heard an operatic voice," one Icarian recalled. The
two Italian doctors and three paramedics provided the Icarians with some
medicine and medical assistance, and showed compassion for the handicapped. In Aghios Kyrikos, soldiers with musical instruments gave
recitals twice a month, and even offered their musical services for private
affairs. When Italian soldiers went on parade, some winked at girls or nod-
ded to acquaintances. A sense of fun and humanity took priority over military efficiency. Though they were an occupying force, they did not regard
the Icarians as lowly occupants of some racial scale. They participated
discreetly in holidays, even those fostering Greek patriotism. After the
Italians departed, life was rather drab.[61]

While Icarians got on with enlisted men, they clashed with some officers over official policy. One issue that led to conflict was the practice of
teaching Italian and presenting propaganda films at the high school at
Aghios Kyrikos. Students tended to boycott the films, and made little
effort to learn Italian. Authorities retaliated by putting the high-school
principal under house arrest, and occasionally detaining teachers from a
half-day to two days for carrying out anti-Axis propaganda.[62]

The attempts at teaching Italian were doomed to failure because the educational system had broken down. The high school at Aghios Kyrikos functioned for only a couple of months during the academic year, and when the Italians closed it in March 1942 the learning process had already been in decline.[63] Icarian high-school students never enjoyed, as did those in Samos, a daily ration of food. Teachers, remunerated with worthless paper drachmas devalued a thousandfold, demanded compensation in olive oil. Even the students who could raise some of this commodity were often too malnourished to concentrate on their studies.[64]

The most sensitive issue between the Icarians and the Italians was not culture but food. When Italians discontinued food rationing, olive oil became the currency of preference. Icarians bartered it with the soldiers for victuals. In the spring of 1942, Italians collected a tithe on olive oil, and deposited this valuable commodity in the bank in Aghios Kyrikos. Entrusting olive oil to bankers proved to be a disaster. The manager and clerk of the bank went into business for themselves, embezzling oil, trading it for Italian goods, and selling them on the black market. The Italians imprisoned the swindlers, and proceeded to take control of the olive presses on the island. The occupying forces now were enjoying the lion's share of this life-sustaining product, and this development led to clashes.[65]

By February 1942, a number of minor incidents had taken place. For instance, an Italian officer, surprising a boy singing the derisive tune "*Coroido Mussolini,*" slapped him for satirizing Il Duce, and threatened him and his family with prison. But conflicts soon became more serious. EAM commemorated Greek Independence Day on March 25, 1942, by painting slogans on walls such as "Long live liberated Greece!" and "Long Live the Allies." The Italians arrested and menaced some high-school students. Considering schools as hotbeds for nationalism and resistance, the military authorities demanded complete control of students and curriculum. The principal refused, and thus the Italians closed the school. In protest to terminating the school year, a high-school girl scribbled "Basso Mussolini," on a wall. An Italian soldier caught her in the act, and put her in confinement. She feared that her parents and brothers would also be punished, and the possibility of the family escaping to a refugee camp in the Middle East was remote because one brother was severely handicapped. Her cousin, however, a friend of an Italian officer, managed to secure her release.[66]

While the students were writing slogans, the women were demonstrating in the main square for more food. As they were marching to the commandant's residence, a huge lady, renowned for her strength, slapped the officer leading a squadron to break up the demonstration. Driven back for a moment, the Italians recovered and pursued the women to the beach where they hid behind the hulks of deteriorating fishing boats. An Italian doctor restrained the exasperated soldiers from punishing the women who sneaked from their hiding places to their homes. Two days later, provisions came from Samos, and the Italians agreed to cancel the tithe on agricultural products. The women in Evdilos and Raches staged demonstrations in May and June and obtained similar concessions. But this measure cut down Italian access to local meat and olive oil, and soldiers began roaming villages either begging or confiscating these items.[67]

From March 1942 to the day in September 1943, when the Italians withdrew from the war, there were numerous cases of Italians confiscating food from Icarians, or civilians pilfering from the soldiers. The natives were aware of a significant Italian supply depot at Fanari. One evening in the spring of 1943 the garrison there invited some girls from Tsouredos to a party featuring *loukoumades,* a type of doughnut fried in oil and drenched in honey. A man from Tsouredos, getting wind of the affair and correctly deducing that the soldiers would be so preoccupied with the girls that they would not be guarding the depot, pilfered most of the Italian *galetta,* hardtack. The following day, the Italians learned of their loss and displayed a rage and violence uncharacteristic of their previous behavior. Rounding up several innocent men in Fanari, they tortured them the entire day. The matter was eventually settled when a certain Italian Lieutenant Pica came from Aghios Kyrikos and arranged with a shepherd to provide sheep to cover the cost of the stolen provisions.[68]

Pica, who was a professor of Greek and Latin in civilian life in Italy, was probably the main reason why the situation did not spiral into violence. He had an Icarian mistress, and he was by no means a Fascist. Indeed, he discreetly taught some Icarians to sing the worker's anthem, *Avanti Popolo.* He often displayed sympathy for the oppressed Icarians. On one occasion, two Italian soldiers went to Meliopon where they clashed with two shepherds over animals. The shepherds, veterans of the Albanian war, brandished knives and sickles and drove away the *makaronades.* Pica defended the shepherds and reprimanded his men.[69]

But in the summer of 1943, a Blackshirt officer replaced the mild Pica and reinstituted the tithe on olive oil and extended it to animals. Soldiers were instructed to deploy ruthless measures, if necessary, in collecting the tax. In once case, soldiers threw a grenade at a recalcitrant shepherd. The wounded man died in Aghios Kyrikos despite the care of the Italian doctor. The confiscated olive oil did not solve the Italian supply problem. While officers had special food, ordinary soldiers began to eat cats. They ranged through villages charging housewives to prepare meals, and confiscated any edibles in sight. Resistance to the new predatory policies led to minor disputes and the imprisonment of about twenty people who were held in Therma and Aghios Kyrikos.[70]

The individual protests against Italian policy grew into organized opposition. EAM advocated that the Icarians not pay the tithe. According to one EAM slogan "even one onion to the Italians is another link in the chain of slavery."[71] In Chrysostomos the Italians, using information supplied by an informer, arrested and beat to death the proprietor of an olive press because he was suspected of engaging in the illegal production of olive oil. EAM gave the man a hero's burial because he refused to surrender an essential commodity to the Fascists.[72] Apparently, at this time EAM began to form a list of informers who would be punished at the appropriate time. By August 1943 events were heading toward the type of violent confrontation that was occurring in Samos, and it was only the withdrawal of Italy from the war that prevented this from happening.[73]

The Exodus

Icarians had begun to leave the island in large numbers in the winter of 1942. The men joined the approximately twenty thousand Greeks from various regions who made the trek across the sea to join the Greek army forming in Egypt while women and children entered refugee camps in the Middle East and Africa. Among the number of Greek refugees was the future prime minister, Konstantinos Karamanlis, who in August 1942 left Athens for Tenos. From there he went to Chesme, Izmir, Aleppo, and finally Cairo. Many Icarians made a similar voyage.[74]

The exodus began in 1942. Although the Italians declared flight a capital crime, boats of various kinds loaded with refugees regularly plied the sea between Icaria and Asia Minor. The Italians never executed anyone for trying to flee as the Germans did in Chios and Mytilene. Captain Phocianos, the Icarian Scarlet Pimpernel, in the service of the OSS, Office of Strategic Services, forerunner of the CIA, took hundreds to Turkey. Others escaped on large rowboats.[75]

Perhaps as many as two thousand people left Icaria for refugee camps in 1942 and 1943. For most of them, the outskirts of Chesme was the first step of the trip. Turkish authorities opposed entry of Greek refugees by sea, so captains usually dumped their passangers in some rural area ten or so miles south of Chesme providing them with vague instructions on how to get there. Generally, Turkish peasants and shepherds provided food and shelter, and their service to Icarian refugees has never been acknowledged. But the dread of robbery and murder was foremost in the minds of the wanderers as they roamed through rural areas seeking the safety of a city. The Greek community in Alexandria, Egypt, read lurid newspaper reports about Greek refugees murdered in Turkey. One of the most dreadful accounts dealt with two Turkish soldiers raping and murdering a Greek woman and then slaying her twelve male companions near an isolated Turkish military base south of Chesme. Indeed a group of seven Icarians vanished in this very area, and it was assumed they suffered a similar fate. In Icaria, there was little contact with the outside world. People who remained on the island hoped that the men who had left were in the Greek army, and that the women and children were in refugee camps.[76]

On a spring day in 1942, an informer led Italians to Tsouredos where they confiscated a buried cache of potatoes and tins of olive oil from a mother. She had been doling out food from this supply to her two young children. Her husband was in America, and thus with no prospect to obtain new supplies she decided to leave Icaria with her offspring. Paying their passage with sheep, they sailed with a about ten people who had gathered at Fanari, and arrived somewhere south of Chesme. By the time they had traversed a forest and reached the city, the woman was suffering from malaria. With the help of a relief agency in Chesme, they reached the Belgian Congo where they remained four years in a refugee camp with other Icarians. There she regularly received checks from her husband in America.[77]

There was greater security in large numbers, and people tended to leave in groups of around fifty. One such band gathered near Armenistis but was unable to depart immediately because of bad weather. They resorted to stealing food in the area. The locals reported them to the Italian authorities but they took no measures to stop the flight. Eventually, a captain transferred them to Asia Minor, dumping them in that rural area south of Chesme where most Icarian refugees landed. A Turkish shepherd provided them with food and allowed them to sleep in his sheep pen in exchange for clothing. Most of this party of Icarians had relatives in

America. One such young girl eventually reached Palestine where, receiving monthly checks from her father in Pittsburgh, she passed the remainder of the war in the relative comfort of a monastery. Somewhat later another group of Icarians landed in the same area and were apprehended by Turkish shepherds whose leader, a man of menacing appearance clad in what appeared to be pajamas and who exhibited a number of watches on both wrists, placed them in detention. They feared for their lives but one a teenage boy, escaped and brought officials from Chesme who released them.[78]

A third party departed from Armenistis and again arrived somewhere south of Chesme where a shepherd fed and sheltered them and then guided them to Chesme. A relief agency arranged for their passage on a Turkish boat to Cyprus, but an inexperienced captain sank the ship off Antalya. Seventeen of fifty-eight passengers survived by clinging to wreckage through a stormy night. They were put in a refugee camp near Antalya where one of the survivors worked in a restaurant. With his earnings, he supplemented the fare of the entire group. He spurned his Turkish employer's offer for a partnership and his Muslim daughter in marriage; he went on to Egypt, joined the Greek navy, and after the war married the girl he had saved from the shipwreck.[79]

Captain Phocianos made some trips directly into Chesme. By identifying himself as an OSS officer, and bribing port officials to accept his passengers as shipwrecked and not refugees he could get them directly to the city and thus eliminate the dangerous trek through the rural areas south of the city. While Phocianos enjoyed a salary from the American government and did not charge fees for his service, other captains demanded high fares that were in view of the danger and ordeal justified. Communists, however, singled out captains who exacted too much in gold sovereigns, animals, and clothing as war profiteers.[80]

Few Icarians fled to Athens during the war. In the first two months of 1942, three hundred thousand people starved to death in the capital. Likewise Icarians trapped in Athens tended to stay put, and those who returned generally regretted their decision. For instance, a woman took her children on a caïque and made the dangerous voyage back to her native village of Daphne to find conditions there worse than at Athens. In the capital, unlike Icaria, there were food-allocation programs, and this family survived with a ration card. The lady with her children soon returned to Athens. For the first six months of the occupation of Icaria, the Italians issued ration cards, but gradually stopped distributing food on a regular basis. Thus an Icarian widow, who had lost her husband, an officer on the Albanian front, decided not to return to her native village but waited out the war in Athens where she was given permission to dine in a military canteen. A man from Tsouredos teaching in a high school in Athens received a daily allowance of rusk, bread baked twice, or lentils in the school cafeteria. By standards in Icaria, these were sumptuous meals.[81]

Armistice with Italy

In Samos, matters were coming to a climax. On March 25th, 1943, a teacher at the Vathi high school made a fiery speech to the student body convened in one large lecture hall about the valiant deeds of 1821. The situation in Vathi became tense, and in the mountains operations of Samian guerrillas against Italian soldiers expanded.[82] The Italian command in Rhodes dispatched a division trained in eradicating guerrillas. There were several minor clashes and on July 26, 1943, the day Mussolini was deposed, guerrillas ambushed an Italian patrol killing several men. On August 30, 1943, the Blackshirts retaliated by executing twenty-seven innocent villagers from Kastania, seventeen from neighboring villages, and burning a large section of forests on the mountain slopes of Cerkis.[83]

In Icaria, the news of Mussolini's fall demoralized the Italian soldiers. The small garrison in Pharos invited the best musician on the island to entertain them with song and *bouzouki,* a type of guitar. After drinking much wine, the garrison requested the forbidden *"O Corodios O Mussolini."* Fearing punishment, the musician hesitated but finally plunged into the tune. The Italian garrison joined in singing the lyrics with gusto. Through the night, the hills behind Pharos rang with the rich voices of Italian soldiers singing "Mussolini, you silly clown," and other lyrics satirizing Il Duce and Italian martial valor. In the next several weeks, there were similar incidents in other parts of the island. EAM, therefore, assumed that the entire Italian garrison on the island was ready to surrender and took steps to take over. EAM unfurled the Red flag in Evdilos and Raches, informed the gendarmerie that it was now under their supervision, and declared that the exodus to Turkey was over because Icaria needed its people to prepare for the future.[84]

Apparently, EAM's assertiveness snapped the Italian garrison out of its lethargy and war weariness. On September 3, 1944, upon news of the armistices, Italian soldiers confiscated mimeographed EAM newsletters circulating throughout the island.[85] But they did not carry through on their threats to punish the distributors, and within a few days Italian officers were conferring with EAM about surrender. On September 9, General Soldarelli dispatched about fifty of his most militant Blackshirts to Icaria. Soldarelli who at this time had transferred civilian authority to the Samians, feared that these firebrands would undermine his efforts to establish peace in Samos, and thus isolated them in Icaria, an area where they presumably could do little damage. In Icaria they immediately changed the chemistry of the Italian garrison. They arrived as negotiations were taking place for surrender and pressured their fellow soldiers to retain their weapons. A disgruntled Dr. Stavros Stavrinades, head of EAM, felt the Italian officers, who had negotiated with him several days before the arrival of the Blackshirs, had broken their word, and warned them that EAM would take Italian arms by force.[86]

On the evening of September 9th, EAM attacked the small Italian post at Cape Papas. The captain telegraphed to Leros before surrendering. There were no casualties. EAM then cut the telephone line between Aghios Kyrikos and Evdilos, and all telegraphic connections linking Icaria to the outside world. At the same time, armed with outdated weapons, EAM began its siege of Evdilos. Endeavoring to repeat the military operations deployed against the Turks in 1912, Dr. Stavrinades intended to seize Evdilos, then Raches, and thus force the isolated garrison in Aghios Kyrikos to surrender. Stavrinades guaranteed the Italians their personal safety, but the commander, who could have wiped out the bedraggled Icarian force with one good round from his machine gun, had received instructions from Leros just before communications were disrupted not to surrender Italian arms. The garrison commander declared his loyalty for the deposed Il Duce and warned EAM to disperse immediately or he would commence firing. Stavrinades waited till evening, and then ordered his men, well protected and from a good distance, to fire shots throughout the night. The enemy not threatened and without a visible target, held its fire. In the morning, another round of negotiations convinced the Italians of their isolation. All of the soldiers, nine officers and fifty-two enlisted men, surrendered. The Icarians confiscated sixty-six rifles, five small machine guns and one large machine gun, ammunition, and grenades.[87]

Now impressively armed with Italian weapons, EAM ordered the Italians in Raches to surrender. The garrison, consisting of forty serviceman and six officers, arrested the EAM envoys. Several of the officers, who were well-known for womanizing and for confiscating olive oil and sheep, dreaded falling into the hands of a vindictive EAM. When the commander realized that the machine guns pointed at his headquarters had belonged to his comrades in Evdilos, he yielded. There were no reprisals. One of the Italian officers was popular among the Rachiotes, and helped defuse tensions. As this officer left Raches to join his fellow Italians in a camp in Evdilos, he made a farewell speech inviting any Icarian who passed through Rome to visit his father's ice-cream factory, and enjoy the product at his expense. The people, however, were more interested in nearby delicacies and broke into the Italian food depots. EAM appropriated the weapons and all the provisions for its armed men. This action was EAM's first step toward serving the interests of its membership rather than those of the entire community.[88]

While the Italian garrisons in Evdilos and Raches were surrendering, the Germans had persuaded about ten thousand Italians in the Aegean to continue the war. Unaware of these developments, a jubilant EAM force reached a point overlooking Aghios Kyrikos as Italian reinforcements were arriving by boat from Leros; an Italian airplane, which dropped several bombs on Raches and Evdilos, supported the new force. Despite the shelling, Raches and Evdilos continued to fly the Greek flag, and a marriage, which had been arranged for that day, was duly celebrated in Evdilos, though an Italian bomb damaged the house of the bride's father and destroyed the wedding presents, the only harm the island suffered from that aerial attack. But this was enough of a show of force to encourage the Blackshirts, who had arrived from Samos the previous week. They ordered their soldiers to gather outside Aghios Kyrikos. The approximately four hundred EAM soldiers, though well armed, were no match for the strengthened Italian garrison in Aghios Kyrikos which now numbered fifteen hundred. EAM retired to the mountains waiting for British support from Samos.[89]

The Arrival of the British

While EAM was perched over Aghios Kyrikos pondering its next move, five German agents from Leros reached Aghios Kyrikos by motorboat. In a one-day stopover, they assured the Blackshirts that the Germans were willing to send a garrison to Icaria. German agents were also at work in Samos encouraging Italian soldiers to reject the armistice. Thus General Soldarelli was losing control of events, and feared that fighting between EAM and Italians might resume and spiral out of control. At this point an adventurous British soldier entered the picture. Major Michael Parish was serving in special operations in Izmir, assisting Noel Rees, the vice-consul, in establishing a covert naval base on the Izmir peninsula. The British operation was similar to the American OSS mission in nearby Kuşadasi. Both enterprises assisted Allied soldiers and Greek civilians escaping from the Germans and Italians, gathered intelligence, and provided relief. Parish therefore knew something about conditions in the islands. Upon hearing of the armistice, Parish decided rather than continuing his official activities he was going to drive the Germans out of the Aegean and win the war.[90]

Parish shared Churchill's view that the Aegean was the jugular vein of the Nazis. From air bases in the Aegean, the Allies could force Turkey into the war, bomb Romanian oil fields, and thus deprive the Germans of their main oil source. The concept of a Balkan front was based on developments in the First World War when the Allies took control of Salonika in 1916, an event that greatly contributed to the collapse of the Central Powers. At the beginning of World War II, the Soviet Union also supported an Aegean theater as a foundation of a Balkan front, but reversed its position in the fall of 1943, and agreed with the Americans that the Allies could not take Rhodes and Rome at the same time.[91]

Rees disagreed with Parish's strategic concepts, and suggested that he wait for orders from their superiors, but on September 9th, Parish, acting unilaterally, dashed to Samos. General Soldarelli welcomed the British soldier. Parish did not know that Soldarelli had been for the past several months in contact with the Greek government in exile, and was showing a willingness to cooperate with the Allies. During the next nine days, Parish and Soldarelli worked out an agreement. As Parish left Samos, two divisions of Blackshirts arrived from Rhodes with instructions to sabotage the cease-fire and keep Italy in the war. Tidings arrived from Icaria that the Blackshirts whom Soldarelli had recently dispatched there had been reinforced by soldiers from Leros, and were about to exterminate the Icarian EAM. This report was not accurate because EAM had retreated to the mountains and had no intention of resisting a well-equipped Italian force. Soldarelli, nonetheless, urged Parish to go to Icaria to prevent bloodshed. Soldarelli, realizing that Parish alone could not sway the Blackshirts, dispatched with the British officer General Pejrolo, who was *il Vice-Commandante* of the Blackshirt Division, and apparently amenable to the armistices.[92]

Parish, a huge man with fair hair, arrived in Armenistis on September 18th in a motor torpedo boat (MAAS). At first he was taken for a German. Once he established his idenity he was well received. He was accompanied by General Pejrolo, second commander of the Cuneo Division, Colonel David Pawson, Admiral Levidas, a representative of the Greek government in Izmir, and George Pasvanes, a zealous Communist who had just arrived in Samos as one of the Icarian EAM representatives. Soldarelli deemed Pejrolo's presence necessary to placate the Blackshirt element, and that of Pasvanes to appease EAM. The MAAS continued to Evdilos and then worked its way to Aghios Kyrikos where Parish persuaded the Italians to cooperate with the British and warned the Icarian EAM that any further attack on the Italians at Aghios Kyrikos would be considered an act of belligerency against the Allies. Allowing the Italians to retain their arms, Parish declared them Allies in the struggle against the Germans. Parish overestimated both the willingness of Italians to fight against the Germans, and of the *andartes* to cooperate with the British. The Icarian KKE construed Parish's support of the Italians as evidence of British collaboration with the enemy during the war, and proof that the British sanctioned the recent mass execution of Samians near Kastania. Anti-British sentiment, which was about to sweep through leftwing elements in Greece, seemed to surface first in Icaria.[93]

Pasvanes, who had close connections with Samian Communists, was, as we have seen, a major figure in the Icarian KKE. He was a firebrand Bolshevik, anti-British, incorruptible, charismatic, and ready to risk his life for his political beliefs. He was more outraged than anyone else at having the former enemy thrust upon the Icarians as Allies. He forewarned EAM that Parish represented the first step in a British scheme to control Greece. Pasvanes did not know that Pawson, Parish's colleague, had left-wing sympathies and agreed with much of the KKE program. Pasvanes feared that the British were planning on killing him. Parish was equally ignorant of EAM's suspicions and Pasvanes' animosities, and did not understand why Pasvanes refused to accompany him to other islands and persuade guerrillas to cooperate with the Italians. Parish completed his mission in Icaria in one day, and that evening his party, without their guerrilla representative, sailed for Fourni.[94] As Parish left Icaria, a Blackshirt in Aghios Kyrikos heard a wireless broadcast that Colonel Otto Skorzeni had rescued Il Duce from his mountain prison, and that Mussolini had nullified the armistice, and had declared Pietro Badoglio a traitor. This information was discretely passed on to the Italians in the

MAAS. Oblivious of these developments, Parish was astounded when the Blackshirts on the MAAS tried to arrest him off the coast of Fourni. Parish resisted and was wounded. The Icarians heard the gunfire, and could see some commotion on the boat; they later learned that Parish and his party were sent to Leros and then to Germany where they spent the remainder of the war in captivity. The Icarian KKE was delighted that the British were duped by the very people they were urging the Icarians to befriend.[95]

Soldarelli informed the Italians in Icaria that despite Mussolini's restoration and the Parish affair, the armistice was still in effect. The Blackshirts in Aghios Kyrikos, however, took another view, assumed a martial air, and on one occasion a soldier pointed a rifle at several Icarians listening to a BBC news report from a wireless radio in a café. But without support from either Samos or Rhodes, the militant Fascists in Icaria gradually became less assertive. Within a week of the rifle incident, EAM, threatening violence, persuaded the Italian soldiers to remain in their quarters. Supplies were now only trickling in from Samos, and Italy was loosing its Dodecanese Empire as British forces were occupying Samos and other islands. Like the garrison in the film *Mediterraneo,* the Italians in Icaria were practically cut off from the world.[96]

Icarians began sailing to Samos seeking rations and medicine. They observed British forces fortifying the island against an anticipated German assault from bases in Rhodes. The British were also making arrangements with Governor Admiral Mascherpa on Leros for support and a base. From camouflaged points in Turkey, the British raided German positions.[97] The German ambassador to Turkey, von Papen, who possessed photographs taken by reconnaissance planes from Rhodes of British bases, complained in vain to Turkish authorities that their country was violating international laws regulating neutral nations.[98]

While a new round of war between British and German forces in the Aegean was brewing, a fury of political activity was taking place in Icaria. With the Italian armistice, Samos and Icaria became the first liberated areas of Greece, and the Greek government, which was in exile in Alexandria, Egypt, sent representatives to Samos who invited the Icarian EAM to send three delegates to Samos. Pasvanes, who would earn the reputation in Samian Communist circles as the "Saint of Icaria," garnered the most votes, but was reluctant to serve because his sole attire consisted of patched trousers and a jacket lacking a sleeve. Clothes, however, make the ambassador, and he went to Samos with his impoverished appearance as a statement about conditions in Icaria. He knew, as all

Icarians did, that some three hundred years earlier the slayers of the cadi exploited their ill-clad appearance in a Turkish court to gain the favor of the judge. True to the ways of his ancestors, he flaunted his poverty to make a point. Pasvanes was well received by Bishop Irineos who realized that Icaria needed more aid and its representative a new wardrobe. He provided him with a document permitting him to obtain clothing at the British military supply station. There the British employed Samian personnel and these men were conservatives and took an instant dislike to Pasvanes. Not only did they ignore the bishop's instructions and refuse to issue Pasvanes apparel, they marked him out as a dangerous man.[99]

As we have seen, September 1943 marked a turning point for the Icarian EAM. It was no longer an organization mainly concerned with dealing with the occupying powers, but rather a political force with left-wing agenda that aimed at establishing a people's government, *Laokratia*. It would be fair to say that the leadership of EAM was Communist, but also that the majority of the people supported it. With encouragement from the Greek government in Samos, the Icarians elected a provisional council, in effect a branch of EAM, with broad legislative and judicial functions. While the Italian garrison remained passive in Aghios Kyrikos, the council fined so-called black marketeers, shaved the heads of some women who had consorted with Italians, imprisoned animal thieves, and forced alleged collaborators into custody. The best known of these was Dr. Amaxis who supposedly cooperated with the Italians. The provisional committee, in power for most of September 1943, anticipated support from Russia in establishing a society on the Soviet model, and suspected that the British were in league with the Greek fascist-monarchist party to sabotage the interest of Greece.[100]

Before dawn on September 26, 1943, Captain John Pyke, a former gunner, now a Civilian Affairs Officer (CAO), arrived in a caïque from Samos to Aghios Kyrikos.[101] Pyke, who had a working knowledge of Greek, led a company of thirty-six soldiers from the Royal West Kent Regiment. Mindful of the fate of Parish, he anticipated trouble with the Italians, but not with EAM, for he had no idea that anti-British emotions were simmering. Waiting until daybreak, he stepped ashore and went directly to the Italian quarters, and, as a goodwill gesture, put aside his revolver. The Italian officers were accommodating and seemed, with the exception of an ardent Fascist, Captain Pavane—not to be confused with the Communist Pasvanes—desirous of collaboration with the Allies. Pyke aimed to create goodwill among the Italians, and make them useful against the imminent German assault. Pyke later discovered that many of the cordial officers were Blackshirts and not disposed to cooperate with the British.[102]

After the Royal West Kent regiment marched from one end of the island to the other, Pyke dispatched all his forces, save two men, to Samos. Pyke then set out to restore the collapsed social and economic structure of the island. Accompanied by a translator, who was an Anglo-Greek from Alexandria, Egypt, he made a second tour of the island, distributing food and opening schools that the Italians had closed the previous year. As he entered villages on a mule, he was enthusiastically welcomed with English flags, banners, and cheers. The general population did not yet share the anti-British sentiments of EAM's leadership. Bedraggled, malnourished children, dressed in their pre-war Sunday best, dashed out of the crowd to kiss his hand.[103] In Chrysostomos, he was astonished by an Icarian-American, who had been trapped in Icaria by the war, wearing a tie but without shoes, looking very much like harlequin and who greeted him with a well-enunciated "welcome." They honored Pyke with a key to the village, a latchkey to a barn, and he in turn dispensed tinned goods.[104]

Winning over the general populace was easier than converting the leadership of EAM to his goals. Pyke's superiors in Samos were operating on the assumption that the Aegean was strategically relevant. They informed him that the British considered Samos as a potential base for war matériel to be shipped to northern Greece for guerrilla forces opening up a second front. The British, therefore, needed to control Icaria to protect Samos, rapidly becoming a significant supply depot. In pursing this policy, Pyke hoped to convert EAM into a fighting force to stop the Germans.[105]

Pyke's superiors in Samos informed him that there were five hundred armed Icarian guerrillas, identified as members of ELAS the fighting branch of EAM. Pyke, however, registered only three hundred soldiers, and about half were without weapons. The *andartes* were expecting to expropriate the remaining Italian arms and receive more from the British. Pyke, therefore, had to walk a fine line between the guerrillas' expectations and the morale of the Italian soldiers who were potential British allies. On October 1, 1943, Dr. Stavrinades escorted Pyke on his third tour of Icaria beginning in Aghios Kyrikos and going through Xylosertis, Chrysostomos, to Raches. The alleged purpose of the tour was to build good relations between EAM and the British, but the real reason was to show Pyke the degree to which EAM controlled the island. As they passed through the villages, people offered honey, grapes, and ouzo. He saw EAM emblems everywhere. Pyke gathered, as Dr. Stavrinades had intended, that EAM had the support of the majority of the people. Pyke, however, reported to his superiors in Samos that EAM leaders, with the exception of Dr. Stavrinades, lacked administrative ability and would, if they seized power, mismanage affairs and abuse the conservative minority. The fifty quisling gendarmes on the island feared for their lives and had no role in maintaining law and order.[106]

Pyke received orders from Samos to continue to cooperate with EAM and to endeavor to win them over to the Allies. Thus, at the end of September 1943, Pyke added ten rifles to EAM's arsenal of 76 rifles and 9 submachine guns, and provided them with biscuits, flour, meat, peas, rice, beans, sugar, margarine, and tea from British supplies in Samos. A second shipment of Red Cross food arrived. Pyke distributed the provisions in the following fashion: the families of the *andartes,* which officially represented sixteen percent of the population, and the utterly destitute, representing twenty-three percent, received supplies gratis. Families with relatives in America, forty-four percent, promised to pay as soon as dollars arrived. The remaining seventeen percent had funds to reimburse the Red Cross. When some Icarians began to complain that EAM was garnering the bulk of the Red Cross shipment, EAM condemned Pyke for arranging the allocation of food in this way for the purpose of fostering dissension among Icarians. EAM leaders, however, did not volunteer to share what surpluses they had collected with the nonmilitary element of the population. Furthermore, EAM leaders considered the supply of only ten rifles too little and a sign that the British did not trust them.[107] Almost immediately after receiving the supplies and rifles, EAM arrested about thirty "collaborators" and "traitors." On September 27th, Pyke informed Major Dagge and Brigadier Baird, the military governor of Samos, about the situation. They urged Pyke to obtain the release of these prisoners from custody. EAM officials protested, giving details about what these "esteemed gentlemen" had done. EAM released everyone from custody, including Dr. Amaxis, and the bank manager and his clerk who had embezzled olive oil, but they did not dispatch any of them to Samos to stand trial.[108]

Pyke told EAM leaders that more supplies from Samos were only available if Icaria was stable, and if law and order broke down and men like Dr. Amaxis were persecuted, British authorities in Samos were ready to dispatch the West Kent regiment to the island. As far as EAM was concerned, Pyke had crossed the Rubicon in offering protection to people considered collaborators. The Communists maintained that he had been in Icaria for nearly a month, made three tours of the island, and should have known how dangerous these people were. One of the characters in S. Tsirkas' novel *Drifting Cities* pondered the situation in the Aegean. "Badoglio has surrendered the islands of Cos, Leros, Icaria, and Samos to us, but British agents are sowing dissension everywhere, and the Allies will not permit us to send our troops there." In Icaria the British role was not quite that sinister. Pyke's mission was to control the indigenous EAM/ELAS forces, and to build a united front against the Germans that encompassed all elements of the population including non-Fascist Italian forces. But he was not succeeding in doing this. By the end of October EAM, doubting that the British were disposed to send troops to Icaria, was again incarcerating the "collaborators" including Dr. Amaxis. Furthermore, EAM was cracking down on criminals, particularly goat thieves. Pyke was shocked by EAM's methods. For instance, the EAM police force, the gendarmerie was no longer performing its duties, had apprehended two brothers suspected of stealing sheep. Incarcerated in separate quarters, one brother heard a rifle shot, was informed that his sibling had just been executed, and was shown a fresh dug dummy grave. The thief quickly confessed to a number of crimes.[109]

Pyke realized that he could not again obtain the release of the "collaborators," but hoped to establish due process for criminals. He appealed to Dr. Stavrinades to do something about practices such as mock executions and other Draconian measures, arguing that such tactics would lead to chaos. Dr. Stavrinades agreed with Pyke, but admitted that he could not control the more extreme elements in EAM. Indeed, the zealots were anxious to go beyond mock executions. There were rumors that EAM had had in addition to the people already under detention a proscription list with the names of seventy "traitors" and "black marketeers." Conservatives were extremely nervous. Pyke realized that he no longer had the authority or prestige to avert a pogrom, so he endeavored to turn EAM's attention from the "collaborators" to a raid on the German base in Myconus. Refugees from Myconus had recently arrived in Icaria providing Pyke information about the German encampment. Pyke drew sketches of German military installations, worked out a plan of attack, and presented them to EAM and offered to lead an EAM force. Dr. Stavrinades summarily rejected the scheme. A disappointed Pyke concluded that his usefulness in Icaria was over, and requested from the command in Samos a new assignment. Headquarters replied, "You are at liberty to return but the Brigadier (Baird) hopes that this will not be necessary in view of possible loss of prestige."[110]

It is not clear what British authorities expected Pyke to accomplish in Icaria, but there seems to have been some unrealistic hopes that he could still organize resistance against the Germans, and maintain political stability. Just after Pyke requested his transfer, his authority was suddenly reestablished in Icaria. At the end of October a representative of the Greek government in exile in Alexandria, Egypt, Emanuel Sophoulis, a Venizelite, arrived in Samos. On October 30th, Sophoulis, who was a nephew of the prime-minister Themistocles Sophoulis (1924, 1945–1946, 1947–1949), appointed Archbishop Irineos Governor General of Samos, Icaria, and Fourni. The Greek government in exile conferred upon Sophoulis, who was a native of Samos and had married a woman from Icaria, extensive powers in establishing a civilian government in Samos and Icaria. Sophoulis in effect made Pyke his representative in Icaria and requested from the British captain a report on political conditions on the island, and the feasibility of free elections. Pyke, who now fully understood that EAM had an agenda contrary to the interests of the Allies, reported to Sophoulis that free elections would produce a Communist regime. Pyke recommended that Dr. Malachias be the dominant member of the body, and nominated two other conservatives and two radicals from the upper echelons of EAM. Thus Pyke's committee would consist of three pro-British members and two Communists. Sophoulis took Pyke's advice not to have elections but reduced the committee from five to three members.[111]

On October 28th, Sophoulis, in a handwritten note to Dr. Malachias, appointed him, "By the Name of King George of the Greeks," as president of the council with a deciding vote, but rejected Pyke's nomination of Dr. Tsantiris, who had never joined EAM. Sophoulis wrote, "I am designating two of your compatriots from the democratic elements, to complete the council." These two "democrats," Pasvanes and Karimalis, were among the men Pyke considered extremist and dangerous. He deemed the former "a nasty customer," and the latter "a man with an itchy trigger finger." Sophoulis had some sympathy with EAM. Before the war the Metaxas government inaccurately branded him a Communist and placed him in detention with other Communists. Although he knew some of the Icarian Communists not only from his pre-war days of imprisonment, but also through his wife, an Icarian woman, he did not share their views. For a short time, Sophoulis with the aid of his wife had formed a resistance organization in Samos that briefly cooperated with EAM. By rejecting Tsantiris and appointing Pasvanes and Karimalis, Sophoulis displayed the government's independence from the British, and a willingness to cooperate with EAM, but not to empower it. Sophoulis thus gave the council a "democratic" façade. As president of the council, Dr. Malachias had veto power and the deciding vote. EAM, however, was not satisfied with Sophoulis' arrangement and unleashed a vicious propaganda campaign against Dr. Malachias, who in effect controlled the committee, accusing him of being a British lackey, corrupt in the distribution of Red Cross provisions, profiteering from the sale of British supplies at exorbitant prices, and a defender of the black market. It was true that Dr. Malachias as a Venizelite belonged to a party that had long ceased to have a policy relevant to Icaria, and that he worked closely with Pyke and was in touch with American OSS agents in Turkey. The doctor was becoming obsessed with curtailing the rising tide of Communism on Icaria, and sought the support of the British, American, and Greek governments to this end. But he had a long record of humanitarian service to the island and was an honest man.[112]

The council never met, but the Pyke-Sophoulis arrangement convinced the Icarian EAM that the Greek government with the support of the British was stifling the will of the people of Icaria. While Sophoulis was empowering Dr. Malachias in Icaria, the Germans were preparing to take the island. Nazi agents had been swarming the area for months. In late September, four Germans in civilian clothes, claiming to be archaeologists, were in Fourni. On October 26th, a Greek arrived from Myconus with a radio concealed in the paneling of the caïque. Pyke assumed he was a German spy. In the first few days of November, several caïques arrived from Myconus with refugees, some of whom were German agents sent to encourage the Italians to support the imminent German assault. EAM undertook emergency powers. In early November, EAM arrested three men believed to be Germans in a boat near Armenistis. EAM continued to arrest "collaborators," took over the Italian telegraph cable and telephone, and expropriated property allegedly for the defense of the island. Some items such as tools and pack animals became the private effects of EAM leaders. On November 6th, 1943, Pyke issued an order forbidding the *andartes* from making any further arrests and expropriating property. It was his last official act in Icaria and was ignored.[113]

Pyke was also losing control of the Italians. Blackshirts, led by Pavane, became openly truculent ignoring the orders of Soldarelli in Samos to cooperate with the British. German agents apparently had informed them of the pending German assault, and the return of the Germans to Icaria. Pyke wrote in his diary on November 6th, 1943, that there were "too many fascists and weaklings for my liking," among the Italians. The most militant of the Italians were going about the island intimidating the populace. In Raches, they defied a local ordinance and cut large trees around the village for firewood. Pyke recommended to an Italian officer in Aghios Kyrikos, who was pro-British, that they purge the Fascist element in the garrison, provide more arms for EAM, and join the guerrillas with Italians who were ready to fight the Germans. The officer discouraged Pyke from pursuing such a strategy, explaining that the anti-Fascist Italians would not fight the Germans and "the *andartes* would only take the arms and run to the hills."[114]

On November 12th, the Germans began the offensive to drive the British from the Aegean, "Operation Poseidon." At that time, there were approximately five thousand British soldiers scattered throughout the Aegean opposing a vastly superior German force. In Samos, British authorities informed Pyke that "you will be thin on the ground" but still cherished hope that EAM and the Italians would bolster British forces enough to stop "Operation Poseidon." The job, however, could only be achieved with massive Allied reinforcements, and without additional support in Icaria and throughout the Aegean the British forces in the area were sacrificial lambs. The British would have been better off simply retreating from the Aegean in 1943, or concentrating all their forces on Cos or Leros to protect the most useful airfields in the Aegean. Thus when the German assault of Leros began, there was no stopping it. The British forces, about five hundred men, and their Italian allies, fought bravely and were massacred. The loss of Leros proved the old adage that in war half measures are catastrophic. While the Icarians, who could hear the German bombardment of Leros, continued to travel to Samos for supplies, EAM withdrew to the mountains and the Italians recovered telegraph and telephone operations. Realizing that a German attack on Icaria was only a matter of days away, Pyke telegraphed Major Dagge for last-minute instructions, concluding, "a speedy reply would be greatly appreciated." The Italian operator would not send the message, and Pyke was unable to relay the memorandum over the wireless that had broken down. Pyke dashed to Samos in a motorboat where his superiors told him to use his own judgment about defending Icaria. Without any forces on the island and with the growing hostility of the guerrillas and Italians toward the British, it took considerable courage on the part of Pyke to return to Icaria.[115]

As Pyke reached Icaria, the Germans launched an air campaign against Samos. During the morning of November 17th, bombs destroyed the seaside road, killed many British and Italian soldiers, leveled homes including the house of a German family who had settled in Vathi in the 1930s, and demolished the hospital. Icarians who were in Samos for supplies or medical services were trapped. About five hundred British soldiers withdrew to Turkey, followed by most of the guerrillas and a few Italians. The crisis took on a festive air. The British left their supplies for the Samians who hoarded food and gulped down bacon, biscuits, marmalade, and canned tidbits, consuming as much as possible before the Germans arrived and confiscated British stores.[116]

Three days later, a German force appeared at Tigani in hydroplanes. A larger occupying force followed. For the most part these soldiers were recovering from wounds or too old for active service. They issued identity cards to the Samians, searched homes for British supplies, gave receipts to people turning over stores, arrested suspected hoarders, and recruited able-bodied men to provide tools and work on fortifications and women to gather fodder for the German pack animals. The Germans permitted Italian soldiers who wished to continue the war to keep their arms, and placed troops no longer willing to fight in a tobacco warehouse on short rations. Samians smuggled food to these prisoners who were eventually shipped to Piraeus. Apart from requisitioning food and labor, this brief German occupation was moderate. For instance, a German doctor performed an appendectomy in a tobacco warehouse on an Icarian woman who had gone to Samos before the German assault for medical treatment. But the Germans came close to carrying out a bloodbath. At the end of November, soldiers on an English torpedo boat, apparently based in Turkey, landed at Marathonkambos, wiping out a German patrol. The Germans arrested one hundred Samians, most of them from that area. A mass execution was averted at the last minute when evidence was discovered that the British had carried out the raid.[117]

In Aghios Kyrikos early in the morning of November 18th, the schoolmistress stood over Captain Pyke, who was in deep sleep, shouting, "the Germans are here." Accompanied by two guerrillas, he fled Aghios Kyrikos on foot, and at a point above the capital, where the Italians had a supply depot, leveled his revolver at two Italian guards and ordered them to open it. He observed in amazement as malnourished men carried off two-hundred-fifty-pound sacks of flour. Pyke had assumed that the Germans would land at Aghios Kyrikos. He, therefore, kept a a caïque on the other side of the island at Evdilos. As he departed from Aghios Kyrikos Pyke had to deal with Major Scerbas and several other Italian anti-Fascists who wanted to leave with him because they were too compromised by their pro-British activities. He did not have room for them on his small vessel. In Chrysostomos a woman was standoffish, mistaking him for a German, but this was the only exception to an otherwise supportive reaction as Pyke made frequent stops in villages for ouzo, water, and raisins as he crossed to the northern side of the island. In his diary entry for that day, he marveled at Icarian hospitality that prevailed even in such times of disaster and chaos.[118]

Pyke tarried in Evdilos for a day while the Germans were establishing themselves in Aghios Kyrikos. On November 19th, he wrote to Dr. Malachias thanking him for his support, handed the letter to a trusted messenger, and sailed for Chesme just as a German patrol boat arrived firing at Pyke's departing caïque.[119]

Captain Kostas

About one hundred Germans, part of a special boat operation, and not an occupying force, landed on Icaria. The German news agency reported that the unit had taken two hundred fifty Italian prisoners and a quantity of arms. There were, of course, hundreds of Italians who were loyal to the Germans and not made prisoners. From this group the Germans appointed Captain Bingi, a wealthy man who had strong Fascist ties and who had recently arrived from Samos, to single out the most ardent supporters of Badoglio. The most prominent of this faction was Major Scerbas who believed British reports that he would be maltreated if he fell into the hands of the "Huns." When Pyke was unable to help him escape to Turkey, Scerbas with about twenty men, fled to the mountains. EAM hid these men, escorted some of them to Evdilos and later ferried about a dozen to Turkey. Aware that EAM was aiding these Italians, the Germans learned from collaborators the names of EAM leaders and burned their houses before they left on November 25th. They announced that they would soon be back with a larger garrison.[120] Reports soon circulated in Icaria that the Germans had sunk a boat conveying approximately two hundred fifty pro-armistice Italians near Fourni, and that the bodies of some of these men had allegedly washed up on Icarian shores. Such an event never happened though it was widely believed that it did, and people insisted that a number of Italian soldiers were buried in Icaria. These Italian soldiers in fact reached Piraeus, and from there were dispatched by train to Germany. Partisans, however, liberated some in Yugoslavia.[121]

The Germans did not return immediately, and for the next seven months Icaria remained unoccupied, but the German presence in Samos and Leros was conspicuous, and an occasional German patrol boat called on Aghios Kyrikos. In June 1944, about sixty Germans arrived with Italian Blackshirts who had previously been on Icaria. EAM again retreated to the mountains while the enemy released the imprisoned collaborators, and rounded up men at random in Aghios Kyrikos and threatened a mass execution if Italian weapons and supplies seized by EAM were not returned.[122] EAM officials from Akamatra suddenly appeared with two mules loaded with arms. The Italians ascertained that several machine guns and a number of rifles were missing, but wishing to avert an incident did not report this to the Germans. The Italians then went about the business of collecting their mules, but made no attempt to recover food supplies.[123]

A certain Captain Kostas, apparently trained by the *Abwehr* in anti-guerrilla activity, was in charge of the German garrison. His Greek was fluent but marked with a slight accent. Rumor had it that he was from Izmir, or from Patra but had lived in Germany for many years. It is most likely that he was reared in Alexandria, Egypt, where his German father was a bank employee. He enjoyed earthy jokes. Once he told a group of men in Aghios Kyrikos that in his youth he had been a shoeshine boy, and had devised a mirror system that provided him with intimate views of his female clients. In Athens he claimed to have served as a translator for the German army, and on one formal occasion instructed a German officer to unwittingly use a crude Greek expression in welcoming distinguished Greek guests. But Kostas was more interested in terrorizing the Icarians than entertaining them with coarse jokes. He paraded through Aghios Kyrikos with two holstered guns strapped to his side, and it was suspected that two more were secured under his shirt. His sphere, apparently, included Icaria, Fourni, Leros, Patmos, and Myconus, and his assignment was to neutralize EAM, and defend his area against raids from British Special Boat Squadrons (SBS). Though no such raid hit Icaria, Kostas had to fight off British forays into Patmos and Myconus. He never had more than seventy men, often fewer, and on occasion seemed to be alone, though on nearby islands German soldiers were at his beck and call. One evening he strolled through Aghios Kyrikos and announced that he was alone and intended to spend that night in a certain house at Therma with an Icarian woman. He would be much obliged if this information were conveyed to the guerrillas. EAM tarried near Akamatra, Oxe, and Droutsoula, never venturing near Therma or Aghios Kyrikos while Kostas was on the island. With a heavily armed motor torpedo boat, he regulated traffic going through the channel stopping caïques by firing over their bow, appropriating a share of the cargo, and searching for members of EAM. He occasionally dashed to Evdilos and Armenistis, but the northern part of the island remained essentially free of German supervision, a circumstance exploited by the Americans who sent an agent, Nicholas Kyrtatos, from an OSS base in Turkey, to Evdilos where he obtained information about the Germans, and distributed supplies to the people. Kyrtatos sailed on a caïque of about ten tons that maintained a speed of around ten knots. A native of Evdilos who was captain of a slower but larger ship, a seventy-ton merchant vessel operating out of Alexandria, Egypt, managed to make two shipments of supplies to Evdilos. While Kostas was unable to stop the relief effort, he arrested members of the man's family. Apart from not being able to patrol the entire island single-handedly, there was one other chink in Kostas' armor. He feared dentists, and when the only available one in Aghios Kyrikos, a staunch member of the KKE, could not promise a painless procedure, he canceled his appointment.[124]

When Captain Kostas arrived in Icaria he ordered, apparently from his second incarceration, the release of Dr. Amaxis, who went directly to the public square in Aghios Kyrikos and accosted a certain Theodorakis, a well-known member of EAM. He vainly demanded that he return the revolver Theodorakis confiscated when Dr. Amaxis was taken into custody in late October. A quarrel ensued, and Dr. Amaxis left, issuing threats. Shortly thereafter the Germans torched several more houses belonging to high-ranking EAM officials and detained about twenty Icarians, among them Theodorakis, whom Kostas transferred to a German camp in Leros. For the next several months, Dr. Amaxis provided medical services for the Germans, who did not have a doctor in their ranks, and allegedly withheld such assistance from some fellow Icarians. His principal patient was Captain Kostas, who was often seen at his house. It was generally believed that the doctor was providing him with information about Communists rather than medical treatment. Otherwise how did the Germans know what houses to torch and whom to put in detention? But if Dr. Amaxis was collaborating with the Germans he was not the only one. Kostas relied on a group of *roufianoi,* and also on the gendarmes who had been earlier dismissed by EAM but were now reinstated to their old positions.[125]

At the end of August 1944, the Germans began to withdraw from the islands. Some forces rendezvoused in Syros and then sailed to Piraeus while other forces sailed directly north. On September 11th, Germans departed from Icaria, Lesbos, and Chios sailing to Salonika. Kyrtatos, as agent of the OSS, had slipped into Icaria from a base in Turkey and counted the German ships as they sailed north. Kostas retreated either to Leros or Patmos where he became part of a vulnerable rear guard and was slain. A member of the Icarian EAM claimed he followed Kostas there to settle scores. Kostas probably died fighting the British. This withdrawal marked the end of the war for Icaria, but the German exit took place smoothly and was calculated to cover their retreat from the Aegean so that the people on Icaria were uncertain whether Kostas and his garrison were gone for good, or simply lurking on some other island ready to pounce on them again.[126]

By mid-September the Icarians realized that the Germans were really gone. EAM emerged from the mountains and took over an island devastated by the war. Most buildings had fallen into disrepair; the people were in rags and emaciated from hunger. EAM radical leadership, now in control of the island, had specific plans for a better tomorrow, and to achieve their goals intended to punish certain people and exterminate others.

---

1. Karl Baedeker, *The Mediterranean: Seaports and Sea Routes* (Leipzig, 1911), pp. 9, 492; *McMillan's Guide to the Eastern Mediterranean: Greece and the Greek Islands, Constantinople, Smyrna, Ephesus, etc.* (London, 1904), did not allot one word to Icaria. *Murray's Hand-Book: Turkey in Asia, Constantinople* (London, 1878), pp. 198–199. Dilys Powell, *Remember Greece* (New York, 1943), pp. 15–16, discusses her frustration in not finding information on Icaria in guidebooks. A generation after her trip to Icaria, *Les guides bleus, Grèce* (Paris, 1962), provided fifteen sentences on Icaria noting Kataphygion, Therma, and Perdiki while E. Bradford, *The Companion Guide to the Greek Islands* (New York, 1963), did not mention Icaria. Odd people: Margarita Lymperake, *Ta Psathina Kapela* (Athens, 2001), in a novel originally published in 1946, pp. 184–187, 272–273, 370–371, portrays Rhodia, a cook from Icaria employed in Kifisia, as an eccentric person telling stories about the crazy people of Icaria.

2. Powell, *Remember Greece* pp. 15–17,

3. Powell, *Greece,* p. 18. There were apparently two automobiles on the island: John Pyke, *Secret Report,* Oct. 13, 1943. All references to Pyke's reports, letters, diaries, are to records in his private papers. I am indebted to John Pyke, Chester, South Wirral, England, for making these available to me.

4. Powell, *Greece,* p. 19. For Mylonas, see X. Chochilas' "E Ikaria os topos exoria," *Kathemerine,* 21, April 1998, 13. Nicholas Battouyios as a boy in Frantato remembered Mylonas reporting every morning to the gendarmes; interview June 12, 2003, Aghios Kyrikos, Icaria. I. Moulas, from Frantato, remembered his remarks about agricultural conditions in Icaria; interview Aghios Kyrikos, Icaria, June 20, 2004. The number 2,000: Margaret E. Kenna, *The Social Organization of Exile: The Greek Political Detainees in the 1930s* (Amsterdam, 2001). The Icarian Communist newspaper published clandestinely, *Laokratia,* Sept. 3, 1938, noted that Metaxas held 4,000 prisoners in Greece. Apparently half were on the mainland. Harsh conditions in Gyaros and Anafi: B. Birtles, *Exiles in the Aegean: A Personal Narrative of Greek Politics and Travel* (London, 1938), pp. 126–139, 323–329. The government forced one Communist held in Aghios Kyrikos to make a public renunciation of his ideology, a *dilosis* in exchange for the recovery of his civil-service position; interview Dimitri Mougannis, June 2, 2002, Aghios Kyrikos, Icaria, who witnessed the affair. Emile Y. Kolodny, *La population des îles de la Grèce: essai de géographie insulaire en Méditerranée orientale* (Aix-en-Provence, 1974), II, 488–489, notes the increase of the population in Aghios Kyrikos from 944 in 1928 to 1,072 by 1940, and concludes that the 128 newcomers were prisoners. There are no figures for exiles like Mylonas confined to small villages. The Athenian politician felt cut off from the world as Pliny had (*Ep.* 7. 4. 3), when weather-bound in Icaria for several days. Roman emperors exiled troublesome senators to the more inhospitable Seriphos and Gyaros; see Tacitus, *Ann.* 4. 13; 4. 21. In a similar fashion, in 1946 and 1947, the Greek government dispatched General Sarafis from Icaria to Seriphos and more hostile types to Gyaros.

5. Powell, *Greece,* 19. Therma: Interview, Th. Vassilaros, Therma, Icaria, June 12, 2003. Anna Adamos, interview, Lincoln Park, Michigan, July 1, 1994. She left Icaria in the fall of 1939 with her six-year-old son. The shipping line extended credit to cover the increased portion of the return ticket.

6. Mario Cervi, *The Hollow Legions: Mussolini's Blunder in Greece 1940–1941,* translated by Eric Mosbacher (New York, 1971), pp. 31–33; Charles Cruickshank, *Greece 1940–1941: The Politics and Strategy of the Second World War* (New Jersey, 1976), p. 29.

7. *The Ciano Diaries, 1939–1943,* ed. Hugh Gibson (New York, 1946). In the entry for August 15, 1940, p. 284, Ciano expressed embarrassment over the barbaric character of the act and blamed it on Count Cesare Maria De

Vecchi, the governor of the Italian Dodecanese. Ciano was nonetheless for a war against the Greeks; see A. Petacco, *La Nostra Guerra, 1940–1945: L'Avventura bellica tra bugie e verità* (Milan, 1995), pp. 9–18, who refers to the carnage in Albania as Ciano's war. N. Koklanaris, interview, Aghios Kyrikos, Icaria, June 7, 2001, heard the report of the sinking of the *Helle* from a wireless radio in Panaghia.

8. G. Katsas, *Etan O Dromos Sostos? Apo Ikaria, Athena, Intzedia, Aegina* (Athens, 1992), p. 23.

9. See Cruickshank, *Greece,* p. 33.

10. For the Italian bases and the strategic value of the Aegean, see Peter Charles Smith and Edwin R. Walker, *War in the Aegean* (London, 1974), pp. 22–23, 66–67. For the Salamis parallel, see Nikos Noou, *Ta Paidia tes Thyellas* (Athens, 1993), pp. 9–10.

11. For the need of the Aegean air force in the Albanian front, see Visconti Prasca, *Io ho aggredito la Grecia* (Rome, 1946), p. 211. See Cervi, *The Hollow Legions,* p. 259, for a discussion of international politics. Lightning assault: Ciano, *Diaries,* Oct. 22, 1940, p. 303. Value of Aegean front: Winston Churchill, *The Grand Alliance* (Boston, 1950), p. 226.

12. For EON: Koklanaris, Interview, Lincoln Park, Michigan, December 31, 1993. Flight to mountains: Katsas, *Dromos Sostos,* pp. 23–24.

13. Katsas, *Dromos Sostos,* p. 25.

14. As the British war effort in Greece collapsed, Turkey offered to occupy Chios, Mytilene, and Samos; see S. Deringil, *Turkish Foreign Policy during the Second World War: An Active Neutrality* (Cambridge, England and New York 1989), p. 121. Frank G. Weber, *The Evasive Neutral: Germany, Britain, and the Quest for a Turkish Alliance in the Second World War* (Columbia, Missouri, 1979), pp. 82, 85. Stalin proposed to give the Dodecanese to the Turks in talks with Anthony Eden in January 1942; see Winston Churchill, *The Grand Alliance* (Boston, 1950), pp. 628–629. The fear persists in these islands that Turkey covets Icaria, Samos, and Chios. A Turkish map, allegedly in the Turkish foreign ministry, displays these islands as possessions of Turkey; see *The Athens News,* November 24, 1998.

15. *Extracts from the War Diaries and Associated Documents of the 164th Infantry Division and Other German Army Units in Greece, from 27 February 1941 to 31 May 1941.* Captured Records Section, Adjunct General's office, United States Army, Washington, D.C. Microfilm No. 888. Katsas, *Dromos Sostos,* pp. 27, 250; Captain John Pyke, *Secret Report to SCAO, Samos,* on St. [Ag.] Kyrikos, September 27, 1943.

16. P. Lombardas, *Taragmena Chronia: Katoche, Ethnike Antistase Emphylios Polemos sten Ikaria* (Athens, 1987), p. 11; and J. Tsantes, *To Chroniko tes*

Katoches tes Ikarias (1940–1944) kai Sentome Episkopise ton Gegonoton tes Metakatochikes Periodou (Athens, 1977), 11–12. Koula Poulos, interview, April 27, 1997, Wilmington, North Carolina, protested in vain as the Germans confiscated twenty-two chickens from her chicken pen in Panaghia. The Germans considered all victuals in Greece property of the Third Reich; see Betty Watson, *Miracle in Hellas: The Greeks Fight On* (New York, 1943), pp. 58–65, who reported Germans looting Athens and gave a graphic description of a German soldier shooting a man for his cow. German units arriving in Chios did not have motor vehicles and requisitioned pack animals from the natives as they did in Icaria; see Argenti, *Occupation of Chios,* p. 23. Suspicious foreign hikers: interview D. Mougiannis, Aghios Kyrikos, June 12, 2004. The Italians made maps of Icaria on the scale of 1:250.000 perhaps clandestinely in the late 1930s but more likely during the occupation around 1941–1943. These maps are in the Istituto Geografico Militare in Florence. The Wehrmacht made copies of these maps. I am indebted to Nicholas Purcell for this information.

17. For a discussion of the British stragglers, see A. Heckstall-Smith and H. T. Baille-Grohman, *Greek Tragedy 1941* (New York, 1961), pp. 217–224. Stragglers in Icaria: Interview, J. Kyprios, Aghios Kyrikos, June 7, 2004, and M. Tsangas and K. Lignou, *E en Ikaria Italike Katoche 1941–1943* (Athens, 2004), p. 46. The New Zealand prime minister Fraser (the author was unable to make out the date which seems to be 1974) sent a letter to the people of Proespera expressing the gratitude of the people of New Zealand for protecting New Zealand soldiers in April 1941. On July 10th, 1941 Frederick Lawrence from Herefordshire, England, and William Beazeley from Victoria, Australia, arrived in Livadi from Naxos. Concealed by the Mamatas family, they were taken to Turkey at the end of July. A captain Andreas Peris stole their revolvers and charged them an exorbitant 18,000 drachmas for their fare. The Mamatas family later petitioned Captain Pyke for the expense of sustaining these two men for two weeks. The Mamatas petition and the Peris affair are in the papers of John Pyke. There were then fewer than 10 families in Livadi and about 20 people. When some of these villagers years later heard about the Mamatas petition, they felt that it should have been in the name of the entire village, for the upkeep of the British stragglers had been a communal affair. Swimming drills and slap: interview, D. Mougiannis, June 29, 2004. Thermopylae: Nick Koklanaris, interview December 31, 1993, Lincoln Park, Michigan. For Salamis, see above, note 10. Em. Sophoulis, unpublished diary, May 1941, referred to the Spartan 300 as he urged resistance and wrote, "people who cherish freedom do not calculate odds before resisting the enemy." Hades: John Tsantes, *Chronia Katoches,* p. 117, whose view is similar to Jeanne Tsatsos, *The Sword's Fierce Edge: A Journal of the Occupation of Greece 1941–1944* (Vanderbilt, Tennessee, 1969), pp. 76, 97. Tsatsos, who survived the German occupation of Athens, compared the Nazis to the deranged whip-wielding Aias while the Greeks drew their source for rational behavior from their classical heritage.

18. Tsolakoglou: *Acropolis,* March 25, 1942, cited in Haris Sakellariou, *E Paideia Sten Antistasi* (Athens, 1984), pp. 127–128. Sakellariou makes some good observations about the doublethink rhetoric of the occupation. Rallis: Mark Mazower, *Inside Hitler's Greece: The Experience of Occupation 1941–1944* (New Haven, Connecticut, 1993), p. 322. Many of the leading members of the quisling government were officers in the Albanian campaign. A charitable interpretation of their collaboration with the Germans was their desire to restore stability; see G. Roussou, *E Neotere Istoria tes Ellados, 1886–1974* (Athens, n.d.) 7, 401. While beholding the present through the lenses of the fifth century B.C., the Greeks received a boost in their morale, but such views distorted strategic realities, and led to dangerous wishful thinking; see Noou, *Ta Paidia,* pp. 9–10, who noted how the Samians, despite the obsolete Greek navy, were expecting a Salamis-type victory in the Aegean.

19. At the start of the war, Germans were highly regarded in Icaria: Katsas, *Dromos Sostos,* p. 19. Also in Samos: Kostas Ptinis, *Chronia Katoches: Symbole Sten Istoria tes Samos 1941–1944* (Samos, 1986), p. 284. Philip P. Argenti, *The Occupation of Chios,* p. 43, discusses the extensive German exploitation of the Chian economy, including the appropriation of the Chian mastic production. Chicken thieves: Interview, Koula Poulos, the victim of the theft, Wilmington, North Carolina, April 12, 1997. Laird Archer, *Athens Journal 1940–1941: The Graeco-Italian and the Graeco-German Wars and the German Operation* (Manhattan, Kansas, 1983), p. 106, cited under May 29, 1941, a German officer telling a Greek that "we will take everything and eventually you'll be so poor and weak you will not be able to commit suicide." Archer goes on to note that by the end of May 1941 malnutrition had taken such a toll that people required twice the time to do their work. Mazower, *Hitler's Greece,* pp. 23–24, discusses the Germans' predatory policies in Greece. Hagen Fleischer, *Im Kreuzschatten der Mächte: Griechenland 1941–1944 (Okkupation, Resistance, Kollaboration)* (Frankfurt am Main, 1986), I, 76–78, ignores such evidence when he defends the German occupation of Greece not as brutal but rather as insensitive, lacking *Fingerspitzengefühl.*

20. Threatened execution: Katsas, *Dromos Sostos,* p. 24. The Italians disapproved of the German policy of the excessive confiscation of food in Greece; see Ciano, *Diaries,* entry for July 22, 1942. In 1943, the Italians became guilty of the same practice, but not to the same degree. Nick Koklanaris, interview December 31, 1993, Lincoln Park, Michigan, became an American citizen, served in the American occupying forces in Berlin in 1952. While supervising German workers on an American base, one informed him that he had belonged to the XVIII A.K. division and did a tour in Icaria, which he contrasted favorably to his next assignment in Russia. For the next several days, Koklanaris treated the man harshly. The puzzled man never comprehended the reason for his boss's rage.

21. Katsas, *Dromos Sostos,* pp. 23–25.

22. Cervi, *Hollow Legions,* p. 300.

23. Noou, *Paidia,* pp. 12–14, 17–18, 23–25, 85, 105, and Ptinis, *Chronia Katoches,* pp. 13–15, 61. Em. Sophoulis, *Unpublished Diary,* entry August 30, 1941, criticized the pro-Fascist gendarmes on Samos, and poured especial scorn on a certain Bafas.

24. Noou, *Paidia,* pp. 12–18, 23–25; Ptinis, *Chronia Katoches,* pp. 14–17. Em. Sophoulis, *Unpublished Diary,* May 1941, emphasized the patriotic character of the bishop.

25. British blockade: A Gerolymatos, *Red Acropolis, Black Terror–The Greek Civil War and the Origins of Soviet-American Rivalry, 1943-1949* (New York, 2004), pp. 40-41. Difficulties for Italian navy: J. Greene and A. Massignani, *The Naval War in the Mediterranean 1940–1943* (London, 1998), pp. 144, 236. Informers and guerrillas: Noou, *Paidia,* pp. 12–25.

26. Philip John Carabott, "A British Military Occupation under a British Military Governor but without a British Military Administration. The Case of Samos: 8 September to 18 November 1943," *Journal of Modern Greek Studies,* 7, 2, (1989), 287–290. Carabott, who provides an excellent analysis of this period, notes the hatred between Samians and Italians. Such a view does not acknowledge good relations between many Italian enlisted men and Samian natives. Remark about *piccola,* interview with G. Baloukas, a Samian guerrilla, Vathi, Samos, August 6, 1998, and Noou, *Paidia,* pp. 20–21, 57–64, who appreciated Italian leniency in the mild enforcement of regulations. Noou, *Paidia,* p. 193, quotes an Italian soldier telling some Samians *"una razza, una facca,"* a marked contrast to German racial views. There was a great difference in the living standards between enlisted men and officers, and this perhaps was one reason why the common soldier identified somewhat with the natives. General Soldarelli had excellent Italian chefs; see Parish, *Aegean Adventures,* p. 209. Noou, *Paidia,* pp. 29–30, contrasts rations of Italian solders, who roamed villages looking for edibles, with that of the officers. For further discussion of Greek-Italian relations, see below n. 60.

27. "We'll go to the Aegean and we will take the Piraeus, and if all goes well, we'll take Athens too"; see Cervi, *The Hollow Legions,* p. 7.

28. Interview with eyewitness S. Kyprios, May 29, 1996, Aghios Kyrikos, Icaria. Also see the comments of P. Lombardas, *Taragmena Chronia,* p. 11. Katsas, *Dromos Sostos,* p. 27. Lombardas, *Taragmena Chronia,* p. 11. In Chios, young boys threw stones at an Italian contingent; see Argenti, *Occupation of Chios,* p. 10. K. Baloukas, a guerrilla in Samos during the civil war, interview, Vathi, Samos, August 6, 1998, asserted that the Icarians readily acquiesced to the Italian yoke, and only displayed a spirit of resistance after the Italian armistice.

29. Captain John Pyke, *Secret report to SCAO, Samos,* on St. [Ag.] Kyrikos, September 27, 1943, based on information supplied by the mayor, M.

Karras. Pyke also reported that in 1943 the sum of $50 remained on one man's account in the Bank of Athens in Aghios Kyrikos.

30. This was the estimate of the mayor; see John Pyke, *Secret Report to SCAO, Samos,* St. [Ag.] Kyrikos, September 27, 1943. The Icarians, however, to gain maximum supplies reported a pre-war population figure of 11,593 in September 1943 when they applied for Red Cross aid, John Pyke, *Icaria and Phourni: Population and Animal Statistics,* no date.

31. General diet: Tsantes, *Katoches,* p. 18. One family in Platania lost a mule to old age. They immediately buried the creature, but somehow people from Karavostamos heard of the dead mule, came at night, quartered it, and took it back to feast in their barren village. Interview with the former mayor of Aghios Kyrikos, George Plakidas, Aghios Kyrikos, May 29, 2001. Partridges: Nikolaos Kyrtatos, an OSS agent who operated in Icaria from Jan. 1944 to Jan. 1945, described the plethora of partridges which developed during the war years because the occupying forces did not allow anyone to shoot or even possess a hunting rifle; interview, Cephisia, Athens, June 29, 2003.

32. Restriction of boats: Ptinis, *Chronia Katoches,* p. 67. Abandoned boats: Elias Pardos, Interview, September 9, 1994, Harrisville, Michigan. Lack of fishing nets: John Pyke, *Diary,* October 21, 1943. John Pyke issued the following statement in the name of the British Military Mission Icaria, Oct. 26, 1943, "I wish to emphasize that no person whatsoever shall be permitted to fish or use any water-borne craft during the hours of darkness." Pyke limited fishing to a daytime activity and only with a permit. The British were concerned that nocturnal boat traffic might convey German spies or sabatoeurs.

33. Tsantes, *Katoches,* p. 21. Soap: Lombardas, *Taragmena Chronia,* p. 14. Price of ouzo: Pyke, *Diary,* November 11, 1943.

34. Petition of the Mamatas family, Sept. 21, 1943, in Pyke's papers. Further comments on Icarian hospitality, see note 116. Mass funerals: Tsantes, *Katoches,* pp. 21–26. According to Aris Poulianos, *E Proeleuse ton Ellenon,* (Athens, 1988), p. 101, some Icarians visiting gravely ill friends challenged Charon to a wrestling match. There is no evidence that this practice survived the war, or in fact that it ever existed in Icaria. The alleged Icarian custom is not mentioned in local folk song, and does not correspond to the modern personification of death in Greece; see M. Alexiou, "Modern Greek Folklore and Its Relation to the Past: The Evolution of Charos in Greek Tradition," in S. Vyronis, ed. *The Past in Medieval Greek Culture,* (Malibu, California, 1978), pp. 221–236.

35. Medicine: Pyke's *Report* Dec. 1943, and, for general conditions, Pyke's secret report to SCAO, Samos, St. [Ag.] Kyrikos, September 27, 1943. Good general health: Interview with Manolis Stanzos, Raches, Icaria, June 12, 2003; for Samos, see Noou, *Paidia,* pp. 31–34. Around November 10,

1943, I. Adamas, a pharmacist, appropriated the stock of Italian medicine. When the Germans arrived on the island about a week later, they failed to recover the medicine from Adamas who went into hiding; interview, A. Koutsounamendos, Aghios Kyrikos, Icaria, June 12, 2003.

36. Statistics for Karavostamos: *Nea Ikaria,* October 19, 1946, and Tsantes, *Katoches,* pp. 24–25, 36. The starvation in rural areas in other parts of Greece was generally lower. For instance, during the winter of 1942 there was one death due to starvation in the village of Ambeli, Euboea; see J. du Boulay, *Portrait of a Greek Mountain Village,* (Oxford, 1974), p. 245. Unprepared Karavostamiotes: Louis Tsouris, interview, Tsouredos, Icaria, June 14, 1994. Tsouris, from the interior of the island, reflected a common view from his region about the soft people of coastal villages. Like Aesop's shiftless insect, which did not work in the summer to stockpile supplies for the winter, the Karavostamiotes were allegedly lazy and thus responsible for their plight. In the remote and fertile village of Akamatra, people upheld agricultural production during the hard years, and also considered the people who starved in seaboard villages as indolent; interview, Mr. Liares, café proprietor, Akamatra, Ikaria, June 8, 2001.

37. Tsantes, *Katoches,* pp. 21–26. Touloumi: interview, May 28, 1994, Aghios Kyrikos, Icaria, with Jesamine Kavoures, who was a young girl in Karavostamos during the occupation.

38. Bread: Interview, May 21, 1994, Aghios Kyrikos, Icaria, with Elias Manolis, who was in Maganiti during the occupation. Making bread in this fashion went back centuries; see the remarks of J. Georgirenes, *Description of the Present Sate of Samos, Nicaria, Patmos and Mount Athos* (London, 1677), p. 62, "a little before dinner they take as much corn as will serve that meal, grind it with a hand-mill, and bake it upon a flat stone." Schoolteacher: Interview, May 29, 1994, with Dr. Omilios Karoutsos, Portorafti, Attica, who was taken to Proespera by his father during the occupation.

39. Canada of Icaria: Interviews with Maria Pourize, Raches, Icaria, May 23, 1994, and John Tsantiris, Armenistis, Icaria, May 24, 1992. Both spent the years of occupation in Proespera.

40. Bread and children: Interview, December 31, 1993, Lincoln Park, Michigan, Nick Koklanaris. Interview with Pantelis Poulos, April 27, 1997, Wilmington, North Carolina, who did not know what bread was.

41. Irineos' Policy: Noou, *Paidia,* pp. 29–34; P. Argenti, *The Occupation of Chios,* pp. 44–46, discusses Red Cross relief to the islands. See the comments of Mark Mazower *Hitler's Greece,* pp. 48–49. For the Red Cross Report on Icaria, see Kostas Ptinis, *Chronia Katoches: Sembole sten Istoria tes Samou 1941–44* (Samos, 1985), pp. 112–114, 120, and the comments of Carabott, "British Military Occupation," 287–290.

42. Ptinis, *Chronia,* pp. 122–123.

43. Ptinis, *Chronia,* pp. 122–123.

44. Theft in Aghios Kyrikos: Interview John Pastis, July 29, 2002, Wilmington, North Carolina. Georgaki: Katsas, *Dromos Sostos,* pp. 23–31.

45. Thucydides' (1. 81) remarks about the moral decay brought about by the hardships of the Peloponnesian War are instructive. Ax: N. Koklanaris, interview Aghios Kyrikos, Icaria, June 27, 2003.

46. J. Pyke, *Field Message Book,* Oct. 9, 1943, notes a case in Akamatra where an *agrophylax,* a rural policeman, ensnared a man stealing a goat and shot him to death. In another case, Pyke endeavored in vain to transfer the venue of the trial of a goat thief from an EAM court in Icaria to Samos.

47. Tsantes, *Katoches,* p. 23.

48. Tsantes, *Katoches,* pp. 24–25.

49. Though the work of J. K. Campbell, *Honour, Family and Patronage: A Study of Institutions and Moral Values in a Greek Mountain Community* (London, 1964), deals with the Sarakatsani, perhaps a non-Greek people and in a very different circumstance, his comments about public shame and honor, pp. 264, 320, are relevant here. Also see the comments of Peregrine Horden and Nicholas Purcell, *The Corrupting Sea: A Study of Mediterranean History* (Oxford, 2002), p. 523.

50. Italian Price Control: Ptinis, *Chronia,* pp. 98–99. Lombardas, *Taragmena Chronia,* p. 16. Some Communist doctors treated patients without fees; see Kalambogias, *Kokkinos Vrachos,* pp. 20–22. Most of these privileged clients had the "correct" political views. A. Koutsounamendos, interview May 23, 2000, Aghios Kyrikos, Icaria, though not mentioned in *Taragmena Chronia,* was the merchant with the bar of soap. He defended the price as accurately reflecting the exchange rate of the period, and pointed out that Communists demanded high prices or services for their goods from non-Communists, and that it was hypocritical to assert that people with left-wing views were altruistic and conservatives were selfish.

51. The statement of Anonymous, *Sklavonetai,* p. 7, that merchants closed their stores, hid their goods, and thus created the black market is misleading because everyone bartered for survival. No shelves in stores: A. Koutsounamendos, interview, Aghios Kyrikos, Icaria, May 28, 2002. For large-scale urban speculators, see Mazower, *Hitler's Greece,* pp. 61–62, where a few unscrupulous individuals became rich. Interview in Aghios Kyrikos, Icaria, May 28, 2003, with Gregory Stagiannis, who as a boy exchanged cigarettes and prophylactics for bread with German soldiers in Athens. Turkey allowed supplies to flow to Greece; see Smith and Walker, *Aegean,* p. 195. The Turkish goods that made their way to Icaria came through the OSS; see note 52 below.

52. Sex: Tsantes, *Katoches,* p. 34, and Katsas, *Dromos Sostos,* p. 31. For the development of hedonism among young people in Athens during the war, see Mazower, *Hitler's Greece,* p. 114. N. Kyrtatos, OSS agent operating in and out of Icaria, supplied the people with needles in August 1944; interview, Cephisia, June 29, 2003. Inventory of Italian stocks: Captain John Pyke, *Secret Report to SCAO, Samos,* St. [Ag.] Kyrikos, September 27, 1943. Pantelis Lakios, Aghios Kyrikos, May 22, 2003, remembers among the few items remaining from his father's store was rope which he sold in small amounts during the war. Manolis Koklanaris, February 19, 1997, Wilmington, North Carolina, found, with his brother, a case of Italian bullets which they bartered. Argenti, *Occupation of Chios,* p. 36, reports that standard exchange rates were established in Chios. For instance, a doctor there received about 1 kilo of flour for a house call.

53. Tsantes, *Katoche,* pp. 12–13, and Katsas, *Dromos Sostos,* pp. 31–35.

54. Piano: Noou, *Paidia,* pp. 31–34.

55. Windswept to Chios: P. Argenti, *The Occupation of Chios,* p. 78.

56. Karimalis, *Antistasi,* pp. 27–28.

57. EAM services: Karimalis, *Antistasi,* pp. 20, 29–31. The only wireless in Raches: operated by N. Vitsaras who used a small windmill to recharge the batteries, obituary N. Vitsaras, *Nea Ikaria,* Feb. 1992. Law and order: Anonymous, *Sklavonetai,* pp. 19–24. Murder for stealing food and mock executions: John Pyke, *Field Book,* October 3, 1943. The need for such methods: Tsantes, *Katoches,* pp. 61–62. By 1947, there were no EAM newsletters from the occupation period extant, a loss keenly lamented by Anonymous, *Sklavonetai,* p. 3. Organizers of EAM: Gerakes, Mavrogeorges and Karnavas. Lombardas, *Taragmena Chronia,* pp. 12–13. John Pyke, *Secret Report on Raches,* Oct. 3, 1943, estimated that in Raches 50% of the population were enrolled in EAM, and about 40% were sympathetic. This figure applies to the entire island.

58. On Malachias and Tsantiris, see Anonymous, *Sklavonetai,* pp. 5–9.

59. EAM: Ch. Makkas, *E Istoria tes Kommounistikes Organoses Ikarias* (Athens, 1980), pp. 58–59; P. Lombardas, *Taragmena Chronia,* pp. 12–13; Tsantes, *Katoches,* pp. 75–76. For its positive role, see G. P. Lombardas, "Gia to EAM tes Ikarias," *Ikariaka,* 42 (2001), 46. Not in EPON: Pantelis Lakios, interview, May 10, 1994, Tzitzifies, Athens. His father, a merchant, had lived in America for many years. He resisted pressure from his teacher to participate in EPON activities. He was nominated to lead an EPON parade because of his high academic achievement, but declined the honor and was publicly insulted by his teacher. Constantinos Papadakis, one of the most successful merchants in Aghios Kyrikos, would not allow his sons to join; interview, Charalambos Papadakis, Aghios Kyrikos, Icaria, June 12, 1969. M. Theodorakis, *Oi Dromoi tou Archangelou* (Athens, 1986), II,

22–25, notes the social bonds developed in EPON. Palamas: *Nea Ikaria,* January/February, 2003.

60. For the type of soldiers used in these garrisons, see Commander Marc Antonio Bragadini, trans. G. Hoffman *The Italian Navy in World War II* (Annapolis, 1957), pp. 333–334. For specific deployment of Italian troops in Icaria, see A. Aldo Levi and A. Giuseppe Fioravanzo, *La Marina Italiana nella Seconda Guerra Mondiale: Attività dopo l'Armistizio. Avvenimenti in Egeo* (Rome, 1957), pp. 426–427. Political character of Italian garrison: Captain John Pyke, *Secret Report to SCAO, to Samos,* from St. [Ag.] Kyrikos, September 27, 1943. The 100 Blackshirts: Pyke, Interview, October 15, 2000, Greenville, North Carolina. In contrast with the normal Italian garrison on Icaria, the character of the Blackshirts was violent and ruthless. Laird Archer, *The Balkan Journal* (New York, 1944), p. 149, describes how the Blackshirts executed villagers as the Italian army retreated from Greece in 1941.

61. See comment of Katsas, *Dromos Sostos,* p. 29. Food policy: Ciano, *Diaries,* entry for July 22, 1942, p. 506. Medical corps: Captain John Pyke, *Secret Report to SCAO, Samos,* on St. [Ag.] Kyrikos, September 27, 1943. Italian soldier displaying pictures of his mother: Philippos Bratses, interview May 25, 2000, Aghios Kyrikos, Icaria. Loved children and mild punishment: Ch. Makkas, *Kommounistikes,* p. 58. Interview, Athens, June 1, 1996, with I. Spanos, who recalled that Italian soldiers shared rations with children in Raches. Operatic voices: Interview Themistocles Speis, June 17, 2003, Perdiki, Icaria. The Italian soldiers were socially integrated in nearby Fourni; see Ptinis, *Chronia,* p. 122. Ptinis, *Chronia,* p. 145, reports how they learned Greek in Samos and admired local traditions and customs. Ettore Caccialanza, as part of the occupying force in Icaria, remembered a cold reception, but soon the Italians were "*bene accolti.*" He, like most of the soldiers, admired the Icarians, and often returns to vacation on the island; telephone interview, Nov. 21, 1999. Marc Antonio Bragadini, *The Italian Navy,* pp. 333–335, notes that soldiers on these remote islands were reserves or men from older draft categories and were assigned to such places chiefly to uphold civil order. In Anafi, people considered the Italians "*kala paidia,*" good lads; see M. E. Kenna, *Greek Island Life: Fieldwork on Anafi* (Amsterdam, 2001), p. 158.

62. General policy of Italicization: Carabott, "British Military Occupation," 288. "Katsas, *Dromos Sostos,* p. 33. Captain John Pyke, *Secret Report to SCAO, Samos,* St. Kyrikos, September 27, 1943.

63. Katsas, *Dromos Sostos,* p. 32. Tsantes, *Katoches,* pp. 44–46.

64. Katsas, *Dromos Sostos,* p. 33.

65. The Italians decided to register all olive presses, and take the lion's share of the production: Katsas, *Dromos Sostos,* p. 31. Bank fraud: Captain John

Pyke, *Secret Report to SCAO, Samos,* St. [Ag.] Kyrikos, September 27, 1943.

66. Coroido Mussolini: M. Mougiannis; interview, Icaria, May 11, 1996. Slogans: Anonymous, *E Ikaria Sklavonetai* (New York, 1948), pp. 12–13. For Italian policy on schools in the Aegean, see Z. Tsipanles, *Italokratia tou Anthropou kai Perivallontos,* (Rhodes, 1998), pp. 140–166. Gymnasiarch who issued *"ochi"* statement: George Katsas, "Necrology," *Atheras,* March–April 1995. Arrest and officer's girlfriend: *Unpublished Diary of Koula Lakios,* entry March 25, 1943. In September 1943, after the armistice, a *laikon dikasterion,* people's court, sentenced many of the women who had associated with the Italians to have their heads shaved in public. Pyke saw such women wearing headscarves when he arrived in Icaria on September 23, 1943 and learned that many of them were planning on leaving Icaria and settling in Athens after the war was over; interview J. Pyke, Chester, South Wirral, England, September 21, 1998. Makkas, *Kommounistikes,* p. 70, criticized the retribution against these women whom he considered patriots, but forced to consort with Italians because of their extreme need. Makkas, nearly 100 years old, vigorously repeated his defense of these fallen "Cariotines"; interview, Monasteri old age home, Icaria, May 31, 2000.

67. Katsas, *Dromos Sostos,* pp. 34–39. Despina Pamphilys slapped a certain Raphael. Toula Moraitis took part in the demonstration; interview, Dec. 29, 1994, Lincoln Park, Michigan. For the goals of the demonstrators, see Karimalis, *Antistasi,* p. 33. There is a controversy about whether the demonstrations took place in 1942 or 1943; see G. Lombardas, "Gia to EAM tes Ikarias," p. 47.

68. Tsantes, *Katoches,* p. 60. Anna Fountoules, interview, Aghios Kyrikos, Icaria, May 28, 2002, recalled details of the affair. George Karafas was one of the innocent bystanders who were tortured; interview, Wilmington, North Carolina, Oct. 7, 1997.

69. Tsantes, *Katoches,* p. 66. Picca's Left-wing sympathies: unpublished diary Koula Lakios, entry March 25, 1943.

70. Tsantes, *Katoches,* pp. 48–56; Lombardas, *Taragmena Chronia,* 73. Interview with Christos Spanos, Raches, Icaria, August 7, 1986. Katsas, *Dromos Sostos,* p. 21. For a similar circumstance in Samos, see Ptinis, *Chronia,* pp. 72–78. Cats: Noou, *Paidia,* pp. 33–34.

71. Onion: Anonymous, *Sklavonetai,* p. 8.

72. People knew the names of the informers: Interview with Papas Paremeros, Tzitzifies, Athens May 14, 1994. Interview with Manolis Moraitis, June 6, 1996, Panaghia, Icaria. Moraitis was a guerrilla for nineteen months in the Icarian mountains, and singled out two prominent informers. People suspected that merchants, the *archousa taxi,* collaborated with the pro-Italian

gendarmerie to help them collect prewar debts; Louis Tsouris, interview in Tsouredos, Icaria, May 26, 1996.

73. The Italians' conciliatory reaction to the women's food demonstration in Aghios Kyrikos is in glaring contrast to the way they responded to such situations in Samos; see Carabott, "British Military Occupation," 315, n. 2., and Ptinis, *Samos,* pp. 109–145. Noou, *Paidia,* pp. 43–47, and Bishop Irineos, *E Dynameis tou ellenochristanikiou Pneumatos* (Athens, 1948), pp. 41–46; however, do not think the Italians were needlessly brutal.

74. Karamanlis: C. M. Woodhouse, *Karamanlis: The Restorer of Greek Democracy* (Oxford, 1982), pp. 20–22.

75. Evacuating people to Turkey, interview with Phocianos, May 27, 2000, Aghios Kyrikos, Icaria. Witnessed executions in Mytilene. A. Rakatzis, interview, Aghios Kyrikos, Icaria, June 17, 2003.

76. For a general account of the flight to Asia Minor, see Anonymous, *Sklavonetai,* pp. 11–13. I interviewed 18 Icarians who were refugees, and most of them had favorable experiences with the Turks. An example is Aspasia Trata Malachias, who in a poem sent to the author, May 5, 1980, related her flight of 1942 and expressed her gratitude to a Turkish farmer who provided nourishment for her party. Malachias' encounter probably represents 80% of what refugees experienced, but the atrocities committed by Turks received more publicity. For instance, in 1942 John Pyke saw a sail ship arrive in Carpathos. A number of people had starved on the boat which had been driven away from Marmaras, on the Turkish coast, after the Turks had raped five women and stolen jewelry and other valuables from the passengers; see Mike Beckett, "The Aegean Adventures of Captain John Pyke: Royal Artillery, Civilian Affairs Officer Attached to the Special Boat Squadron," *The Bulletin of the Military Historical Society,* vol. 46, no. 184 (May 1996), p. 186. Pyke vividly recalled the incident more than fifty years later; interview, John Pyke, Chester, South Wirral, England, September 21, 1998. Similar stories: Noou, *Paidia,* pp. 33–34, and Karimalis, *Antistasi,* p. 24. Pyke was unable to acquire information from the British command in Samos about certain Icarian men who had fled to Turkey; John Pyke, *Field Message Book,* Letter, Oct. 13, 1943.

77. Interviews with Mary Tsouris Papalas, March 18, 1994, Lincoln Park, Michigan, and with Louis Tsouris, May. 24, 1995, Tsouredos, Icaria. Louis Tsouris had been in the merchant marine in the late 1930s, jumped boat in America and gained citizenship by joining the armed forces.

78. Interview, Irene Achidafty, Lincoln Park, Michigan, July 12, 1991.

79. Interviews with Antonis Kastanias, June 8, 1996, Gialiskari, Icaria, and with Basilis Yakas, June 7, 1996, Raches, who remembered the extra rations provided by Kastanias.

80. Phocianos: Interviews with Phocianos, Aghios Kyrikos, Icaria June 4, 1996, and his OSS superior, N. Kyrtatos, Cephisia, Athens, June 29, 2003. Stephanos Glaros, a spry, astute octogenarian, recalled details of a trip with Phocianos directly to Chesme; interview, Aghios Kyrikos, Icaria, May 24, 1994. He had published the account in an issue of *Ikariake Phoné* which I was unable to consult. Dr. Kostas Saphos, interview May 14, 1994, Tzitzifies, Athens, considered the fare for his passage, gold coins and a sewing machine, exorbitant. Saphos believed that the captain should have offered his services *aphilokerdos*, without the thought of profit.

81. Starving family: Interview, Demosthenes Galiktiadis, San Francisco, September 3, 2000. War Widow: Interview, Maria Sotilis, Tzitzifies, Athens, May 21, 2000. Teacher in Athens: Elias Papalas, interview, Tsouredos, Icaria, May 21, 1993.

82. Ptinis, *Chronia,* pp. 219–220; Noou, *Paidia,* pp. 105–106.

83. Ptinis, *Katoche,* pp. 221–227, 241–245, esp. p. 226, places the responsibility for the bloodshed on Pierolla who brought the Blackshirts from Rhodes. Carabott, "British Military Occupation," p. 291.

84. Renowned Icarian musician Themistocles Kyprios: "That man would have made a fortune if he had gone to Athens," interview, John Pyke, October 15, 2000, Greenville, North Carolina. Incident at Faros: Interview with son of entertainer, John Kyprios, Aghios Kyrikos, Icaria, May 27, 2002. Pyke, Letter to author, October 23, 1998, "from day one of the Italian armistice the political struggle, communism versus status quo, surfaced in earnest." Red flag: John Pyke, *Secret Report, SCAO, Samos,* St. [Ag.] Kyrikos, September 9, 1943.

85. Lombardas, *Taragmena Chronia,* p. 17.

86. Blackshirts: John Pyke, Interview Chester, South Wirral, September 21, 1998. Also see A. Kédros, *La Résistance Grecque, 1940–1944* (Paris, 1966), pp. 325–326; Carabott, "British Military Occupation," 290–291; Tsantes, *Katoches,* pp. 71–75; Anonymous, *Sklavonetai,* pp. 20–25.

87. Lombardas, *Taragmena Chronia,* pp. 18–19. Anonymous, *Sklavonetai,* pp. 20–25. Levi, *La Marina Italiana,* pp. 243–244, 426–427, and p. 566, document 56. For a general picture of events in the Aegean, see Smith and Walker, *Aegean,* p. 73. L. Lind, *The Battle of the Wine Dark Sea: The Aegean Campaign 1940–1945* (Maryborough, Australia, 1996), p. 124.

88. Aris Poulianos, who later received a Ph.D. in anthropology in Russia and had learned Italian during the occupation, negotiated the surrender. Ice cream: Stamatoula Spanos, a schoolteacher in Raches, remembered the name of the officer, perhaps inaccurately, as Lieutenant Motta; interview, Raches, Icaria, June 18, 1961. Also see Tsantes, *Katoches,* pp. 73–74. Anonymous, *Sklavonetai,* pp. 21–24.

89. Italian reinforcements: Levi, *La Marina Italiana,* pp. 580–581, and document 115; Italian maltreatment of people in Aghios Kyrikos: Anonymous, *Sklavonetai,* pp. 21–22. Wedding presents: Pyke, *Restitution of Lost Property Form,* Oct. 2, 1943. The bride's father petitioned the British for compensation.

90. John Pyke, *Secret Report, SCAO, Samos,* September 9, 1943, St. [Ag.] Kyrikos, 1943. Lieutenant-Commander Noel C. Rees not only used British funds but also invested his personal fortune in the operation; based on a phone interview the daughter of Rees, Mrs. Zoe Woolrych York, Denver, Colorado, March 2, 2002. An undated letter to the author from York, received June 7, 2000, discussed her father's commitment to Greek refugees. For MI 9 operations, see M. R. D. Foot and J. M. Langley, *MI 9: The British Secret Service that Fostered Escape and Evasion 1939–1945 and its American Counterpart* (London, 1979), pp. 91–92, who note the valuable role of Rees.

91. Mike Beckett, "The Aegean Adventures of Captain John Pyke," p. 187, provides a version of the domino theory in the Aegean: the capture of Rhodes would force Turkey into the war on the side of the Allies; the Allies would supply Russia through the Dardanelles rather than through the more difficult Arctic route, and this would speed the collapse of the German eastern front. This was essentially the position of Winston Churchill, *The Grand Alliance* (Boston, 1950), p. 405, and accepted by Michael Woodbine Parish, *Aegean Adventures 1940–1943 and the End of Churchill's Dream* (Sussex, England, 1993), pp. 194–201, 226. Philip P. Argenti, *The Occupation of Chios by the Germans 1941–1944 (*Cambridge, England, 1966), p. 91. Argenti, not a military historian, supports the more conventional view that the islands were strategically irrelevant, a position more fully developed by Jeffrey Holland, *The Aegean Mission: Allied Operations in the Dodecanese* (New York, 1988), pp. 46–50. Russian position: V. Mastny, *Russia's Road to the Cold War: Diplomacy, Warfare, and the Politics of Communism, 1941–1945* (New York, 1975) pp. 124–125.

92. Unilateral action of Parish: Phone interview with Zoe Wollrych York, Denver, Colorado, March 3, 2002, and an undated letter to the author, received June 7, 2000. Rees tried to dissuade Parish from making the trip, and suggested that he wait several days to clear it with his superiors. Soldarelli in touch with Greek government: phone interview with Kostas Sophoulis, son of Emannuel Sophoulis, June 29, 2003, and e-mail message of July 2, 2003. Emmanuel Sophoulis, who was minister of Welfare and Refugees, in the summer of 1943 made contacts with Soldarelli about humanitarian issues. It seems that Soldarelli displayed some interest in cooperating with the Allies before the armistice. For the influence of Pejrolo over the Blackshirts, see *La Marina Italiana Nella Seconda Guerra Mondiale* (Rome, 1957), 5, 416–417.

93. Parish, *Aegean Adventures,* pp. 220–221. The memoirs of Gianni Zapheris, who organized the Samian guerrillas, published in the *Samiako Bema* in

December 1978 and reprinted in Ptinis, *Katoche,* pp. 226–228, blames the slaughter at Kastania on Churchill's policy. Also see Carabott, "British Military Occupation," p. 298.

94. The political views of Pawson and Parish: letter from Mrs. Michael Woodbine Parish to the author, April 12, 1997. Mrs. Zoe York recalled that her father, Noel Rees, complained that Pawson was too liberal in distributing British funds to left-wing forces after September 1943; phone interview, Denver, Colorado, March 3, 2002. The alleged plan to kill Pasvanes: Anonymous, *Skalvonetai,* pp. 22–23. Elias Zizes remembered that Parish was well received in Aghios Kyrikos interview, Aghios Kyrikos, June 27, 2003.

95. Tsantes, *Katoches,* pp. 78–83; Lombardas, *Taragmena Chronia,* p. 20; Anonymous, *Sklavonetai,* pp. 24–26. Parish, *Aegean Adventures,* pp. 220–221, gives an account that varies slightly from Tsantes, Lombardas, and Anonymous. The Icarians saw the motorboat zigzag and assumed the erratic movement was a result of a struggle on board, but Parish reports that the Blackshirts overwhelmed his party upon landing on Fourni. An Italian naval document refers to this incident as "the rebellion of the MAS 522," and notes the arrest of Parish, but not the scuffle. The lookout at Cape Pharos observed the MAS begin in a northerly direction and then swerve to the west; see Levi and Fioravanzo, *La Marina Italiana,* pp. 416–418. Carabott, "British Military occupation," pp. 314–315, notes the incident.

96. Anonymous, *Sklavonetai,* pp. 25–26.

97. John Lodwick, *Raiders from the Sea: The Story of the Special Boat Service in World War II,* (London, 1947; reprint, 1990, Annapolis, Maryland, with a new foreword by Lord Jellicoe), pp. 91–93, 159, 165, 195. Pitt, *Special Boat Squadron,* pp. 98–100. A. Petacco, *La Nostra Guerra 1940–1945:* pp. 181–183. Interview with Captain Phocianos, Aghios Kyrikos, Icaria, May 27, 2000.

98. Smith and Walker, *Aegean,* pp. 54–63. The Germans in fact understood that Noel Rees was the key figure in these operations; see National Archives and Record Service, Washington, Abschrift, Sturmdivision Rhodos, Betr: Spionage Dodekanese; no. 49, Sept. 28, 1943.

99. Anonymous, *Sklavonetai,* pp. 27–28. Karimalis, *Antistasi,* pp. 52–54, who identifies a certain Tsalapantes as Pasvanes' main enemy. Saint of Icaria: Interview, Noou, Vathi, Samos, August 5, 1998. For Pasvanes, see, *Nea Ikaria,* June 1990.

100. Anonymous, *Sklavonetai,* p. 27, identified by initials, certain men in the group of "*prodotes,*" traitors, under arrest. Also see Lombardas, *Taragmena Chronia,* pp. 210–211. Tsantes, *Katoches,* p. 76; Soviet model: Anonymous, *Skalvonetai,* p. 5. The author seems to be retrojecting views of 1948 onto 1944. Stalin was not opposed to insurgency but did not support it; see Stavrakis, *Moscow,* pp. 48–127.

101. For Pyke's military career in the Aegean, see Mike Beckett, "The Aegean Adventures of Captain John Pyke." pp. 182-186. Beckett deals mainly with Pyke's post-Icaria activities, but for Pyke his Icarian sojourn was the highlight of his military career. Indeed he became a hometown hero for his adventures in Icaria; see *Birkenhead News,* May 27, 1944, "From Rookie to Ruler," noting how the peacetime jeweler became "king of Icaria."

102. Pyke, *Secret Report to SCAO, Samos,* on St. [Ag.] Kyrikos, September 27, 1943. "Putting aside my revolver at that moment was the bravest thing I did during the war"; interview with John Pyke, Chester, South Wirral, England, September 21, 1998.

103. Interview with John Pyke, Chester, South Wirral, England, September 21, 1998; letter, October 23, 1998, and unpublished diary, entries September 26–29, 1942. Katsas *Dromos Sostos,* p. 42, describes the scene in Chrysostomos in a similar manner.

104. Pyke, letter to author, October 23, 1998. Key and American: Katsas, *Dromos Sostos,* p. 40. Pyke was still in proud possession of the key, and remembered the shoeless American who in his efforts to be decently attired resembled a harlequin; interview, Pyke, South Wirral, England, September 21, 1998. Makkas, *Kommounistikes,* p. 77.

105. For Churchill's view that the Aegean was a decisive theater, see above, note 93. This conviction was anticipated in a 1939 memorandum of Admiral Sir Percy Noble; see J. Greene and A. Massignani, *Naval War in the Mediterranean,* pp. 308–311. Instructions to Civilian Affairs Officers in Aegean: Public Record Office: War Office 201/1720. Pyke summarized his assignment in Icaria in an interview, October 20, 2000, Greenville, North Carolina. Pyke was briefed on this policy during his training as a CAO officer in Alexandria, Egypt, in 1942.

106. John Pyke, *Report on Interview with guerrilla leaders from Ikaria,* Sept. 24, 1943; Supplies: Pyke, *Diary,* Oct. 23, 1943. Ouzo: Pyke, *Diary,* entry October 1, 1943.

107. Captain John Pyke, *Secret report to SCAO, Samos,* St. [Ag.] Kyrikos, September 27, 1943. Anonymous, *Sklavonetai,* pp. 25–28. Elias Zizes witnessed at this time EAM blatantly appropriating supplies from needy people and became a staunch anti-Communist; interview, Aghios Kyrikos, June 12, 2003. In the postwar years, during the Cold War, Pyke emerged as a villain in the memoirs of KKE participants. Tsantes, *Katoches,* p. 79, writes about EAM's distrust of Pyke. Pasvanes accused Pyke of being a "malevolent" person sowing seeds for civil war in Icaria; see Karimalis, *Antistasi,* pp. 38–39, 79–80, who details a clash between Pasvanes and Pyke, but Pyke, interview South Wirral, England, September 21, 1998, had no recollection of a clash with Pasvanes, or any sharp quarrel with EAM, though he realized they had their agenda, that he had lost his influence with them by the end of his mission on the island, and that certain EAM leaders distrust-

ed him. It was Pyke's main goal in Icaria to establish a cooperative relationship with the guerrillas in Icaria; see Public Record Office: Foreign Office 371/37226. R9058. In his last two weeks in Icaria, *Diary,* entry for November 6, 1943, Pyke saw that it was hopeless to work with the guerrillas. Their animosity to the British was surfacing as the German counteroffensive was clearly coming to Icaria. Pyke's difficulties with the guerrillas coincided with Churchill's disapproving statements about the KKE; see Stavrakis, *Moscow,* p. 13.

108. John Pyke, *Field Message Book,* October 14, 1943. 120. Anonymous, *Sklavonetai,* p. 27, makes the case against the collaborators. Release of Amaxis: letter from J. Pyke, October 23, 1998. Bank: Captain John Pyke, *Secret Report to SCAO, Samos,* on St. [Ag.] Kyrikos, September 27, 1943. This enabled the two hundred and fifteen bank depositors to have access to their accounts.

109. S. Tsirka, *Akyvernetes Politeies, E Nychterida* (Athens, 2000), p. 23. Sheep thieves: Pyke, *Diary,* entry, November 6, 1943. Malachias: diminished authority: Captain John Pyke, *Secret report, SCAO-Samos,* on St. [Ag.] Kyrikos, September 27, 1943.

110. List of seventy: The proscription roll allegedly was seized and kept in the gendarmerie where in 1947 Andreas Katsas claimed to have seen it; interview, San Francisco, September 2, 2000. It is doubtful, however, that the gendarmes possessed such a document for it would have been eventually published for propaganda purposes. The merchant A. Koutsounamendos, interview, Aghios Kyrikos, May 24, 2000, heard of such a document, and despite being a merchant did not think his name was on it. Pyke believed there was such a list and speculated that Dr. Amaxis, the gendarme Koutsouflakis, Zoe Marinakis, and Leonidas Spanos were on it, "Notes between Murray and Pyke," Nov. 3, 1943, Field Security Section in Cairo. When the Communists took over Icaria in September 1944, conservatives panicked and many escaped the island. For instance, Leonidas Spanos fled to Turkey, e-mail message from his niece Bibi Spanos Ikaris, Dec. 14, 2004. Perhaps his escape was assisted by the OSS. Dr. Malachias on September 9, 1944, wrote to an OSS agent in Turkey arranging the evacuation of certain Icarians who he thought were in danger; in collection of Nicholas Kyrtatos, Cephisia, Athens. Anonymous, *Sklavonetai,* p. 111, notes initials of collaborators. Sketches for the raid on Myconus are in the papers of John Pyke. At liberty to return: British Military governor Samos to Pyke, Oct 7, 1943.

111. For Sophoulis: Philip John Carabott, "British Military Occupation," p. 290. On Sophoulis' mission, see the Tsouderos files 13 in the Gennadios Library, Athens. John Pyke, *Diary,* Entry October 1, 1943; Captain John Pyke *Secret Report, SCAO-Samos,* on St. [Ag.] Kyrikos, September 27, 1943. On December 15, 1945, Dr. Malachias wrote to John Pyke thanking him for his services. In what seems to be the only extant document dealing with Dr. Malachias' views on Icarian Communists, he expressed gratitude to

England as well "for its disinterested help in spite of the foolish activities of rebels in the guise of communism."

112. Malachias: Captain John Pyke, *Secret report, SCAO-Samos,* on St. [Ag.] Kyrikos, September 27, 1943. E. Sophoulis, "Action by the name of King George B [II] of the Greek government," Nov. 1, 1943, Pyke *Papers.* Sophoulis, who had led Venizelite guerrilla forces in Samos, was aware of the Communist agenda in Icaria and Samos and was eager to control it; phone interview with Kostas Sophoulis, June 17, 2003. Dr. Malachias made known his strong anti-Communist views to Pyke in a letter dated December 15, 1945, in the Pyke papers. Major Dagge, *Secret Report: Notes on Political Policy and Treatment of EAM and Andartes on Samos, Icaria, and Aegean Isles,* no date, probably early November 1943. Anonymous, *Sklavonetai,* pp. 27–30, reports hostility between Malachias' committee and the people, and objected to the policy of selling supplies, but Pyke, interview South Wirral, England, September 21, 1998, thought that supplies were given away if people did not have the means to purchase them. Pyke expected that when communication with America would be reopened the approximately ten thousand Icarian-Americans could contribute to the purchase of supplies; see J. Pyke, *Secret Report, SCAO, Samos* on St. [Ag.] Kyrikos, September 27, 1943. For the establishment of the council, letter from J. Pyke, October 23, 1998, and Pyke's *Diary,* entry October 6, 1943, notes that EAM expected two of the three council seats. An October 11, 1943, telegram from the bishop in Samos to Pyke discusses some sort of EAM proposal, which Dr. Malachias rejected as a ruse to gain power. Pyke did not remember what the EAM artifice was, but apparently EAM attempted to nullify Dr. Malachias' veto authority. Malachias and American government: letter to OSS Agent Nicholas Kyrtatos, Sept. 9, 1944, in possession of the author. Malachias and British government: letter of Pyke to Malachias, Nov. 19, 1943, copy of which is in Pyke's *Field Book.* Humanitarian service: Ioannis Kyprios saw him give patients money to purchase medicine; interview with Kyprios in Aghios Kyrikos, Icaria, June, 27, 2003. Such stories about Dr. Malachias are still current on the island.

113. German spies: Pyke: *Report Aghios Kyrikos to Vathi,* November, 1, 12, 1943; Italian telegraph cable and telephone: Pyke, *Report on the Islands of Icaria and Fourni* undated, Arrests: British Military Mission at Aghios Kyrikos November 6, 1943, to EAM Headquarters in Evdilos. *EAM communiqué* signed by Stavrinades to Pyke, Nov. 12, 1943. Appropriation of private property: Interview, Panagiotis Kefalos, Aghios Kyrikos, May 27, 2000, who added, "They were uneducated and full of the devil and would have executed a lot of people." Pyke had a similar view, *Secret Report to SCAO Samos,* September 27, 1943, and *Field Message Book,* October 4, 1943.

114. John Pyke, *Field Message Book,* October 14, 1943, October 18, 1943. Too many Fascists: Pyke, *Diary,* November 10, 1943. Demeanor of Italians: Nov. 14, 1943 Pyke *Report to Samos. Andartes* take the weapons and run:

Pyke *Secret Report,* no date. Firewood: Pyke to Italian commandant. November 10, 1943.

115. Leros: Lodwick, *Raiders,* pp. 91–93, Pitt, *Special Boat,* pp. 98–100. A. Petacco, *La Nostra Guerra,* pp. 181–183, notes the heroic effort of the eight thousand Italian soldiers and two thousand marines. Mascherpa, commander of Leros, and Campioni, the supreme commander in the Aegean, were taken to Italy and executed for their support of the armistice. Bragadini, *The Italian Navy,* pp. 333–335, singles out the bravery of Admiral Mascherpa but reduces the number of Italians to fifty-five hundred. He argues that they fought heroically with the British against the Germans who nonetheless prevailed because they could send reinforcements while the British could not. Admiral Sir Andrew Bourne Cunningham, *A Sailor's Odyssey* (New York, 1951), p. 582, repudiates any suggestion of a solid Italian military contribution at Leros. Italians encouraged by operation Poseidon: John Pyke, *Report on Italian Garrison in Icaria,* Nov. 15, 1943. Secret and Confidential. Report of delight at German success: Pyke to Headquarters, November 15, 1943. Pyke to Italian commandant, November 15, 1943. "Ayez la bonté, s'il vous plait, de faire une enquête et de me faire connaître les resultats." Failed wireless set: *Letter to Headquarters* November 17th, 1943, and *Field Book,* October 10, 1943. Pyke's wishful thinking: *Andartes* will doubtless join the regular troops: Pyke's *Diary,* Nov. 15, 1943. Churchill on foothold and private initiative: Winston Churchill, *The Grand Alliance* (Boston, 1950), p. 405. Also see above, note 93. For the view about converging all British forces on Cos, see N. A. Petropoulos, *Anamneses enos Palaiou Nautikou* (Athens, 1971), pp. 47–49.

116. Icarians in Samos: Tsantes, *Katoches,* pp. 37–38. Anonymous, *Sklavonetai,* p. 34. Destruction of hospital: Interview, Toula Moraitis, June 1, 2002, Kountoumas, Icaria. For the German assault on Vathi and behavior in Samos, see Noou, *Paidia,* pp. 188–200. Also see, Smith and Walker, *Aegean,* pp. 82–83.

117. Aborted execution: interview with Noou, Vathi, Samos, August 5, 1998. Identity cards: Ptinis, *Chronia,* p. 138. Operation: Interview, Toula Moraitis, August 3, 2000, Lincoln Park, Michigan. Shovels and fodder: Ptinis, *Chronia,* p. 141. The Earl Jellicoe was one of the soldiers who escaped. In a letter of October 20, 1997, to Mrs. Zoe W. York, he describes his flight to Turkey and the assistance provided by Noel Rees.

118. *Field book,* John Pyke Nov. 19, 1943. Interview, John Pyke, South Wirral, England, September 21, 1998.

119. A copy of the letter, Nov. 19, 1943, is in Pyke's *Field Book.* Dr. Malachias' name is crossed out, apparently to protect him if it fell into German hands.

120. The report of a German news agency was noted in *Echo,* November 20, 1943. (newspaper clipping found in Pyke's papers). Lombardas, *Taragmena*

Chronia, pp. 20–21. Anonymous, *Sklavonetai,* pp. 31–33. Pitt, *Special Boat,* pp. 108–110.

121. Churchill's remarks about the brutality of the "Huns" got back to the Italians; see Richard Lamb, *War in Italy: A Brutal Story* (New York, 1993), p. 145. Smith and Walker, *Aegean,* p. 105 note the sinking of German transport ship by the British with eighteen hundred Italian prisoners, most of whom drowned. Katsas, *Dromos Sostos,* p. 43, claimed that Italian corpses were washed to Icarian shores. Makkas, *Kommounistikes,* p. 75, repeats the story. Noou, *Ta Paidia,* pp. 151–157, notes the correct version. The number of Italian defectors: Lombardas, *Taragmena Chronia,* pp. 22–23. Italians in hiding: Interview with P. Lakios, May 12, 1994, Tzitzifies, Athens. John Pyke, *Report on Italian Garrison in Icaria: Secret and Confidential,* Nov. 15, 1943.

122. G. Baloukas, an officer in the Samian guerrilla army; interview, Vathi, Samos, August 6, 1998, suggested that the Icarians were chicken-hearted soldiers. Papas Glaros, interview Xyloserti, Icaria, August 9, 1993, was astonished at the caution exhibited by the guerrillas over a handful of Germans.

123. Lombardas, *Taragmena Chronia,* pp. 24–25. EAM officials: S. Stavrinades, G. Economos, J. Adams, and P. Lombardas. Interview with Irene Tsouris, May 21, 1994, Tsouredos, Icaria, who noted that her fourteen-year-old brother George returned a stolen mule, which he had hidden in a stable in Tsouredos, after Italians threatened to shoot him.

124. For the general picture in this area, see B. Pitt, *Special Boat Squadron: The Story of the S.B.S. in the Mediterranean* (London, 1983) 87–94; and Beckett, "Pyke," 180; Seventy Germans: Lombardas, *Taragmena Chronia,* p. 25. Kostas' sense of humor: A. Koutsounamendos who had an acquaintance who knew Kostas' father in Alexandria, Egypt: interview Aghios Kyrikos, Icaria, May 27, 2002. Torched houses: Tzermingkas in Mavrato, Mavrekes in Mavrekato, G. Pasvanes in Oxe, Karpete in Perdiki, and Phantoustis in Ploumari. Personal encounters with Kostas: Interviews, Elias Pardos, September 9, 1994, Harrisville, Michigan; Pantelis Lakios, May 12, 1994, Aghios Kyrikos, Icaria; V. Seringas, July 12, 1995, Lincoln Park, Michigan. Also see the comments of Tsantes, *Katoches,* p. 85. OSS officer: Nicholas Kyrtatos, interview, Cephisia, Athens, June 29, 2003. Blockade runner: Photis Spanos, his obituary in *Nea Ikaria,* Dec. 1991; and interview with his uncle, Christos Spanos, May 29, 1994, Raches, Icaria, and with his cousin, Nicholas Battuyios, June 28, 2003, Aghios Kyrikos. Battuyios avoided detention by sleeping in the woods, but Kostas apprehended his cousin and aunt. Kostas' dental problem: Lombardas, *Taragmena Chronia,* pp. 24–25, 112.

125. Quarrel in square: witnessed by A. Koutsounamendos; interview, Aghios Kyrikos, Icaria, May 27, 2002. General deportment of Kostas: Lombardas, *Taragmena Chronia,* p. 22. Tsantes, *Katoches,* p. 41. Interview, Tsouredos,

Icaria, May 12, 1994, with Irene Tsouris who was held prisoner in Therma. She complained that Dr. Amaxis treated German soldiers but ignored her injured arm and ailments of other detainees. Sent to Leros: George Theodorakis and Michalis Pouilanos.

126. Lars Barentzen, "The German Withdrawal from Greece in 1944 and British Naval Inactivity," *Journal of Modern Greek Studies* 5 (1987), pp. 237–239. Pitt, *Special Boats,* pp. 138–140. Tsantes, *Katoches,* 86–87. Lodwick, *Raiders,* p. 116, notes one German killed on Patmos, perhaps Captain Kostas. Nicholas Kyrtatos, an OSS agent in Icaria in November 1944, from a position in the mountains gathered information about the number of German vessels steaming for Salonika; interview OSS agent N. Kyrtatos, Cephisia, Athens, June 29, 2003.

CHAPTER 6

The Red
Island

B Y THE TIME the war ended, the overwhelming majority of people in Icaria supported EAM. The leadership of EAM was Communist, and had raised on occasion the hammer-and-sickle flag. The extremists in EAM were Bolsheviks and proud to be so called. On the other hand, the preponderance of the Icarians considered themselves leftists and readily accepted the following identifications: *philoleutheroi* (liberals), *prodeutikoi* (progressives), *aristeroi* (leftists), or *demokratoi* (democrats). They were not total believers, but were inclined to support Communist candidates. The Icarians expressed their political leanings in the September 1, 1946, plebiscite on King George II (reigned, 1922–1923, and again, 1935–1947). While the majority of the Greek electorate favored the return of the king (he had fled to Crete and then to England during the Nazi occupation of Greece) by 68 percent, in Icaria nearly 65 percent voted against his reinstatement. In some instances, Icarians felt that conservative elements were putting pressure on them to vote for the return of the monarchy. In 1964, when some Icarian Communists had regained their civil rights and ran for elective office, Communist candidates swept all local posts. In the first decades after the war, when given the opportunity, about 65 percent of the Icarians consistently voted for either Communists or other left-wing candidates.[1]

Radicalism did not sweep over the island during the war but like the waves that make toward its rugged shore came gradually, indeed having started two decades before the war. The first ripples reached Icaria in the early 1920s. The Greek Communist Party, KKE, initially aimed at converting the urban unemployed, and exhibited little interest in rural areas. Many of the founders of the party came from urban areas, and dismissed the peasantry as politically irrelevant, particularly the type that toiled in underdeveloped Aegean islands. Marxist ideas, nonetheless, began to slip into the island in the 1920s. Some of the first Communists in Icaria were refugees from Asia Minor, and a few were fairly well-educated, but they had little impact on the people because most of the more enlightened members of the Asia Minor diaspora found Icaria too confining, and left for Athens. On the other hand, teachers who accepted positions in the new high school in Aghios Kyrikos in the late 1920s and the 1930s had a decided influence on their students' political outlook. The majority of these teachers were sympathetic to Marxism, and, although they did not actively proselytize their students, they tended to open their eyes to new political ideas. It was widely believed by the mid-1930s that anyone who had a high-school education had acquired left-wing views. But the poorest inhabitants of the region, the several thousand occupants of the neighboring island of Fourni, who did not have a high school of their own, were generally too poor to send their offspring to the high school in Aghios Kyrikos and thus the Fourniotes, who had many reasons to be left-wing, tended to be more conservative than the Icarians.[2]

Elias Viores, apparently, made the first effort to organize Communist activity in Icaria. Immigrating to America before the First World War, Viores became a factory worker and joined the Communist party in the Pittsburgh area. About 1920, he returned to Icaria and established a following in his native village of Petropouli and then took the new ideology to other poor villages in the central mountain range. Adding money collected from natives to dollars he had conveyed from America, he established a party fund. His most talented disciple was Ioannis Koutsouphlakes, known as Kapelas. Viores appointed him treasurer of the fledgling local party. A strong orator with a special appeal to young people, Kapelas was charismatic and extremely anticlerical. He encouraged some of his young followers to desecrate a church in the small village of Kyparisi. On several occasions, after Mass on Sundays he would hurl obscenities at the priests as they emerged from church, branding them as Rasputins and leeches on society. On one occasion he publicly insulted a bishop who was making an official tour of the island. The majority of his colleagues did not share his anticlericalism. Indeed many Icarian priests became staunch Communists, and it was commonly believed that any son of a priest was a radical. Kapelas' greatest fault was his penchant for drinking and gambling. Viores, who disapproved of the way Kapelas was using party funds, attempted to expel him from the movement. Both men were discredited in the quarrel. Viores concluded that Icaria was not fertile soil for Communism and decided to return to America about 1927.[3]

Viores left Icaria when people were still optimistic about the future. In 1926, a very modern high school, funded by the Icarian community in America, was completed in Aghios Kyrikos and there were plans to attract tourists and develop Therma into a major spa and build hotels and restaurants in Raches and a harbor in Evdilos. Since the government would not provide funds for these projects, Icarians hoped their relatives in America would continue to invest in Icaria and they themselves purchased stocks in Icaros, a corporation established to carry out these works. In 1927, one of the most encouraging developments was the excellent steamship connection with Athens. Eight steamers were in this service, and the *Frinton,* one of the finest passenger ships in the Aegean, made its maiden voyage to Icaria in the spring of 1927.[4]

Indications of the Great Depression surfaced in Icaria earlier than they did in other parts of Greece. The first signs of a great economic decline in Icaria appeared in 1928. While neighboring Samos was being electrified, Icaria was not. A greater source of distress was the breakdown of six of the eight passenger ships servicing the island. On several occasions, travelers were stranded in the middle of the Aegean on a disabled steamer. Eventually the owners of the ships sent them to the scrap heap. Furthermore, people lost all the money they had invested in Icaros when the corporation went bankrupt for reasons not entirely clear. Living standards on the island were rapidly declining under the government of Prime Minister Alexander Zaimis (November 1926 to July 1928), who was obliged to negotiate a loan with European powers of six million pounds sterling. According to one of the many terms spelled out in the so-called Geneva Accord, the Greek government had to maintain a budget surplus. Thus Zaimis intensified the regressive system of taxation that now drew more than three-quarters of the state's revenues from indirect taxes, a policy that hit rural areas very hard. The government sent tax collectors to Icaria to attempt to exact revenue on every animal and all crops, even on goats that roamed the Atheras range and isolated fruit tree. In May 1928, gendarmes took two farmers who had been eluding these tax officials to headquarters in Evdilos and hit them with their fists. Several days later, the gendarmes slapped a farmer because he was a Communist, apparently the earliest recorded clash between a Communist and the authorities in

Icaria. For the first time, Icarians began to criticize Greece and not just a particular Greek government. An editorial in the *Ikariake Enosis,* a newspaper published by the Icarian community in Athens, complained that Turkey never hounded Icarians for taxes or drafted men for cannon fodder, as did "Mama" Greece.[5]

While Viores had given up on Communism for Icaria, other Icarian-Americans recommenced his work. Nikolaos Tsermingkas, who had immigrated to the United States around 1920, joined the Communist party and eventually became a friend of Gus Hall, the American Communist leader. In 1928, Tsermingkas published a letter in the *Ikariake Enosis,* announcing that the government's exploitation of Icaria must stop. He declared that the Icarians had the support of the American Communist party, that they should be patient and courageous, and that the final "victory will be ours." Tsermingkas sent $21, about two weeks wages in America and a substantial sum for Icaria, to help establish the Communist party in Icaria and regularly dispatched *Embros,* a Greek Communist newspaper published in the United States, to his sister in Mavratos, his native village. Tsermingkas wrote occasional editorials for this newspaper which circulated from hand to hand and contributed in radicalizing the people of the village that eventually acquired the nickname "Little Stalingrad."[6]

Eleutherios Venizelos, who had been out of office for some years, assumed power again in July 1928. Many Icarians were deeply disappointed in Venizelos' administration. The politician they had idolized for his role in aiding Icaria to break away from the Ottoman Empire continued the harsh tactics of the previous government to raise taxes. Venizelos was now primarily interested in foreign affairs, and his "Great Idea," the dream of uniting all Greeks within a single, enlarged Greece, proved to be an all-consuming political passion and an expensive scheme. After 1922, the Icarians had already begun to feel that Venizelos did not have a progressive policy for the rustic areas of Greece, and in 1928, when he resumed political power, they began to abandon Venizelos' Liberal Party for the KKE.

One of the Icarians who read *Embros* was Nicholas Amaxis, a distant relative of Dr. Amaxis. In the mid-1920s, he became a university student of mathematics and was the chief editorial writer of the *Ikariake Enosis.* From 1926 to 1927, he wrote nonpolitical essays on various Icarian matters. In 1928, he apparently joined the Communist party in Athens, and under the pseudonym Nicaris wrote a series of editorials blaming capitalism for the prevailing poverty in Icaria. In an essay published in *Ikariake Enosis* in June 1928, he reported that Communism was spreading like mushrooms in Icaria, and that the authorities were trying to eradicate Bolsheviks, a term now coming into usage on the island. Around 1930, Amaxis returned to Icaria and, while giving private lessons in mathematics, he set up Communist cells in various villages. For instance, in the summer of 1930, he addressed a number of men in a secluded spot in Tsourdeos, and converted everyone to his views. "We thought he was a god," one man remembered. Avoiding the sort of disputes that had undermined the efforts of Viores and Kapelas, he established a solid foundation for the movement in Icaria before the Metaxas government dispatched him to a prison in Amorgos and in 1936 jailed some of his followers in Samos and Aghios Kyrikos. By the mid-1930s, there was a firm core of Communists on the island. In 1934, the people in Daphne elected a local council of five consisting entirely of Communists, and in the following year there were similar results in Frantato. In *Laokratia* (Power to the People), a handwritten, mimeographed newspaper which circulated clandestinely on the island, the Icarian Communists called for a general uprising in solidarity with colleagues being held in Metaxas' prisons.[7] Although we have no record of how many joined the party, we do know the names of the three most prominent: Ioannis Salas, George Pasvanes, and Olga Malachias. They were all born just before the First World War and were all killed in the civil war in the late 1940s.

Salas, born in 1909, was the only one who gained national prominence, and it is thus appropriate that we digress to review his early career. In the mid-1920s he fell under the sway of Viores and Koutsouphlakes. After finishing primary school in Frantato, he went to Athens to further his education. What exactly he studied is not clear, but it was there that he displayed a flair for writing. He returned to Icaria and soon became the leading Communist on the island. In 1934, in a clash with the gendarmes, he suffered a hand wound, but continued his Icarian mission until 1936 when the Metaxas government placed him in a concentration camp. He escaped during the Axis occupation of Greece, joining the Greek army in exile. He became an important member of the KKE cadre in the armed forces which were instrumental in forming the KSO *(Kommounistike Stratiotike Organosi)*. Under Salas' leadership, this association developed into the Antifascist Military Organization (ASO), an umbrella organization for Communists in the army. He edited its newspaper *Antifasistas*. In it, he took a strong anti-British position before the Greek Communists generally held this view. His editorials, which invariably criticized the government-in-exile, exerted enormous influence in the party and in the armed forces. In March 1944, Salas supported military officers who had recently formed the Political Committee of National Liberation (PEEA) in the Greek mountains. These left-wing officers demanded the formation of a new government led by PEEA, and on March 24th sparked a mutiny in the armed forces in the Middle East. Admiral Petros Voulgaris, commander-in-chief of the Greek navy, put down the rebels and restored order by the end of April.[8]

In May, George Papandreou, enjoying British support, became prime minister and invited politicians from all parties to meet in Lebanon. Moscow encouraged the KKE to accept five unspecified ministers out of twenty in the new government. Salas, out of touch with international developments and Moscow's wishes, was outraged at the compromise, and wrote a letter to one of the new Communist ministers criticizing KKE leadership for collaborating with the people who had exterminated colleagues in the April mutiny. After December 1944, when the British and KKE clashed in Athens, Salas' letter proved prophetic. By then the Communist hierarchy wished to absolve itself from its decision to cooperate with the British. Salas became an embarrassment to the leadership because he had predicted a confrontation with the British at the time the leadership was urging cooperation with British forces in Greece. Zachariadis who had been the prewar Secretary General of the KKE and had, after emerging from prison, regained control of the party in May 1945, considered Salas a rival. Zachariadis thus had him demoted to a low-ranking position. Several years later, Salas reemerged as the political advisor to the Samian guerrillas and recruited Icarians to Samos to fight against the govenrment.[9]

George Pasvanes, born in the first decade of the twentieth century, joined the party in the mid-1920s. In 1936, the Metaxas government incarcerated him in Akronaflia, a military prison, and then dispatched him to the small island of Aghios Evstratios. At the beginning of the war, he returned to Icaria and became a leader in the Icarian EAM. He supervised the people's court, which tried "collaborators" in the fall of 1944, and it was generally believed that no KKE decision was made in Icaria without his final approval. Right-wing forces assassinated him in Samos in the fall of 1944.[10]

Olga Malachias, born around 1912, fell under the political sway of her Communist father, and that of her friends Nikos Kastanias and Ioannis

Salas. She enrolled in a program for nurses in Athens, found a position in the hospital Evangelismos, and joined the Communist party. In 1936, Metaxas' gendarmes arrested her. They placed her in a room packed with other women. Many were Icarian women who worked as domestics in Kolonaki, the wealthy section of Athens. The gendarmes, hoping to break their spirits, doused the women periodically with ice water. Malachias refused to sign a declaration renouncing Communism, or to provide the authorities names of colleagues and information about the meetings she had attended. The government transported her to Anafi, and then through the influence of Dr. Malachias, a distant relative, transferred her to Aghios Kyrikos. In October, during the general disarray caused by the Italian invasion in western Greece, she slipped out of Icaria and returned to Athens. She volunteered to serve as a nurse on the Albanian front, but the government rejected her application because of her political beliefs. She returned to her old job in the hospital where she worked until the Italians arrested her and then sent her to a concentration camp in Larissa. There she became well-known for helping ill and wounded Greek prisoners. After the war, she continued her political activism in Athens where she stayed one step ahead of the police. In September 1947, she wrote from Athens to her parents, "please do not seek me in Athens. I must go where duty calls." Duty was in the Karpenisi, at that time the main Civil War theater. She became a guerrilla officer in the Democratic Army of Greece (the Communist armed force), fought in the mountains until 1949 when General Alexander Papagos cleared out the rebels from that area. She refused to join her comrades fleeing to friendly Communist countries, and was thus apprehended and executed in 1950.[11]

Salas, Pasvanes, Malachias, and other activists had already made converts in Icaria when the Metaxas (1936–1941) government exiled about one hundred and fifty political opponents to the island. As we have seen in the previous chapter, in 1939 a correspondent of the *New York Times* had come to Icaria to interview one of them. The dictator selected this backwater as an exile site to isolate political enemies who consisted mainly of Venizelites, Royalists, and Communists. Confinement was not unduly harsh, and these prisoners had contacts with natives. Icarians were generally impressed with these well-educated and reasonable people.[12]

At the beginning of the war, Icarian Communists, who had acquired organizational skills lacking in the general population, assumed the leadership of the Icarian EAM, the National Liberation Front. During the first grim years of the war, they instilled the people with a sense of hope in the future and thus won the confidence of the Icarians. By 1943, about eighty percent of the men on the island belonged to EAM, which included some conservatives. The choice was simple. The gendarmerie and the quisling government in Athens were indifferent to the problems of the people while EAM made efforts to help the Icarians through the years of crisis.[13]

Icarians who left the island and did not join EAM were nonetheless radicalized by their experiences outside the island, and when they began to trickle back after the war, they generally supported left-wing forces on the island. One man who had gone to Palestine where he enlisted in the pro-Communist ASO organization and read its newspaper edited by Salas, the *Antifasistas,* confessed: "I believed everything they told me and everything I read in their newspaper. But if my father had been an industrialist I would have told them to go to the devil." Another left Icaria half-starved, not having seen bread for a year. He joined the Greek army in exile where ASO officers spoke to him of a system that did not permit starvation or poverty, and a program of democratizing the army and purging Greece of fascist elements. The government incarcerated another Icarian, who had joined the army in Egypt, for supporting a Communist rally. While he was in prison, a Greek officer indoctrinated him with Communist ideology, and gave him copies of the *Antifasistas.* He became a staunch Communist clinging to the views he had been then exposed to for the rest of his life. By the later part of 1943, the Greek government began to weed out Communists from the officer ranks.[14]

For some Icarians the instructions they received from Communist cadres were the culmination of their educational experience. For the academic year of 1941/1942, there were only about sixty days of school. In March 1943, the Italians closed the high school, and the village schools faded away. As we have seen, the British reopened the schools in September 1943, but by then most of the teachers had departed to join the Greek army in the Middle East. During the war only a limited school schedule was maintained. For many Icarians, the only serious reading they ever undertook was under the supervision of the ASO.[15]

In September 1944, rebuilding the educational system in Icaria was not high on EAM's agenda. They wanted to seize political control. When it became evident that the Germans and their Blackshirt confederates would not return to Icaria, EAM took steps to right the wrongs of the capitalistic system. In the prewar era, there were complaints about the *archousa taxis* in Icaria, an upper class consisting of about one hundred people, mainly merchants and some men who had returned from America with money and lived better than the rest of the people. During the war, many merchants were regarded as black marketeers. The merchants of Icaria represented a substantial part of the 17% of the population who had the means to pay the Red Cross for food. They were not as visible as the Samian retailers and large landowners who in prewar years made up a middle class that enjoyed fine musical instruments, chocolates, and servants. Icarians, who were again making frequent trips to Samos, observed a reemerging Samian bourgeoisie. The KKE pamphlets that circulated in Icaria, promising a world without hunger and social inequalities, were in some measure directed at such a class.[16]

At the end of August 1944, EAM, in control of Icaria, decided to abolish these inequities by regulating merchants and ending the black market. Anyone selling goods required a permit from EAM. Unaware of the new order, a woman from a mountain village conveyed a load of walnuts on her shoulders to Aghios Kyrikos. When she failed to produce the required document, an EAM official hurled her produce into the sea. The committee ordered merchants to obtain licenses to sell certain goods at fixed prices and to fill the store shelves with merchandise. Not only did retailers lack goods, they also did not have a place to exhibit them. During the war, they had bartered away display cases and the wood from the shelves. Such conditions did not deter EAM from fining merchants for hoarding wares.[17]

EAM proceeded to reestablish a "People's Court" which was active in September 1943 after the Italian armistices but which went into abeyance with the arrival of the Germans in November 1943. Most of the proceedings were held in a building next to the main square in Aghios Kyrikos while people waited outside for the verdict to be announced. The court exacted fines in olive oil from some merchants who allegedly had overpriced their goods, and ordered that certain women who had consorted with Italians have their heads shaved in a public place. In Aghios Kyrikos, an EAM official, with a pistol strapped to his side, supervised these degrading sentences. Some of these compromised women had good connections with the KKE and went unpunished, but many of the others whose heads were shaved could not endure the public disgrace and abandoned Icaria to settle in Athens.[18]

The humiliation of female "collaborators" was not the major item on EAM's agenda. It was time to settle scores with their male counterparts. The "People's Court" tried a number of collaborators and fined some and exonerated others who had collaborated but were related to EAM officials. But the chief act of retribution was settled outside the "People's Court." On September 5, 1944, about twenty men, presenting themselves as members of ELAS, the military branch of EAM, marched from Raches to Aghios Kyrikos and arrested Dr. Amaxis. Friends had warned him that his enemies were about to take action, and he himself suspected as much since EAM had on two previous occasions, when they were briefly masters of the island, threatened his life and placed him under detention. He was armed and in the public square in Aghios Kyrikos when the contingent arrived. He decided not to resist and made a futile effort to hide his revolver in a café.[19]

These firebrands, who had seized control of EAM, led Dr. Amaxis to his home in Fleves. There they encountered a woman seeking aid for her young son recently injured by a mule. The mother panicked at the sight of arms. The men gave leave to Dr. Amaxis to treat the boy, his last patient, and informed him that they were taking him to Evdilos. There men allegedly waited with a vessel to convey him to the Middle East for a trial at EAM headquarters. Granting him time only to pack a small valise, they marched this sixty-two-year-old man through narrow footpaths. Despite being well nourished, he was not a nimble walker and before he reached Panaghia, the village above Aghios Kyrikos, he was exhausted. Outside the village the men encountered two boys with a mule, but were unable to borrow it. In Panagia, Dr. Amaxis rested at the café of an ardent Communist, who was troubled by the scene, and while offering him water, spoke a few encouraging words. The twenty men nudged the doctor back to his feet, and marched him further into the mountain. Drenched in sweat he was now carrying his suit jacket over his shoulder, but had not taken off his necktie. At Mavratos, despite its sobriquet "Little Stalingrad," he sought help in a café. By now he realized that there was no boat waiting for him on the northern coast to take him from the island. Here the armed men found a mule, conveyed the doctor to Fardi, a forested area. On the previous day, on their march to Aghios Kyrikos, they had stopped there to dig a grave. While the doctor was taking a rest a member of the escort shot him three times in the back of the head. Dr. Malachias, who feared that he was in danger, went into hiding for two days. People panicked in Aghios Kyrikos fearing that there would be no doctors to care for them. On September 7th, Dr. Malachias reappeared and was apprised of the location of the grave in Fardi. He took a mule and with an assistant dug up the remains of Dr. Amaxis and brought them back to Aghios Kyrikos for proper burial rites. The decomposition of the body prevented the service from taking place in a church, but a multitude of people in silent protest to the murder attended the service in the main square.[20]

Dr. Amaxis did not have a trial, and therefore never had an opportunity to answer the charges of conspiring with the enemy to harm Icarians. It was widely reported that he was a confidant of a certain Italian officer to whom he provided names of guerrillas and of people preparing to escape to Turkey. Later, he was often seen with German officers, particularly Captain Kostas. Houses of Communist families seemed to go up in flames soon after Italians or Germans talked with Dr. Amaxis.[21] His supporters argue that, if he collaborated with the enemy, he was not the only one. It was widely believed that a number of Icarians helped the enemy, and they went unpunished. The Italians obtained information from their girlfriends, and both Italians and Germans received intelligence from the gendarmes. There were about fifty Icarians who were in the service of the occupying force providing information, particularly about hidden food stocks, in return for supplies. Furthermore, in other parts of Greece the Germans and Italians combated guerrillas with machine guns, grenades, and flamethrowers destroying entire villages, and carrying out mass executions. In Icaria, there was not one execution, and the enemy burned only about ten houses. Furthermore, the occupying forces never effectively impeded people from escaping to Asia Minor. Dr Amaxis' defenders maintain that he used his influence to control the level of German-Italian reprisals, abhorred violence, and dispensed medicine acquired from the enemy to the people.[22]

Some Icarian Communists claimed that the order for the execution of Dr. Amaxis came from EAM headquarters in the Middle East while others maintained that the British enjoined the *andartes* to shoot him. Both explanations are very unlikely. Why would the EAM command center, which had not given any such orders for any other part of Greece, single out Dr. Amaxis? The British had no reason to eliminate the doctor. When Captain Pyke was in Icaria in the fall of 1943, he secured the release of Dr. Amaxis from a KKE jail, and years later vehemently denied that the British had any interest in harming the man, but, quite the contrary, considered him a source of information and an asset. The decision to eliminate Dr. Amaxis was most likely made by a radical element of the Icarian KKE in Aghios Kyrikos. News of the event inspired an Icarian Communist to compose a poem entitled *The Reckoning of the Traitors* writing "every fascist and informer must be slain and killed, and the righteous passion of the people fulfilled."[23]

Around the time of the shooting of Dr. Amaxis, it was inaccurately reported in Icaria that a Communist, who had been arrested by the Germans, presumably on the recommendation of Dr. Amaxis, and sent to Leros, had been shot. The report of the alleged execution galvanized the guerrillas into action. But there were more issues involved in eliminating Dr. Amaxis than collaborating with the enemy. Over several decades he had antagonized many people on the island. He allegedly would not provide medical treatment for everyone under any circumstance. During one of his early incarcerations one of his patients, a Communist, sought medical assistance but the doctor would only provide it if EAM released him from custody for several days and granted him certain privileges. On an other occasion he allegedly refused to offer medical assistance to a woman with a broken arm because she had Communist connections. Some people maintained that he did not observe the Hippocratic oath in dealing with female patients. There were rumors that in the 1920s, when Dr. Amaxis went to study medicine in Paris, he borrowed money from a lady who anticipated a marriage proposal. He neither repaid the money nor married the lady. Some people felt that he was aloof and unfriendly to certain people, and tended to flaunt his possessions, even food during the time of starvation. In Icaria, where most people were connected through blood ties, his behavior was considered irregular.[24]

Dr. Amaxis had a number of legal problems before the war. In the early decades of the century, Icarian doctors supplemented their income by practicing dentistry and dispensing medicine. By the 1930s, the Greek government barred such practices to doctors, but Dr. Amaxis illegally continued to provide these services. In the prewar era, there were only a limited number of people who had money to pay for health care, and competition among the few medical people on the island was fierce. His irregular practices brought him into legal difficulties with the dentists and the pharmacist of Aghios Kyrikos. His most serious legal issue, however, was related to his role in a scandal that took place around 1933. A young girl died while working for Dr. Amaxis. Rumors about foul play spread throughout the island. Authorities exhumed the remains of the girl and arranged for an autopsy that revealed that poison was the cause of her death. Accused of homicide, Dr. Amaxis hired a renowned lawyer who skillfully changed the venue of the trial to secure a favorable jury that acquitted him on grounds of insufficient evidence. During the trial, several witnesses including the local poet Georgiades, who was considered the best Icarian orator of his generation, defamed the doctor's character.

An OSS base in Turkey about 50 miles northwest of Izmir at Rhasadia. The code name was "Boston." Nicholas Kyrtatos, the OSS agent who had several missions in Icaria, is at the far left. At the far right is an Icarian who worked as the cook for the mission. (N. Kyrtatos' collection)

While distributing supplies and gathering information about German activities, Kyrtatos took this picture of two young girls outside of Evdilos in the fall of 1944. (N. Kyrtatos' collection)

Kyrtatos took this picture of two sisters outside of Evdilos sometime in the spring of 1944. One of the girls does not have shoes. (N. Kyrtatos' collection)

OSS agent Nicholas Kyrtatos,
taken about 1944. (N. Kyrtatos'
collection)

Nicholas Kyrtatos in a rowboat at OSS base "Boston,"
around 1944. (N. Kyrtatos' collection)

Evdilos, probably around 1943. It depicts the desolation of the war years and matches the Red Cross description of the village. (Ch. Malachias' collection)

Nicholas Kyrtatos in the "Aghia Triada," an OSS boat some-where off the coast of Turkey. John Caskey, his immediate superior in the OSS and a scholar of classical antiquity, christened the boat. This photo depicts Kyrtatos perhaps evacuating refugees to Turkey. (N. Kyrtatos' collection)

Olga Malachias (fifth from left) with the Democratic
Army of Greece. This photo was taken around 1947 in
Rendina, Karpenisi. (Spyros Meletzis' collection)

Olga Malachias (far right) somewhere around
Karpenisi 1947. (Olga Malachias' family collection)

Political prisoners, more accurately termed internal exiles, milling about Evdilos, around 1947. (Ch. Malachias' collection)

The Icarians had elected most of these men to local councils around 1960. The government had accused them of being members of the Communist party and placed them under detention. Here they have just returned from Samos, where they had stood trial. (Ch. Malachias' collection)

A group of prisoners around 1947. (Ch. Malachias' collection)

Miki Theodorakis (far right), who became a famous composer, with fellow prisoners in Evdilos around 1947. Note the fine attire of the prisoners. (Ch. Malachias' collection 1947)

Miki Theodorakis (left), probably in Vrakades around
1946. (Ch. Malachias' collection.)

Captain Megaloeconomus,
around 1954, taken shortly
before he conveyed the last
of the Icarian guerrillas to
Albania. (Ch. Malachias' collection)

Prisoners receiving their rations, around 1947. (Ch. Malachias' collection)

I. Melas, the historian of Icaria and former member of parliament, with two
friends in Raches, 1980. (author's collection)

Boy walking with a ram in inter-village lane
1980. (author's collection)

A gendarme supervising activities in the public square, Raches 1961 (author's collection)

Prosperous fish merchant in Aghios Kyrikos holding up lobsters for the Myconus market, taken around 1982. (author's collection)

At the far left, Dr. George Tsantiris, with constituents and patients, Raches 1961. (author's collection)

Theophanes Loukatsos, Mayor of Aghios Kyrikos, opening the Aegean
Symposium, 1980. (author's collection)

Member of parliament Zacharias Kratsas addressing Aegean symposium,
1980, at the Toula Hotel, which was reopened for this occasion. (author's
collection)

Icarian fisherman Armenistis, 1983. (author's collection)

Indeed Georgiades' philippic was so stirring that Icarians who heard it memorized parts of it and recited it years after the trial. It could not, however, be determined who administered poison to the girl. The truth of this matter will never be known, but in the minds of many Icarians Dr. Amaxis was guilty. He offended public sentiment when his supporters arranged a reception at the dock to celebrate his return as an innocent man.[25]

The decision to murder Dr. Amaxis was most likely made in a Star Chamber session of KKE officials in Aghios Kyrikos. These men summoned the executioners from the northern part of the island, people who were not known in Aghios Kyrikos. Dr. Amaxis did not have important friends, as other alleged collaborators did, in the decision-making clique of KKE. The execution, however one wishes to see it in moral terms, was a strategic mistake for the KKE.[26]

It was among the first acts of the *Laokratia,* and, in the minds of many, a harbinger of a reign of terror. In the words of a contemporary, the KKE had "picked up the island and was about to give it a good shake." The KKE had allegedly drafted a list of seventy people who were to be either executed or otherwise punished. The Icarian EAM, in a white paper published in 1948, denied the existence of such a proscription list and claimed that the elimination of Dr. Amaxis was the only act of vengeance EAM desired, and this execution settled matters with collaborators. The Communists, however, prepared such lists in other parts of Greece, and it is likely that one was drafted in Icaria. People lived in terror. Two weeks after the execution of Dr. Amaxis, a merchant from Aghios Kyrikos wrote to the EAM committee in control of Icaria. He suspected that there was a proscription list that included Dr. Malachias. The merchant argued that the doctor had not sold out to the Germans and Italians. He did not, however, defend the late Dr. Amaxis but noted that he was not one of the more sinister collaborators. There were men who had actually brought Italian and German soldiers to the homes of Icarians to either arrest men or confiscate olive oil. He named such men including a rival merchant. He concluded that if justice were not maintained, Icaria would descend into a civil war.[27]

By the end of September, the pro-monarchist *Ieros Lochos,* the Sacred Battalion, a commando unit composed of conservative officers and supported by the British, arrived from Samos where they had been engaged in disarming EAM and supporting conservative elements. The Sacred Battalion stopped in Icaria for only several days, and would return in March for a longer stay. It obliterated EAM's emblem in Aghios Kyrikos,

collected EAM's weapons, mainly malfunctioning rifles, and then sum-
moned EAM officials and anti-Communists for a meeting in Aghios
Kyrikos. The most prominent anti-Communist at the meeting was Dr.
Malachias. After the execution of Dr. Amaxis, officials of EAM were
openly charging that Dr. Malachias was a tool of the British, and that he
allegedly favored friends in distributing Red Cross supplies. Dr.
Malachias believed that he was in danger and saw the arrival of the Sacred
Battalion as an opportunity to protect himself and stabilize conditions in
Icaria. At the meeting, the doctor demanded the punishment of the men
who killed Amaxis, and the suppression of the Communists who were
allegedly displaying hammer-and-sickle emblems in various villages. The
commander of the battalion reinvested the gendarmes with full police
power and instructed the sublieutenant of the gendarmes, *anthepomerarchos,* to suppress the Communist movement and find the slayers of Dr.
Amaxis. The battalion departed, however, without leaving reinforcements. For the next three months, there was a political stalemate in Icaria.
The gendarmes were officially in control, but EAM retained the bulk of
its arms, and enjoyed the support of the majority of the people. Neither
side attempted to push matters. The sublieutenant, *anthepomerarchos,*
made a token effort to apprehend some of the twenty armed men who had
arrested Dr. Amaxis and particularly the gunman who had killed him. The
case was never solved. A year later, a detachment from the regular army
arrived to support the gendarmes. The chief army officer dismissed the
ineffective sublieutenant because he had not rooted out Communism and
solved the Amaxis case. The man immigrated to the Congo. For the KKE,
he emerged as a heroic figure who refused to persecute left-wing elements
on the island, but he in fact was forced out because of a sex scandal.[28]

During the fall and winter of 1944, agents representing the Office of
Strategic Services (OSS) helped stabilize the situation in Icaria. The OSS,
which in the postwar years would develop into the CIA, had bases in
Turkey. The OSS code name for the base in the small bay at Rhasadia,
fifty miles northwest of Izmir was "Boston." The station at Kusadasi was
known as "Key West." Among the Greek OSS agents at "Boston" was
Nikolaos Kyrtatos, a man who had learned English in Roberts College in
Turkey and taught English in Athens. He joined the Greek resistance and
on January 26, 1944, entered the service of the government of the United
States as a member of the OSS. In the summer of 1944, Kyrtatos was slipping in and out of Icaria, operating mainly in the Evdilos region, where he
collected information about enemy forces on the island, and on one occa-

sion nearly fell into the hands of a German military vessel. He saw more poverty and starvation in Icaria than he did in any other place in Greece during the war, but due to German patrols was unable to bring supplies. OSS officials, however, provided him with fifty gold sovereigns to be used for specific military objectives. Kyrtatos lent 34 of these gold sovereigns to the poorest Icarians with the understanding that they would reimburse him when contacts with America were resumed. Kyrtatos was never repaid, and experienced difficulties from OSS authorities who accused him of being too liberal with the money. When the Germans vacated Icaria at the end of August, he urged greater shipments of supplies, and on August 24, 1944, his superior, the eminent Classical scholar, John Langdon Caskey, wrote to him, "I want you to take part in the shipping of wheat and other supplies to Icaria and to be responsible for the distribution. *Aghia Tridas,* the caïque for Icaria was held up, as you know. She should be back soon from her latest mission. When she comes back I want her to carry out the Icarian plan." In September, as the Germans quit the Aegean, Kyrtatos stayed in the northern part of the island tallying German ships sailing past Icaria to Salonica. While he was collecting this information, messengers arrived from Aghios Kyrikos delivering letters from Dr. Malachias describing the growing Communist threat on the island, and the execution of Dr. Amaxis. Dr. Malachias thought that OSS intervention might eventually be needed and requested that Kyrtatos immediately remove two men from danger by taking them back to "Boston."[29]

At that time, reports were reaching the American embassy in Athens, which had been recently reestablished, that islands such as Mytilene had fallen to the Communists. The OSS dispatched the *Aghia Tridas* with canned goods and medicine and several armed men to Icaria. As Kyrtatos distributed the supplies, he informed EAM officials that he had forces at his disposal in Turkey and was ready to intervene should circumstances warrant. Kyrtatos believed that his allusion to troops had a sobering effect on the Communists, and may have been responsible for preventing several episodes from spiraling into violence. One such incident took place on an October evening in 1944. During an EAM festival in Aghios Kyrikos a notorious collaborator, a man who helped the Italians confiscate olive oil from the people and had provided the enemy with information about EAM but had been exonerated by the People's Court because of personal connections, lurked in a dark area outside the party allegedly collecting intelligence about Communist activities to be given either to the Ieros Lochos, on their return to Icaria, or to OSS agents in Evdilos. Moschos Mazares, who would become the foremost Icarian *andarte* (guerrilla), surprised this man, threw him to the ground and was about to slit his throat with a butcher's knife when the musician of the festival, a conservative, intervened. Mazares, who knew about the OSS presence on the island possibly reflected on the results of bloodshed, and decided not to kill the man. In early November, the Greek destroyer *Aetos* arrived in Aghios Kyrikos bringing British and American officials, perhaps more OSS agents, with the provisional governor of the Aegean islands. At a meeting in Aghios Kyrikos, Dr. Malachias again branded EAM as a terrorist organization "supporting Bolshevik policies."[30]

The governor of Samos, Icaria, and Fourni instructed the Icarians to elect a three-man committee that would assist him in administering the *nomos,* the district of Samos and Icaria. In the ensuing elections, Communists took all the seats. Pasvanes was the chief member of the council and in the first week of December 1944 led the Icarian delegates to Samos. As a youth in Icaria, Pasvanes was known as a dapper man, but he arrived in Samos in rags, a jacket without a sleeve, the proper attire to represent his proletariat constituents. At that time, Major Tzigantes, commander of the Sacred Battalion, was attempting to disarm the Samian EAM/ELAS, now a Communist guerrilla operation. British troops reinforcing the Sacred Battalion clashed with guerrillas.[31]

On December 3, 1944 Communists clashed with government forces in Athens. Violence reigned in Athens and as the conflict spread to other parts of Greece the British entered the fray. Dr. Malachias feared that armed conflict would break out in Icaria, and that his life and the stability of Icaria were in jeopardy. But it was not Dr. Malachias but rather Pasvanes who was in harm's way. On December 13th, British forces in Samos assisted the Sacred Battalion in apprehending a member of the KKE who was trying to foment trouble in Vathi. The man was detained in a British ship. Pasvanes endeavored to have the man released by going into the streets of Vathi, shouting out slogans about British supporting fascist gendarmes, and calling for a mass uprising. At that very moment, there were Samian Communist guerrillas fighting in the mountains, and it was possible that their supporters might take to arms in the city. That evening, as Pasvanes stepped out of his residence, a gunman assassinated him.[32]

The Samian police chief, a political conservative, thought it was imperative to solve the case. Otherwise the extremists would consider it open season on the Communists. The police chief feared that the KKE would retaliate and unleash an armed conflict. It was common knowledge that the assassin belonged to a faction of one hundred members from the wealthiest families in Samos, and the identity of these people was well-known. Without evidence, the police chief did not have the authority to interrogate anyone from this elite group. He, therefore, arrested all the Icarians in Samos and the following day circulated a rumor that the assassins, allegedly several Icarians who happened to be in Vathi, had confessed. Placing agents in various taverns to observe excessive merrymaking, he discovered that a gathering of men, suspected members of the Samian oligarchic club, was celebrating the apprehension of the "assassins" of Pasvanes. He arrested one of the revelers, a chauffeur, and pretending to know the details of the killing, obtained a confession with all the names, including that of the assassin, who was an army officer and the scion of an important Vathi family. He reported the results of his investigation to his superior who, instead of taking action, accused him of Communist leanings, had him imprisoned for ten days, and coerced him into dropping the matter.[33]

The slaying of Pasvanes was as vile as the murder of Dr. Amaxis and took place in the context of bitter fighting between the KKE and conservative forces throughout Greece in December 1944. Churchill and Eden flew to Athens on Christmas day and called for a conference chaired by Archbishop Damaskinos. The Communists, who were included in the discussions, rejected the terms. War broke out again, but the parties soon agreed to a truce on January 13, 1945, and a political settlement, the Varkiza agreement, was concluded a month later. The guerrillas yielded the bulk of their arms, and General Plastiras, serving as prime minister, made a number of concessions and reforms including amnesty for political crimes. Varkiza, however, was not a definitive settlement but rather a prelude to a greater conflict. Aris Velouchiotes, the ardent guerrilla chief, withdrew to the mountains in the spring of 1945 and resumed the struggle. In the meantime, right-wing extremists instituted a witch hunt against EAM/ELAS. Prominent guerrillas and particularly anyone who had been involved in the "People's Court" were subject to reprisals. Neither the government of Papandreou nor the British could restrain these acts of vengeance. Thus by 1946, gendarmes in Icaria were persecuting and arresting prominent members of the Icarian EAM. They were particularly interested in apprehending the men who were involved in the murder of Dr. Amaxis. Some Icarians began to flee to the mountains.[34]

The Civil War

A. Samos

From 1946 to 1955, there were four developments that took place simultaneously: the guerrilla operation in Samos, the emergence of guerrillas in Icaria, the creation of a political prisoner camp in Icaria, and the gendarmerie's despotic rule of Icaria. These topics must be treated separately at the expense of some overlapping.

When the civil war began in earnest, Zachariadis, the general secretary of the KKE, championed guerrilla combat in the Aegean islands, despite the fact that the government controlled the sea making it practically impossible to reinforce and supply the insurgents. Zachariadis was willing to sacrifice men on the islands to demonstrate that the guerrillas represented a genuine national movement not supported by foreign governments as were the rebels on the northern frontiers of Greece. Furthermore, fighting on the islands, mainly Crete, Euboea, and Samos, tied up government forces that would otherwise be deployed on the mainland. The Samian guerrillas fought aggressively, and to some degree cooperated with the Icarian guerrillas. Thus a review of the Samian conflict is appropriate.[35]

In September 1943, following Italy's surrender, the British registered four hundred and thirty Samian guerrillas. Only three hundred and fifty-three were armed, and many were in rags and without shoes. Expecting them to join anti-Fascist Italians to fight the Germans, the British provided them with food, clothing, and rifles. Since nearly a quarter came from Karlovassi, the most impoverished part of the island, some men apparently presented themselves as guerrillas only to obtain supplies.[36]

We have seen in the previous chapter the events that took place in August 1943. The Italians massacred people in the village of Kastanias, and later in Icaria betrayed a British captain to the Germans. Thus the Samian guerrillas were not inclined to integrate their forces with Italians. When the Germans assaulted Samos, in Operation Poseidon, the guerrillas fled to the hills, and many joined the approximately twelve thousand Samians who had deserted the island during the years 1941–1943 going to Asia Minor and then finding refuge in various parts of the Middle East. When the Germans began to withdraw from Samos in August 1944, the natives began to return, and among them were EAM veterans radicalized during the war and also during their sojourn in the Middle East. The core of the guerrillas came from these EAM veterans. There was a smaller guerrilla force unconnected with EAM, the "Independent Organization of Democratic Reserve Officers." This unit consisted mainly of Venizelites and conservatives who demobilized after the Germans had withdrawn and were openly opposed to those guerrillas who resisted the nomarch's (governor's) attempt to collect their arms in 1945.[37]

Initially, the Samian Communists operated in bands ranging from five to seven, occasionally ambushing gendarmes. The rebels did not tarry near any inhabited area for long because there was no village in Samos like Droutsoula in Icaria where everyone was a Communist. They did not enjoy great support from the inhabitants. The KKE delegations entered Samian villages endeavoring to recruit men, and collect supplies, but they feared informers who had connections to right-wing political elements in Vathi, Pythagorion, and Karlovassi. Such villagers frequently betrayed the guerrillas to the National Guard, a militia unit commanded by right-wing officers who supplemented and in some cases replaced the gendarmerie. Such treachery took place in Icaria but it was the exception to the rule. Icarian informers were responsible for the death of possibly four *andartes,* but in Samos the number was much greater.[38]

The Samian and Icarian guerrillas plied the channel between the islands mainly by rowboats, exchanging goods and services. They sent messages by fire signals from the peaks of their respective mountains. The Samian guerrillas had garnered money from a bank robbery in Karlovassi and shared the windfall with their Icarian associates.

In the winter of 1948, the Samian KKE communicated with their Icarian counterparts that a wounded Samian guerrilla with a gangrenous arm needed medical attention. OKNE, the KKE youth organization, met the man and his party at Fanari. They hid the boat in bushes, cleared the sand of footprints, placed this desperately ill man on a litter and set out into a moonless night filled with rain and fog to rendezvous with a doctor in a secluded mountain village. One of the stretcher-bearers fell off a footpath down a cliff to his death. In a house in Monokampi a doctor, a political prisoner who had slipped out of the village in which he was confined, amputated the arm without anesthetic. The amputee returned to Samos by the same route.[39]

In the spring of 1948, the Samian guerrillas seized a defensive position, and challenged the army to a pitched battle. The guerrillas won the encounter. The villagers in the vicinity of the battle serenaded the guerillas with "*zeto e andartes,*" (long live the guerilllas). Such a strategy, however, resulted in casualties, and the guerrillas were in need of reinforcements, and the only source was Icaria. The Samians appealed to their Icarian comrades, who had become too numerous to remain safely concealed. About fifty *andartes* volunteered to go to Samos. They gathered at Myliopon where the villagers, all supporters of the KKE, provided a midnight feast for the men who then slipped into Fanari under cover of darkness and commandeered two fishing boats. Although there was adequate space for the entire group, only fifteen embarked. One of the deserters claimed that when the captain discovered that the entire force destabilized the boat, he ordered about thirty-five to disembark. It is more likely that the bulk of the men panicked at the last minute. Dodging patrol boats, the fifteen arrived during a skirmish, but managed to steal into the foothills of Cerkis. The Samians, who were expecting a contingent of fifty, were disappointed and considered their Icarian colleagues as shirkers.[40]

Salas, the political commissar in Samos who knew these men and was related to some, was on the spot to welcome them. He doubtless had something to do with recruiting them, but at some point must have had misgivings about their participation in this suicidal mission. As we have seen, Salas had fallen from a position of eminence in the Communist party. In the rapidly changing political atmosphere of the postwar era, the KKE leadership dropped Salas from a place of importance to a lowly position, and may have tried to assassinate him before dispatching him to Samos. He allegedly opposed Zachariadis' monolithic concept of the party. While the ideological differences between the two men may not have been particularly sharp, their personalities were dissimilar. Salas was an open and charismatic man while Zachariadis had a brooding and paranoid nature. Contrary to the facts, Zachariadis apparently believed that Salas collaborated with the British in 1944. Many Communists later considered Salas, who provided the model for the idealistic, self-sacrificing Phanis in Tsirkas' *Drifting Cities,* an advocate of a democracy based on the principles that governed EAM/ELAS in 1941 and 1942. It may have been these qualities that aroused Zachariadis' envy. For whatever reasons, he instructed his underlings to set Salas, as David had Uriah, "in the forefront of the hottest battle that he may be smitten and die."[41]

The Samians introduced the Icarians to a new type of guerrilla warfare. As we have seen *roufianoi* (informers and traitors) were legion, and thus the guerillas had to keep their distance from villages and arrange the purchase of supplies with funds in part obtained from a bank robbery in Karlovassi. In September 1949, the guerrillas again changed tactics and openly challenged government forces outside Pythagorion where Salas, who had been in poor health since he arrived in Samos, was wounded. The gendarmes roped him to a tank, and he died as he was being dragged to Vathi where his mangled corpse was put on public display. Despite his brutal death, the KKE accused Salas of being a British agent. A medical student from Icaria, who had come from Athens and had been assigned to attend Salas, was shot in the back of the head while he was drinking at a public fountain. Other men were captured and executed in jail. The losses suffered by the Samian Communists in this battle, for all practical purposes, ended the guerrilla war on the island, but a remnant continued to fight. Realizing the desperate nature of their situation they made a pact to kill badly injured colleagues to prevent anyone from suffering the fate of Salas. In the summer of 1950, the National Guard trapped the remaining guerrillas in a remote part of the island killing most of them. Two Icarians committed suicide with grenades. Apparently, only three of the fifteen Icarian *andartes* who had come from Fanari in 1948 survived. Despite the contribution of Salas, Pasvanes, and the sacrifice of about twenty Icarians (not all Icarians in Samos had come in the 1948 expedition), the Samian Communists generally considered the Icarians as inadequate guerrillas. The Samians argued that since there was scarcely any fighting in Icaria the guerrillas who declined to come to Samos should have given their arms to their Samian colleagues who would have put them to better use.[42]

B. The Men of Atheras

There is some basis to the Samian position that they went to the mountains to fight while the Icarians were mainly fleeing authority. The idea of withdrawal was a strong theme in Icarian history. In earlier centuries, men had settled Icaria escaping the oppression of the Ottoman government. Retreating to the mountain was a passive act similar to the behavior of men in late Classical antiquity who fled military and tax obligations as the Roman Empire declined. In the eastern part of the Roman Empire the authorities referred to this illegal act as *anachoresis,* and Icarians in the mid-twentieth century were resorting to a type of *anachoresis*, withdrawing from a society that seemed to be breaking down. Many had simply avoided the draft, had been compromised by their association with EAM, or were persecuted for personal differences with gendarmes or neighbors.

In 1946, there were few Icarian guerrillas. Most of them did not wish to be conscripted into the Greek army. In the ensuing two years, the brutality of the local gendarmes drove more men to their ranks. One such case took place in the winter of 1946 when a group of young people gathered in Kerame to celebrate a birthday. The music from the gramophone attracted the attention of the gendarmes who considered it an illegal gathering because there were several Communists in attendance from other villages without travel permits. The gendarmes arrested and with their fists beat some of the guests. The host fled to the mountains joining the guerrillas. He was one of the fifteen who volunteered to fight in Samos where he was killed in 1949 in the battle outside Pythagorion.[43]

In 1947, a man chaperoning his cousin to a festival denied a gendarme permission to dance with her. The officer persecuted the man, driving him to the mountains where he was eventually killed. In another similar case, a man opposed the courtship of a female relative with a gendarme, and was killed while attempting to prevent a rendezvous. The government sentenced the gendarme to a four-year prison term. A similar incident took place on December 25, 1949, when a man was celebrating Christmas with friends in his home in Aghios Pantelemonos. A gendarme entered the home with a drawn gun, angry because the celebration had lasted too long and too many left-wingers were enjoying themselves. He threatened the group and accidentally shot the host who lost his leg as a result of the wound. The government sentenced the gendarme to two years in jail but released him after one.[44]

For some, it was better to join the *andartes* than to be exposed to such abuse. In the summer of 1947, one man who had witnessed the types of incidents described above fled to the mountains. He rarely saw his comrades or anyone else. He had recurrent nightmares about fighting his brother who was in the navy, theoretically his enemy. Once he spotted a shepherd, a man from his village, and approached him to inquire about his family, but the frightened man made gestures signifying he wanted no contacts. After a month of this life, he threw away his rifle, slipped back to his village, denied he had been a guerrilla, and after a brief incarceration, returned to normal life.[45]

Many men, such as the guerrilla noted above, stayed in the mountains for a very short period, and it is therefore difficult to establish the maximum number at any given time. The records of the gendarmes had guerrilla forces peaking at slightly fewer than two hundred in 1948, with 76 armed men and 120 unarmed. The armed men operated in four detachments of about twenty men each. These bands never joined forces, as they did in Samos, to challenge the gendarmes in a major battle. The men spent their idle hours with card games and books. Entertainment came in the form of practical jokes, and discussions. For some guerrillas it was this part of their life rather than the hardships and the constant fleeing that was most vivid in their memories. Guerrillas found shelter in caves but never stayed long in one place suspecting the authorities knew about some of their hideaways. Occasionally they came into villages and collected food and supplies from friends and relatives, some of whom were conservatives. The National Guard was aware of this support, and hated these sympathizers more than they did the guerrillas. The impoverished villagers, however, could not afford to provide all necessities such as medicine and shoes. Most guerrillas had some dollars in their possession, and some earned money making charcoal and selling it to their supporters in Karavostamos. In the beginning, many of the guerrillas turned over their money to the treasurer of the local KKE who kept it until they required funds. The treasurer also controlled the Icarian share of the money from the bank robbery in Karlovassi. As the needs of the guerrillas for medicine and clothing increased, requests for funds mushroomed and disputes developed within their ranks over money.[46]

A new sublieutenant of the gendarmes, *anthepomerarchos,* Em. Apostolatos, arrived in Icaria in 1946, replacing an ineffective but popular predecessor. Apostolatos had served in Evdilos in this capacity before the war and participated in Metaxas' purge of the KKE, and was very much disliked by Communists who half a century later compared his physical appearance to that of an ape. At the beginning of his second tour of duty in Icaria, he set out to apprehend the murderers of Dr. Amaxis and not to hunt guerrillas. The event that changed his policy and brought the government's focus onto the guerrillas came in May 1948, when Communists in Athens assassinated the Minister of Justice, Christos Ladas. The government responded by a crackdown on leftists throughout Greece, and charged Apostolatos to clear off out any irregular forces in Icaria. He decided to begin operations in the western part of the island and sweep through to the eastern tip. In June 1948, he dispatched troops to the vicinity of Xyloserti to wipe out a half dozen *andartes* hiding between Chalkia and Chrysostomos. Some of these men had become guerrillas when they refused to be demobilized from EAM and forced into the Greek army. Though most were armed, they had not committed any violent acts and they enjoyed the support of most of the people from Xyloserti. An informer among the guerrillas, allegedly in exchange for canned goods, apprised the gendarmes of their whereabouts when he was carrying out his assignment to bring water to his comrades. The National Guard trapped the group, and shot and killed one of them, Nestor Niapas, as he stepped out to give up. The gendarmes later claimed he threw a grenade, but those who were apprehended with him deny that he possessed explosives and maintained it was an outright execution. The soldiers mobilized several men from a nearby village to place the corpse in an improvised coffin, and take it to the house of Niapas' mother. The commandant, a fierce anti-Communist from the Peloponnese, taunted Niapas' mother, "Old lady, we present you with this dead beast. Skin it and make it a leather pouch for cheese." Whether the officer said this or anything comparable is uncertain, but practically everyone on the island believed such words were uttered.[47]

Apostolatos then focused his attention on the central mountain range near Droutsoulas, a village wedged in a mountainous terrain riddled with caves and encircled by forests and then only accessible by a winding footpath from Evdilos. In this village, which today still retains a strong proletarian look, there were fewer than one hundred inhabitants, all Communists, who paid scant heed to injunctions not to help the *andartes* and who indeed contributed generously to their upkeep. Because there was not one *roufianos,* informer, in the area, the gendarmes pitched their camp on the outskirts of the village and from there monitored the villagers requiring all Droutsoulites to carry identity cards even when working in their fields. Frustrated because they were unable to snare guerrillas picking up supplies hidden in the fields, or slipping into the village, the gendarmes ransacked homes, abused the people, and damaged personal property.[48]

In June, the gendarmes retired to Evdilos, and suddenly reappeared in July hoping to trap guerrillas resting in the village. Issuing directives through a bullhorn they ordered the villagers to stay in their houses. Not understanding the command, a man stepped from his home, and was shot dead.[49] Rather than recoil from their atrocity, the gendarmes increased the pressure on the Droutsoulites. The guerrillas, to spare the villagers further harassment, retreated to the area near Arethousa, another village entirely supportive of the guerrillas. Here the gendarmes were successful in trapping some rebels on the outskirts of the hamlet. In the exchange of gunfire, Moschos Mazares, a leader of the *andartes,* killed two gendarmes, one of whom had allegedly shot Niapas.[50]

The National Guard retreated to Evdilos, appealed to Athens for help, and suspended operations while it waited for reinforcements. A large contingent of well-equipped soldiers arrived in August. By then many of the guerrillas had slipped back to their old haunts near Droutsoula. The gendarmes again settled outside the village, harassing the Droutsoulites, and forcing about fifteen guerrillas to slip across the mountain to Mavratos, a village perched high over Aghios Kyrikos. On a misty November morning, while the *andartes* were resting in the outskirts of the village near the church Aghios Enoufrios, the gendarmes, apparently acting on information provided by an informer, suddenly appeared. Mazares' Italian weapon misfired, and the gendarmes slew him.[51]

Mazares had been forced into action by the rapidly fading mist, the cover the *andartes* needed to break out of the gendarmes' snare. An Icarian guerrilla and a man who had escaped from one of the prison quarters on the island to join the *andartes* were apprehended as they retreated toward a forested area. They were taken to Samos where they were tried and executed. In the meantime, the National Guard displayed the remains of Mazares in Aghios Kyrikos in the public square. Though spattered with blood, his clothing was in good condition, and he wore relatively new shoes, a detail that the impoverished people were quick to note. The priest of Aghios Kyrikos, Papas Kouloulias, was a man who had played a key role in expelling the Turks in 1912 and in the late 1930s was a strong supporter of the Metaxas regime. He refused to participate in the funeral and allegedly abused and anathematized the corpse. To most people, however, Mazares was a valiant soldier for the right cause, a *pallikari,* a hero. A priest from a neighboring village, though a political conservative, ran the risk of angering the gendarmes by providing Mazares with proper burial rites.[52] After this battle, the National Guard received offers to negotiate with the guerrillas. A meeting was arranged and when one of the guerrillas, George Beletakis, emerged into the view of the soldiers they shot him. His comrades escaped. The gendarmes beheaded Beletakis, perhaps while he was still alive. These gendarmes came from regions in Greece where severed heads rated bonuses, and so they conveyed the trophy to Aghios Kyrikos for their reward. Halting at Chrysostomos, they displayed the severed head in a tree outside a village café while allegedly guzzling ouzo. In what may well be an apocryphal story, one gendarme joked with the proprietress that she was welcome to take the head and make brain soup.[53]

One band of about fifteen guerrillas never retreated from the Droutsoula area for long. At the end of December, the National Guard

raided the region again. The guerrillas avoided clashes with the gendarmes realizing that the death of a gendarme resulted in repressive measures against villagers and political prisoners in Icaria. But in an exchange
of fire the guerrillas killed the gendarme who beheaded Beletakis. The
guerrillas viewed the slaying of this man as *theia dike,* divine justice.
Despite the anticlerical position of the early Icarian Communists, many
guerrillas remained religious. The National Guard, unable to uncover the
guerrillas, retaliated by burning two houses in Droutsoula and four in
Arethousa. A young mother from Arethousa, who had recently given birth,
was one of the villagers driven from their homes. She became ill and
died.[54]

In 1948, as we have seen, fifteen Icarian guerrillas volunteered to
fight in Samos, and in the same year two Icarian Communists, a veteran
political organizer and a priest, went to Chios with arms to endeavor to
foment resistance. They were apprehended and executed. These were
more or less the last aggressive acts of Icarian communists. The national
guards' pressure on the villagers supporting the guerrillas proved effective. By the beginning of 1949, as the civil war was ending in Greece,
there were probably fewer than thirty men left in the Icarian mountains.
One may wonder why the government invested so much in trying to exterminate a few inactive guerrillas who simply would have withered away if
neglected. Perhaps Athens feared that even a small number of men were
capable of exporting Communism to other islands. The main reason, however, in going to such expense to eradicate this group was that the existence of any band of guerrillas, however small, was an embarrassment to
the government.[55] In the summer of 1949, the government decided to liq-
uidate the remaining Icarian guerrillas, and from Samos dispatched the
military governor (*dioeketes*) and Major (*tagmatarches*) Euthymios
Kamoutses who was a specialist in antiguerrilla warfare. Amalgamating
his fifty soldiers with the gendarmes based there, Kamoutses destroyed
the guerrillas' supply network by a systematic evacuation of certain "red"
villages. The inhabitants of Droutsoula, Meliopon, Ploumari,
Monokampos, Neia, Mavratos, Oxe, and Kataphygion were ordered to
vacate their villages in 24 hours as the army and their informers looted
what the residents could not take with them. The informers were chiefly
interested in the goats and sheep that the owners were unable to round up
before they vacated their villages. Then the army proceeded to the mountain areas where they believed guerrillas were hiding and burned trees and
bushes. Now the guerrillas emerged only at night. They moved through a

burned out landscape, scrupulously placing their feet in tracks only trod by them avoiding the frequented footpaths. In pitch darkness, they knew every inch of the way. The incinerated *maquis* darkened their hands, faces, and clothes giving them the appearance of their ancestors, the Icarian *carbonieri.*[56]

While Kamoutses was making headway against the guerrillas, international events were going badly for the Greek Communists. The rebels in northern Greece had enjoyed the support of Albania, Bulgaria, and Yugoslavia. General Tito, the head of the Yugoslav government, broke with Stalin in 1948, and in 1949 closed his frontier with Greece. At the same time, General Alexander Papagos cleared the guerrillas out of the Peloponnese and then defeated them in northern Greece. The KKE central committee ceased to encourage Aegean guerrillas to continue the insurrection. In Samos the end came for the Communists in 1950, when the gendarmes wiped out their last stronghold. At this point, the secretary of the Icarian KKE advised his comrades to capitulate. He allegedly had negotiated terms for an amnesty. The bulk of the guerrillas, weary of the hopeless struggle, and believing that they would be given a pardon, surrendered but the government had given no assurances on this matter, and summarily dispatched them to Makronisos, a harsh concentration camp. Some accused the secretary of betraying the movement, maintaining he was never committed to Communism, had girlfriends in various villages, and put his personal pleasures above the interest of the party. Whatever this man's character may have been, his recommendation to yield to the government, at this point, was reasonable. But eight men remained in the mountains, and they would stay there for seven more years.[57]

C. Political Prisoners

The role of Icaria as a place of internal exile may have gone back to Byzantine times. In the 1920s, Venizelos dispatched a few royalist opponents to Icaria, and in the late 1930s, Metaxas, as we have seen, exiled about one hundred and fifty left-wing politicians and civil servants. In the summer of 1946, the Tsaldaris government announced that Icaria, Fourni, Makronisos, Yaros, Lemnos, and Aghios Efstratios were to serve as detention centers for Communists. The first detainees—these people were in fact prisoners, although internal exiles may be a more appropriate term, for they were not confined to quarters and at times enjoyed the right to move about the island—appeared in Icaria in the fall of 1946, and by

October there were 125, ranging from 16 to 65 years in age. With a government allocation of 10 drachmas, about 30 cents, a day, they lacked housing and the means to survive. Nevertheless, many lived with the civilian population under conditions significantly better than in other places of exile. The authorities recognizing that the bulk of the Icarians were sympathetic to Communism did not consider it necessary to segregate the detainees from the people by holding them in camps, but allowed them to live in various villages. Until 1948, the prisoners were free to move around the island. The Icarians, who were themselves utterly impoverished, began collecting food and clothing for the detainees, particularly woolen underwear much needed for the coming winter for men who lived in shacks and stables. In subsequent years as many as five thousand exiles were on Icaria at any one time and about thirty thousand eventually passed through the island.[58]

The islands designated for prisoners, excluding Icaria, were thinly inhabited with inadequate supplies of potable water, and even trees providing shade were in short supply. Indeed, the harsh environment and the absence of flora and fauna contributed to the deconstruction of the prisoners' personalities. The aim was to isolate them from the rest of the population, alter their political views, and persuade them too abjure Communism by signing a formal statement. Furthermore, conditions were often unhealthy. For instance, the government packed ten thousand exiles on Yaros, an island of seventeen square miles. Many of them died from dysentery.[59]

Although the Icarians welcomed these people, they resisted the conversion of Icaria into a penal colony, and were angered at the government for sending such a large number to the island. There were rumors that some politician in Athens had a grudge against the island, and other Icarians believed that the strong vote against King George in the referendum of September 1946 had provoked the government to deposit more exiles than it had originally intended. At any rate, the government's policy exposed the citizens to financial ruin and psychological pressures. Generally, prisoners were allowed to make their own arrangements for lodging, and one who secured a room in the home of an Icarian described the repeated suicide attempts of his host. His landlord felt as if he were a prisoner himself. An editorial of December 3, 1946, in *Nea Ikaria,* argued that the government aspired to punish Icaria by packing so many people into it, and criticized Athenian officials for not affording the prisoners adequate food and shelter, and appealed to "all democratic Icarians to save their comrades from starvation." Conditions were worse for the prisoners on Fourni, two small neighboring islands with little agricultural production. In September 1946, the people of Daphne, a village in the central part of the island, set an example by sending canned goods, fruit, vegetables, and ten thousand drachmas for their upkeep.[60]

In Icaria, the detainees were exclusively men; women prisoners only passed through to be relocated. Icaria was still a relatively unknown part of Greece, and the prisoners arrived with some trepidation, but quickly discovered that they were in what they considered to be "Free Greece." Many of the prisoners were highly educated. Exiled doctors assisted local medical people in difficult cases. Some men gave lessons in foreign languages and lectures on literature. Engineers, architects, and agricultural experts offered their services gratis or in exchange for food or shelter. On one occasion, the prisoners volunteered to help construct a road between Armenistis and Christos. The overwhelming majority of Icarians regarded the prisoners as dynamic and decent people, and fell under their intellectual sway.[61]

By 1949, the island's population, a combination of civilians and prisoners, was about 17,000. In every village, there were detainees often lodging free of charge, repairing and living in old houses, and even staying in barns. Although there were Icarians who collaborated with the gendarmes and denounced prisoners for petty infractions, these people were treated as pariahs and utterly despised, even by the right wing. The government's decision to continue to use Icaria as a locale for exiles without investing in the infrastructure of the island or in the upkeep of the prisoners completed the pauperization and radicalization of Icaria. On July 12, 1950, upon hearing that the government was planning on shipping more prisoners, the people demonstrated in Aghios Kyrikos, Evdilos, and Armenistis, threatening to oppose by force the arrival of more detainees. They maintained that the quartering of so many Communists had labeled Icaria the "Red Island," a reputation that dissuaded tourists from coming to the spas, and generally impeded the development of the island. The mayor of one of the villages complained to the commander of the National Guard that facilities to maintain such a multitude were inadequate. Either Athens should provide housing and more support for the prisoners or find other islands to relocate the excess. The commander replied that he could not allow these prisoners to go to civilized islands and corrupt innocent people. It was better that they should be placed among a populace already indoctrinated. Icarian officials took their case to the minister of internal security in Athens. The Athenian government was unconcerned that thousands of Communists were unsheltered in Icaria when nearly 7,000 patriotic families were living in sheds in the Athens-Piraeus area. The minister proposed that the Greek armed forces drop a bomb on Icaria extinguishing detainees and Icarians alike and thus delivering Greece from the cancer of Icaria.[62]

Among the most eminent detainees was General Stefanos Sarafis, not a Communist but head of wartime ELAS. He was held in Aghios Kyrikos in 1946 for a short period. When he left the island, he thanked the Icarians for their hospitality and praised them as "a gentle and civilized people who have made great sacrifices to support those who have rendered service to Greece." General Bakirtzis, an eminent EAM officer, was held in Icaria for a short period, and then transferred to Fourni where he reportedly committed suicide. Dimitris Partsalidis, general secretary of EAM and later prime minister of the provisional democratic government, and Andreas Tzimas, a high official in the KKE, were briefly in Icaria. The composer Mikis Theodorakis, then an unknown young man, spent the summer of 1947 in Icaria and returned for another stay in 1948. The government quickly learned to dispatch important Communists to more secure detention centers. Indeed, many of the internal exiles in Icaria were not Communists, but merely men with left-wing sympathies. It was generally from this non-Communist element that the government recruited spies to report on the detainees.[63]

Theodorakis and Sarafis, who came from middle-class families, did not depend on the government's allocation of ten drachmas a day, but paid for food and lodging from their own family funds. They lived comfortably and dressed not only more elegantly that the other prisoners but even better than the natives. Sarafis never appeared in public without a suit and tie. The class distinctions among the prisoners were somewhat reduced by the willingness of men to share what money and food they received from their families, but this was not necessarily done on a systematic basis. There were complaints about certain prisoners hoarding the contents of packages sent from home. Some of the higher-status prisoners maintained that they needed more nutrition because they were providing leadership and had to do make decisions for the group. But no one, thanks to the natives, suffered malnutrition. One man, who spent a year in Frantato with about one hundred other exiles, had lost four members of his family during the civil war and had no resources. Without the assistance of the *philotimoi* Icarians, as he called them, he would have perished. One would have expected the man to have said either "generous," or "hospitable." The concept of *philotimia* is roughly honor and self-respect and is the basic element in the relationship between a patron and a client. The prisoners in Icaria had given everything to a cause dear to the majority of Icarians. Most people on the island therefore assumed the role of patron and felt a sense of responsibility for the welfare of the prisoners.[64]

There were approximately one hundred and thirty prisoners who suffered from tuberculosis. The government quartered these men in the monastery of Mounte in Raches. Though many realized they were dying, they maintained an orderly life exchanging their labor according to their former occupations. One of the men stricken with tuberculosis happened to be a doctor and provided basic medical service with the help of Dr. Tsantiris, the doctor of Raches, who obtained medicine from the Red Cross. The poet Louis MacNeice, who lived near the monastery in the summer of 1951, received reports about gendarmes maltreating prisoners endeavoring to force them to sign a document renouncing Communism. As he walked in the vicinity of Mounte, he heard the tubercular coughs from the confined men, and was astonished that "they would not agree to sign for their freedom."[65]

There were three hundred national guardsmen on the island, the bulk in Aghios Kyrikos and Evdilos. In small villages, there were generally several gendarmes supervising as many as a hundred prisoners. During politically calm periods, prisoners free of tuberculosis had some liberties and acquired permits to visit neighboring villages. When the civil war intensified on the mainland, or when some incident took place on the island, the gendarmes confined prisoners to their quarters, and randomly abused them. In December 1947, two high-ranking EAM officials, Partsalidis and Tzimas, escaped from Icaria. The authorities imposed a total curfew on the island. In searching for the missing men, the gendarmes ransacked homes, and molested prisoners and Icarian citizens alike. The gendarmes began to regard people who lodged prisoners as confederates of the Communists. Spot inspections were means of depriving them of their civil liberties, and during one surprise search, the gendarmes mistook the landlord, a conservative, for his lodger, and began to maltreat him. They did not apologize for their behavior, for the master of the house had not reported that his two lodgers (a doctor and a lawyer), in violation of the permit law, were visiting a nearby village.[66]

There was a core group of brutal gendarmes. Mikis Theodorakis believed they were given positions of authority because they were psychopaths who were useful in maintaining an atmosphere of fear. Unlike the other gendarmes, they did not associate with the natives, and since they did not have contact with normal people their violent instincts were intensified. They allegedly battered Theodorakis for refusing to sign a *dilosis,* a statement renouncing communism, cast him into a sewer where he remained unconscious several hours, and labeled him a "homosexual Bulgarian bastard." On the other hand, one gendarme, who stayed on the island after these hard years and eventually married an Icarian woman, claimed that he never witnessed the type of cruelty described by Theodorakis. While the degree of gendarme violence is debatable, it cannot be denied that the gendarmes resorted to brutality. They openly beat someone for missing a roll call, slapped citizens who displayed sympathy for the detainees or were in violation of the curfew, and restricted people to their homes for smuggling food to prisoners on short rations. But the harm inflicted on the prisoners and Icarians was certainly more mental than physical. In public, the gendarmes routinely addressed sympathizers of the prisoners as "Bulgarians" and "whores." Each day a citizen had to walk a fine line between humanitarian support for the prisoners and insults from the gendarmes. It is difficult to assess the psychological damage suffered by people exposed to such pressure, but deep depression was not uncommon.[67]

The prisoners formed an organization, OSPE, and according to article ten of their charter, courting local women was prohibited. This restriction derived from the ascetic EAM/ELAS practices that forbade *andartes* from indulging in sex. Theodorakis recounts how he and his friends tried to adhere to article ten by averting their eyes from village girls who teased them: "Comrades, didn't they teach you to say hello in your part of Greece? Comrades, why do you not talk to us?" Despite article ten there were relationships between local women and detainees. On the other hand, some gendarmes carried out successful courtships, married local women, and stayed on the island.[68]

The Reign of the National Guard—Lourian Justice

In 1946, the government of Tsaldaris and Maximos mobilized the resources of the state to stop the rising tide of Communism. It was, in their words, a crusade of the *ethnikophrones* (nationalists) against the *anarchikoi* (anarchists). One weapon in the state's arsenal was the reconstituted educational system. School superintendents, *ephitheorites,* arrived in

Icaria to purge the school system of left-wing teachers. In the prewar days, teachers had instructed their charges that the Turks were not human because they were not baptized, but now because of the cordial relationship between the two countries they were obliged to inform their students that Turks were friends and allies. Furthermore, teachers had to explain why Orthodox Russians, Serbs, and Bulgarians, coreligionists but Communists, were now the enemy. Educators who did not toe the official line were dismissed. Furthermore, teachers who collected money for the support of the political prisoners, or took part in left-wing gatherings were either fined or dismissed.[69] In 1946 the gendarmes reopened the Dr. Amaxis case by arresting eight citizens, and restricting the movements of all the *aristeroi,* left-wing Icarians. A large segment of the population could not travel from one village to another without permits. In November 1946, a man in Aghios Polikarpos went to purchase cigarettes and encountered three gendarmes who, apparently drunk, were singing nationalistic songs. Assuming he was violating a curfew regulation, and without asking him questions, they beat him as they sang, "EAM, ELAS, EPON," in ridicule of the guerrillas' claim that they sang as they fought.[70]

In the summer of 1947, the Tsaldaris government imposed martial law and arrested prominent Communists in mainland Greece. They also drafted a list with the names of over one hundred Icarian citizens to be detained. In late July, the government telegraphed the names to Icaria. A postal worker, a Communist who had managed to hide his political ideology and thus retained his civil service post, saw the telegram, and relayed the information to KKE officials who then helped about a dozen men escape to the mountains. In the early hours of July 24th, gendarmes arrested about one hundred and twenty people. Many went to prison in pajamas and slippers. The authorities were furious that some eluded the dragnet, and discovering the source of the leak, incarcerated the postal worker, maltreated him, and dismissed him from his position. While this act deprived him of his coveted civil-service post, it launched his political career, and in 1964 provided him with enough prestige to gain the position of mayor of Aghios Kyrikos, the highest elective office on the island.[71]

One of the men arrested on July 24, 1947, provided a graphic account of his ordeal. Although his book is riddled with hyperbole, he had a novelist's eye for colorful details, and he captures the essence of the era. One hundred and twenty men were detained at the high school in Aghios Kyrikos for over a week. On August 3rd, the gendarmes packed them onto a boat sailing to Piraeus and then herded them into a prison so crowded that men could not sleep with legs extended. The toilet facilities were limited, and the prison was filthy. The Greek government was, as we have seen, a penurious jailer allocating daily no more than a piece of dried bread, and a bowl of lentils or beans. Adequate clothing, fresh bread, pencils, paper, and postage stamps were luxuries supplied by relatives, usually wives and mothers, who visited the prison. These women were often sexually harassed and occasionally violated by guards who promised to deliver their packages or give favorable treatment to their men on certain conditions. The prisoners were periodically beaten and constantly pressured to sign statements denouncing Communism. The process of making a *dilosis* included a statement in some public place before fellow villagers denouncing not only Communism but also old comrades. Several of these men who resisted signing such a document were transported to Makronisos. Only 65 kilometers from Athens, this uninhabited and isolated island afforded the government the opportunity to maltreat the prisoners far from the eyes of the world.[72]

The government had earlier in the year established anti-Communist local militia in Icaria as they had in other parts of Greece. Icarians served reluctantly and went through the motions of pursuing Communists and had nothing to do with the mass arrests. Nevertheless on August 6, 1947, the Athens daily *Kathemerine* reported that local committees responsible for security carried out the arrests.[73]

Quite to the contrary, the Icarians were horrified at the pogrom, especially when it was directed against many of the high-school students. The bulk of these young people were members of EPON, and they were among the most ardent Communists. They published a mimeographed newspaper, *Phlogia: Organo Epon,* that criticized the government's repressive measures, and appealed for funds to purchase food and clothing in Piraeus for the detainees in Icaria. Some of these supplies found their way to the guerrillas in the mountains. The gendarmes suspected, with some justification, that EPON was, in part, a guerrilla commissariat, and in the fall of 1948 vainly entreated the ministry of education to shut down the high school. By 1949, as the situation for the guerrillas became utterly hopeless, a group of students aspired to arrange an amnesty, and as part of such a strategy circulated a document calling for international peace in the name of the brotherhood of man. Regarding this as a Communist-inspired ploy, the gendarmes again moved to close the school. J. Tsarnas, the principal, who had liberal political views and enjoyed great prestige on the island, calmed down the students and placated the gendarmes.[74]

While the authorities did not dismantle EPON, they persecuted its members and interfered with its activities. On one occasion, EPON arranged a dance to raise money for the prisoners. In the course of the evening, a gendarme, a Don Juan type, crashed the gathering and procured a dance with an attractive girl. The Italian occupation had liberated women somewhat from the strict prewar sexual mores, and EPON females enjoyed a greater social freedom than Icarian women of the prewar period who rarely met males from outside the island. But consorting with gendarmes was as bad as fraternizing with Italians. A male associate discreetly reminded the young lady that the gathering was for the pleasure of EPON members. She turned down the gendarme's subsequent invitation, and other girls, taking her cue, rebuffed him as well. The jilted officer, who saw the rejections as a Communist scheme, stopped the dance, and in the ensuing weeks drove the proprietor of the establishment out of business with fines for alleged infractions of the code governing the operations of cafés.[75]

There were many unwritten rules governing the relationship between gendarmes and people. It was understood that no one would purchase Communist publications such as *Nea Ikaria* and *Rizospasti,* the official organ of the KKE, in the presence of a gendarme or read it in a public place. By allowing Communist newspapers to circulate until October 1947, the government claimed freedom of the press, learned the views of its adversaries, and kept track of Communists. But readers of the suspect publications slipped them under acceptable journals, or hid them in a shopping bag, and took them home for perusal. Natives observed these rules but some Icarian-Americans, who began to return in 1946, were unaware of the intricacies of life in postwar Icaria and transgressed the practice. On one occasion, a visitor from America acquired a *Rizospasti,* went to a café, and by spreading it open was inadvertently waving a battle flag. He was immediately invited to the gendarmerie for questioning. Politics in postwar Icaria were like sex in Victorian England. Everyone thought of it constantly, but no one dared to speak about it in public. Words such as "democracy," "Fascist", "peace" or "poverty" could not be uttered openly. Articulated too loudly (it was difficult for an Icarian to speak in hushed tones) or with too much emphasis, these terms might imply a criticism of the present government or of the National Guard. It was in the area of speech that the Icarians occasionally failed to maintain the unwritten code, for their natural volubility led to candid outbursts on political matters, and this was regarded as a challenge to the gendarmes.[76]

In the late 1940s, Icarian-Americans were wealthy by Icarian standards. Icarians believed that these *Broklides* (plutocrats from Brooklyn) had enough dollars in their pocket to buy an entire village, and in some cases this was more or less true. Americans often spent their money in a manner that was offensive even to the gendarmes. For instance, an American visiting his family in Mavratos, "Little Stalingrad," wished to celebrate his birthday on a large scale, and obtained permission from the head of the gendarmes. He invited all the villagers, who with the exception of one were Communists, hired two musicians, and provided food and drink to entertain the guests all night. In a society where abundance was rare, invitations to such affairs were highly prized. Two gendarmes supervising the event, who rejected an invitation to join the festivities because they did not wish to break bread with so many "Bulgarians" but who would have enjoyed the lavish food, became angry when the affair went into the morning hours. Why were these "gangsters" having such a great time while they were being deprived of sleep? They suddenly opened fire, shooting over the heads of the people, scattering the merrymakers, and ending festivities.[77]

Returning veterans from the Greek army also had difficulties adjusting to the new conditions. Their service in the government's army in northern Greece endowed them with anti-Communist credentials, but they were not prepared to repudiate Communist friends and relatives. In 1950, a veteran raised money to pay a fiddler to play at a festival in Tsouredo. Late in the evening, Peloponnesian gendarmes—most of the gendarmes in Icaria were from that region—supervising the festival ordered the fiddlers to play a tune from their region rather than the local "Bulgarian" music. When the veteran intervened, arguing that he was paying the fiddler to play "our tunes," the gendarme aimed his revolver at him. The next day, the veteran appeared in full uniform before the police chief and demanded an explanation. What right did gendarmes have to terrorize him in Icaria after he had spent the last two years fighting Communists in the mainland? In one of the few concessions ever made to the civilian population, the government transferred the trigger-happy officer.[78]

Army veterans who had fought on the side of the government forces during the civil war and conservatives generally enjoyed immunity from such abuses. A few misused their leverage with the authorities for personal gain, particularly to attain property in legal disputes, or to have an enemy sent to Makronisos. But most of these privileged people used their influence with the authorities to help fellow Icarians. For instance, a man in Raches angered the gendarmes for singing an allegedly revolutionary song at a festival. Dr. Tsanteris, a strong anti-Communist, went to the police station to save the man from physical abuse. Upon another occasion, the gendarmes had seized a man for some minor infraction in Chrysostomos and were cudgeling him in headquarters in Aghios Kyrikos. It so happened that the sister of the famous movie actor Lambros Konstantaras, who resided in Chrysostomos, was a friend of the victim. She wrote a letter to the police chief, who was a great fan of her brother. He immediately released the prisoner.[79]

In Raches, Louras, a *stathmarches,* a station chief of the gendarmes, is typical of the period. In his position, he exercised police power as well as some judicial functions prosecuting Communists and doing little else. On one occasion, a hotheaded young man assaulted an elderly farmer in a dispute over land. The younger man raced to Louras and lodged a complaint against the injured elder who, running at a slower pace, arrived after his assailant had given a distorted version of the affair. Louras, seeing that it was not a political matter, informed the winded elder that the case was closed, invoking the principle that he made up on the spot: "justice goes to the swiftest." On a number of occasions, he told men not to lodge complaints against younger, stronger men because "you may be assaulted." The people of Raches referred to this as the era of Lourian justice.[80]

Louras, however, was diligent in prosecuting left-wing Icarians. He built dossiers on all suspects, often based on hearsay or flimsy evidence. When he could produce no proof, he resorted to harassment. In one case, he prosecuted a suspected Communist for selling oranges without a license. The trial was in Samos, where the man pleaded innocent and noted in court that he was so impoverished he could not afford a kilo of sugar or a box of matches. Although he won his case, his six-day stay in Samos, which included the expense of maintaining a witness for the time of his trial, was very costly. In a similar case, Louras accused the president of the athletic association of Raches, a stanch Communist, of indoctrinating athletes with Communism, and dispatched the man to Aghios Kyrikos for a pretrial hearing. Because of a recent snowstorm, he was weather-bound in Aghios Kyrikos for ten days. The judge found no evidence against the athletic trainer but ruled that he could no longer serve as president of the athletic association. The cost of going to Aghios Kyrikos was in effect a heavy fine.[81]

The worst fear was to be sent to Makronisos, and the final determination for that punishment was made not by Louras but rather by an official in Evdilos. There, a certain gendarme, a man who had allegedly executed thirty-two prisoners in Gytheion, southern Greece, would conduct the interrogation. If the "Butcher of Gytheion" could not persuade the accused to reform his ways and renounce Communism and sign a *dilosis,* he dispatched them to Makronisos. Rumor had it that the ships transporting the prisoners were equipped with torture chambers.[82]

The government would not allow anyone with a tainted dossier to emigrate, sail as a merchant marine, obtain a civil-service job, or even find work as a laborer for certain large firms. The regime barred qualified children of parents besmirched with Communism from matriculating in universities, but it would withdraw all restrictions and disabilities against a Communist and his family if he renounced Communism. A man agreeing to such a *dilosis* in Athens or any urban area might slip into an anonymous life and elude disgrace. In Icaria, however, the community regarded a man who made a formal renunciation as false to himself, to his friends, and to the movement. Rather than commit a threefold perjury, most men preferred prison, and financial ruin. A man who endured the pressures applied by the state earned the rank of *kalos agonistes,* a man who had fought the good fight. Though this appellation resonated well in Icaria and gave the person a high though unofficial status, a *kalos agonistes* remained a second-class citizen in Greece.[83]

The Last of the Guerrillas

In May 1952, the *tagmatarches* (major) of the National Guard offered to the "peace-loving citizens of Icaria," a reward of fifteen million drachmas for the capture of any of the eight guerrillas still at large, and ten million for information leading to the arrest of any of them. A wanted poster proclaimed that these men had been carrying out criminal activity against the state since 1941.[84]

Nonetheless, the beleaguered guerrillas persisted for three more years, generally in groups of two or three. They all faced capital punishment. Occasionally, they found temporary asylum in the house of a friend. Gendarmes were constantly showing up in villages demanding to know the whereabouts of the "gangsters" or "Bulgarians." One old man received a slap when he replied that over the years he had seen Turks, Germans, and Italians in Icaria but never Bulgarians. In 1952, the

National Guard nearly apprehended two guerrillas in Kountoumas. They eluded capture, but the gendarmes imprisoned their hosts, increased surveillance of various villages, and raised the level of persecution on the inhabitants.[85]

For the sake of eight men, the entire island was held hostage. In the winter of 1955, the government dispatched a new major with broad powers to capture the eight, and to renew once again, apparently for the third time, the investigation into the Dr. Amaxis affair. The constitutional rights of the Icarians, already minimal, were suspended as the gendarmes raided houses without permits, and arrested people on suspicion of aiding guerrillas.

Everyone on the island was eager to have the eight depart, but not to be arrested. The Icarian KKE, finally taking measures to settle the matter, appealed to an experienced seaman, Captain Megaloeconomus, to remove the eight men. While he had left-wing sympathies, he was not at first an active Communist. Around 1950, the gendarmes had demanded that he sign a *dilosis*, and when he refused to do so, the government confiscated his boat. At this point, he became a committed Communist. The Icarian Communists offered this man a good seaman's position in Albania, and promised to support his wife and six children in Greece if he would obtain a boat in order to evacuate the guerrillas from Icaria. Borrowing money, he purchased a vessel, and on July 16, 1955, unbeknownst to his wife, sailed out of Evdilos with his 16-year-old daughter as a deckhand.[86]

That evening, near Cape Papas, eight men waited in a rowboat hidden in the shadow of the silhouetted mountains. Megaloeconomus came along the dark shore, picked up his passengers and then sailed into the open sea. The guerrillas looked back to see the sunset illuminate patches on the high ridges of the island near one of their old hideaways. Clutching Icarian earth in her hand, the captain's daughter strove to store in her memory the image of the island to which she might never return. They eventually reached Albania where the authorities confiscated the captain's boat, and assigned him to a factory job. The captain never came back to Greece, and now rests in a corner of some foreign field. The daughter found employment in a factory where her health was broken. She returned to Icaria many years later to write about her difficult sojourn and died prematurely. Some of these men raised families in strange lands and several returned as old men. The captain's wife did menial work while struggling to pay off her husband's debt for purchasing the boat. She raised five children without a drachma of aid from the KKE. Meanwhile the gendarmes harassed her for allegedly being involved in the scheme to evacuate the guerrillas.[87]

With the departure of the eight, the persecution of the general population diminished, and gradually people began to recover their constitutional rights. Icarian-Americans, who were trickling back to Icaria after the war, now came in greater numbers. People from distant places like New York, Chicago, Pittsburgh, and Detroit were the island's main postwar resources, and during these difficult times provided the foundation for the return to normal conditions.

1. Hammer and sickle: Lombardas, *Taragmena Chronia: Katoche, Ethnike Antistasi Emphylios Polemos sten Ikaria* (Athens, 1987), pp. 31–32. Plebiscite: *Nea Ikaria,* Sept. 14, 1946, notes that out of the 3003 voters, 1935 were against the king. According to Ch. Kochilas, interview, Raches, April 12, 2003, in Aghios Dimitrios, he received colored paper ballots, each color representing a different party, as he stepped into the polling station in Aghios Dimitrios. Kochilas cast his vote in a small one-room building without a curtain under the supervision of a gendarme who could determine his vote. Civil servants who voted against the king's return ran the risk of losing their jobs. Some conservative doctors expected their indigent patients who could not pay for medical services to vote for the king. Merchants who sold on credit applied pressure on certain impoverished customers during elections. Several Icarian doctors and merchants purchased steamer tickets for Icarians residing in Athens so they could return to Icaria to vote for the king. It is possible that these pressures gained an additional two percent in votes for the king. But Theophanes Loukatsos, a Communist and an elected official in Icaria in the 1970s, did not remember the government exerting any pressure; interview, Kountomas, Icaria, June 19, 2004. In 1964, Theologos Fakaros, a Communist, was elected *Proedros Kenotes* of Aghios Kyrikos. In the following year, that position was upgraded to mayor. In 1964, a leftist candidate Sakoutis in Aghios Polikarpos secured 67.8 percent of the vote. In Raches, H. Spanos, a leftist, received 48.1 percent while his two conservative opponents split the remaining 51.9 percent of the vote. For the election results, see *Demokratike Ephemeris tes Samou kai Ikarias,* Karlovassi, July 17, 1964, under the rubric *"Thriambos tes Aristeas."* In 1975, T. Loukatsos, a Communist, received 575 votes against his opponents 368, and in 1982, 546 while his two rivals secured 362 and 466. In 1982, I. Karimalis, openly running as the KKE candidate, received 52.9 percent in Aghios Polikarpos while M. Karaftis, KKE, collected 57.5 percent in Raches. For these results, see the Samian newspaper *Ellas,* March 31, 1975.

2. Nature of early KKE: G. D. Katsoulis, *Istoria tou Kommounistikou Kommatos Ellados* (Athens, 1976), 1–10. Rural poverty: Antonis Kalambogias, *Ikaria: O Kokkinos Vrachos* (Athens, 1975), pp. 4–5; Poverty

driving Asia Minor Greeks to communism: Bert Birtles, *Exiles in the Aegean: A Personal Narrative of Greek Politics and Travel* (London, 1938), p. 147. Makkas, *E Istoria tes Kommounistikes Organosis Ikarias* (Athens, 1989), pp. 19–21; A. Plakidas, *It Could Only Happen in America* (Athens, 1966), pp. 18–19. Byron Zachariadis, the pharmacist in Raches, came from Izmir, and was a schoolmate of Aristotle Onassis. In the 1960s he was the best-educated person in Raches, and being an Asia Minor Greek did not have that sense of inferiority Icarians generally felt. I did not know his political view. Kostas Kalokairinos, who came from Asia Minor with his widowed mother, was a resolute Communist. See his obituary in *Rizospsastis,* Jan. 4, 2001. Left-wing teachers: Interview, C. Makkas, Monasteri, Icaria, May 31, 2000. Fourni: an anonymous Fourniotes provides this analysis in *Nea Ikaria,* August 1, 1946.

3. Kapelas: Makkas, *Kommounistikes,* pp. 5, 24–25. Rasputins: Interview Andreas Katsas, San Francisco, September 2, 2000. Radical priests: Papas Xenakis was a Communist who was captured exporting arms to Chios. P. Argenti: *The Occupation of Chios by the Germans 1941–1944* (Cambridge, England 1966), p. 112. Also see Kalambogias, *Kokkinos Vrachos,* p. 58. Stephanos Glaros, the son of a priest, believed that the overwhelming majority of male children from Icarian clergymen were Communists. Stephanos was a staunch Communist in his youth and had been imprisoned in Makronisos. Interview with Glaros, Aghios Kyrikos, Icaria, May 22, 2000. Radicals and clergy: The three sons of Papas Xeros from Akamatra were involved in the terrorist activities of the group known as "November 17th." For the Xeros brothers, see chapter 7, note 38.

4. Public Works and Shipping: *Ikariake Enosis,* December 1926, March 1927. Vasilike Mavrikes in 1927 purchased 100 shares in Ikaros, a stock company for public works in Icaria. The certificate, which became worthless in the following year, is in possession of her daughter, S. Koutsounamendos, Aghios Kyrikos, Icaria.

5. Steamers and abusive gendarmes: *Ikariake Enosis,* May, June, July 1928. Taxation policy: A. Lykogiannis, "The Bank of Greece, 75 Years: 1928–2003," *Journal of Hellenic Diaspora* 21.1 (2003), 85.

6. S. Papagiannis, *Apo Evelpis Andartes: Anamensis enos Kommouniste Axiomatikou* (Athens, 1991), p. 6, was influenced by *Embros,* which circulated in his native village of Mavratos. Tsermingkas wrote editorials in *Ikariake Enosis,* June 1928. I obtained much information about Tsermingkas in an interview with his nephew, Michalis Betsakos, Aghios Kyrikos, Icaria, June 7, 2003.

7. Makkas, *Kommounistikes,* pp. 48–49. Nicholas Amaxis as God: Interview with one of his converts, E. Tsouris, May 21, 1994, Tsouredo, Icaria. Christos Mavrogeorgis was jailed in Samos in 1934 and again in Aghios

Kyrikos in 1936; see the biographical note on back of his *Odysseia: Stes Niotes ta Chronia se Xenes Patrides* (Athens? 2002). Revolt: *Laokratia,* Sept. 3, 1938.

8. Early years: Ch. Mavrogeorgis, *Ioannis Salas* (Athens, 1998), pp. 9–14. E. Spyropoulos, *The Greek Military (1909–1941) and the Greek Mutinies in the Middle East* (New York, 1993), pp. 190–193. For the PEEA, see Peter J. Stavrakis, *Moscow and Greek Communism, 1944–1949* (Ithaca, New York, 1989), pp. 17–19.

9. S. Tsirkas, *E Nechterida, Akyvernetes Politeies* (Athens, 2000), pp. 407–422, esp. pp. 418–419, bases Phanis on Salas. Professor Papatheodorou in an undated letter received by the author August 7, 2002, discusses the Salas/Phanis character. For more on Salas, see below n. 41.

10. S. Karimalis, *Antistasi sten Ikaria* (Athens, 1993), pp. 4–9, 85–87. Antonis Kalambogias, *Kokkinos Vrachos* (Athens, 1975), p. 9.

11. Influences on Olga Malachias, interview with Olga's sister, Eleni Malachias, Raches, May 30, 2003. The letters between Salas and Olga were destroyed during the civil war. There seems to have been some romantic bantering in the correspondence. Also see Eleni Malachias "Memorial essay in honor of O. Malachias," *Nea Ikaria,* Feb. 1992. In July 1947, Olga took her niece, who was ill, to a hospital. At that time, the police in Athens had picked up Olga's trail. Her niece never saw her again. Interview with the daughter of Eleni Malachias, Raches, Icaria, May 30, 2003. Letter of Olga to her parents from Athens, September 1947, in possession of Eleni Malachias. A fellow guerrilla, Diogennes Kermanides, in a letter to Olga's sister, August 8, 1991, described her last days. For the career of Nikos Kastanias, executed in 1949, see Strates Tzambes, *Sto Dromo tou Kathekontos: 80 Chronia tes Kommatikes Organoses Nautergaton tou KKE* (Athens, 2001), p. 345. The role of Communist women: Tassoula Vervenioti, "Left-Wing Women between Politics and Family," in *After the War Was Over: Reconstructing the Family, Nation, and State in Greece, 1943–1960,* ed. Mark Mazower, (Princeton, Oxford, 2000), p. 106.

12. For number of refugees, see, E. Kolodny, *La Population,* 2, 489.

13. Philippos Mavrogeorgis, who joined the party in the 1930s and served as a guerrilla in Icaria, knows of no record of Icarians enrolled in the party before the Second World War and would not even venture to estimate their number; telephone interview from Icaria, Nov. 7, 2002. EAM's Communist background has been well established; see J. C. Louis, *The Greek Communist Party, 1940–1944* (London, 1982), pp. 39–58. While in Icaria conservatives did not have an option, in Samos conservatives formed a resistance organization, the Independent Organization of Democratic Reserve Officers, led by Manolis Sophoulis and his wife Evangeleia. The

members of this organization were in contact with EAM, but did not join because of the overwhelming Communist orientation of the EAM group; e-mail message, Kostas Man. Sophoulis, Sept. 26, 2003, and unpublished diary of M. Sophoulis, May, 1943.

14. Communist officer in Egypt: A. Kastanias, interview Galiskari, June 6, 1984. Go to the devil: interview with Stephanos Glaros, Aghios Kyrikos, Icaria, May 22, 2000. No bread for a year: interview, G. Cavarlingos, Aghios Kyrikos, May 27, 2002. How an empty stomach led to Communism: Birtles, *Exiles in the Aegean,* p. 172. Weeding out: Pyke, interview, South Wirral, England, Oct. 16, 2000, reported that he provided a list of the foremost Icarian Communists to the British Intelligence. Pyke's report on the political conditions in Icaria is replete with information about the *andartes,* and his diary contains political and psychological profiles on some of them. Ch. Makkas, *Anamneses Mou Apo Tin Mesi Anatole (Ikaria,* 1981), pp. 19–20, bitterly complained that when he arrived in Palestine, he fully expected to be made an officer in the Greek army because of his university education, but Greek officials there, on the basis of information allegedly provided by Pyke, nullified his application. Makkas felt betrayed claiming that he had delivered Pyke from the grasp of the Germans in Icaria. Pyke vaguely recollected a man who accompanied him to Evdilos while he was fleeing the Germans in November 1943, but did not recall the situation as especially dangerous. He admitted that he probably did provide the secret service with the name of Makkas, as he did that of any well-known Icarian Communists. "That was part of my job"; interview with J. Pyke, Chester, South Wirral, England, September 21, 1998.

15. Ch. Sakellariou, *E Paidia Sten Antistasi* (Athens, 1984), pp. 100–102, cites remarks about the general rate of illiteracy and other educational problems discussed at conferences in 1944 in Evretania, Karditsa, and Trikkala. In those regions, students paid their teachers in kilos of grain; see pp. 83, 143. But EAMite teachers allegedly did not take food, and were only interested in indoctrinating their students. For instance, in Evretania, EAM taught their students that they were children of the people and that they should become the teachers of their parents; see Sakellariou, *Paidia,* pp. 80–81.

16. The EAM Communist pamphlet, Anonymous, *E Ikaria Sklavonetai* (New York, 1947), pp. 11–21, plays on the class theme. Noou, *Paidia,* pp. 53, 58, describes the Samian middle class that led a life quite distinct from anything in Icaria. G. Katsas, *Etan O Dromos Sostos: Apo Ikaria, Athena, Intzedena, Aigena* (Athens, 1992), p. 65, notes how class distinction became visible through nutrition and appearance. "Look how robust that man is. He must be wealthy."

17. Walnuts: Interview with Alice Koklanaris, Lincoln Park, Dec. 26, 1994.

18. Lombardas, *Taragmena Chronia*, pp. 27–28; Tsantes, *Katoches*, p. 58. Pistol-packing *Ethnikes Politophylakis:* Basilis Tsaganas, interview, Manolis Koklanaris, February 19, 1997, Wilmington, North Carolina, who viewed the revolver as unnecessary. G. Lombardas, *"Gia to EAM tes Ikarias,"* p. 50, notes the importance of Tsaganas' work.

19. Interview, John Tsantes, Aghios Kyrikos, June 22, 2003.

20. Boy injured by mule: Christos Moraitis, interview, Aghios Kyrikos, May 29, 2000. Makkas, *Kommounistikes,* p. 80, condemned the execution, but notes that the right wing was more vicious. According to Makkas, pp. 95–96, the gunman was not an Icarian but a refugee from Asia Minor who later, driven by guilt, became an alcoholic. By most accounts, the trigger-man was an Icarian, and people knew who committed the act. Makkas' dis-avowal of an Icarian connection emphasizes a general Icarian aversion to violence. Witness of escort: Manolis Koklanaris, who was a boy at the time on an errand with a mule, interview Manolis Koklanaris, Feb. 19, 1997, Wilmington, North Carolina. The widow of Dr. Amaxis remained on the "Red Island." She referred to the assassins as "anarchists," to distinguish them from decent Communists; interview, Vangelis Seringas, July 22, 2000, Lincoln Park, Michigan. Elias Zizes attended Amaxis' funeral; interview, Aghios Kyrikos, June 21, 2003. There were rumors that the killers buried a mortally wound but not dead Dr. Amaxis; interview, Ioannis Kyprios, Aghios Kyrikos, June 12, 2003. This was not the cause of death in Dr. Amaxis' death certificate, no. 20, volume 2, 1944, Aghios Kyrikos, which notes three bullets in the back of the head ended his life. For a brief description of the murder of Dr. Amaxis, see Dimitris Stephanadis, *Samaiache Echo,* Oct. 5, 2002.

21. Open contacts with the enemy: Karimalis, *Antistasi,* p. 9. Katsas, *Dromos Sostos,* p. 42, reports that Dr. Amaxis studied in Germany, and that the people were indifferent to the murder. Amaxis in fact received his medical training in France; interview with his niece Anna Rakatzis, Aghios Kyrikos, June 19, 2003. The number of people attending the Amaxis funeral suggests how shocked the Icarians were by the event. P. Lombardas, *Taragmena Chronia,* pp. 26–27, and G. Lombardas, *"Gia to EAM tes Ikarias," Ikariaka,* 42 (2001), p.44. argue that the evidence for Dr. Amaxis' collaboration with the Germans and Italians was overwhelming, and as a "quisling collabora-tor," he merited his fate. Tsantes, *Katoches,* pp. 92–93, who is sympathetic to left-wing views, condemns the execution.

22. Amaxis' patients defended his character and refuted charges of collabora-tion: interviews with Dimitri Phocianos, Aghios Kyrikos, May 24, 1994; Koula Tsalis, Kostia Koklanaris, Isabella Logizos, January 1, 1994, Lincoln Park, Michigan; Koula Poulos, April 27, 1997, Wilmington, North Carolina.

23. Philippos Mavrogeorgis, a member of EAM and a guerrilla in Icaria, maintains the order came from the British; interview, Athens, June 16, 1997. Pyke, *Diary,* Nov. 2, 1943, was concerned for the safety of Amaxis. Years later, Pyke maintained that it is absurd to claim that in 1944 EAM would be willing to do the bidding of the British. In 1944, the British had no forces in Icaria, and in the fall of 1943, when Pyke was there, he scarcely had any influence over EAM; interview, Chester, South Wirral, England, September 21, 1998. The type of men who took over EAM leadership were similar to those described by Thucydides (3. 82) during the civil war in Corcyra in the fifth century B.C. "Any idea of moderation was an attempt to disguise one's unmanly character; the ability to understand a question from all sides meant that one was totally unfitted for actions. Fanatical enthusiasm was the mark of a real man." Some compared Dr. Amaxis to Evangelos Drosos, a Samian whose collaboration with the enemy led to the death of many Samians, but Dr. Amaxis was not responsible for any deaths. For Drosos, see Kedros, *La Resistance,* p. 328. Makkas, *Kommounistikes,* p. 78, despised Dr. Amaxis and considers the execution a minor matter in the context of all the persecutions endured by the Communists, but nonetheless condemns it as a mistake. Poem composed Sept. 17, 1944: Mavrogeorgis, *Odysseia,* p. 55. Although the Icarian EAM did not receive orders from EAM central headquarters to execute Dr. Amaxis, they had the ability to communicate with the supreme command; see C. M. Woodhouse, *Apple of Discord* (London, 1948), pp. 146–147, who marveled at the capacity of EAM to stay in touch. "Communications in the mountains, by wireless, courier . . . have never been so good . . . their communications extend as far as Crete and Samos." Interview, Irene Tsouris, Tsouredo, May 21, 1994, who was imprisoned in Therma because her brother was a guerilla, and observed Dr. Amaxis provide medical treatment to German soldiers while ignoring injured or sick Icarian prisoners. She, in fact, was suffering from an injured arm and claimed that Dr. Amaxis took no interest in her problem.

24. The Germans allegedly executed a certain Theodorakis. The rumor proved false. Dr. Amaxis had quarreled with this man about a gun, and probably reported him to the Germans. Interview with A. Koutsounamendos, who witnessed the quarrel between the two men; interview, Aghios Kyrikos, May 17, 2001. Also see Tsantes, *Katoches,* pp. 92–93, and *Samaiache Echo,* Oct. 5, 2002. Shunned patients: Toula Moraitis, interview, July 23, 2000, Aghios Kyrikos. Broken arm: Irene Tsouris, interview, Tsouredo, May 21, 1994. Dr. Amaxis negotiates with EAM to treat patient; interview, Theophanes Loukatsos, Kountoumas, Icaria, June 17, 2004. Unpaid debts: B. Glaros, interview, Aghios Kyrikos, Icaria, May 30, 2000. Unfriendly behavior: N. Achidafty, interview, Lincoln Park, July 1, 1994. A. Koutsounamendos, however, saw Dr. Amaxis take petitions from people to plead with the Germans, and witnessed him turning one lady away saying "I am willing to help in other matters, but I cannot intervene to get back your lamb"; interview, Aghios Kyrikos, May 17, 2001.

25. Themistocles Speis knew people who furtively delivered medicine for Dr. Amaxis to various villages; see interview, Perdiki, Icaria, May 27, 2003. Alecos Xylas recalled the professional rivalry between one of the dentists in Aghios Kyrikos and Dr. Amaxis; interview, Aghios Kyrikos, June 24, 2003. Professional rivalries rather than politics explains a number of executions carried out by the Communist throughout Greece, see A. Gerolymatos, *Red Acropolis, Black Terror—the Greek Civil War and the Origins of Soviet-American Rivalry, 1943-1949* (New York, 2004), pp. 167-171. Violation of Hippocratic Oath: E. Zizes, interview, Aghios Kyrikos, June 27, 2003, and N. Batouyios, Aghios Kyrikos, June 19, 2003. Nick Diamantides, September 1, 1996, Washington, D.C. Diamantides, as a young man in Icaria, discussed the autopsy with Doctor A. Klikos who had completed it. The local poet: interview, Alecos Xylas, Aghios Kyrikos, Icaria, June 1, 2003.

26. Makkas, *Kommounistikes,* p. 79.

27. For more negative views of Dr. Amaxis, see Tsantes, Katoches, p. 59; Anonymous, *Sklavonetai,* pp. 36–38, and Karimalis, *Antistasi,* pp. 90–92. Pick up island: Panagiotis Kefalos, interview, May 27, 2000, Aghios Kyrikos. Letter denouncing alleged collaborators and defending Dr. Amaxis, Christos Kratsas to EAM Governing Committee, Sept. 18, 1944, in possession of Vasso Kratsas Spanos, Athens, Greece. For the existence of such Communist blacklists in other parts of Greece, see Mark Mazower, "Three Forms of Political Justice: Greece, 1944–1945," in *After The War Was Over,* pp. 27, 40, n. 7. In Icaria both sides seem to have kept a register of opponents. Pyke, interview, Chester, South Wirral, England, September 21, 2000, passed on the names of prominent Icarian Communists to the Secret Service.

28. Lombardas, *Taragmena Chronia,* pp. 31–32. For the importance of the Sacred Squadron in combating EAM, see John O. Iatrides, *Revolt in Athens: The Greek Communist "Second Round," 1944–1945* (Princeton, 1972) pp. 152–156. For Dr. Malachias on proscription list, Sifis Stenos, interview, May 20, 1996. According to Stenos, EAM attempted to arrest Dr. Malachias, but he simply refused to leave his house. Rumors about EAM's plans to harm Dr. Malachias may have prompted Christos Kratsas' letter in defense of the doctor to the EAM governing committee of Sept. 18, 1944. The hostility EAM harbored against Dr. Malachias may be detected in the 1948 EAM pamphlet, *E Ikaria Skalvonetai,* pp. 28–29, 45, which characterized Dr. Malachias as an enemy of EAM because he was reluctant to join EAM, had urged reconciliation with the Italians, lacked toughness and decisiveness, and had not lived up to the reputation he had acquired in playing a prominent role in expelling the Turks from Icaria in 1912. Dr. Malachias was aware of the threats to his life and wrote to both a British officer and an American OSS agent for help to curtail EAM activities in Icaria. There are letters of Malachias in both John Pyke's papers and Kyrtatos' papers.

For Kyrtatos, see note 29. An editorial writer in *Nea Ikaria,* October 5, 1946, comments on the irony of Dr. Malachias, a Venizelite, supporting the king in the referendum of September 1946. Anti-EAMikos: *Nea Ikaria,* Nov. 2, 1946. Lombardas, *Taragmena Chronia,* pp. 31–32, characterized Papaioannes as "a democrat" who stood up to Dr. Malachias and refused to persecute Communists and thus lost his job and went to Africa where he became a successful businessman. *Ikariake Phoné,* September 5, 1946, praises Papaioannes because he did not harass the population. He was not removed from office because he was too tolerant of left-wing elements. Elias Zizes, interviewed May 28, 2003, recounted the sex scandal he witnessed in 1946 that drove the officer from Icaria. In the 1970s, Zizes met the former police chief in the Congo where he observed him pursuing his alternate lifestyle with a freedom not permitted in Icaria.

29. OSS base Kusadasi: A. C. Brown, *The Last Hero: Wild Bill Donovan* (New York, 1982), p. 439. OSS Agent in Icaria: interview, with Nikolaos Kyrtatos, Kephisia, June 29, 30, 2003. A certificate of service, signed by William J. Donovan, dates Kyrtatos' tenure in the OSS from January 26, 1944, to January 2, 1945. Transfer of men: letter of Dr. Malachias to Kyrtatos, dated Sept. 9, 1944. At the same time, perhaps arranged through Dr. Malachias, Angelis Tsantes, one of the wealthiest men on the island, was removed to "Boston" where he found employment as a cook. Irene Tsantes Papanikolaou believed her father was on the list of seventy because he had made a fortune in America and returned around 1924 to live the good life in Icaria; interview, Aghios Kyrikos, June 21, 2003. Kyrtatos lost most of the letters from Dr. Malachias in a basement flood in his home in Cephisia. The IOUs, for which he was never reimbursed, survived the flood. OSS humanitarian aid was a general policy in the fall of 1944; see J. Iatrides, *Ambassador MacVeagh Reports: Greece, 1933–1947* (Princeton, 1980), pp. 608–609.

30. Alleged fall of Mytilene: Iatrides, *Ambassador,* p. 628. Malachias' appeal for help: interview with Nikolaos Kyrtatos, Cephisia, June 29, 30, 2003. Malachias' accusations: Lombardas, *Taragmena Chronia,* pp. 8, 29. Mazares and butcher knife: Interview with eyewitness, Ioannes Kyprios, May 23, 2002, Aghios Kyrikos, Icaria.

31. Lombardas, *Taragmena Chronia,* pp. 8–9. Carabott, "Samos," 300; Kedros, *La Resistance,* pp. 326–327. Pyke worked with Tzigantes on several operations and had a high regard for his leadership abilities; interview, South Wirral, England, Oct. 16, 2000. For the elections in Icaria, see Karimalis, *Antistasi,* pp. 59–61.

32. Tsantes, *Katoches,* pp. 91–92; Stephanos Karimalis, *Nea Ikaria,* June 1990, and Karimalis, *Antistasi,* pp. 86–87, who based his account on a witness to the murder, Manolis Moraitis; interview with Moraitis, May 12, 1996,

Panaghia, Icaria. In an interview with the author, Moraitis identified the triggerman as a certain Tsalapataves.

33. Ioannis Christodoulos' memoirs. I. Christodoulos, *"E Dolophonia tou Grammataia tou K. K. tou Nomou Samou,"* Ikariaka, 34 (1992), 168–169.

34. See Edgar O'Ballance, *The Greek Civil War, 1944–1949* (London and New York, 1966), pp. 97–110, for a military perspective. Also see Peter J. Stavrakis, *Moscow and Greek Communism, 1944–1949* (Ithaca, New York, 1989). For the right-wing witch hunt, see D. Eudes, *The Kapetanios Partisans and Civil War in Greece 1943–1949* (New York, 1972), pp. 252–256, and especially M. Mazower, "Three Forms of Political Justice in Greece, 1944–1945," in *After the War Was Over,* pp. 32–33.

35. N. Noou, a Communist who was a teenage witness to the Samian civil war; interview, Samos, Vathi, August 5, 1998, emphasized the futility of the fighting in Samos, and blamed Zachariadis and the monolithic structure of the party for the fiasco, but admitted that a partisan movement in the Aegean had propaganda value. George Baloukas, a Samian guerrilla leader (*tagmatarchis*), emphasized the propaganda benefit from having a government army tied down by a clearly indigenous movement in Samos; interview, Vathi, August 5, 1998. Stalin did not need to apologize about anything that was happening on the islands while he was embarrassed by developments in northern Greece where foreign aid from Communist powers reached the KKE; see the comments of John O. Iatrides and Nicholas Rizopoulos, "The International Dimension of the Greek Civil War," *World Policy Journal,* Spring 18, 1 (2000) 98. For the war on the islands, see Georgios Margarites, *Istoria tou Ellenikou Emphyliou Polemou, 1946–1949,* (Athens, 2001), I, 423–452.

36. Pyke Papers. *Secret Report* Sept. 24, 1943. K. Ptinis, *Chronia Katoches: Symvole sten Istoria tes Samou 1941–1944* (Samos, 1985), p. 259.

37. Refugees to Asia Minor: I. Saphiris, *O Agonas tou Demokratikou Stratou sti Samo* (Athens, 1987), pp. 13–14. Samians after Varkiza: Margarites, *Emphyliou Polemou 1946–1949,* I, 425–426. V. Tsantiris, *Nea Ikaria,* June 1991; Interview with the former Samian guerrilla, G. Baloukas, Aug. 6, 1998, Vathi, Samos.

38. Guerrillas came to the house of G. Mortos of Spatharei in 1946 to recruit him, but he joined the army. He thought about fifty percent of the village was Communist; see interview on the steamer *Samina* outside Karlovassi, August 6, 1998. Droutsoula: Makkas, *Kommounistike,* p. 55, *"oloi ekei etane dikoi mas."*

39. Kalambogias, *Kokkinos Vrachos,* pp. 24–35, described the amputation in detail. For general EAM communications: Woodhouse, *Apple,* pp. 146–147.

Communications between Samos and Icaria: I. Saphiris, *O Agonas,* pp. 189–190. G. Plakidas, the former mayor of Aghios Kyrikos, claimed that the amputee later betrayed his Icarian benefactors, and that Samians were not to be trusted; interview, Aghios Kyrikos, June 7, 2002. Samians felt the same way about Icarians; see the comments of Baloukas, below in note 40. The assertions of Plakidas and Baloukas may be understood in the context of a long-standing rivalry between Samos and Icaria that goes back, at least, to Bishop Georgirenes in the 17ᵗʰ century.

40. Destabilized the vessels: Christos Parianos, *O Demokratikos Stratos Ikarias* (Athens, 2002), pp. 27, 44–45. Second thoughts: The KKE chief in Raches recruited Manolis Stanzos, not a guerrilla, to join the group. A staunch Communist friend, S. Karimalis, who wrote *Antistasi Sten Ikaria,* told him not to go because it was certain death; interview with Manolis Stanzos, May 26, 2003, Raches. For a charitable Samian view of this event, see Ptinis, *Chronia,* p. 259. The Samian guerrilla Baloukas, interview, Vathi, August 6, 1998, argues that the men who did not go were cowards, and the Icarians generally lacked aggressive qualities.

41. Ch. Mavrogeorgis, *Salas,* p. 20. S. Tsirkas, *E Nechterida, Akyvernetes Politeies* (Athens, 2000), pp. 407–422, esp. pp. 418–419. J. Papatheodorou interviewed the author. S. Tsirkas, "Sto Ergastirio tou Mythostorigraphou," *Diavazo,* 171 (1983), 31, explains the connection between Phanis and Salas. Papatheodorou refers to the Salas/Phanis letter, *Nechterida,* pp. 413–414, analyzing events in the spring of 1943 and believes, as Tsirkas suggested, that it is somewhere in KKE archives. This letter, if published, will possibly enhance Phanis/Salas' prestige that was damaged by attacks from the "*anthropaki,*" P. Pankalos, a fictionalized party hack *Nechterida,* pp. 414–416. Professor Papatheodorou in an undated letter received by the author August 7, 2002, argues that certain left-wing elements were not disposed to recognize Salas as Phanis. Such a connection would put Zachariades in a bad light. Papatheodorou has not been able to verify the assassination attempt; see *Nechterida,* p. 414. S. Tsirkas, *Nechterida,* pp. 407–422, esp. pp. 418–419, establishes the ambiance of this period. M. Anagnostakes, *Poems, Postscriptum* (Athens, 1992), p. 10, doubtless was referring to Salas' demotion and humiliation after the war in the lines, "Not one of them knew who John Salas was." One may argue that Zachariadis actually believed victory was possible in Samos, and so did not purposefully send Salas on a suicide mission; see V. Bartziotas, *O Agonas tou Demokratikou Stratou Elladas* (Athens, 1982), p. 35.

42. N. Zachariadis, *Deka Chronia Palis* (Nicosia, 1950), pp. 9–10, accused Siantos, general secretary of the KKE and ELAS of British sympathies, and apparently tarred Salas with the same brush. At his death, Salas/Phanis had an expensive pair of shoes. His critics in the KKE asserted this was a sign of his corruption; see Tsirkas, *Nechterida,* pp. 412–413. In an interesting parallel, Moschos Mazares was wearing a good pair of shoes when he was

killed, but there was no criticism of him on this account; see below, note 53. On Zachariadis' totalitarian position, see V. Bartziotas, *Exenta Chronia Kommounistes* (Athens, 1986), p. 301. Zachariadis may have viewed the Aegean as a viable military option. The harsh imprisonment he endured in Corfu and Dachau perhaps rendered him incapable of making clear and rational decisions; see Bartziotas, *O Agonas tou Demokratikou Stratou Elladas* (Athens, 1982), p. 35. In retrospect, the rank and file recognized the blunder. Kalambogias, *Kokkinos Vrachos,* p. 41, concludes that the decision to fight in Samos was a strategic mistake, a view shared by the Samian guerrilla, G. Baloukas; interview, Vathi, Samos, August 6, 1998. While Baloukas was critical of Zachariadis' leadership, he was more derogatory of the Icarian contribution. "They only reacted when they were cornered. The Icarian guerrillas never offered one great battle." He regarded the Samian support of the Icarians as a bad investment. The money allotted to Icaria from the Karlovassi bank robbery could have been better used elsewhere. Indeed the Icarians may be less aggressive than their neighbors. Argenti, *Occupation of Chios,* p. 66, argues that the Communist movement in Chios did not produce excesses because the people were comparatively moderate, while the Mytileneans did commit savage acts because they incline toward violence. Medical student: S. Karoutsos. Hours before leaving Athens, a friend visited Karoutsos and was taken by his determination to fight in Samos; see interview, Nikos Karimalis, Aghios Kyrikos, May 26, 1999. Battle description: Baloukas, interview, Vathi, August 6, 1998. Two men blew themselves up with a grenade. Those not killed were sent off to Makronisos, and many of them were condemned to death. General Plastiras, as prime minister, commuted their sentence to life in prison, and in 1955 George Papandreou released them. Karimalis, *Antistasi,* pp. 128–130, 136, based on an interview with one of the survivors, V. Tsantiris. Grenade: Kalambogias, *Kokkinos Vrachos,* p. 57.

43. G. Margarites, *Emphyliou Polemou 1946–1949,* I, 432, correctly states that many of the Icarian guerrillas were deserters from the army. Also see Lombardas, *Taragmena Chronia,* pp. 33–35, 50–51.

44. For these incidents, see Papageorgakis, *Ikaria sten Thyella,* p. 17, and Lombardas, *Taragmena Chronia,* pp. 37–38, 55–56.

45. One month as unarmed guerrilla: interviews with George Karafas, Wilmington, North Carolina, April 27, 1997.

46. The official number of guerrillas is provided by Panagiotes Kourouvanes who served as a gendarme in Icaria from 1948 into the late 1950s. The number may be based on Pyke's report that EAM seized 76 rifles from the Italians in September 1943. Pyke added 10 rifles, but in November 1943 the Germans arrived and confiscated some of these arms. Kourouvanes is an avid reader of the memoirs of the Icarian guerrillas, and professes that the gendarmes really did not know, as the guerrillas suspected, their hideouts.

He settled on the island marrying the cousin of a prominent Communist. He felt, as did his fellow soldiers, that the villagers supporting the guerrillas were worse than the guerrillas; interview, Kountoumas, Icaria, May 29, 2003. Manolis Moraitis, who served as a guerrilla for 19 months, emphasized the policy of avoiding skirmishes. J. du Boulay, *Portrait of a Greek Mountain Village,* (Oxford, 1974), pp. 240–243, describes the normal rather than the Icarian pattern of guerrilla behavior when *andartes* raided villages, forced young people to join the movement, confiscated property, and killed people with whom they had private quarrels. Cheerful report of guerrilla life in Icaria: Philip Mavrogeorgis, interview, Athens, Greece, Feb. 29, 1998, who remained nearly two years in the mountains. S. Papagiannes, *Evelpis,* p. 101, describes jokes and light moments among the guerrillas he led in northern Greece. G. Baloukas, interview, Vathi, Samos, Aug. 6, 1998, recalled passing much of his time both in the mountain and in Makronisos in studies and contemplation. Kalambogias, *Kokkinos Vrachos,* pp. 100–101, whose book Baloukas dismissed as inaccurate, admits there were some positive activities, but pp. 93–94, maintains that the hardships were legion and diversions infrequent. Some supplies from Athens: Katsas, *Dromos Sostos,* p. 67. Financial problems and work: Parianos, *Demokratikos Stratos,* pp. 60–78. In the film of Leonidas Vardaros, *Ouli Emeis Efendis,* there is a particularly effective scene where a conservative hides a fugitive Communist in his cellar while fanatically denouncing Communists to a gendarme who is seeking the man. Papagiannis, *Evelpis,* p. 159, notes that while he was in prison he received money from the only conservative in Mavratos, his home village.

47. Lax policy till 1948: When his superiors sent Panagiotes Kourouvanes, a gendarme, to seek guerrillas, he found a comfortable place and waited out the day. His superior officer probably knew that his men were not making great efforts to locate guerrillas, but generally did not mind; interview, P. Kourouvanes, Icaria, May 29, 2003. The killing of Niapas: Katsas, *Dromos Sostos,* p. 58–59, and Karimalis, *Antistasi,* pp. 76–77, 109–110. The crude remark to Niapas' mother: Kalambogias, *Kokkinos Vrachos,* pp. 20–21, reported by Triandafilos Poulos, whose father, Stelios, was one of the men mobilized to convey the corpse to the mother's house and heard the gendarme say *"Grae pare to psopho sou."* [Old Lady, here's your dead beast.] Interview, Aghios Kyrikos, May 20, 2002. Deranged state of gendarmes: Mikis Theodorakis, *Archangellou,* II, 191. On May 24, 1995, I sat with a group at a café in Aghios Kyrikos and overheard Niapas' brother blame the death of his brother on "Fascist American imperialism." Canned goods: Panagiotis Kefalos, interview, Aghios Kyrikos, May 27, 2000. Draft dodgers and surrender of arms to guerrillas: interview, Andreas Katsas, San Francisco, September 2, 2000, and Papas Glaros; interview, Glaridos, May 25, 2002. Katsas claimed that in January 1947 the guerrillas came to his house and forced him to yield his father's First World War rifle and his own service revolver. For the assassination of Ladas and the ensuing Draconian measures, see reports in the *Manchester Guardian* and London *Times,* May

6, 1948. Following the assassination of Ladas,109 political prisoners were executed in the mainland; see Polymeris Voglis, "Between Negation and Self-Negation: Political Prisoners in Greece, 1945–1950," in Mark Mazower, ed. *After the War Was Over,* pp. 82–83. The name of the informer was well-known in Xyloserti. He died some years later as a result of a fall, and nearly everyone, radicals and conservatives alike, assumed that death was divine retribution for his act of treachery; interviews, Triandafilos Poulos, Aghios Kyrikos, May 20, 2002, and Panagiotis Kefalos, Aghios Kyrikos, May 27, 2000.

48. Karimalis, *Antistasi,* p. 150. On May 27, 2001, Peter Green and I visited Droutsoula, hoping to interview veteran guerrillas. There were laundries on clotheslines, a door in one of the houses was open, and people were possibly taking an afternoon siesta, but there was no sign of life. It seemed as if we had stepped into a time capsule and, as was their wont a half century before when strangers suddenly appeared, the Droutsoulites had fled to the surrounding maquis.

49. Papageorgakis, *Ikaria,* pp. 31–35. Man shot dead: Xeros.

50. Lombardas, *Taragmena Chronia,* p. 48. Interview with Philip Mavrogeorgis, Athens, February 29, 1998, who was a guerrilla for three and a half years and fought in the Droutsoula battle.

51. Lombardas, *Taragmena Chronia,* p. 49. Interview with a veteran of the battle, Manolis Moraitis, May 24, 1996, Kountoumas, Icaria. Katsas, *Dromos Sostos,* p. 60, notes a fifty percent failure of the old Italian rifles. Panagiotes Kourouvanes, a gendarme who did not fight in the battle, heard in headquarters from comrades who did that Moschos had provided cover for his fellow guerrillas, and when they reached a certain defensive position were supposed to do the same for him, but they panicked and continued to flee; interview, Kountoumas, Icaria, May 29, 2003.

52. Ioannis Kyprios, interview, Aghios Kyrikos, June 12, 2003, the grandson of Papas Stelios Kyprios who performed the funeral rites. The Kyprios family was politically conservative, but they all admired Mazares. Papas Kouloulias was a strong nationalist, and a conservative who did not collaborate with either the Italians or the Germans; see Lombardas, *Taragmena Chronia,* p, 46, and Karimalis, *Antistasi,* p. 134. This priest retained a prominent position on the island during the 1950s; see Leotsakos, *Ikaria,* p. 87. Lombardas, *Taragmena Chronia,* p. 58. Katsas, *Dromos Sostos,* p. 76, graphically describes the insults directed at the corpse that included kicks. Ioannis Kyprios, interview, Aghios Kyrikos, June 12, 2003, witnessed the priest's behavior. But Petros Lakios, who was mobilized to bury Moschos, saw Kouloulias merely walk past the corpse. He did, however, witness people taking Mazares' shoes, coat, and also a pack of aspirin from his shirt pocket. In 1946 in Icaria a good pair of shoes was a luxury. It is interesting

that Mazaraes' decent attire and fine shoes did not raise questions about his integrity as it did in the case of Salas/Phanis; see Tsirkas, *Nechterida*, pp. 412–413.

53. Negotiations: Parianos, *Demokratikos Stratos*, pp. 32–33. Lombardas, *Taragmena Chronia*, p. 58. The man who allegedly beheaded Beletakis was a specialist in torturing prisoners; see Katsas, *Dromos Sostos*, p. 70. Kalambogias, *Kokkinos Vrachos*, pp. 40–41, reports that the gendarme placed the head on a café table in Xyloserti and danced around the table. Papageorgakis, *Ikaria*, p. 46, notes that the beheading took place before Beletakis expired. A gendarme, who served in Icaria at the time, denies that his fellow gendarmes behaved in this way; interview with P. Kourouvanes, Kountoumas, Icaria, May 29, 2003. On November 11, 1947, the *Daily Mirror* published a photograph of gendarmes swinging the severed heads of women partisans by their ample hair as they rode into town to collect their bounty. It outraged western sentiments, but the Minister of Justice, Rendis, stated that it was a tradition he could not alter. Kalambogias, *Kokkinos Vrachos*, pp. 99–100, discusses the price range, informer's reward, and promotions for severed heads.

54. Lombardas, *Taragmena Chronia*, p. 55. Divine Punishment: Karimalis, *Antistasi*, p. 124, and pp. 130–131 where he attributes the death of a Samian informer, who had turned in an Icarian guerrilla fighting in Samos, to the same force. The Samian *roufianos* got drunk, fell off a mule, and died. On the other hand, Karimalis wonders why God did not similarly punish the many "Fascists" who prospered and enjoyed life after persecuting Communists. V. Tsantiris, one of the Icarian guerrillas who survived the war in Samos, became a successful baker in Raches and in the 1980s won the national lottery. His father maintained that it was God's way of repaying him for his suffering; interview with Tsantiris, June 12, 1982, Raches, Icaria. Policy of not killing gendarmes: Interview with a veteran Icarian guerrilla, Philip Mavrogeorgis, Athens, February 29, 1998.

55. Petros Andriotis and Papa Xenakis: Argenti: *Chios*, p. 112, and Kalambogias, *Kokkinos Vrachos*, p. 58.

56. Lombardas, *Taragmena Chronia*, pp. 59–62, notes, p. 61, that Kamoutses brought special incendiary devices to burn the landscape. Using paths: Interview with P. Mavrogeorgis, Athens, February 29, 1998, who boasted of a sixth sense when walking at night. He eventually surrendered and was sent to Makronisos. Some supplies from Athens: Katsas, *Dromos Sostos*, p. 67. Burned out landscape: A. Kalambogias, *Kokkinos Vrachos*, pp. 81–82. Furthermore, Kalambogias, pp. 85–86, writes, "wherever there were roads and lanes, there were traps."

57. Hopeless mission: Interview with Samian guerrilla, Baloukas, August, 6, 1998, Vathi, Samos. Kalambogias, *Kokkinos Vrachos*, p. 58. Veteran guer-

rillas like Baloukas were utterly disillusioned but not surprised by the 1998 publication of the diary of Bulgarian Communist leader Georgi Dimitrov, who reported that Stalin considered the Communist insurgency in Greece an act of folly; see *To Vima,* March 22, 1998.

58. Dr. X. Chochilas, "*E Ikaria os topos exoria,*" *Kathemerine,* 21, April, 1998, 13, provides a useful sketch of the period and repeats the local tradition that Byzantine authorities used Icaria as a place of exile. In 1923, Venizelos sent a political opponent, the royalist General Napoleon Sotilis who had won fame in the Balkan Wars, to Icaria. Sotilis was expecting harsh treatment from primitive people but was charmed by their moderate behavior; interview, Maria Sotilis, his daughter-in-law, Tzitzifies, Athens, May, 2001. First exiles: *Nea Ikaria,* Oct. 18, 1946. For Yaros see, E. Kolodny, *La Population* I, 447. Kalambogias, *Kokkinos Vrachos,* p. 90. Lombardas, *Taragmena Chronia,* pp. 53–54; Anonymous, *Sklavonetai,* p. 42, gives a figure of 15,000 exiles in 1947, but that figure doubled in the next three years. J. Melas, in a speech in parliament, noted a total of 30,000 "*ektopismenoi*"; see *Ikariake Phoné,* April 30, 1962. Mikis Theodorakis, in *Ikaria,* with A. Papalas and others (Athens, 2003), p. 10, contrasts the freedom he enjoyed in 1947 with the confined conditions of 1948.

59. The government managed to conceal the harsh treatment of prisoners at Makronisos until 1950, when a liberal member of parliament wrote an article in *Machi,* May 20, 1950, detailing the cold-blooded terrorism. G. Malachias was held in Yaros, but along with other Icarians was shielded from the worst conditions because the chief military officer on the island was an Icarian; interview, Aghios Kyrikos, June 27, 2003. The *dilosis* procedure: Polymeris Voglis, "Between Negation and Self-Negation: Political Prisoners in Greece, 1945–1950, in Mark Mazower, ed. *After the War Was Over,* pp. 76–77.

60. Suicide: unpublished memoirs of Vangelis Athanassopoulos, in the personal archives of Christos Malachias, Raches, Icaria. Daphne: *Nea Ikaria,* Dec. 3, 1946.

61. Makkas, *Kommounistikou,* p. 92, apparently knew Sarafis, who told him that "progressive Greece will always remember Icaria for what it did for the prisoners." Free Greece and Lessons: M. Theodorakis, *Archangellou,* II, 105. 118–119. Sarafis' speech: *Nea Ikaria,* Dec. 3, 1946. In April 1949, the government sent 1,200 women exiles to Icaria before dispatching them to the deserted Trikeri; see Tassoula Vervenioti, "Left-Wing Women between Politics and Family," in *After the War Was Over,* p. 115. Daphne: *Nea Ikaria,* ibid. The same issue of *Nea Ikaria* published a list of the 28 officers confined to Icaria. A doctor who was being held in Icaria assisted Dr. Malachias in a difficult delivery; interview, J. Lygizos, Lincoln Park, July 27, 2000. Former detainees taking the cure at Therma: Makkas, *Kommounistike,* p. 92. Road: unpublished memoirs of Vangelis

Athanassopoulos, in the personal archives of Christos Malachias, Raches, Icaria.

62. Demonstration: *Kathemirine,* 12 July 1959. S. Leotsakos, *Ikaria to Nesi Tou Radiou* (Athens, 1953), pp. 104–105, a journalist and convalescent at Therma, describes his uneasiness about the political prisoners on Icaria. He feared the island would develop into such a large penal colony that it would extinguish the *loutropolis.* He witnessed the uprising, and concluded that it was so intense that one could no longer call Icaria the "Red Island." Leotsakos' book with its unfortunate title, *The Island of Radioactivity,* seems to have been subsidized by Icarians promoting the thermal baths, and he intentionally misinterpreted the demonstration as being against Communists rather than against the government for pitting the bulk of the burden of maintaining so many prisoners on the Icarians. The book, while deficient in analysis of any kind, is valuable in capturing the mood of the 1950s. The people of the island of Anafi, like the Icarians, felt that the government intentionally kept their island undeveloped to have a place for prisoners; see Margaret E. Kenna, *The Social Organization of Exile: Greek Political Detainees in the 1930's* (Amsterdam, 2001), pp. 72–73. Unsheltered families in Athens-Piraeus: D. Pentzopoulos, *The Balkan Exchange of Minorities and its Impact upon Greece* (Paris and the Hague, 1962), p. 227. Bomb: Makkas, *Kommounistike,* p. 56. Also *Nea Ikaria,* Dec. 3, 1946. The figures for 1949 are unavailable but in 1950 5,782 registered to use the baths. In 1952, as times became normal, 9,816 registered for the baths; see *Panikariake Adelfotes Athenas Yearbook,* 1957.

63. Sarafis' statement: *Nea Ikaria,* Dec. 3, 1946. For Sarafis also see, Anonymous, *Sklavonetai,* p. 146. Katsas, *Dromos Sostos,* pp. 51–53. M. Woodhouse, *The Struggle for Greece, 1941–1949* (London 1976), pp. 215–216, notes that Icaria was for the more moderate members of the KKE while aggressive Communists were sent to Makronisos, Leros, Partheni, and Lakki. For informers planted among the prisoners, see Papageorgakis, *Ikaria sten Thyella,* pp. pp. 23–24. The exiles maintained records in code about their fellow inmates, and probably knew who these informers were. There is a document in code from the exiles in the archives of Christos Malachias, Raches, which seems to deal with this issue.

64. Sarafis: *Nea Ikaria,* Dec. 3, 1946. Themistocles Speis saw Sarafis in Aghios Kyrikos always impeccably dressed and revered by the people; interview, Perdiki, Icaria, June 3, 2000. M. Theodorakis, *Archangellou,* II, 189–191. Kalambogias, *Kokkinos Vrachos,* p. 13, discussed the charity of the locals to the prisoners, a point stressed in the unpublished memoirs of Vangelis Athanassopoulos, a detainee from 1947–1948. His memoirs are in the personal archives of Christos Malachias, Raches, Icaria. According to Papageorgakis, *Ikaria,* pp. 22–28, a conservative provided furnished quarters to refugees rent-free because he was afraid the gendarmes would commandeer it. Having his house occupied by people persecuting the villagers

would have made him a social pariah. *Philotimoi:* Interview with Christos Stasinopoulos, Athens, June 16, 1997. Stasinopoulos, who later wrote a multivolume study on Kolokotronis, was eventually sent to Makronisos where he was maltreated. The comments of Kenna, *Social Organization,* p. 56, about certain inequities in food distribution is relevant to Icaria, though it refers to Anafi in the pre–World War II period. *Philotimia:* E. Friedl, *Vassilika: A Village in Modern Greece* (New York, 1962), pp. 34–35, and J. K, Campbell, "Traditional Values and Continuities in Greek Society," in Richard Clogg, ed., *Greece in the 1980's* (London and New York, 1983), pp. 184–204.

65. Conditions: Dr. Dimitris Dalianes, *1948–1949, To Sanatorio Exoriston tes Ikarias* (Larissa, 1999), pp. 30–38, 48. Dalianes later became a specialist in tuberculosis. Beatings: J. Skarpetis, interviewed by Dalianes, pp. 77–78. L. MacNeice, "The Island" in *Ten Burnt Offerings* (London, 1951), p. 59. Jon Stallworthy, *Louis MacNeice* (London, 1995), p. 383, notes that Kevin Andrews, who passed through Raches before MacNeice came, told MacNeice about the sanatorium. Apparently, Andrews returned to Icaria after MacNeice's sojourn there, and stayed a year.

66. Escapees: C. M. Woodhouse, *Struggle,* pp. 215–216. For their importance, see D. Eudes, *The Kapetanios,* p. 314; Stavrakis, *Moscow,* pp. 36–38. Abuse of citizens: Karimalis, *Antistasi,* p. 150. Ioannis Kyprios, as the electrician who maintained the power for the gendarmes, was one of the few men allowed to leave his house; interview, Aghios Kyrikos, June 24, 2003. Nikos Kyprios witnessed the cudgeling of the men, which took place in his father's house; interview, July 24, 1994, Lincoln Park.

67. Papageorgakis, *Ikaria,* pp. 23–25. Kalambogias, *Kokkinos Vrachos,* pp. 10–11, notes that the gendarmes generally referred to the Icarians as "Bulgarians." Number of gendarmes: Anonymous, *Sklavonetai,* p. 46. Theodorakis, *Archangellou,* II, 189–191. The English version Theodorakis, *Journals of Resistance,* translated by G. Webb (London 1973), pp. 14–15, is condensed and leaves out important material. Panagiotes Kourouvanes, who arrived in Icaria to serve as a gendarme in 1948, repudiates Theodorakis' account of gendarme ruthlessness; interview with Kourouvanes in Kountoumas, Icaria, May 29, 2003. The former gendarme clearly has a good reputation on the island, for he became a merchant in Aghios Kyrikos and enjoyed the patronage of left-wing clientele. L. Kefalos knew a brutal gendarme in Aghios Kyrikos and met him twenty-five years later in New York. He was surprised at the man's mild manners; interview, Port Jefferson, New York, March, 12, 1982. Inadequate records of treatment of prisoners: Kalambogias, *Kokkinos Vrachos,* p. 14. Other prisoners in Icaria fled to the mountains because they were anticipating a transfer to Makronisos, Karimalis, *Antistasi,* p. 145. Mental depression: unpublished memoirs of Vangelis Athanassopoulos, in the personal archives of Christos Malachias, Raches, Icaria. Stephanos Glaros was kept in a cellar for sever-

al days in the police station in Icaria and then sent to Makronisos. "I was never really abused, though in Makronisos guards slapped me on several occasions," interview, Aghios Kyrikos, June 24, 2003. For the weeding out process and treatment in Makronisos, see Eudes, *Kapetanios,* pp. 357–358, and Major General Stefanos Sarafis, trans. Sylvia Moody, *ELAS: Greek Resistance Army* (London, 1960), pp. lxxiv–lxxv, and Katsas, *Dromos Sostos,* p. 58.

68. Article Ten OSPE: Katsas, *Dromos Sostos,* pp. 53–54. M. Theodorakis, *Archangellou,* p. 105. Theodorakis spoke of the extremely friendly girls when he returned to Icaria and gave a lecture, August 23, 1997, in Raches.

69. *Nea Ikaria,* August 1, 1946, notes an *epitheortes,* school inspector, harassing schoolteachers in Aghios Polikarpos and Aghios Dimitris. An anonymous editorial writer of *Nea Ikaria,* Nov. 2, 1946, accused Dr. Malachias of falsely charging the schoolteacher in Oxe of collecting money for the detainees and participating in Communist festivals.

70. Beating: *Nea Ikaria,* Jan. 1, 1947. Anonymous, *Sklavonetai,* p. 42. Lombardas, *Taragmena Chronia,* pp. 33–35, 50–51.

71. Karimalis, *Antistasi,* pp. 115–116. Kalambogias, *Kokkinos Vrachos,* p. 10. Postal worker: Theologos Fakaros, Mayor of Aghios Kyrikos, 1963–1967. For the 1964 election, see n. 1. During his incarceration, the gendarmes inflicted such physical abuse on him that he contemplated suicide; interview with Theologos Fakaros, Xyloserti, July 29, 1974. A nephew of Fakaros took food to his uncle, but was driven away by the jailers with insults, "Get out of here, you damn Bulgarian"; interview, Vangelis Seringas, Lincoln Park, Michigan, July 12, 2003.

72. The Communists in Icaria were so opposed to British policy in Greece that they demonized the British and apparently invented incidents to prove their point. Lombardas, *Taragmena Chronia,* pp. 36–37, writes that while he and his fellow prisoners were being transferred in Piraeus from one point to another, he was mocked by a drunken Englishman with a Greek prostitute. We may take this, as we should much of what he writes, with a grain of salt. The account of C. Makkas is also unreliable on this matter. In his *Anamneses Mou apo ten Mesi Anatole* (Ikaria, 1981), pp. 18–30, he maintains that the British ran the refugee camps in Palestine on a preferential system, taking better care of the Greek upper class; that the Secret Service took pictures of Greek girls as they were being deloused and scrubbed in showers to be sold on the pornography market; that Greek children died at the hands of incompetent British doctors; that the camp hospital was for every sick person a certain grave, and that British soldiers ran a large-scale burglary operation stealing from Greeks. For more anti-British sentiment, see Anonymous, *Sklavonetai,* pp. 46–50. Smothers and McNeil, *Report on Greece,* p. 47, discuss the March 1947 arrest of six hundred Communists in

Athens followed by more arrests in July leading to imprisonment without trial. Also see *Atheras* June–July 1994. Seclusion in Makronisos, see S. Abdoulou, *To Phainomeno Makronesos* (Athens, 1998), pp. 37–39.

73. Katsas, *Dromos Sostos,* p. 117, and p. 63. For "*symmorites,*" gangsters. Also see, Lombardas, *Taragmena Chronia,* pp. 59–62.

74. Katsas, *Dromos Sostos,* p. 60. Tsarnas: Karimalis, *Antistasi,* pp. 194–195. For the purge of Communist teachers under Metaxas, see Sakellariou, *Paidia,* pp. 20–25.

75. Dance: Papageorgakis, *Ikaria,* pp. 29–30. Dancing with a gendarme at an EPON gathering was a very serious breach of etiquette even in an organization where women enjoyed equality with men and were very loyal to male members; see Tassoula Vervenioti, "Left-Wing Women between Politics and Family," in *After the War Was Over,* p. 106. For the ELAS/EAM position on sex, see Mazower, *Hitler's Greece,* pp. 3–5. Sexual mores in Icaria from 1941 to 1943 had been rather altered by the Italians. Indeed, it was widely rumored that the Italians were more sophisticated in lovemaking, and that it was difficult for Icarians to satisfy their women after the Italians left; interview, Argyri Koutsounamendos, Aghios Kyrikos, May 27, 2002, and Elias Zises, Aghios Kyrikos, June 14, 2003. But by 1946 sexual mores had returned to prewar standards. Unlike the *andartisa* who served in the mountains, young women of EPON retained traditional views about sex and did not condone sexual relations with their male colleagues. But in the late 1940s and early 1950s, virginity was expected from marriageable women. For Icarian endogamy, see the remarks of Georgirenes, *Nicaria,* p. 66, "of all the isles of the archipelago this only admits of no mixture with strangers in marriage." At this time, 98 percent of the marriages were endogamous. Most matches were made in the same village, though many families negotiated marriages between couples in neighboring villages such as Tsouredo and Kountoumas, or Xyloserti and Chrysostomos.

76. Eudes, *Kapetanios,* p. 245, discusses problems of selling lawful Communist newspapers in 1945. Smothers and McNeil, *Report on the Greeks,* pp. 48, 126–127, analyze the issue of the so-called free press, but do not address the way the government harassed these papers. The government imposed 36 fines on *Nea Ikaria* in its first year of publication; see ibid., Dec. 3, 1946. Leftist newspapers were finally suppressed in 1947. Anonymous, *Sklavonetai,* pp. 50–51, complains that *Nea Ikaria* was repressed without any explanation, forcing the KKE to publish it illegally. Interview with Lilos Pardos, Tsourdeos, June 7, 1996, who witnessed in 1946 the harassment of an American for reading the *Rizospasti* in a public place. Karimalis, *Antistasi,* pp. 201–202, while in Samos trying to resolve his legal problem, was harassed by two gendarmes, dressed in civilian clothing, for reading a Communist paper in a café.

77. Wealthy Americans: In the unpublished memoirs of Vangelis Athanassopoulos, who was a political prisoner in Icaria in 1947 and 1948, there is a reference to a man who returned from America with allegedly enough money to purchase the entire village of Aghios Polikarpos. Athanassopoulos' memoirs are in the personal archives of Christos Malachias, Raches, Icaria. Celebration: Interview with Nikos Kyprios, July 24, 1994, Lincoln Park, Michigan, who was one of the musicians at the affair. People who exercise autocratic power do not like to be indisposed while inferiors are enjoying themselves, see Tacitus, *Histories* 3. 38–39, and the comments of P. V. Jones, "Critical Appreciations: Tacitus, *Histories* 3. 38.9," *Greece and Rome,* 24, no. 1 (1978), 70–72.

78. Interview with the returning veteran Nick Skaros, Philadelphia, and September 1, 1994. Interview with Lilos Pardos, Tsouredo, June 7, 1996, and Pantelis Tsouris, Tsouredo, May 27, 1994.

79. A man allegedly got away with robbery and rape because he was a royalist; see *Nea Ikaria,* Sept. 14, 1946. Tsantiris: Interview, Mitsos Gerales, Raches, June 1, 1996. There were a number of left-wing songs that praised Zachariadis, the leader of the Communist Party, or alluded to the National Guard as creatures of darkness; see Katas, *Dromos Sostos,* p. 52. The sister of the famous actor Konstantaras: see *Eleutheroudakis' Enkyklopaidikon Lexicon,* s.v. "Konstantaras"; she lived in Chrysostomos during the war years; see Katsas, *Dromos Sostos,* p. 77. S. Glaros, interview, Aghios Kyrikos, Icaria, June 22, 2003, claimed that a neighbor with whom he had a dispute about property informed the gendarmes that he was a Communist. As a result, Glaros was dispatched to Markonisos.

80. Lourian justice, interview with George Stenos, Raches, May 23, 1994. *"protos erthes, dikio echeis."*

81. Karimalis, *Antistasi,* pp. 198–200. Lilos Pardos, a Communist who ran a fish market in Aghios Kyrikos, incurred so many fines for petty infractions that he was forced to sell his business to Antonis Pirovolikos, who became through the same establishment one of the wealthiest men on the island; interview, Lilos Pardos, Tsouredo, May 6, 1993, and Antonis Pirovolikos, May 27, 2000, Aghios Kyrikos. For such harassment also see Lombardas, *Taragmena Chronia,* p. 55, and Stephanos Karimalis, "E Ikaria sten Antistasi," Nea Ikaria, Oct. 1992, and Kalambogias, *Kokkinos Vrachos,* pp. 104–105. Itchy trigger finger: Captain John Pyke, *secret report to SCAO, Samos,* on St. [Ag.] Kyrikos, September 27, 1943.

82. Karimalis, *Antistasi,* pp. 199–200. Lombardas, *Taragmena Chronia,* pp. 56–58; Stephanos Karimalis, *"E Ikaria sten Antistasi," Nea Ikaria,* Oct. 1992, and Kalambogias, *Kokkinos Vrachos,* pp. 105–106.

83. Brutal guard: Karimalis, *Antistasi,* pp. 156–157. Perhaps this man had been trained by the Germans. Fleischer, *Kreuzschatten,* I, 459, discusses the German deployment of brutal and violent men to fight the Communists. Many of these later became members of the National Guard. Also see K. Andrews, *The Flight of Ikaros,* p. 159. *Kalos agonistes:* Kalambogias, *Kokkinos Vrachos,* p. 157, Torture on boat: K. Karapatake, *Ikariaka,* 84 (1987). The *dilosis* procedure: Polymeris Voglis, "Between Negation and Self-Negation: Political Prisoners in Greece, 1945–1950," in Mark Mazower, ed. *After the War Was Over,* pp. 76–77. In some cases those who signed a declaration of renunciation experienced mental breakdowns; see Tassoula Vervenioti, "Left-Wing Women between Politics and Family," in *After the War Was Over,* p. 109. For daughter not becoming nurse, other disabilities, and refusal to sign a *dilosis,* see Karimalis, *Antistasi,* pp. 160–162.

84. Wanted poster of May 22, 1952, in the collection of Christos Malachias. See Kalambogias, *Kokkinos Vrachos,* pp. 106–113 who was one of the eight.

85. Papageorgakis, *Ikaria,* pp. 79–80; Lombardas, *Taragmena Chronia,* pp. 68–72; Kalambogias, *Kokkinos Vrachos,* pp. 106–107. For the sea captain, Kostas Megaloeconomos, see Makkas, *Kommounistike,* pp. 93–95. There is an excellent dramatization of this event in the 1997 film *Ouli Emeis Efendi,* directed by Leonidas Vardaros.

86. Government confiscation of boats: Ch. Plakidas, *Nea Ikaria,* July, 17, 1946. Megaloeconomos: interview with the widow of Kostas Megaloeconomos, Irene Stamoulou, Evdilos, May 27, 2002, and telephone interview, July 1, 2002.

87. Makkas, *Kommounistike,* pp. 93–95. Lombardas, *Taragmena Chronia,* pp. 70–72. For the view of a fading Icaria, see Omorphoula Megaloekonomou-Moschovake, *Matia Poiematia* (Ikaria, 2000), pp. 17, 21, 26. Interview with the widow of Kostas Megaloeconomos and mother of Omorphoula, Irene Stamoulou, Evdilos, May 27, 2002, and telephone interview July 1, 2002. "I went to them (the Communists) once and told them, "My husband took your damn *andartes;* how about giving me a sack of flour?" But they claimed they couldn't do it because they would get in trouble. "After that, they would always hide when they saw me coming."

CHAPTER 7

Widening Horizons

American Aid

T HE WAR had devastated Icaria. In 1946, agriculture production was down more than 50 percent from that of the prewar years, and only 10 percent of the people had money to purchase store goods. Cigarettes were a luxury cut into halves and smoked to the ashes. They purchased matches in lots of ten rather than by the box. Staple food items were beyond most people's means. The situation was particularly grim in Karavostomos, the village most overwhelmed by the war, where there was fear of another winter of famine comparable to that of 1942. In the summer of 1946, forty men from Karavostomos left to resume their prewar occupation making charcoal in various parts of Greece, but only sixteen found work, and the others scarcely had enough money to return to Icaria. In the winter of that year, bread was scarce throughout the island, and the price of olive oil was exorbitant. Many students did not have enough clothing even to attend school.[1]

In 1946, the Greek government sent aid to Icaria, but in the following year Athens, with limited resources and a Civil War on its hands, eliminated the relief program, even stopping the supply of milk to children. Gradually, agricultural production recovered its prewar level. By 1950, there were a few positive developments. The government began to release Icarian Communists held in Samos, and then men started to return from other detention centers as well. A decade after the war, non-Communist members of the community regained their constitutional rights. The Greek government, however, was not disposed to invest in the infrastructure of the "Red island."[2]

In the first two postwar decades, the Icarians relied greatly on their American brethren, and indeed the émigré community was in a position to help, for the war which had destroyed Icaria had brought affluence to the Icarian-Americans. Men who had lost their jobs in the depression of the 1930s returned to steel mills in the 1940s and worked long hours earning excellent wages. Others established restaurants, bakeries, industrial roofing and sheeting companies, and various other small businesses. In 1946, at the annual Pan-Icarian convention in Youngstown, Ohio, the members collected clothing, canned goods, and money for the island. Thus the Icarian-Americans assumed the burden of supplying the people with essentials, sending not only food, but also tools, seed, and even vines to restore the vineyards ravaged in the early decades of the century by phylloxera. Some of the funds went toward a printing press for *Nea Ikaria,* a left-wing publication. It soon became evident that the editorial opinions of the publication were contrary to the views of most of the Icarian-Americans who had become thoroughly Americanized by the military service performed by family members and the economic opportunities created by the war.[3]

In 1948, the Pan-Icarian Brotherhood met at the Statler Hotel in Detroit for its annual convention. Although there had been postwar conventions in Pittsburgh, Youngstown, and Cleveland, the Detroit meeting was a watershed. People arrived in new automobiles and fine clothes and had money to squander. They were impressed with their own prosperity, especially as they contrasted it to the plight of their impoverished relatives in Icaria.[4] At the business council of the Detroit convention they resolved to revive the island by financing public works rather than continue to patch the economy with relief programs. This policy became the main aim of the Pan-Icarian Brotherhood for the next generation. Members felt a new sense of responsibility and importance. The national officers, to distinguish themselves from the functionaries of local chapters, assumed high-sounding titles—supreme presidents, supreme vice presidents and supreme treasurers. Such nomenclatures, translated into Greek, were even more showy and persuaded people on the island that the association was of great importance in the United States. In later years, the Icarians were able to lure Herbert Humphrey, who was serving then as vice president of the United States, to one of their banquets. Humphrey who spoke after the presentations of the supreme national officers referred to himself as "the plain old vice president of the United States." Indeed, the Pan-Icarian Brotherhood reached its peak of prestige in the 1960s when Archbishop Iakovos invited the Supreme President of the Brotherhood on several occasions to meet with visiting Greek officials and American politicians.

The efforts of the Pan-Icarian Brotherhood of America to rescue Icaria from the devastation of the war were initially hindered by the presence of so many prisoners on the island and the survival of a handful of guerrillas in the mountains. Overcrowded conditions obstructed public-works projects. Moreover, the Greek government was suspicious that some of the parcels with food and clothing were aiding the prisoners and even falling into the hands of the guerrillas.[5] It was only after the prisoners departed and the last guerrillas withdrew in 1955 that the Icarian-Americans were able to implement a systematic program not only to revitalize Icaria, but also to provide relief on a large scale.

In 1955, declaring that it was the only resource the island had, the editor of one of the local newspapers appealed to the Pan-Icarian Brotherhood of America to establish a permanent fund for the relief of Icaria. An event illustrating how much the Icarians depended on their American relatives took place in December 1955 when a relentless rainstorm struck Icaria. Amalou, the village near ancient Langadha on the northwestern tip of the island, was devastated. Deforestation had created conditions favorable for landslides so when torrential rains hit the village they carried away some houses, a section of the school, crops, trees and even swept animals and a man into the sea. No traces of the man ever surfaced. While the Red Cross and the Greek government offered minimal assistance, the people, about 300, remained destitute, and the schoolhouse, which they had built before the war at their own expense, was in disrepair.[6]

On March 22, 1956, the schoolteacher from the village wrote to the Pan-Icarian Brotherhood of America, describing the Amalouites as hospitable people who kept their doors open for strangers despite their poverty. Before the war, half their men tended about four thousand sheep and goats, and the others found work making charcoal in various parts of Greece. The great herds were now gone, and there was no work for the men on the mainland. Thus their primary income came from the sale of lemons in the winter, and in the summer from vegetables planted on steep and rocky terrain. The teacher found it impossible to describe *ta chalia tous,* their misery. The villagers lost everything including their *tsarouch-*

ia, a type of rustic shoe in use only in this part of the island. Nearly a half-year had passed since the disaster, and 49 students were exposed to primitive conditions in a half-wrecked schoolhouse. The president of the Pan-Icarian Brotherhood of America released $780.00 to restore the school, and collected clothing and other items for the people of the ravaged village. He recommended that a three-man committee consisting of a priest, the highest elected official of the village, and another trusted person handle the funds and benefactions.[7]

The war and subsequent troubles had deprived many Icarians of the means to further their education. In 1955, the Icarian-Americans established a fund to grant annual stipends of $1,000, approximately three-times the yearly salary of a worker in Greece, for indigent Icarian students to study in Athens. Furthermore, the organization engaged in many acts of private charity. For example, in 1955 a lady born in Frantato who had settled in Athens appealed for help. She had been doing menial work in Athens since her husband was killed in the war against Turkey in 1922. He had left the Pittsburgh community to join the Greek army. As a result of the recent hard times, she had no roof over her head. The Icarian-Americans responded to her appeal.[8]

During the war, all the schools, particularly the high school in Aghios Kyrikos, had fallen into disrepair. In 1946, the Icarians petitioned the government to renovate the building, and add a teacher of English so the youth of the island would be able to converse with their American relatives, some of whom had been born in America and did not know Greek, and were likely to visit Icaria. There were expectations that the new generation of Icarian-American men would find brides in Icaria. Not only did the Tsaldaris government refuse to appoint a teacher of English, but it also did not immediately replace four teachers, half the teaching staff, who requested, because of the horrible conditions on the island, transfers to other regions. Thus in 1946, the high school in Aghios Kyrikos was reduced to four teachers who had to teach in a decrepit building. Gradually, the government restaffed the high school, but did not restore the building. In 1956, the Pan-Icarian Brotherhood sent over $18,000 to recondition and expand the high school in Aghios Kyrikos, and $3,750.30 for the restoration of primary schools in the Evdilos area, and even dispatched pencils and writing pads to children who lacked basic educational material.[9]

Apart from a six-bed clinic in the house of Dr. Malachias, Icaria could boast of no hospital. In those years, it was not uncommon to see fatally or nearly fatally hemorrhaging women, or other seriously ill persons, being conveyed by stretcher to a steamer headed for Piraeus. John A. Vassilaros, a New York businessman importing and roasting coffee, had long dreamed of a medical facility for Icaria. While over the years he had made generous contributions to various Icarian public-work projects, he had set aside money of his own and apparently collected funds from other Icarians for a hospital. In 1955, he persuaded the Pan-Icarian Brotherhood of American to participate in the venture and add to the fund he had already amassed. The organization paid for the architectural plans, and members initially pledged over $11,000 for the facility. In the summer of 1956, Vassilaros went to Icaria to supervise the construction of the hospital in Aghios Kyrikos, and discovered that certain features in the architectural plans were impractical and unilaterally decided to modify the Pan-Icarian blueprint. In an effort to launch the project and bring it to a swift completion, accounting procedures became slapdash. It was not clear who was to have legal possession of the building, or exactly how much of his own money Vassilaros was putting into the project. A number of people surfaced claiming that over the years they had made contributions but had not been given credit for their donations. The American organization decided to withdraw from further participation in the enterprise as financial records became vague. When the hospital was completed at the end of the decade, it was reported that $65,000 came from other Icarian-Americans and $40,000 from the Vassilaros family. Icarians envisaged a facility packed with doctors and nurses clad in immaculately white medical attire looking like angels of mercy. It was, however, difficult to staff the hospital, and at first it did not deliver the medical services anticipated. Helicopters transported emergency cases to more sophisticated medical centers. While the philanthropy and sincerity of Vassilaros were greatly appreciated, it took decades before many issues related to the hospital were resolved.[10]

The Icarians realized that without a good port and a road unifying the island their economy would continue to stagnate. Thus the main economic issue of the postwar period was a road connecting Aghios Kyrikos with Evdilos. The economy of the island was in shambles. Dr. George Tsantiris, a native of Raches and a member of parliament, representing the *nomos* of Samos-Icaria, was determined to use his political influence to have bulldozers pierce the mountain and unite the island with a road. Konstantinos Karamanlis, the minister of public works, was at that time undertaking a great road-building program for all of Greece. Karamanlis had achieved an excellent reputation for efficiency and honesty. When Tsantiris approached him about the Icarian road, Karamanlis explained that the government earmarked money only for those roads classified as national and provincial. He considered the Icarian road as a local project not meriting the government's backing. Tsantiris had another card to play. He had a brother-in-law in America, John Manta, a wealthy Chicago businessman who wanted to establish personal relationships with members of the Greek government. In 1954, Tsantiris informed General Alexander Papagos (Prime Minister 1952–1955) that Manta was ready to make a substantial contribution toward completion of the Aghios-Evdilos road, which Tsantiris unilaterally classified as a "national road," *Ethnike Othos,* and promised additional American funds from the Pan-Icarian Brotherhood of America. Papagos instructed Karamanlis to put the Icarian road in the public-works budget.[11]

The Papagos government agreed to build the Aghios-Evdilos road, allegedly 30 kilometers, if the Icarian-Americans would contribute $25,000, about one-sixth of the estimated cost. The original budget was $5,000 per kilometer, a figure partly based on wages of about $2.00 a day for a mid-1950s Greek construction worker. Furthermore, the minister of public works kept costs down by assigning state-owned bulldozers and some labor from the armed forces to the road construction. Karamanlis agreed to launch the construction of the Icarian road on July 1, 1956, if the Icarian-American subsidy arrived before October 1, 1955. The Icarian-Americans were reluctant to issue a check to the name of individuals, but after some months Dr. Tsantiris convinced them to do so, for if the draft was assigned to the ministry of public works, the money might be allocated to some other project. Thus in June 1955, the Icarian-Americans dispatched a check of $25,000 in the name of Papagos and Tsantiris.[12]

By the time the American funds arrived, Papagos had become seriously ill and was too sick to endorse the check. He died on October 4, 1955. King Paul summoned Karamanlis to form a government. In the meantime, the road engineers, who had been making a preliminary study of the Aghios-Evdilos road, reported that the road was 37 and not 30 kilometers, and had to be cut through a mountain of especially tough granite. Thus the cost for the road was not $5,000 a kilometer but rather $10,000. On Oct. 18th, the new minister of public works informed Karamanlis that the project required at least twice the budget, and thus suggested that the work be spread out over three years, and that operations start as soon as the Icarian-Americans reissued their check of $25,000. Karamanlis balked at the new figures and agreed only to allocate enough to build about 10 kilometers at some unspecified date. The Icarian-Americans would have to fund the remaining 27 kilometers. At this point, the Icarian-Americans began to reconsider their position. Tsantiris, who saw the great goal of his political career slipping through his fingers, wrote to the Icarian-Americans on October 28, 1955, "A beginning is half of the whole task." He proceeded in earnest rather than eloquent language to recommend that the Americans build the road as far as Oxe at their own expense. Then the Greek government, inspired by *philotimia,* a sense of honor and self-esteem, would complete the project. Tsantiris implied that the American funds would create a patron-client relationship between Greece and Icaria, and that the Greek government would thereafter take care of Icaria. He, therefore, urged the Icarian-Americans to reissue the check in his name, and he would see the project through.[13]

In the meantime, Karamanlis was occupied in forming his National Radical Union Party (ERE). In the general election in February 1956, Karamanlis, securing a majority of 10 in parliament, earned a narrow victory. In Karamanlis' 1956 budget for public works, there was a decided increase in expenditures for roads, but the allocation for the Aghios-Evdilos highway was dropped. There were several reasons for Karamanlis' decision in this matter. In his first months in office, he had to deal with the Cyprus crisis that was threatening to draw Greece into a war with Turkey. In the event of war, the main theater would be in the northern provinces, and highways in that area were vital for moving military personnel and equipment. It would be impractical to defend Icaria, near a major Turkish military base, and any investment in that island at that time would be ill-advised. When matters with Turkey were resolved and the government again turned to public works in nonessential military areas, Karamanlis earmarked funds to sections of Greece more supportive of ERE than "the Red Island."[14]

When Tsantiris realized that the Karamanlis government was not going to carry through Papagos' commitment to Icaria, he proposed that the Icarian-Americans fund the road entirely out of their pockets, and beseeched them to contribute $200,000 in four annual installments of $50,000. Tsantiris pleaded that the Greek government was poor, but the Pan-Icarian Brotherhood was rich, and the sum for the road would not be a great burden to its members. Tsantiris assured the Icarian-Americans that this would be the last favor the people from the island would ask of their relatives in America. With the completion of this great highway, the

Icarians would enjoy prosperity and financial independence. The transport of goods and people in Icaria would be more efficient, tourism would develop, and the island would finally step into the modern world. Students in Evdilos would be able to commute to the high school in Aghios Kyrikos. And Tsantiris concluded that the Icarian-Americans could bring their automobiles and tour the island rather than going about on donkeys. John L. Manta was the president of the Icarian Radioactive Hot Springs Corporation of America and major stockholder. As we shall see below, the corporation formed in 1950 to develop Therma into a tourist area, was about to be dissolved. Manta decided to use some of its funds for the road and thus wrote a check from the corporation's funds for $25,000 and instructed his brother George to arrange the affair. On November 17, 1955 George Manta sent the check to the treasurer of the Hot Springs Corporation and wrote, "Let's help this man Tsantiris who is doing his damnest to have a road built uniting the south with the north of the island. We will then have our automobiles with us next time we visit the island." The treasurer wanted assurances that the Greek government would make a commitment to the road, and when such assurances were not forthcoming he refused to sign the check. The construction of the Aghios Kyrikos-Evdilos road would have to wait for another decade to be funded not by Icarian-Americans but by the Greek government.[15]

Local and National Politics

Without this road or any other major public works from Athens, the Icarian economy lagged behind that of the rest of Greece, and its people persisted in embracing left-wing politics. The government continued to clamp down on Communists, denying them passports, civil-service jobs, and access to higher education. It was difficult for a Communist to prevail in a legal dispute concerning property, and the gendarmes constantly summoned Communists to court for minor offenses. Such cases were adjudicated in Samos where a stay of several days and the expense of a trial proved ruinous to indigent peasants. For instance, in 1964, the gendarmes accused fifteen Icarian farmers, all with Communist leanings, of selling products without proper permits. They stood trial in Samos on three different occasions, and though finally exonerated were financially crushed.[16]

The trial of these fifteen men came at a time when Greek national politics was undergoing changes that would result in a temporary slackening of repressive conditions throughout Greece. In 1963, the Central Union party of George Papandreou rose to power, and restored the civic privileges of many Communists who now could vote and run for local office, but not as Communists, for the Communist party remained outlawed. Thus Communists ran for office either under the aegis of the EDA—the United Democratic Left—or locally with the affiliation of "Aristera," the left-wing party. The local elections of 1964 marked a political watershed. The Communist postal worker who in 1947 had relayed information to his associates about their imminent arrests and was imprisoned for this act became *proedros tes kenotes,* equivalent to mayor, in Aghios Kyrikos, the most important office on the island with 50.4 percent of the vote. In 1965, this position was upgraded to the office of mayor. The voting results were more striking in the interior villages. In Arethousa, one of the "red villages," the Communist candidate had no opposition and received 100 percent of the vote.[17]

For the next three years, Communists controlled local government in Icaria. During that period, the left-wing citizens of Icaria regained a measure of their constitutional rights, particularly in legal matters. Gendarmes no longer dispatched men for minor infractions to Samos for expensive trials. All citizens could initiate litigation to recover property in the local courts. The process of reconciliation, however, came to an end in April 1967 when a group of Greek colonels led by George Papadopoulos seized power. The junta immediately arrested 7,000 people and among them were about twenty leading Icarian Communists. The government put them in "reeducation" centers for several months, and then released them to their villages under the supervision of the gendarmes. The new regime dismissed most elected officials in Icaria and replaced them with conservatives who were in no position to decline the appointment. Local government gave way to the fiats of the *Nomarchos* (governor) of Samos and Icaria.[18]

The overwhelming majority of the Icarians despised the junta even though it was composed of men who had peasant backgrounds similar to the people of Icaria. Papadopoulos and his colleagues, suspicious of Athenian high society, proudly acknowledged that they were "from the class of toil." Moreover, like the majority of Icarians, the colonels were antimonarchists, and had purged the army of the king's supporters. When the king attempted a countercoup in December 1967, they forced him out of the country. Most Icarians viewed this as a positive development. One of the more active Communists on the island sent a telegram to the local police chief congratulating the junta for its actions. He later explained, "Most of the suffering we Communists endured came from the palace. These were the early days of the Junta. Of course, we were against colonels, but they were better than the king, and might not be bad for Icaria."[19] Indeed the colonels, despite erratic policies and repressive measures, in certain ways were generous to Icaria.

Around 1970, the colonels advanced funds to an entrepreneur to build the Toula Pallas Hotel in Lefkada, the suburbs of Aghios Kyrikos. The junta made this investment not because it had a special interest in Icaria but as part of a national program to bolster tourism that was not developing as rapidly as the junta had anticipated. Europeans were discovering Turkey, and were reluctant to visit a country under military rule. Critics of the junta argued that the Greek economy was being carried by the economic initiatives of the previous government, and that the colonels were not contributing to the long-term prosperity of Greece.[20]

Members of the Pan-Icarian Brotherhood of Athens believed they could deal with the junta. On December 22, 1970, a committee consisting of three of its members appealed to the head of the government, George Papadopoulos, for a subsidy to host the 1972 annual convention of the Pan-Icarian Brotherhood of America in Aghios Kyrikos, to build a road and harbor, and to complete other public works in Icaria. The members of the committee had strong conservative credentials and they stressed the island's firm support of the Greek Orthodox Church. They reported that there were 8,000 Icarian families in America, and that they had formed the first Greek-American association there and were among the most important Greeks in the United States, particularly successful in business. The committee resorting to hyperbole characterized the Icarians in America as dedicated Greek Orthodox who maintained the Greek language on foreign shores. Their generosity and philhellenism were reflected in many acts of charity, particularly in the high school and hospital which they had built in Icaria. The Papadopoulos government was impressed with requests couched in nationalistic rhetoric. Furthermore, a subsidy to entertain the Icarian-Americans was a way to launch the new hotel in Icaria, a venture that the government had supported, and to circumvent the boycott the junta's enemies were imposing on Greece. The colonels, moreover, desired to demonstrate to the Icarian-Americans that they were not un-Greek, not the Fascist beasts that the Council of Europe claimed they were, to show off the new road, which they had built between Aghios Kyrikos and Evdilos, and to stimulate tourism in the Aegean.

Papadopoulos earmarked a substantial budget for the event, and to prepare for the American visit began work on the road from Aghios Kyrikos to Evdilos by deploying M.O.M.A., a military construction entity. The government also began work on the port at Aghios Kyrikos.[21]

Icarian-Americans, however, showed a reluctance to make a commitment. About half the members disapproved of the junta. The Icarians in Canada, who had formed the Nesos Ikarias chapter in Toronto in 1969, were generally recent immigrants with strong anti-junta feelings. In the same year, Andreas Papandreou had accepted an academic appointed in Toronto at York University, and formed PAK, an anti-junta organization to which many of the Toronto Icarians belonged. Indeed, Papandreou became acquainted with some Icarians and employed several in renovating his house. One Toronto Icarian was shocked that the Icarian-Americans were thinking of going to Icaria. "The junta had forced me out of Greece. I was so opposed to the colonels that I even stopped sending money to my needy parents because I did not want to provide the dictatorship with foreign currency."[22]

There was another problem about transporting so many Icarian-Americans to Icaria. Most of the children of the immigrants had never visited Greece. Could the island provide modern comforts, decent quarters, and especially plumbing, for 2,000 guests? The Athenian organization sent their secretary to the United States to tour the various Icarian communities. He assured them that not only would plumbing be up to American standards, but also he spoke of free hotel rooms and even the construction of a golf course in Icaria. The president of the Pan-Icarian Brotherhood of America was hesitant about endorsing the excursion. "Finally, I decided it was the best thing to go through with the trip and not to jeopardize the public works projects in Icaria."[23]

As one of the charter planes left New York, the Toronto chapter, by unanimous vote, seceded from the organization. The government was disappointed to discover that less than 1,000 Icarians came. In Athens the government lavishly entertained the Icarian-Americans with several banquets. Some enjoyed free hotel rooms and the junta provided Pullman buses for excursions to Delphi and comparable sites. Some of the group were embarrassed by the junta's generosity and shunned its hospitality. The group went to Icaria on the *Ionion,* a ship hired by the junta that stayed in port and provided beds for three nights at a low rate. Others found rooms at the Toula Hotel at fees subsidized by the government. Several days after arriving, the president of the Icarian-American association received a telegram from America informing him of several more chapters threatening secessions. Ultimately, the president resigned. The organization was seriously divided, and it took several years to patch up the rift.[24]

The 1972 Icarian-American convention revealed the differences between the two Icarias. In the course of the trip, the Icarian-Americans, an odd combination of half-Greek and half-American who came seeking their roots, discovered that they were really Americans. To the people on the island they were a curious lot, speaking atrocious Greek, and exhibiting crude manners. They were not the benevolent relatives whom they had imagined, but a pack of capitalists interested in supporting a Fascist government and taking possession of family property. And now that Athens had financed the Aghios-Evdilos road, it was understood that in the future the Greek government, whatever its political persuasion might be, and not the Icarian-Americans, was responsible for the welfare of Icaria. The Icarian-Americans were superfluous. The two Icarias began to go their separate ways.

The junta was the first Greek government that did not write off Icaria as an insignificant frontier province or as the "Red Island." But it failed to gain the support of the people because of its heavy-handed politics. As the junta physically united the island with a road, it politically divided the people by posting everywhere slogans on blue and white notice boards that "Communists are traitors to the nation." The government revived the practice of keeping a dossier on left-wing citizens, which included about half the Icarian population, and required civil servants to sign a type of loyalty oath, "the certificate of social beliefs, *Pistopiotika Koinonikon Fronimaton.*" Some teachers lost their positions, and seamen were denied a *Nautiko Fyladion,* a permit to sail, if they could not produce such a document. While Icaria collectively benefited from the colonels, many individual Icarians were harmed.[25]

In 1974, prices soared in Greece. The term "inflation" became one of the taboo words prohibited in public. In July 1974, perhaps attempting to cover economic problems and unite the country, the junta became involved in a conflict with Turkey over Cyprus, lost control of events, and fell from power. K. Karamanlis returned from exile in France and assumed control of the government. He came to a temporary understanding with the Turks, legalized the Communist party, and called for national elections. In the 1975 local elections, a man who had been maltreated by the gendarmes for his Communist beliefs in the late 1940s, as a KKE candidate, won the office of mayor in Aghios Kyrikos with 61 percent of the vote. Communists took all the elective positions on the island, and continued in power until 1982 when PASOK under the leadership of Andreas Papandreou won the general election. Papandreou completed the restoration of normalcy by recognizing the legitimacy of the leftist resistance, and allowing political exiles to return. Local Communist politicians had now to compete with candidates from PASOK, a rival socialist party but continued to dominate local elections throughout the 1980s. During these decades, Icarians backed a candidate because he was a *kalos agonistes,* one who had fought the good fight, and not for his abilities. Unfortunately, some of the men who gained office in these years simply because they had left-wing political credentials were ill-qualified to hold public office, and were unprepared to lead Icaria into the rapidly changing world of the 1970s and 1980s. The inadequate leadership of these men was one of the reasons the island lagged behind its neighbors in the last decades of the 20th century.[26]

These two decades marked important shifts in the people's political attitudes. The fear of Turkey, always a factor, reached levels of paranoia. During the 1974 war with Turkey over Cyprus, Icaria was defenseless. There were no armed forces on the island. Thus middle-aged men patrolled the coast with hunting rifles, while people read stories in Greek newspapers of alleged Turkish atrocities on Cyprus. Had the war been expanded, as Karamanlis contemplated, Icaria would have fallen to the Turks in a matter of hours. To defend Icaria, the Karamanlis government, despite the 1923 treaty of Lausanne which stipulated that the island must be demilitarized, installed several machine-gun nests manned by small garrisons.[27]

The increased anxiety about Turkey was connected to a growing anti-Americanism. The majority of the Icarians felt that the United States had forced Turkey as a pseudo-ally on Greece, was partially responsible for the Turkish occupation of about forty percent of Cyprus, and would not lift a finger to save Icaria from a Turkish invasion. The general feeling in Icaria was that American policy had been too supportive of the junta, and that American "monopolies," never specifically identified, were preventing Greek industry from growing while draining the country of its natural resources, and that Americans were coveting the only natural resource Icaria had, the spas at Therma. Indeed, it was widely believed that American capitalists were conspiring to acquire the spas.[28]

Tourism

By the mid-1950s, tourism had become Greece's third main industry, but only a trickle of tourists passed through Icaria during this period and they left little money. They were not the preferred foreigners with plenty of cash but rather Greeks with limited funds. Some of them had been Communists who learned about the spas during their detention in Icaria, and ironically were returning to recover their health in the very place where it had been broken. But fewer came to Therma to benefit from the spas than before the war. Raches, which had attracted a small stream of Athenians and a few foreigners in the 1920s and 1930s, was now ignored for more developed areas in the Aegean. The register from the Politis Hotel in Raches for the decade of the 1930s reveals mainly civil servants, and professional people from Athens. During this period about ten foreigners stayed in the hotel. Between Therma and Raches, there were about three hundred visitors who came to spend several weeks in the summer. The government delivered a blow to tourism in the postwar period when it made Icaria a location for political prisoners. In 1950, a Greek journalist taking the waters at Therma witnessed a demonstration against the government for placing prisoners on the island, and downplayed the tense atmosphere, but implied that such clashes damaged the reputation of Icaria and discouraged tourists from coming. Furthermore, many of the prisoners were ill, and some suffered from tuberculosis, and it was feared that some type of plague would sweep through the island.[29]

In the 1950s, the few European visitors who came to Icaria found it isolated and primitive. There were about six motor vehicles on the island, and limited roads. Most areas remained connected simply by inter-village lanes. People either walked or hired a mule. Only Aghios Kyrikos could boast of electricity and plumbing. In other villages, the inhabitants relied on well water and lanterns. In 1950, the Irish poet Louis MacNeice and his wife rented a house in Raches and spent the summer there. In *Burnt Offerings,* MacNeice contrasted the peaceful rural beauty with the tense political situation, noting "and there are prisoners really, here in the hills."[30]

Several years later, Kevin Andrews, an Anglo-American writer, stayed in Raches for one year. Andrews enjoyed the cold winters in an unheated house without plumbing and electricity. He dressed like a shepherd, going about with the *phylaki,* a shepherd's backpack, and playing his reed flute. One night he accompanied Domna Samiou, the singer who happened to be in Icaria, in an impromptu concert in a café in Aghios Polikarpos. Children loved his flute playing and implored him, *"Barba, pexe allo ena"* (Uncle, play one more!). He rarely turned down a social invitation. People remember his trek over a mountain on a snowy December night to attend a baptism where he gorged himself on dried mushrooms, but avoided wine, telling his host that he was epileptic. On his last evening in Raches, he invited the village to a party and offered large quantities of food and drink. In fact, his cordiality and interest in the island both flattered and baffled people who assumed he was either an English or an American spy. Otherwise why would an Anglo-American want to spend a year in Icaria? Andrews' wife, the illegitimate daughter of the poet E. E. Cummings, was unhappy with the hard conditions and did not like the island.[31]

Most non-Greek tourists to Greece never heard of Icaria, and those who strayed on the island generally shared Mrs. Andrew's negative feelings about it. While other islands in the Aegean were building roads, and hotels, and offering amenities such as electricity and running water, Icaria remained primitive and the home of political prisoners. In 1950, a group of Icarian-Americans decided to do something about the situation. Under the leadership of John Manta, they formed the Icarian Radio-Active Hot Springs Corporation of America issuing 6,000 shares valued at $25 each. Manta was president of the corportion and major stockholder with 200 shares. The shareholders endeavored to acquire most of the coastal property in Therma, providing the landowners with both cash and shares. The directors of the corporation, who intended to invest the profits in roads and an airport, envisaged a resort complex with shopping malls, swimming pools, and the most modern hotel facilities in Greece. The projected spa would have been far too elegant for the clientele of the 1950s. The project stalled when the corporation was unable to secure the land from the locals, and ran into strong opposition from Communists who suspected that American capitalists were trying to swindle the Icarians out of their most precious resources, their thermal springs. The major hotel proprietor from Therma invited American investments but did not wish to exchange his property for shares. Money would not, however, come from America without strings attached. As the project languished, the major hotel owner lashed out at Dr. Malachias, who was representing Icaria in parliament. The hotelier accused the doctor of missing many opportunities to develop Therma. Among Dr. Malachias' alleged blunders was his failure to lure the actress Esther Williams to Therma, who apparently was vacationing in

Greece, to publicize the baths. Not only was Dr. Malachias unable to establish contacts with movie stars, he was losing his influence in the Greek parliament and his requests for funds for Therma were ignored. Dr. Malachias' critics were exasperated that his trip to America around 1950 was not a success. He toured the Icarian communities in America to revive the dormant Icarian Radio-Active Corporation of America. The older generation of Icarian-Americans received him with great reverence and many asked him for medical advice. He wrote scores of prescriptions for these people, some of them old patients. But American pharmacists would not honor the prescriptions, nor would the Icarian-Americans invest more money in the Radio-Active Corporation, and it was finally dissolved in the 1960s.[32]

Despite the failure of the Radio-Active Corporation to provide money to develop Therma, Icarians continued to believe that the spas represented the economic salvation of the island. In 1961, Ioannis Melas, who represented Piraeus but had married a woman from Icaria and had a home there, requested from the Greek government a subsidy for building 10,000 bathing installations and several hotels offering a total of 17,500 beds in Therma. The under minister of communications of Greece pointed out that such an undertaking would absorb about 60 percent of his department's budget. Undaunted, in 1961, hotel owners from Therma invited Dr. Alexander Fleming, the discoverer of penicillin, and then President John Fitzgerald Kennedy, who was experiencing back problems, to benefit from the radioactive baths. The Icarians had no luck in luring celebrities, but thousands of ailing Greeks came that year, and found the run-down facilities at Therma acceptable for their needs. Because visitors with lavish means were not appearing, Icarians generally believed that there was a conspiracy to prevent their spas, which they regarded as the best curative waters in the world, from developing into the foremost spas in Greece. According to this view, the National Bank of Greece, which had invested in spas in other parts of Greece, did not wish to see Therma become a rival to its projects. Even the Greek medical community was allegedly in collusion with the banks. Doctors were recommending to their patients other spas not because they were undermining Icaria, but rather because they feared that the radioactivity at Therma was at a dangerously high level. Such apprehensions were seemingly justified when one of the seven springs at Therma was closed as a health hazard.[33]

The 1972 Pan-Icarian Brotherhood of America convention in Icaria was a great economic boost to the island, but there was no follow-up. The

Toula hotel, which served as the headquarters for the meeting, soon closed its doors. According to the terms of the loan, the developer was not required to repay the government, which provided about 80 percent of the capital, if the hotel, which had about 200 rooms and over 400 beds, failed. The developer engaged local contractors and paid some with stock in the hotel. When the Toula opened in the summer of 1972, the editor of one local paper bragged that it would rival the Hilton in Athens in luxury, and the mayor declared it was the best hotel in the Aegean. These views, however, were not shared by European tourists who felt isolated in Lefkada, far from a beach, and a mile walk from Aghios Kyrikos, a warren of a village without distinction. After several years, the owner declared bankruptcy, and several of the local contractors were left with worthless stock as the hotel terminated operations. Damaged by fire it endured as a decrepit eyesore on the Icarian landscape into the first years of the new century.[34]

Thus by the late 1970s Icaria remained, except for impecunious Greek invalids going to the spas at Therma, unspoiled and undiscovered while adjacent Turkey was swarming with tourists. The belief that the socialist government of Andreas Papandreou, who became prime minister in 1982, would display a special interest in Icaria did not materialize. On one occasion, when Papandreou was visiting Samos, the mayor of Icaria forged through a crowd and personally presented a letter to the prime minister appealing to the government to develop the spas at Therma and build an airport. While Icaria benefited from PASOK's significant investment in rebuilding schools and many social programs, the left-wing Icarians were dissatisfied and suspected that Papandreou was colluding with right-wing elements at the expense of the island. PASOK was making inroads into the Communist vote in Icaria.[35]

The class and number of visitors to Therma did not produce the revenues that other islands were enjoying from tourism in the 1970s. Icarians continued to promote Therma and began to consider ways to attract visitors to other parts of the island. There were proposals to spruce up the interior villages for sightseeing tours, to advertise the forests or what was left of them, and to renovate the monuments of the island. There was even a suggestion to rebuild the small Byzantine church at Myliopon.[36]

While Icarians were devising various inept schemes to cash in on the obsession that well-heeled Europeans were displaying for the Aegean, backpackers were discovering Livadi beach between Armenistis and Gialiskari. The locals never held this area in high esteem, for they did not regard sunbathing or swimming as a leisure activity. The sandy shore was deserted except for the occasional native following a doctor's advice to take the sun or sea for therapy. Bohemian types began to infiltrate a region without hotels or restaurants. They put up tents on the seaside and raided orchards, gardens, and vineyards for food. At first, the locals felt that their section of the island was becoming a *xephrakto ambeli* (open vineyard) for impecunious riffraff who were corrupting the morality of the youth while living off the fruits of the land. Gradually café owners, who had hitherto catered to fishermen, began to build small family-operated pensions. Nudists established a summer community on the Livadi beaches much to the opposition of the locals. In the summer of 1982, an alliance of farmers, Orthodox priests, and Communist officials attacked the nudists with anti-American slogans and threats. There were no casualties, and a compromise was eventually reached. The nudists retreated to the less visible beach at Nas, and the more conventional tourists settled in the Armenisti-Gialiskari area where small lodgings by the late 1980s grew into modern hotels catering to thousands of summer guests spread between Armenistis and Gialiskari.[37]

The next level of development depended on an airport that would enhance the number and class of tourists. The government's delayed response to building an airport was partially a result of local opposition. Despite the resistance, the government completed the airport in 1993. K. Mitsotakis, the prime minister, arrived to inaugurate air service in 1994, and was surprised to be greeted with black flags. The opposition consisted of some landowners from Fanari and neighboring villages, and a group of Communists. The subsidiary roads to the airport and the extension of electricity to outlying regions unleashed complaints that individuals rather than the public tended to benefit from these projects. Complaints, however, faded away as Olympic Air Lines transported many of the tourists who were now staying in Icaria for weeks in the summer. Larger hotels were now built between Armenistis and Gialiskari, but the tourists were still not of the class that went to the other islands. For instance, they would not pay the high price for lobster ensnared off the Icarian so the local fishing capitalists shipped this luxury product to Myconus.[38]

A New Way of Life

The expansion of the Greek economy in the 1960s and the growth of Athens offered economic opportunities. There were over 3,000 Icarian families established in the proletarian sections of Athens and Piraeus. The bulk of the men worked in shipyards, and the factories on the outskirts of Piraeus. Many settled in Perama, the shipyard area of Piraeus, where some had built shacks at night on public land and then claimed possession of the property. Most of these people lived in housing without running water or heating. A decade later, these Icarians enjoyed all urban amenities and were taking their first steps into the emerging Greek middle class, and importing middle-class ways to the island. The approximately 8,000 Icarians who inhabited the island year round benefited from their success-ful Athenian relatives, from tourism which took hold in the 1980s, and from Greece's entry into the European Union in 1981. With sources of income outside the island and subsidies from the EU, people tended to forego traditional occupations. Farmers became less productive, and shep-herds gradually disbursed their flocks because of regulations imposed and subsidies granted to the shepherds by the EU. The decade of the 1980s marked a decrease in the number of Icarians doing physical work, and those who performed such labor demanded high wages. Icarians in many instances preferred Albanians as rural laborers and construction workers to their fellow natives. Immigrants toiled for low wages and without insurance like the first Icarians in Pittsburgh. Tensions between the new arrivals and local workers resulted in several clashes peaking with a melee between Icarians and Albanians in September 1999. As a result of the fray, public opinion has become more sympathetic to the plight of Albanians.[39]

Tourism combined with proximity to Asia Minor also brought traffic in illegal drugs, a problem common to many of the islands. For the older generation, it was shocking to see drug use spreading into a society where alcoholism had not been a problem even in the wretched years of war and poverty. Thousands of young Icarians residing in Athens came to spend part of the summer in their rural homeland. This first generation of urban Icarians joined tourists at seashore nightclubs using drugs and living a free lifestyle. In 1997, a conference of Icarian professional people took place in Athens to discuss the problem. They offered no solution. Their concern was not only about the use of drugs on the island but also the role of Icaria as a transit point. Dealers in speedboats occasionally smuggled narcotics in from Turkey. In 1989, authorities had arrested locals collaborating with Lebanese nationals in such an operation. In the following year, police announced that there were 250 dealers operating in Icaria, a figure that has not been substantiated. The police force is no longer the ruthless instru-ment of law and order that hounded Communists in the 1950s. The approximately 20 gendarmes generally dressed like civilians, blended in with the community, and were reluctant to exert authority. On one occasion, villagers from the remote western region informed the police about the growth of a drug crop. The gendarmes destroyed the substance but were unable to make arrests. Although there are no reliable figures, the general feeling in the island is that the use of drugs by Icarian youth is slightly more than in other areas.[40]

Many of the parents of the 1960s and 1970s had experienced a youth totally different from that of their children. In their days, one began hard physical labor at the age of twelve. As members of EPON and EAM, they had accepted sexual abstinence and self-sacrifice. They were appalled to observe that the youth of the island adhered to the new moral standards that were so different from their own. Both the extreme Right and Left shared puritanical views. Thus to some degree, this moral revolution was also a political statement, a reaction to the austerity of old-fashioned Communist moral tenets, and a rejection of the junta that had declared war on miniskirts, nudists, free love, homosexuals, long-haired hippies, drugs, and music in public places after midnight. PASOK seemed to be more in tune with modern times, more attractive to this generation, by decriminalizing adultery, legalizing abortion, and giving equal rights to women.[41]

The tourist boom enabled people to modernize their homes and purchase cars, TVs, and deep freezes. The unanticipated abundance of the 1990s placed strains on the island's fragile ecology. The authorities had no satisfactory way to dispose of garbage that was dumped into open fields. Rusted frames of automobiles scarred the countryside. In the summers, water was often in short supply. The inhabitants of Aghios Kyrikos pumped in water from Levadia, the monastery several miles west of the city, but it proved inadequate, and new sources were scarce. Even the sparsely settled villages in the interior were experiencing shortfalls. For instance, villagers digging wells at Kosika, Petropouli, and Daphne were squabbling as they tapped into the same source. The tourist and building boom may have contributed to the parched conditions that precipitated the fire of the summer of 1993. A conflagration appeared above Aghios Kyrikos, perhaps started by construction workers tarring a road near a cluster of dry trees, and resulted in the death of 12 people.[42]

While tourism was bringing the island into the modern world, and changes were sweeping through it, the veterans of the world war and of the civil war began to contemplate their role in the brutal decades of the 1940s and 1950s. For years, it had been too painful to contemplate the atrocities, travails, and compromises. Some people simply deleted events from their minds. But in the last decades of the twentieth century, activists began to examine their part in the movement. Aris Alexandrou, not an Icarian, writes about this period in his Kafkaesque novel, *To Kivotio* (The Box). The authorities detain the narrator, a Communist, for one year in Icaria. Eventually, he leaves the island to become a key member in a secret mission to deliver a box to a certain city. If he accomplishes his assignment, Communism will prevail. Though his colleagues perish on the way, and he passes through many dangers and hardships, he delivers the box never knowing what is in it or why it is so important. His superiors open it, find it empty, and punish him. The narrator, while in prison and contemplating his service to the cause, implies that he has wasted much of his life on a fool's errand supporting an ambiguous ideology and serving irrational leaders.[43]

Most of the Icarians, however, who had sacrificed their youth to make a "better tomorrow," who had spent years in the mountains, suffered in Markronisos, faced years of persecution in the postwar period, would have no sympathy for the narrator in the *Box*. They remained convinced that their cause was just and its aim sound. They would not admit that the golden calf had usurped the altar and the dogma. As their colleagues outside the island acknowledged the mistakes of the past and the futility of the movement on the islands, and became Euro-Communists or socialists, the majority of Icarian Communists retained a loyalty to a rigid Stalinist tradition. A few, however, turned to more radical organizations. Three brothers with an Icarian background were members of the November 17th, a Marxist-Leninists group which inaugurated its terrorism with the murder of Richard Wells, the CIA station head in Athens in 1975 and carried out a series of assassination for the next two decades. It is rumored on the island that some of November 17th organizational and strategic meetings took place on Icaria.[44]

While the Icarians are not great readers, they like to write. In the last decades of the 20th Century, books began to appear with such titles as the *Turbulent Years, The Red Island, The Time of the Occupation, The Stormy Age, Resistance in Icaria, the Democratic Army of Icaria, Recollections from Anatolia,* and *Our Course Was Just.* One may regard these books as Edward Gibbon did his ecclesiastical sources, as "bigoted" but nevertheless full of "diligence, and scrupulous minuteness." These books contain extraordinary details though judgment and objectivity are often lacking. These guerrillas-turned-authors had fought the good fight for the just cause. These participants did not criticize the aims of the party, the decision to go to the mountains, but rather complained about colleagues, local corruption, and informers. These Icario-centric accounts never took in the larger picture, or considered the changing world.

These works were the last political acts of the authors. The leading participants were passing away observing a world that was hardly comprehensible. Scarcity had turned to abundance, and individual goals superseded the welfare of the community. The two local Communist newspapers criticized the new trends, but were more interested in praising the dead who had sacrificed their youth to the cause. The encomia-cum-obituaries were the last shot in a war that ended a half-century before. These obituaries reassessed the past, and defined the qualities of the *kalos agonistes*. The deceased, often pictured in work-clothes, were described as good men who had progressive ideas. They subscribed to the local Communist newspapers, possessed democratic courtesy, and had unpretentious manners. The eulogies emphasized their role as reliable providers, and men who left property not only to children but also to grandchildren. Their most important quality, however, was a love for Icaria, a desire to help the people and be buried under its soil. No one seemed to care about the contradictions, the accumulation of property, and the devotion to a region, with the international and nonmaterial objectives of the movement they had fiercely supported. While this was not the "better tomorrow" they had envisaged in their youth, it was not the bondage they had feared.[45]

At the beginning of the 21st century, old Icaria survived in the half-abandoned villages of the interior where democratic traditions are old and run deep. But even here the people have never resolved the discrepancy in their heritage—the individualism expressed in the myth of Icarus and the collective responsibility taken when they hurled a Turkish official from a precipice. Somewhere in a forlorn valley beneath one of these hamlets lie the bones, now some 400 years old, of this haughty Ottoman tax collector. It was into the heart of Icaria that he went seeking taxes. Now the seaboard inhabitants prosper while the people of the interior live in undistinguished quarters. To reach these inhospitable regions, one passes through uncultivated terraced fields where sharp brambles spike the summer air. But the village lanes are inviting and well-shaded with columnar cypresses and olive trees some of which go back to the *Tourkokratia*. The wind rarely ceases to shake their hoary branches, and one may hear it whisper, "ouloi emeis effendi"

1. Fear of another winter of famine: *Nea Ikaria,* November 2, 1946. Karavostomos: *Nea Ikaria,* Oct. 18, 1946. Agriculture figures contrast the production of 1936 with that of 1946. For example, in 1936 Icarians produced 846,000 pounds of currants and 560,000 pounds of various fruits. In 1946, the production dropped for the former to 140,000 and for the latter to 280,000; see *Nea Ikaria,* Jan. 1, 1947. Cigarettes and matches: George Stenos, merchant, interview Raches, Icaria, June 12, 2003. Clothing: the 308 students from the high school in Aghios sent a letter to the Pan-Icarian Brotherhood of America thanking it for the 170 sweaters for the male students and 25 dresses for the women students, *Nea Ikaria,* Jan. 1, 1947.

2. Greek government ends aid: *Flogia: Organo Epon,* March 16, 1947. Vineyards: *Nea Ikaria,* December 3, 1946.

3. General aid from Icarian-Americans and printing press: *Nea Ikaria,* Dec. 3, 1946, and *Nea Ikaria,* Aug. 15, 1946. For professions, see advertisements in Pan-Icarian Brotherhood Year Book, Detroit Convention, 1948.

4. See Pan-Icarian Brotherhood Year Book, Detroit Convention, 1948.

5. *Nea Ikaria,* Oct. 18, 1946, appealed to Icarians to contribute clothing sent from American relatives to the political prisoners.

6. K. Diamantides, editor of *Ikaria Phoné,* in a letter to John A. Papalas, Nov. 3, 1955, wrote, "Our brothers in America are the only hope of our island." The letter of George Glaros, March 22, 1956, to the Pan-Icarian Brotherhood of America, relates the devastation in Amalou. The letter is in *Minutes and Correspondence of Pan-Icarian Brotherhood of America 1956–1957* in Icarian Archives, Verona, Pennsylvania. Glaros' description of the Amalou landslide resembles W. J. Woodhouse's, *Aetolia: Its Geography, Topography and Antiquities* (Oxford, 1897), p. 38, report from the Pindus on the collapse of part of the village Agrapha into a gorge after a long period of rain.

7. Description of prewar Amalou: *Nea Ikaria,* March 6, 1947. For the aid package: letter of John A. Papalas president of the Brotherhood, April 28, 1956, to George Glaros, in *Minutes and Correspondence of Pan-Icarian Brotherhood of America 1956–1957* in Icarian Archives, Verona, Pennsylvania. On Dec. 19, 1956, an Icarian living in Volos, a city in the eastern part of Greece, requested assistance for his adopted city that had been devastated by an earthquake, and in the ensuing flood lost 47 residents, and its olive orchards. There is no record of Icarians responding to

this request but in Jan. 1933 they had sent funds to the people in the Chalcide peninsula after an earthquake, minutes Jan. 1933, Verona archives.

8. Professor A. Plakidas directed the Brotherhood scholarship fund; see *Minutes and Correspondence of Pan-Icarian Brotherhood of America 1956–1957.* Letter of Anastasia Kanidia, Dec. 3, 1955, in Icarian Archives in Verona.

9. Condition of schools and English teacher: *Ikariake Phoné,* September 5, 1946. Number of teachers: *Nea Ikaria,* Nov. 16, 1946. Evdilos schools: October 20, 1956, in *Minutes and Correspondence of Pan-Icarian Brotherhood of America 1956–1957,* Archives in Verona. For general school expenditure, see the account of the president of the Pan-Icarian Brotherhood, John A. Papalas, December 6, 1955, Icarian archives, Verona. In Nov. 1955, the George Spanos chapter of Detroit sent 4,260 pencils and some notebooks to the 1,924 students in the primary schools of Icaria; letter of Michalis Lakas to the school association of Ikaria, Nov. 28, 1955, Icarian Archives in Verona. The Samians noted the great support which the Icarian-Americans conferred on Icaria, and noted it was the only blessing this poor island had; see M. I. Margarones, *Geographia Nomou Samou* (Karlovasi, 1966), p. 144.

10. In the 1920s, John Vassilaros contributed $376.00 for the high school in Aghios Kyrikos. This constituted one of the largest donations; see *Katastatikon tou Philekpaideutikou Syllogou Ikarias* (Cosmos Printing Company, New York, 1926), p. 23. When construction of the hospital stalled because of a lack of funds, Evangelia Sopoulis, president of the Women's Philanthropic Society of Aghios Kyrikos, urged the Brotherhood to continue its support of the project. John A. Papalas, president of the Brotherhood, in a letter dated August 1, 1956, explained that the unconventional accounting procedures related to the hospital fund made it impossible for people having donated money to declare it on their United States federal income-tax forms as charitable contributions. The controversy over the issue of financial records between the president of the brotherhood and Vassilaros became acrimonious; see the letters of Vassilaros to Papalas, August 6, 1957, and Papalas to Vassilaros, August 13, 1957, in the *Minutes and Correspondence of Pan-Icarian Brotherhood of America 1956–1957* Verona, Pennsylvania. Reported final cost: *Ikariaka,* Dec. 1958. Image of angels of mercy: Ch. Mavrogeorges, *Ikariake Phoné,* Aug. 23, 1958.

11. Farmers could not sell their produce—honey, wine, and herbs—because there were no roads or ports; see I. Karemalis, "Pros tous Ikarious," *Ikariaka,* 2, 1958. Karamanlis' designation of roads: Christopher Montague Woodhouse, *Karamanlis: The Restorer of Greek Democracy* (Oxford, 1982), p. 47. John Manta in a letter to John A. Papalas, April, 17, 1955, dis-

cusses the road and his willingness to contribute $10,000 toward its completion.

12. Letters of G. Tsantiris to John A. Papalas, Feb. 28, 1955; July 26, 1955.

13. Discussion of reissuing check, letter John A. Papalas to G. Tsantiris, Nov. 7, 1955, and letter of Dr. Levis to John A. Papalas, Dec. 20, 1955. These letters are in the Icarian Archives in Verona. Document 2406, 1955, Public Works Ministry, and letter G. Tsantiris to John A. Papalas, Oct. 27, 1955, in Icarian Archives in Verona. Machinery: Woodhouse, *Karamanlis,* p. 50. For the concept of *philotimia,* see Irwin Sanders, *Rainbow in the Rock* (Cambridge, Massachusetts, 1962), pp. 283–294, and J. K. Campbell, "Traditional Values and Continuities in Greek Society," in Richard Clogg, ed., *Greece in the 1980's* (New York, 1983), pp. 184–207.

14. Woodhouse, *Karamanlis,* p. 96.

15. John A. Papalas to J. Mylonas, Oct. 10, 1955. Ten thousand per kilometer: John A. Papalas to G. Tsantiris, Nov. 29, 1955; K. Diamantides, editor of *Ikaria Phoné,* in a letter to John A. Papalas, Nov. 3, 1955, discusses the reasons for Karamanlis' deleting the Icarian road from his public-works budget. Tsantiris pleas for more money: Letter G. Tsantiris to John A. Papalas, August 3, 1955. Icarians to build 20 kilometers: John A. Papalas to G. Tsantiris, Nov. 7, 1955. All these letters are in the Icarian Archives in Verona. George L. Manta to John A Papalas, November 17, 1955 letter in possession of author.

16. Discrimination against Communists: In 1961, Theologos Fakaros attempted to lodge a complaint against a neighbor who had encroached on his property. The gendarme dismissed the charges out of hand and evicted him from his office, "Get out of here, you damn Bulgarian." The event was witnessed by his son, John Fakaros; interview, Toronto, Canada, Sept. 1, 2002. Fifteen peasants: *Demokratike: Ephemeris tes Samou kai Ikarias,* Karlovasi, 17 July 1964.

17. Theologos Fakaros, 1964–1967; see note above.

18. Authorities placed Theologos Fakaros, mayor of Aghios Kyrikos, in a detention center. He was not exposed to the type of physical abuse he suffered in Greek prisons in 1947; interview, Xyloserti, June 7, 1975. Other Icarians incarcerated by the junta returned to the island with no signs of having been tortured. The junta appointed Aleco Xylas to succeed Fakaros as mayor. "I did not want to serve, but I could not say no. I put my wife in

my store, and did what I could for Icaria. The junta was not bad. You did not need *rousfeti* (connections based on bribes or personal relationships) to get things done in Icaria. You simply had to persuade them that it was good for Greece. They imposed a discipline, threatened some people, dismissed some from their jobs without good reason, but there was no physical abuse. A lot of stories about torture were simply made up by their enemies"; interview, A. Xylas, Aghios Kyrikos, June 27, 2003. Another conservative; interview, I. Kyprios, June 23, 2003, admired the junta for the discipline it imposed on society and the conscientious management of public affairs, but felt that *rousfeti* was not entirely eliminated, and maintained that an Icarian native, S. Pardos, a military officer and army colleague of Papadopoulos, influenced the colonels to build the Icarian road. Pardos was on the committee that petitioned Papadopoulos on December 22, 1970, for aid to Icaria. See below n. 29.

19. People of toil: T. Papakonstantinou, *Politiki Agogi* (Athens, 1970), pp. 224–226. Junta on the monarchy: David Holden, *Greece Without Columns* (Philadelphia, 1972), pp. 266–267. Sinister monarchy: interview, Th. Vassilaros, Aghios Kyrikos, June 29, 2003.

20. John Pesmazoglu, "The Greek Economy since 1967," in *Greece under Military Rule,* edited by Richard Clogg and G. Yannopoulos (London, 1972), p. 76, estimated the shortfall in tourism and related revenues at 400 million dollars for the period 1967 to 1971. Also see the remarks of C. M. Woodhouse, *The Rise and Fall of the Greek Colonels* (New York, 1985), p. 51. Hilton of the Aegean: *Ikariake Phoné,* October 1974.

21. Letter from Icarian-Brotherhood of Athens, S. Vassilaros (president), S. Pardos (vice president), and G. Kassiotes (secretary), to President George Papadopoulos, December 22, 1970. Pardos was a military officer who had known Papadopoulos during his army days and had a distinguished career fighting with government forces during the civil war. The committee also included a wish list of public works for Icaria among which was the road from Aghios Kyrikos to Evdilos. Convention: *"Peraste kai apo to Spiti Mas," Ikariaka,* 6, 1972, p. 1. An interview and the perusal of the private papers of George Kassiotes, a civil servant, secretary of the Icarian-Brotherhood of Icarians in Athens, who organized the convention, Aghios Kyrikos, May 14, 2002. Kassiotes went to America in the summer of 1971 to make preparations, and to encourage Icarian-Americans to attend the convention.

22. Interview, Vasilis Fratelos, Pittsburgh, Pennsylvania, Sept. 1, 2003.

23. N. Achidafty, interview, Pittsburgh, Pennsylvania, Sept. 1, 2003. Golf course: Speech of Kassiotes, June 17, 1971, Lincoln Park, Michigan, to approximately 50 Icarian-Americans. Dr. S. Vassilaros, who assisted in the arrangements for this affair, believed that the Icarian-American participation in the gathering in Icaria was tied to the public-works projects; interview, Athens, June 30, 2003.

24. N. Achidafty, interview, Pittsburgh, Pennsylvania, Sept. 1, 2003.

25. Loyalty oath: Professor Kalokairinos, from Armenistis, lost his teaching position in the American College in Athens because he did not acquire the loyalty certificate; interview with his son, Angelos Kalokairinos, June 12, 2003, Raches, Icaria, and the official newspaper of the Greek Communist party Rizospastis, Jan. 4, 2001. Vasilis Fratelos lost his permit to sail and became a political refugee in Canada; interview, Pittsburgh, Sept. 1, 2003.

26. Mayor of Aghios Kyrikos: Theologos Fakaros, 1964–1967. In 1965, this position was upgraded to mayor. Theophanes Loukatsos, 1974–1986. In 1975, Loukatsos received 575 votes against his opponents 368, and in 1982, 546 while one of his opponents obtained 362 and the other 466. The results in Raches show greater Communist strength. In 1964, the leftist candidate Sakoutis in Aghios Polikarpos secured 67.8 percent while in Raches H. Spanos received 48.1 percent while two conservatives shared the rest of the vote. In 1982, I. Karemalis, openly running as the KKE candidate, received 52.9 percent in Aghios Polikarpos while M. Karaftis, KKE, collected 57.5 percent in Raches. See Karemalis, *Antistasi,* p. 157, for the concept of *kalos agonistes.*

27. War: Woodhouse, *Karamanlis,* p. 68.

28. An editorial in *Nea Ikaria,* July 17, 1946, defines American "monopolies" as the exploitation of natural resources by a few capitalists. There was a fear that American millionaires would control the profits from the spas at Therma; see Kalambogias *Kokkinos Vrachos,* p. 77. This may be an allusion to to the Icarian Radioactive Hot springs Corporation of America which failed to build a tourist complex at Therma; see below, note 24. The Icarians, particularly the Communists, always overestimated the natural resources of the island and suspected capitalists of wanting them. The editorial on thermal baths, *Ikariaka,* no 7, 1976, takes a more realistic position recognizing the need for an infusion of capital.

29. Fear of widespread infection: Dimitris Dalianes, *1948–1949 To Sanatorio Exoriston tes Ikarias* (Larissa, 1999), p. 29–31. S. Leotsakos, *Ikaria to Nesi tou Radiou* (Athens, 1953), pp. 104–105.

30. Tourists in Raches: Register of Politis Hotel for the decade of the 1930s notes months but not years. MacNeice, "The Island" in *Burnt Offerings,* p. 59, describes political prisoners. Also see Jon Stallworthy, *Louis MacNeice* (New York, 1995), p. 383.

31. During Andrews's sojourn in Icaria, he completed a scholarly book *The Castles of the Morea* (1953). His masterpiece, *Flight of Icarus* (1959), despite its title, does not deal with his Icarian experience. Spy: interview, Nikos Fakaros, Raches, May 12, 1992.

32. E. Bradford, *The Companion Guide to the Greek Islands* (New York, 1963), provides tourist information about the Aegean islands, even noting tiny Pholegandros, but makes no mention of Icaria. J. Saray, *E Architechnike tes Periphimou Loutropoleos Ikarias* (Athens, 1956), and the more detailed English version, *The Icarian Radioactive Hot Springs Corporation of America,* (no date or place of publication). Attack on Malachias Ch. Kratsas, *E Seghronos Exelixis ton Loutron tes Ikarias* (Athens, 1958), pp. 8–10. The main hotel owner of Therma, who was reluctant to trade his real estate for shares, complained about the failure of the corporation to develop Therma and stated that henceforth people on the island would have no confidence in their American compatriots; letter of Christos N. Kratsas, to John. A. Papalas, from Aghios Kyrikos, Aug. 18, 1958, in author's private collection. A majority of the Icarians felt that the people on the island should share the profits from the spas; see *Nea Ikaria,* Aug. 1, 1946. N. A. Vassilaros in a letter dated Jan. 5, 1956, to John A. Papalas notes the lack of progress in developing the spa and the dissatisfaction of the shareholders. Steps leading to dissolution of the corporation: October 20, 1956, in *Minutes and Correspondence of Pan-Icarian Brotherhood of America 1956–1957* in Icarian Archives, Verona. Malachias prescriptions in America: interview Themistocles Speis, Perdiki, June 12, 2004. Speis met Dr. Malachias during his American tour.

33. John Melas' speech in parliament on behalf of Icaria, and the response of the undersecretary of communications recorded in *Ikariake Phoné,* April 30, 1962. Melas noted ten thousand annual visitors to Therma, but this figure seems inflated and perhaps includes native Icarians returning for the summer. Banks: *Nea Ikaria,* Sept. Oct. 1994. Doctors: *Nea Ikaria,* June 1991.

34. John Kyprios installed the electrical facilities and served as a general contractor on the project. He was paid with worthless stock; interview, Aghios Kyrikos, June 27, 2003. Durrell arrived in Aghios Kyrikos shortly after the Toula was completed. In his *Greek Islands* (New York, 1978), p. 167, he described Icaria as a messy and unbecoming island with peculiarly laid out roads. Durrell did not mention the Toula Hotel. After the Toula closed, the inhabitants of Aghios Kyrikos made no great efforts to attract tourists. The authors of *Let's Go Greece* (New York, 1985), p. 333, write that "when you get off the ferry in Aghios Kyrikos you'll notice that a large fraction of the backpackers makes a beeline for the old bus at the end of the deck without so much as a sidelong glance." They are heading for Armenistis and the authors recommend "follow them."

35. See editorial, *Atheras,* January, February 1989, referring to Papandreou as *Tselementes tou PASOK,* "the pastry chef for PASOK," and complaining that he was playing into the hands of right-wing elements. An editorial in *Atheras,* May, June 1989, asserted that both PASOK and Nea Demokratia treated Icaria like a disinherited offspring. In 1994, a member of the KKE proposed in parliament that the government allocate 400,000,000 drachmas to sponsor aerial games in Icaria. PASOK rejected the request because they were not Olympic games, and recommended they be funded privately; see *Nea Ikaria,* March 1994.

36. T. Vassilaros, *Ikariake Phoné,* August 15, 1977. T. Vassilaros, *Ikariake Phoné,* Sept. 1977.

37. N. D. Pavlides, *"Tourismos kai Ikaria,"* *Ikariaka,* 8, May, 1977, 2–5.

38. Two brothers born in Icaria, Zacharias Kratsas and Apostolis Kratsas, who were members of Nea Demokratia, and served in the government, lobbied for the airport. Zacharias Kratsas, who was then representing Samos and Icaria in parliament, discussed the local opposition to the project in *Ikariake Phoné,* May 1977. The visit of Prime Minister Mitsotakis to Icaria: *Nea Ikaria,* Sept. 1993. Apostolis Kratsas, also a member of parliament representing a district in Athens, at that time was serving as undersecretary for transformation and communication. He was the main force for building the airport. "I slipped the airport into the budget by bribing other politicians with telephone lines which were then very scarce. Mitsotakis was a bit surprised when he heard about the airport because it was not in his budget, but he smiled. I allocated these lines to politicians in various parts of Greece, and then did not have enough to satisfy my own constituents. I got the airport, but at great political cost to myself. The most embarrassing moment in my political career came when Mitsotakis saw the black flags. My constituents in Athens, who were demanding telephone connections, were not impressed with my concern for Icaria, and the Icarians were ungrateful for

the airport." Interview, Negia, Icaria, June 27, 2003. Critics of the airport accused Kratsas of profiting from the enterprise by having DEH bring electricity to his house in Negia and for getting asphalt roads built on the island for the benefit of himself and friends. Kratsas pointed out to the author the dirt road leading to his house, and the generator he built for electricity. He was defended against charges of personal profit by J. Tripolas, *Atheras,* Jan. March 1994. Lobsters: Interview with Icaria's most successful entrepreneur, the fishmonger Antonis Pyrovolikos, Aghios Kyrikos, May 23, 2002.

39. Number of Icarians in Athens and Piraeus: Letter of G. Kassiotes, secretary of the Icarian-Brotherhood of Athens, December 22, 1970. Albanians: *Atheras,* May 1993.

40. Drugs: *Atheras,* Sept. Oct. 1989; *Nea Ikaria,* March 1990. Conference: *Nea Ikaria,* Jan. Feb. 1997.

41. Hard life for young Icarians; see essay of J. Liares, *"E Nea Genia Mas,"* *Nea Ikaria,* Nov. 2, 1946, who describes the difficult life of the prewar generation and argues that the postwar youth were more impoverished. Morality propounded by Junta; see pro-regime newspaper: *Eleftheros Kosmos,* 26 Feb. 1971, and remarks of G. Papadopoulos, *To Pistevo Mas* (Athens, 1971), 4, 205.

42. *Atheras,* Sept. Oct. 1989; *Atheras,* April May 1995; *Nea Ikaria,* Sept. 1993; *Atheras,* June July 1994.

43. A. Alexandrou, *To Kivotio* (Athens, 1974).

44. The Xeros brothers are sons of a Greek Orthodox priest who was born in Akamatra, and served as priests in Koutoumas, Icaria. One of the bothers, Christodoulos, spent summers in Akamatra. This is not the place to assess the movement, whether its adherents were primarily interested in living the good life by combining bank robbery with assassinations, or motivated by genuine political ideals.

45. For a typical obituary see, "Eulogy for Kostas Saphos," *Atheras,* June, August 2003. In contrast to the provincial mentality of local Communists was the outlook of the radical journalist Michalis Raptis, born in Icaria, but who was so committed to internationalism that he never alluded to Icaria and claimed he was a citizen of the world. He had an influence on the November 17th gang, who referred to him by his code name Pablos. Raptis broke with its leader Yiotopoulos because he did not believe in violence; see *Eleutherotypia,* July 29, 2002.

Select
Bibliography

Ahrweiler, H. *Byzance et la mer: la marine de guerre la politique et les institutions maritimes de Byzance aux VIIe–XVe siècles* (Paris, 1966).

Alexandrou, A. *To Kivotio* (Athens, 1974).

Alexandris, K. *The Greek Marine in the War of Independence (*Athens, 1968).

Alexandris, A. "Turkish Policy towards Greece during the Second World War and Its Import on Greek-Turkish Détente," *Balkan Studies* 23 (1982), 157–197.

Alexiou, M. "Modern Greek Folklore and its Relation to the Past: The Evolution of Charos in Greek Tradition," In Vryonis, S., Ed. *The "Past" in Medieval and Modern Greek Culture* (Malibu, California, 1978), pp. 221–236.

Anagnostakes, M. *Poems, Postscriptum* (Athens, 1992).

Anderson, Roger Charles. *Naval Wars in the Levant, 1559–1853* (Liverpool, 1952).

Anonymous. *Life of a Midshipman: A Tale Founded on Fact and Intended to Correct an Injudicious Predilection in Boys for the Life of a Sailor* (London, 1829).

Anonymous. *Tourist Brochure: Rachai tes Ikarias: Exochos topos Therines Diamones, Committee for Tourism* (Raches, Icaria, 1931).

Anonymous. *E Ikaria Sklavonetai* (New York, 1948).

Anonymous. *The Icarian Radioactive Hot Springs Corporation of America* (Chicago, 1950).

Anonymous. *Katastatikon tou Philekpaideutikou Sylogou Ikarion "O Sokrates"* (New York, 1926).

Andréades, A. "L'administration financière de la Grèce sous la domination turque," *Revue des Études Grecques*, 23 (1910), 131–183.

Andréades, A. "The Currant Crisis in Greece," *Economic Journal* vol. 16, no. 61 (1906), 41–54.

Angel, J. L. *The People of Lerna: Analysis of a Prehistoric Aegean Population* (Princeton, 1971).

Archer, L. *Athens Journal 1940–1941: The Graeco-Italian and the Graeco-German Wars and the German Operation* (Manhattan, Kansas, 1983).

Archer, L. *The Balkan Journal* (New York, 1944).

Argenti, P. P. *Chius Vincta or the Occupation of Chios by the Turks (1566) & Their Administration of the Island, 1566–1912* (Cambridge, 1941).

Argenti, P. P. and S. E. Kyriakidis. *Chios Para Tois Geographois Kai Periegetais* (Athens, 1946).

Argenti, P. P. *The Occupation of Chios by the Germans 1941–1944* (Cambridge, 1966).

Asdrachas, S., and I. Asdracha. "Vaptistika kai Oikogeneiaka Onomata se mia Nesiotike Koinonia: Patmos" in *Ste Mneme P. Apostolopoulou* (Athens, 1984).

Augustinos, Gerasimos. *The Greeks of Asia Minor: Confessions, Community and Ethnicity in the Nineteenth Century* (Kent, 1992).

Augustinos, Olga. *French Odysseys: Greece in French Travel Literature from the Renaissance to the Romantic Era* (Baltimore, 1994).

Avdoulou, S. *To Phainomeno Makronesos* (Athens, 1998).

Baedeker, K. *The Mediterranean: Seaports and Sea Routes* (Leipzig, 1911).

Barentzen, L. "The German Withdrawal from Greece in 1944 and British Naval Inactivity," *Journal Modern Greek Studies* (5) 1987, 237–239.

Bartziotas, V. O. *Agonas tou Demokratikou Stratou Elladas* (Athens, 1982).

Bartziotas, V. *Exenta Chronia Kommounistes* (Athens, 1986).

Batouyios, N. "The Early Ikarians of the United States and the Pan-Icarian Brotherhood of America," *Ikaria* 24, (2002), 11–14.

Beatty, J. *Colossus: How the Corporation Changed America* (New York, 2002).

Bechmann, Roland. *Trees and Man: The Forest in the Middle Ages* (New York, 1990).

Beckett, M. "The Aegean Adventures of Captain John Pyke: Royal Artillery, Civilian Affairs Officer attached to the Special Boat Squadron," *The Bulletin of the Military Historical Society,* vol. 46, no. 184 (May 1996), 186–194.

Belon, P. *Les observations de plusieurs singularités et choses mémorables trouvées en Grèce* (Paris, 1553).

Berghold, C., and K. Styrein. *Surface Water Storage on the Island of Ikaria, Greece: A Preliminary Feasibility Study* (Stockholm, Royal Institute of Technology, 1993).

Blum, Richard and Eva. *The Dangerous Hour: The Lore of Crisis and Mystery in Rural Greece* (New York, 1970).

Booth, C. D. and I. B. *Italy's Aegean Possessions* (London, 1928).

Bosworth, R. "Britain and Italy's Acquisition of the Dodecanese, 1912–1915", *The Historical Journal 13* (4), 1970, 685–686.

Bragadini, M. A. trans. G. Hoffman. *The Italian Navy in World War II* (Annapolis, 1957).

Brummett, P. "Overrated Adversary: Rhodes and Ottoman Naval Power," *Historical Journal*, 36, 3 (1993), 517–541.

Brummett, P. *Ottoman Seapower and Levantine Diplomacy in the Age of Discovery* (Albany, 1994).

Buondelmonti, C. in Legrand's *Description des îles de l'Archipel* (Paris, 1897).

Bürchner, L. "Ikaros-Nicaria, eine vergessene Insel des griechischen Archipels," *Petermans Mitteilungen* 40 (1894), 256–261.

Campbell, J. K. "Traditional Values and Continuities in Greek Society," in Richard Clogg, ed., *Greece in the 1980's* (New York, 1983), pp. 184–207.

Campbell, J. K. *Honour, Family and Patronage: A Study of Institutions and Moral Values in a Greek Mountain Community* (London, 1964).

Carabott, P. J. "A British Military Occupation under a British Military Governor but without a British Military Administration: The Case of Samos, 8 September to 18 November 1943," *Journal of Modern Greek Studies*, 7, 2, (1989), 287–319.

Cervi, Mario. *The Hollow Legions: Mussolini's Blunder in Greece 1940–1941,* translated by Eric Mosbacher, introduction by F. W. Deakin (New York, 1971, and London, 1972).

Charlemont, James Caulfeild, Lord. *The Travels of Lord Charlemont in Greece and Turkey, 1749* (London, 1984).

Christodoulos, I. "E Dolophonia tou Grammatea tou K. K. tou Nomou Samou," *Ikariaka* (34), 1992, 167–170.

Churchill, W. *The Grand Alliance* (Boston, 1950).

Ciano, Galeazzo. *Diaries, 1939–1943*, ed. Hugh Gibson (New York, 1946).

Clogg, Richard, ed. *Greece in the 1980's* (London, 1983).

Close, D. *The Origins of the Greek Civil War* (London, 1995).

Constantine, David. *Early Greek Travellers and the Hellenic Ideal* (Cambridge, 1984).

Coronelli, P. *Dell'Archipelago* (Venice, 1688).

Cruickshank, Charles Greig. *Greece 1940–1941: The Politics and Strategy of the Second World War* (London, 1976; Newark, Delaware, 1989).

Cunningham, A. B. *A Sailor's Odyssey* (New York, 1951).

Dakin, D. *The Greek Struggle for Independence, 1821–1833* (Berkeley, 1973).

Dalianes, D. 1948–1949, *To Sanatorio Exoriston tes Ikarias* (Larrisa, 1999).

Dallaway, J. *Constantinople Ancient and Modern, with Excursions to the Shores and islands of the Archipelago and the Troad* (London, 1797).

Davais, D. G. *Patmos: The Sacred Island* (Athens, n.d.).

Davison, Roderic H. "Advent of the Electric Telegraph in the Ottoman Empire," in his *Essays in Ottoman and Turkish History, 1774–1923: The Impact of the West* (Austin, Texas 1990, pp. 137–148).

Deringil, Selim. *Turkish Foreign Policy during the Second World War: An "Active" Neutrality* (Cambridge, 1989).

Diamantides, N. "Aristides E. Phoutrides: Harvard's Schizocardiac Scholar," *Modern Greek Studies Yearbook* 8 (1992), 75–93.

Du Boulay, J. *Portrait of a Greek Mountainous* Village (Oxford, 1979).

Economakis, R. *Nisyros: History and Architecture of an Aegean Island* (Athens, 2001).

Edlund-Berry, Ingrid E. M. *The Gods and the Place: The Location and Function of Sanctuaries in the Countryside of Etruria and Magna Graecia (700–400 B.C.)* (Stockholm, 1987).

Eleuthera Politeia Ikarias (Aghios Kyrikos, n.d.).

Eudes, D. *The Kapetanios: Partisans and Civil War in Greece 1943–1949* (New York, 1972).

Evangelides, T. E. E *Paideia epi Tourkokratias* (Athens, 1936).

Evangelides, T. E. E *Mykonos: Istoria tes Nesou apo ton Archaiotaton Chronon mechri ton kath Emas* (Athens, 1914).

Fairchild, Henry Pratt. *Greek Immigration to the United States* (New Haven, Connecticut, 1911).

Field, H. *The Greek Islands and Turkey after the War* (New York, 1885).

Filitti, G. P. "Une visite chez le prince de Samos 1848," *E Samos apo ta Vyzantina Chronia Mechri Semera* (Athens, 1998), 2, 467–472.

Findley, C. V. *Ottoman Civil Officialdom: A Social History* (Princeton, 1989).

Findley, C. V. *Bureaucratic Reform in the Ottoman Empire: The Sublime Porte, 1789–1922* (Princeton, 1980).

Fleischer, Hagen. *Im Kreuzschatten der Möchte: Griechenland 1941–1944* (Frankfurt am Main and New York, 1986).

Foot, M. R. D., and J. M. Langley. *MI 9: The British Secret Service that Fostered Escape and Evasion 1939–1945 and its American Counterpart* (London, 1979).

Fourni: http://www.geocities.com/fournoi2001/greek.htm.

Fortescue, A. K. *The Orthodox Eastern Church* (London, 1916).

Fradelou-Kokkore, C. "Gia ten Paradosiake Foresia tes Ikarias," *Ikariaka* 42 (2001), 207–210.

Friedl, E. *Vassilika: A Village in Modern Greece* (New York, 1962).

Georgirenes, J. *Description of Patmos, Samos, Nicaria and Mt. Athos* (London, 1677).

Gerber, H. "Jewish Tax Farmers in the Ottoman Empire in the 16th and 17th centuries," *Journal of Turkish Studies*, 10 (1986), 143–145.

Gerolymatos, André. *Red Acropolis, Black Terror—the Greek Civil War and the Origins of Soviet-American Rivalry, 1943–1949* (New York, 2004).

Giagourtas, G. *E Oikonomike Zoe tes Ikarias apo ta Mesa tou 19ou os ta Mesa tou 20ou Aeona: E Paragoge kai Emporia tes Staphidas* (Athens, 2002).

González, R. *Embajada a Tamolorán* (Madrid, 1943).

Graham, G. S. "The Ascendancy of Sailing Ships 1850–1885," *Economic History Review* 9 (1956), 74–78.

Great Britain Admiralty Hydrographic Department *New Pilot Directions for the Mediterranean* (London, 1831).

Greene J., and A. Massignani *The Naval War in the Mediterranean, 1940–1943* (London, 1998).

Guilmartin, John Francis. *Gunpowder and Galleys: Changing Technology and Mediterranean Warfare at Sea in the 16th Century* (Cambridge 1980).

Hackett, L. W. *Malaria in Europe: An Ecological Study* (London, 1937).

Haghimichali, A. "L'art populaire Grec : L'île d'Icarie," *Byzantinische-neugriechische Jahrbücher*, 6 (1927–1928), 32–51.

Hanioğlu, Ş. *The Young Turks in Opposition* (Oxford, 1995).

Hasluck, F. W. "Depopulation in the Aegean Islands," Annual *British School at Athens 17 (1922),* 151–175.

Hatzidakis, G. "Peri tes Ikarias Dialectou," *Messaionika kai Nea Ellenika* (Amsterdam, 1990), 2, 397–460.

Hauttecoeur, H. "L'île d'Ikaria," *Bulletin de la Société Géographique d'Anvers* 25 (1900), 329–363.

Heckstall-Smith, Anthony and H. T. Baille-Grohman, *A Greek Tragedy 1941* (New York, 1961).

Heers, J. *Gênes au XVᵉ siècle* (Paris, 1961).

Herlihy, P. "The Greek Communities in Odessa, 1816–1917," *Journal of Modern Greek Studies* 7, 2 (1988), 242–244.

Herzfeld, Michael. *Ours Once More: Folklore, Ideology, and the Making of Modern Greece* (New York, 1986).

Hess, A. C. "The Evolution of the Ottoman Seaborne Empire in the Age of the Oceanic Discoveries, 1453–1525," *American Historical Review*, 75, no, 7 (1970), 1892–1919.

Hirschon, Renée. *Heirs of the Greek Catastrophe: The Social Life of Asia Minor Refugees in Piraeus* (Oxford, 1989).

Holden, D. *Greece Without Columns* (Philadelphia, 1972).

Holland, Jeffrey; foreword by David Lloyd Owen. *The Aegean Mission: Allied Operations in the Dodecanese, 1943.* (New York, 1988).

Horden, P., and N. Purcell. *The Corrupting Sea: A Study of Mediterranean History* (Oxford, 2000).

Horton, G. *Home of Nymphs and Vampires: The Isles of Greece* (New York, 1929).

Iatrides, John O. *Revolt in Athens: The Greek Communist "Second Round," 1944–1945* (Princeton, 1972).

Iatrides, John O. *Ambassador MacVeagh's Reports: Greece, 1933–1947* (Princeton, 1980).

Iatrides John O., and N. Rizopoulos. "The International Dimension of the Greek Civil War," *World Policy Journal*, Spring 18, 1 (2000), 87–103.

Ioannou, N. P. *E Ikariake Epanastasis kata to 1912: Drama eis Praxeis Treis* (Alexandria, Egypt, 1912).

Irineos, Archbishop of Samos and Icaria. *E Dynameis tou Ellenochristianikou Pneumatos: Anamnesis kai Enteposeis apo ten Katoche tes Nesou Samou kai ten Mese Anatole* (Athens, 1948).

Issawi, C. *The Economic History of Turkey, 1800–1914* (Chicago, 1980).

Jacopi, S. "Scavi e richerchi di Nisiro," *Clara Rhodos*, 6–7, 2, 469–552.

Jameson, M. J. "Sacrifice and Animal Husbandry in Classical Greece," in C. R. Whitaker, ed., *Pastoral Economies in Classical Antiquity*, Cambridge

Philosophical Society Supplementary, volume 14 (Cambridge, England, 1988), pp. 87–119.

Jarvis, George. *George Jarvis: His Journal and Related Documents.* Thessaloniki, 1965).

Jennings, R. "The Population, Taxation, and Wealth in Cities of Cyprus according to the Detailed Population Survey (Defter-I-Mufasial of 1572)," *Journal of Turkish Studies*, 10 (1986), 175–189.

Jones, William Henry Samuel. *Malaria: A Neglected Factor in the History of Greece and Rome* (Cambridge, England, 1907).

Kalambogias, A. *Ikaria: O Kokkinos Vrachos* (Athens, 1975).

Karimalis, S. *E Nikaria Sten Antistasi* (Athens, 1992).

Karpat, K. "Ottoman Population Records and the Census of 1881/1882–1893," *International Journal of Middle East Studies,* 9 (1978), 237–273.

Karpat, K. "The Ottoman Emigration to America, 1860–1914" *International Journal of Middle East Studies*, 17 (1985), 175–209.

Karpat, K. *Ottoman Population 1830–1914. Demographic and Social Characteristics* (Madison, 1985).

Kasdagli, A. E. "Gender Differentiation and Social Practice in Post-Byzantine Naxos," in *The Byzantine Tradition after the Fall of Constantinople* (Charlottesville, Virginia, 1991), pp. 61–94.

Kasperson, R. E. *The Dodecanese: Diversity and Unity in Island Politics* (Chicago, 1966).

Katastatikon tou Philekpaideutikou Syllogou Ikarias (New York, 1926).

Katsas, G. *Etan O Dromos Sostos? Apo Ikaria, Athena, Intzedin, Aegina* (Athens, 1992).

Katsaros, T. "Aghios Kyrikos Ikarias," *Ikariaka* (42) 2001, 20–22.

Kenna, M. E. *Greek Island Life: Fieldwork on Anafi* (Amsterdam, 2001).

Kenna, M. E. *The Social Organization of Exile: The Greek Political Detainees in the 1930s* (Amsterdam, 2001).

Kédros, A. *La Résistance Grecque, 1940–1944* (Paris, 1966).

Klehr, H. "Gus Hall," *American National Biography. Supplement,* Vol. 1 (Oxford, 2002).

Kochilas, X. "E Ikaria os topos exorias," *Kathemerine*, 21, April 1998.

Kolodny, E. *La Population des îles de la Grèce: essai de geographiqe en Mediterranée orientale* (Aix-en-Provence, 1974).

Konstantinopoulos, G. "Dodekanesa: Italokratia-Ensomatose," *Ephemerida E Kathemerine Epta Emerai*, 30, Nov. 1997.

Koukoules, Ph. *Vyzantinon Vios kai Politismos* (Athens, 1948–1955).

Koumparou, D. *The Communal Management of the Radi forest on Icaria Island, Greece* (Mytiline, Lesvos, 2001).

Kousoulas, D. G. *Istoria tou Kommounistikou Kommatos Ellados* (Athens, 1976).

Kratsas, Ch. *E Sechronos Exelixis ton Loutron tes Ikarias* (Athens, 1958).

Lamb, R. *War in Italy: A Brutal Story* (New York, 1993).

Landrou, C. "E Lestoperateia sten Samo peri ta mesa tou 19ou Aiona," in *E Samos apo ta Vyzantina Chronia mechri Semera* (Athens, 1998) 181–230.

Langensiepen, B., and A. Güleryüz, *The Ottoman Steam Navy, 1828–1923* (Annapolis 1995).

Legnani, A. *Il Dodecaneso e la sua base navale* (Taranto, 1923).

Leon, G. B. "Greece and the Central Powers, 1913–1914: The Origins of the National Schism," *Südost-Forschungen* 39 (1985), 116–167.

Leotsakos, S. *Ikaria to Nesi tou Radiou* (Athens, 1953).

Levi, A. A., and G. Fioravanzo. *La Marina Italiana nella Seconda Guerra Mondiale: Attività dopo L'Armistizio. Avvenimenti in Egeo* (Rome, 1957).

Lithgow, W. *Travels and voyages through Europe, Asia and Africa, for nineteen years containing an account of the religion, government, policy, laws, customs, trade etc. of the several countries through which the author travelled and a description of Jerusalem and other remarkable places mentioned in sacred and profane history. Also a narrative of the torture he suffered in the Spanish Inquisition and his miraculous deliverance from those cruelties* (Leith, 1814).

Lock, P. *The Franks in the Aegean, 1204–1500* (London, 1995).

Lodwick, John. *Raiders from the Sea: The Story of the Special Boat Service in World War II* (Annapolis, 1990).

Logothetes, M. "E Ensomatose tes Dodekanesou," *Istorika, Eleutherotypia*, 8, March 2001, 24–31.

Logothetes, M. "Oikonomia kai Plethismos," *Istorika, Eleutherotypia*, 8, March 2001, 31–36.

Lombardas, P. *Taragmena Chronia: Katoche, Ethnike Antistase Emphylios Polemos sten Ikaria* (Athens, 1987).

Lombardas, G. *Ikaria etoi Geographike tes Nesou Perigraphe* (Syros, Greece 1903).

Lombardas, G. P. "Gia to EAM tes Ikarias," *Ikariaka*, 42 (2001), 42–46.

Loupes, D. *O Piri Reis (1465–1553), Chartographe to Aigaio: E Othomanike Chartographia kai E Limne tou Aigaiou* (Athens, 1999).

Louis, J. C. *The Greek Communist Party, 1940–1944* (London, 1982).

Luttrell, Anthony. *The Hospitallers of Rhodes and Their Mediterranean World* (Aldershot, 1992).

Lykogiannis, A. "The Bank of Greece, 75 Years: 1928–2003," *Journal of Hellenic Diaspora* 21.1 (2003), 77–98.

Lymberake, M. *Ta Psathina Kapela* (Athens, 2001).

Macfie, A. L.. *The End of the Ottoman Empire, 1908–1923* (London, 1998).

MacNeice, L. *Ten Burnt Offerings* (London, 1951).

Makkas, C. *E Istoria tes Kommounistikes Organosis Ikarias* (Athens, 1989).

Makkas, C. *Oi Anamneses Mou apo te Mese Anatole* (Ikaria, 1981).

Malachias, T. G. *O Gero Kapetan Giannis Malachias* (Athens, 1985).

Malachias, T. G. *Anekdota Diegemata* (Athens, 1967).

Malandrakes, M. "Nesiotika Chronia," *Ellenika* 10 (1937/1938), 69–116.

Margarites, G. *Istoria tou Ellenikou Emphyliou Polemou, 1946–1949* (Athens, 2001).

Margarones, M. *Geographia Nomou Samou* (Karlovassi, Samos, 1966).

Mastny, V. *Russia's Road to the Cold War: Diplomacy, Warfare and the Politics of Communism, 1941–1945* (New York, 1979).

Maurand, J. *Itinéraires d'Antibes à Constantinople, 1544* (Paris, 1901).

Mavrogeorgis, C. *Odysseia Stes Niotes ta Chronia se Xenes Patrides* (Athens, 2002).

Mavrogeorgis, C. Yiannis *Salas* (Athens, 1998).

Mazower, M. *Inside Hitler's Greece: The Experience of Occupation 1941–1944* (Yale, 1993).

Mazower, M. "Three Forms of Political Justice: Greece, 1944–1945," in *After The War Was Over: Reconstructing the Family, Nation, and State in Greece, 1943–1960*, (Princeton, 2000), pp. 32–33.

McNeill, William Hardy. *Plagues and People* (Garden City, New York, 1976).

Mears, E. G. *Greece Today: The Aftermath of the Refugee Impact* (Stanford, 1929).

Megas, G. "Ta Anemotaphia tes Ikarias," *Deltion tes Ellenikes Laographikes Etaireias*, 16, 1 (1956), 250–256.

Megaloekonomou-Moschovake, Omorphoula. *Matia Pelagissia-Poemata* (Ikaria, 2000).

Melas, J. *Istoria tes Nesou Ikarias* (Athens, 1958).

Melas, J. "Georgios Rhodios," *Ikariaka* 8 (1959), 6–15.

Miller, W. *A History of the Greek People, 1821–1921* (London, 1922).

Morton, J. *The Role of the Physical Environment in Ancient Greek Seafaring* (Leiden, 2001).

Murray's Hand-Book: *Turkey in Asia, Constantinople* (London, 1878).

Newton, C. *Travels and Discoveries in the Levant*, vol. 2 (London, 1858).

Noou, N. *Ta Paidia tes Thyellas* (Athens, 1993).

O'Ballance, E. *The Greek Civil War, 1944–1949* (London 1966).

Olivier, G. *Voyage dans l'Empire Ottoman fait par ordre du gouvernement, pendant les six premières années de la République* (Paris, 1801–1807).

Palmer, S. "The indemnity in the London Marine Insurance Market," in *The Historian and the Business of Insurance*, edited by O. M. Westall (Manchester, 1984), pp. 74–94.

Pamphylis, A. C. *To Ikariakon Eidyllion tou 1912 kai Semeioseis peri tes Ikarias* (Athens, 1914).

Pamphylis, Ch. *Istoria tes Nesou Ikarias* (Athens, 1980).

Pamuk, Şevket. *A Monetary History of the Ottoman Empire* (New York, 2000).

Pamuk, Şevket. "Commodity Production for World Markets and Relations of Production," in *Ottoman Agriculture in the Ottoman Empire and the World Economy* (Paris, 1987), pp. 178–202.

Papadopoulos, G. *To Pistevo Mas* (Athens, 1971).

Papageorgakis, G. *Ikaria sten Thyella* (Piraeus, 1985).

Papagiannis, S. *Apo Evelpis Andartes: Anamenseis enos Kommouniste Axiomatikou* (Athens, 1991).

Papakonstantinou, T. *Politike Agoge* (Athens, 1970).

Papalas, Anthony J. *Ancient Icaria* (Wauconda, Illinois, 1992).

Papathanasopoulos, K. "Greek Shipping in Its Historical Context," in *Greece and the Sea* (Amsterdam, 1987).

Papatheodorou, J. "Sto Ergastirio tou Mythistorigraphou," *Diavazo* 171 (1983), 28–32.

Parianos, C. T. *O Demokratikos Stratos Ikarias* (Athens, 2000).

Parish, Michael Woodbine. *Aegean Adventures 1940–1943 and the End of Churchill's Dream* (Sussex, 1993).

Pavlides, N. D. "Tourismos kai Ikaria," *Ikariaka*, 8, May, 1977, 2–5.

Pentzopoulos, D. *The Balkan Exchange of Minorities and its Impact upon Greece* (Paris and the Hague, 1962)

Perry, C. *A View of the Levant Particularly of Constantinople, Syria, Egypt and Greece* (London, 1743).

Pesmazoglu, J. "The Greek Economy since 1967," in *Greece under Military Rule* (London, 1972), 75–108.

Petacco, A. *La Nostra Guerra, 1940–1945—L'Avventura bellica tra bugie e verità* (Milan, 1995).

Petropoulos, N. A. *Anamneses enos Palaiou Nautikou* (Athens, 1971).

Pitcairn Jones, C. G. *Piracy in the Levant, Selected Papers of Admiral Edward Codrington* (London, 1934).

Plakidas, A. *It Could Happen Only in America* (Athens, 1966).

Plakidas, A. "Allo Ena Palio Kariotiko Engrapho," *Ikariaka* 37 (1966), 187–189.

Plakidas, A. "Icarian Phytopathological Remedies," *Pan-Icarian Convention Book* (Youngstown, 1935).

Polites, N. *Paradoseis* (Athens, 1965).

Poulianos, Alexis. *Laika Tragoudia tes Ikarias* (Athens, 1964).

Poulianos, Aris. *E Proeleuse ton Ellenon* (Athens, 1982).

Poulianos, D. "Maria Vatouyios" *Ikariake Phoné*, 31, Oct/Nov. 1963, and *Ikariaka* 27/28, 1963.

Powell, D. *Remember Greece* (New York, 1943).

Prasca, V. *Io ho aggredito la Grecia* (Rome, 1946).

Protopsaltes, E. "E Tyche ton Notion Sporadon kata ten Epanastasin kai met' auten," *Karpathiakai Meletai* 2 (1981), 287–307.

Ptinis, K. *Chronia Katoches, Symvole Sten Istoria tes Samou 1941–1944* (Samos, 1986).

Ptinis, K. *E Samos kai to 21* (Samos, 1990).

Quartert, D. *Social Disintegration and Popular Resistance in the Ottoman Empire, 1881–1908. Reactions to European Economic Penetration* (New York, 1983).

Ramsay, W. M. "A Romaic Ballad," *Journal of Hellenic Studies*, 1 (1888), 293–300.

Randolph, B. Bernard Randolph, *The Present State of the Islands in the Archipelago, (or Arches) Sea of Constantinople, and Gulph of Smyrna; with the islands of Candia, and Rhodes. Faithfully Described by Ber. Randolph. To Which is annexed an index, shewing the longitude and latitude of all the places in the new map of Greece lately published by the same author* (Oxford, 1687).

Redfield, R. "The Folk Society," *American Journal of Sociology*, 52 (1947), 293–308.

Reger, G. *Regionalism and Change in the Economy of Independent Delos* (Berkeley, 1994).

Robert, L. "Les Asklepieis de l'Archipel," *Revue des Études Grecques*, 46 (1933), 423–441.

Roberts, Mr. *Adventures among the Corsairs of the Levant. His Account of their Villainous Ways of Living. Description of the Archipelago* (London. 1694).

Roberts, P. *The Immigrant Wage Economy, Wage Earning in Pittsburgh* (New York, 1911).

Ross, L. *Inselreisen* (Halle, 1913).

Roussos, G. *E Neotere Istoria tes Ellados, 1886–1974* (Athens, n.d).

Rozos, E. *Oi Nesiotes tou Aegaiou ston Agona* (Athens, 1971).

Rozos, E. *O Aigaiopelagitikos Politismos Sta Chronia tes Tourkokratias* (Athens, 1978).

Runciman, Steven *The Great Church in Captivity: A Study of the Patriarchy of Constantinople from the Eve of the Turkish Conquest to the War of Independence* (Cambridge, 1968).

Sakellariou, H. *E Paideia Sten Antistasi* (Athens, 1984).

Saloutas, T. *The Greeks of the United States*, (Cambridge, 1964).

Sanders, I. *Rainbow in the Rock* (Cambridge, 1962).

Saphiris, I. *O Agonas tou Demokratikou Stratou ste Samo* (Athens, 1987).

Sarafis, Stefanos, translated by Sylvia Moody *ELAS: Greek Resistance Army* (London 1960).

Saray, J. *E Architechtonike tes Periphemou Loutropoleos Ikarias* (Athens, 1956).

Saray, J. *The Icarian Radioactive Hot Springs Corporation of America* (no date or place of publication).

Savorinakes, P. *Nesiotikes Koinonies Sto Aigaio: E Periptose ton Ellenon tes Rhodou kai Ko, 19os–20os Aionas* (Athens, n.d.).

Sevastakes, A. *Istoria Neou Karlovassou Samou, 1768–1840* (Athens, 1995).

Seton-Watson, Christopher. *Italy from Liberalism to Fascism, 1870–1925.* (London, 1967).

Shaw, S. J. "Selim III and the Ottoman Navy," *Turcica: Revue d'Etudes Turques*, I (1969), 212–241.

Sherrard, P. *The Greek East and the Latin West* (London, 1959).

Simopoulos, K. *Xenoi Taxidiotes sten Ellada, 333 B.C.–1700* (Athens, 1984).

Siphnaios, E. *Lesvos: Oikonomike kai Koinonike Istoria, 1840–1912* (Athens, 1996).

Sire, H. J. A. *The Knights of Malta* (New Haven, 1994).

Slot, B. J. *Archipelagus turbatus, les Cyclades entre colonisation latine et occupation ottomane c. 1500–1718* (Leiden, 1982).

Smith, P. C., and W. Walker. *War in the Aegean* (London, 1974).

Soucek, S. "A propos du livre d'instruction nautique de Piri Reis," *Revue des Études Islamiques*, 32, 2 (1971), 241–255.

Spanos, L. *Ikariaka Chronika* (Syros, Greece 1925).

Spyridakis, K. "Laographike Apostole eis Ikarian," *Epeteris tou Kentrou Erevnes Laographias*, 15–16 (1962–1963), 230–243.

Spyropoulos, E. *The Greek Military (1909–1941) and the Greek Mutinies in the Middle East (1941–1944)* (New York, 1993).

Stallworthy, J. *Louis MacNeice* (London, 1995).

Stamatiades, Ep. *Ikariaka* (Samos, 1893).

Stamatiades, Ep. *Samiaka* (Samos, 1882).

Stavrakis, Peter J. *Moscow and Greek Communism, 1944–1949* (Ithaca, New York, 1989).

Stavrinou-Valtogianni, C. *Archaologikon Deltion*, 20 (1965), 502–504.

Stewart. C. *Demons and the Devil* (Princeton, 1991).

Stoneman, Richard. *Land of Lost Gods: The Search for Classical Greece* (Norman, 1987).

Tatsios, Theodore George. *The Megali Idea and the Greek-Turkish War of 1897: The Impact of the Cretan Problem on Greek Irredentism, 1866–1897* (Boulder, 1984).

Theodorakis, M. *Oi Dromoi tou Archangelou*, II (Athens, 1986).

Theodorakis, M., and A. Papalas, and G. Depollas. *Ikaria* (Athens, 2002).

Thévenot, J. *Voyage en Europe, Asie et Afrique* (Amsterdam, 1727).

Tournefort, P. *Relation d'un Voyage au Levant, Fait par ordre du roi* (Amsterdam, 1703).

Thrasyvoulos, D. "Agrotike Krisi kai Koinonikoi Mechanismoi: E Penia tou 1854," in *E Samos apo ta Vyzantina Chronia mechri Semera* (Athens, 1998), II, 152–154.

Tripodes, N. J. *History of the Icarian Greeks of Southern California* (South Pasadena, 2001).

Tsantes, J. *To Chroniko tes Katoches tes Ikarias (1940–1944) kai Sentome Episkopise ton Gegonoton tes Metakatochikes Periodou* (Athens, 1977).

Tsapaliares, K. *E Nesos Ikaria* (Athens, 1927).

Tsarnas, I. D. "Istoria tes Ieras Mones tou Evangelismou Leukadas," *Ikariaka*, 37 (1966).

Tsarnas, I. D. "O Patsifikos tes Ikarias," *Ikariaka*, 6 (1972), 4–5.

Tsarnas, I. D. "E Paideia sten Ikaria Sta Chronia tes Tourkokratias," *Praktika Symposiou Aigaiou 1980* (Athens, 1993).

Tsarnas, I. D. *Ioannes Tzelepes, O Mathematikos Didaskalos tou Genous kai Ethnomartyras* (Athens, 1998), pp. 24–25.

Tsarnas, I. D. "Charalambos Pamphylis," *Atheras*, Nov./Dec. 1993.

Tsatsos, Jeanne. *The Sword's Fierce Edge: A Journal of the Occupation of Greece, 1941–1944* (Nashville 1969).

Tsipanles, Z. *Italokratia tou anthropou kai perivallontos*, (Rhodes, 1998).

Tsirkas, S. *Akyvernetes Politeies, E Nychterida* (Athens, 2000).

Tzambes, S. *Sto Dromo tou Kathekontos: 80 Chronia tes Kommatikes Organoses Nautergaton tou KKE* (Athens, 2001).

Tzelikas, A. *Ikariaka Engrapha tou 16ou kai 17ou aiona apo to Archeio tes Panikariakes Adelphotetas Athenon* (Athens, 2000)

Vikelas, D. *Loukes Laras* (Athens, 1988).

Vlachopoulos, A. *Istoria tou Neou Ellenismou* (Thessaloniki, 1964).

Vlachopoulos, A. *Origins of the Greek Nation* (New Brunswick, 1970).

Vryonis, Speros. *The Decline of Medieval Hellenism in Asia Minor and the Process of Islamization from the Eleventh through the Fifteenth Century* (Berkeley 1971).

Vranoussis, E. *Ta Agiologika Keimena tou Osiou Christodoulou Idrytou tes en Patmo Mones Philologikai Paradoseis kai Istorika kai Martyriai* (Athens, 1960).

Ware, T. *Eustratios Argenti: A Study of the Greek Church under Turkish Rule* (Oxford, 1964).

Watson, B. *Miracle in Hellas: The Greeks Fight On* (New York, 1943).

Weber, Frank G. *The Evasive Neutral: Germany, Britain, and the Quest for a Turkish Alliance in the Second World War* (Columbia, 1979).

Woodhouse, C. M. *Karamanlis, the Restorer of Greek Democracy* (Oxford, 1982).

Woodhouse, C. M. *The Struggle for Greece, 1941–1949* (London, 1976).

Woodhouse, C. M. *Apple of Discord* (London, 1948).

Woodhouse, C. M. *The Rise and Fall of the Greek Colonels* (New York, 1985).

Yerasimos, Stefanos. *Les voyageurs dans l'Empire Ottoman, (XIVe–XVIe siècles: bibliographie, itinéraires et inventaire des lieux habités* (Ankara, 1991).

Zachariadis, N. *Deka Chronia Pales* (Nicosia, Cyprus, 1950).

Interviews

Achidafty, Nikos, September 1, 2003, Pittsburgh, Pennsylvania.

Achidafty, Irene, July 12, 1991, Lincoln Park, Michigan.

Adamos, Anna, July 1, 1994, Lincoln Park, Michigan.

Baloukas, G., August 6, 1998, Vathy, Samos.

Battuyios, Nicholas, June 28, 2003, Aghios Kyrikos, Icaria.

Bratsas, Philippos, May 25, 2000, Panagia, Icaria.

Caccialanza, Ettore, telephone interview, November 21, 1999.

Diamantides, Nicholas, September 1, 1999, Atlanta, Georgia.

Fakares, Socrates, June 12, 1960, Raches, Icaria.

Fakaros, Steve, July 2, 1995, Aghios Kyrikos, Icaria.

Fakaros, John, September 1, 2002, Toronto, Canada.

Fountouli, Anna, May 26, 2002, Aghios Kyrikos, Icaria.

Fournos, Antonis, June 2, 2001, Aghios Kyrikos, Icaria.

Fradelos, Vasilis, September 1, 2003, Pittsburgh, Pennsylvania.

Galiktiadis, Demosthenes, September 3, 2000, San Francisco, California.

Gerales, Demetris, June 1, 1996, Raches, Icaria.

Glaros, Stephanos, June 1, 1994, Aghios Kyrikos, Icaria.

Glaros, Priest, August 9, 1993, Xylosertis, Icaria.

Green, Peter, May 27, 2001, Akamatra, Icaria.

Karoutsos, Kyriakos, Dr., May 21, 1994, Portorafti, Attica.

Kavoures, Jesamine, May 28, 1994, Aghios Kyrikos, Icaria.

Kalokairinos, Angelos, May 27, 2002, Raches, Icaria.

Karafas, George, October 7, 1997, Wilmington, North Carolina.

Katsas, Andreas, September 2, 2000, San Francisco.

Kastanias, Antonis, June 8, 1996, Gialiskari, Icaria.

Kefalos, Panagiotis, May 27, 2000, Aghios Kyrikos, Icaria.

Koklanaris, Alice, December 26, 1993, Lincoln Park, Michigan.

Koklanaris, Kostia, January 1, 1994, Lincoln Park, Michigan.

Koklanaris, Manolis, February 19, 1997, Wilmington, North Carolina.

Koklanaris, Nikos, June 7, 2001, Panaghia, Icaria.

Kourouvanes, Panagiotes, May 29, 2003, Kountoumas, Icaria.

Koutsounamendos, Argiris, May 23, 2000; May 28, 2002; June 19, 2003, Aghios Kyrikos, Icaria.

Kyprios, Stelios, May 29, 1996, Aghios Kyrikos, Icaria.

Kyprios, Ioannis, May 27, 2002, Aghios Kyrikos, Icaria.

Kyprios, Nikos, July 24, 1994, Lincoln Park, Michigan.

Kyrtatos, Nicholas, June 29, 2003, Cephisia, Athens.

Kratsas, Vasilis, July 17, 1995, Pittsburgh, Pennsylvania.

Kratsas, Apostolos, June 27, 2003, Negia, Icaria.

Kassiotes, Georgios, June 2, 2002, Aghios Kyrikos, Icaria.

Lygizos, Isabella, January 1, 1994, Lincoln Park, Michigan.

Lygizos, John, September 1, 1999, Atlanta, Georgia.

Magoulakis, Zacharias, September 1, 2001, New York.

Makkas, Christos, June 1, 2000, Monasteri, Icaria.

Malachias, Eleni, May 30, 2003, Raches, Icaria.

Manolis, George, July 7,1955, Allen Park, Michigan.

Manolis, Elias, May 29, 1994, Aghios Kyrikos, Icaria.

Mavrogeorgis, Philippos, June 16, 1997, Athens.

Moraitis, Toula, June 1, 2002, Kountoumas, Icaria.

Moraitis, Manolis, June 3, 1997, Panaghia, Icaria.

Mougiannis, Dimitri, May 20, 2002, Aghios Kyrikos.

Mougiannis, George, July 17, 1994, Lincoln Park, Michigan.

Oeconomou, Angelike, May 25, 2002, Aghios Kyrikos, Icaria.

Papadakis, Charalambos, June 12, 1969, Aghios Kyrikos, Icaria.

Papalas, Elias, June 7, 1994, Tsouredos, Icaria.

Papalas, Marino, August 3, 1994, Lincoln Park, Michigan.

Papasimakes, Philippos, May 23, 2002, Raches, Icaria.

Pardos, Lilos, June 7, 1996, Tsouredos, Icaria.

Pardos, Elias, September 9, 1994, Harrisville, Michigan.

Pastis, John, July 29, 2002, Wilmington, North Carolina.

Phocianos, Nicholas, May 27, 2000, Aghios Kyrikos, Icaria.

Phocianos, Dimitris, May 24, 1994, Aghios Kyrikos, Icaria.

Plakidas, George, June 7, 2002, Aghios Kyrikos, Icaria.

Poulos, Koula, April 27, 1997, Wilmington, North Carolina.

Poulos, Pantelis, April 27, 1997, Wilmington, North Carolina.

Poulos, Triandafilos, May 20, 2002, Aghios Kyrikos, Icaria.

Pouriezi, Maria, May 23, 1994, Raches, Icaria.

Pyke, John, September 21, 1998, Chester, South Wirral, England.

Rakitzes, Apostolos, June 17, 2003, Aghios Kyrikos, Icaria.

Saphos, Kostas, May 14, 1994, Tzitzifies, Athens.

Seringas, Vangelis, July 11, 1995, Lincoln Park, Michigan.

Skaros, Nicholas, September 1, 1994, Philadelphia, Pennsylvania.

Sophoulis, Kostas, June 29, 2003, July 2, 2003, Mytilene, phone interview, Sept. 26, 2003 e-mail message from Mytilene.

Sophoulis, Evangelia, June 3, 1970, Aghios Kyrikos, Icaria.

Sotilis, Maria, May 21, 2000, Tzitzifies, Athens.

Spanos, Christos, July 5, 1974, May 23, 1994, Raches, Icaria.

Spanos, Daniel, June 3, 1996, Raches, Icaria

Spanos, George, March 17, 2002, Piraeus, Greece.

Spanos, Stamatoula, June 12, 1964, Raches, Icaria.

Speis, Themistocles, June 17, 2003, Perdiki, Icaria.

Stanzos, Manolis, May 26, 2003, Raches, Icaria.

Stamoulos, Irene, May 27, 2002, Evdilos, Icaria.

Stasinopoulos, Christos, June 16, 1997, Athens.

Stenos, George, May 23, 1994, Raches, Icaria.

Tsalis, Koula, January 1, 1994, Lincoln Park, Michigan.

Tsantiris, Ioannis, May 24, 1992, Armenistis, Icaria.

Tsouris, Elias, May 26, 1996, Tsouredo, Icaria.

Tsouris, Pantelis, May 27, 1994, Tsouredo, Icaria.

Vassilaros, Thanassis, June 12, 2003, Therma, Icaria.

Yiakas, Vassilis, June 7, 1996, Raches, Icaria.

Xylas, Alecos, June 29, 2003, Aghios Kyrikos, Icaria.

Zizes, Elias, June 27, 2003, Aghios Kyrikos, Icaria.

Unpublished Material

Dagge, Richard *Secret Report: Notes on Political Policy and Treatment of EAM and Andartes on Samos, Icaria, and other Aegean Isles, September 1943.* Pyke papers. Chester, South Wirral, Great Britain.

Pyke, John. *Secret Report.* Oct. 13, 1943. Pyke papers. Chester, South Wirral, Great Britain.

Pyke, John. *Secret Report to SCAO, Samos, on St. [Agios] Kyrikos*, September 27, 1943. Pyke papers. Chester, South Wirral, Great Britain.

Pyke, John. *Report on Italian Garrison in Icaria: Secret and Confidential*, Nov. 15, 1943. Pyke papers. Chester, South Wirral, Great Britain.

Pyke, John. *Icaria and Phourni: Population and Animal Statistics*, (sometime between September 7 and November 2, 1943). Pyke papers. Chester, South Wirral, Great Britain.

Pyke, John. *Field Message Book*, Sept. 7, to Nov. 12, 1943 Chester, South Wirral, Great Britain.

Pyke, John. *Report on Interview with Guerrilla Leaders from Ikaria,* Sept. 24, 1943. Pyke papers.Chester, South Wirral, Great Britain.

Pyke, John. *Report on Italian Garrison in Icaria*, Nov. 15, 1943. Chester, South Wirral, Great Britain.

Reaves, B. *Wilmington's Greek Community: A Brief History* (1982) in the North Carolina Room of the New Hanover Co. Public Library, Wilmington, North Carolina.

ʹrinades, Dr. *EAM communiqué Nov. 12, 1943.* Pyke papers, Chester, South ʹirral, Great Britain.

Select Letters

Caskey, J. L. Letter to N. Kyrtatos discussing OSS aid to Icaria, August 24, 1944 in possession of N. Kyrtatos, Cephissia, Athens.

Gemelos, Fotini. Letter to George Spanos Chapter, June 1991, in possession of Nick Achidafty in Clearwater, Florida.

Kermanides, Diogenes. Letter to Eleni Malachias, August 8, 1991, in possession of E. Malachias in Raches, Icaria.

Malachias, Aspasia. "Flight to Turkey 1942," Letter of May 5, 1980, to author, in possession of author, Greenville, North Carolina.

Malachias, John. Letter to Nicholas Kyrtatos, September 9, 1944, in possession of N. Kyrtatos, Cephissia, Athens.

Malachias, Olga. Letter of September, 7 1947, to her parents, in possession of Eleni Malachias-Karimalis, Raches, Icaria.

Parish, Mrs. Michael Woodbine. Letter to the author, April 12, 1997, in possession of author, Greenville, North Carolina.

Sophoulis, Em. Letter to John Pyke, "Action by the name of King George B of the Greek government," September 27, 1943, in possession of John Pyke, Chester, South Wirral, Great Britain.

Tsantiris, George. Correspondence 1955–1956 in archives of the Pan-Icarian Brotherhood of America in Verona, Pennsylvania.

Wilkinson, Richard. Unpublished Correspondence of British Consul in Greece from 1836 to 1838, in collection of Aeneas Constantine, Harrisville, Michigan.

York, Zoe. Denver, Colorado, June 2, 2000, and March 2, 2002, to author, in possession of author.

Diaries

Athanassopoulos, Vangelis. Diary, 1947–1948, in possession of Ch. Malachias, Raches, Icaria.

Lakios, Koula. Diary 1943, in possession of Koula Lakios, Aghios Kyrikos, Icaria.

Pyke, John. Diary, Sept 7th–Nov. 12th, 1943, in possession of John Pyke, Chester, South Wirral, Great Britain.

Sophoulis, Em. Diary, 1939–1943, in possession of Kostas Sophoulis, Mytiline.

Newspapers

Acropolis
Athens News
Atheras
Birkenhead News
Demokratike: Ephemeris tes Samou kai Ikarias
Eleftheros Kosmos
Ellas
Eleutherotypia
Ikaros
Ikariake Enosis
Ikaria Phoné
Kathemerine

Laokratia
Le Moniteur Ottoman
Londo Times
Manchester Guardian
Nea Ikaria
Pandike
Floga: Organo Epon.
Rizospastis
Samiako Vema
Samiake Echo
Vema
Warren Tribune
Youngstown Vindicator

Index

351

ANCIENT ICARIA

Anthony J. Papalas

This is the only English-language book-length study of ancient Icaria and its people. It traces the history of the island in five different periods: the Bronze Age to the Persian Wars; the fifth century; Spartan hegemony to Alexander; the Hellenistic and Roman period; and the Byzantine period. The book is beautifully illustrated with photographs of key sites and monuments. Also included are an appendix listing the island's main inscriptions and a select bibliography.

This is local history at its very best. It is also compulsively readable.

– Peter Green, F.R.S.L.
Dougherty Centennial Professor Emeritus of Classics
The University of Texas at Austin

BOLCHAZY-CARDUCCI PUBLISHERS, INC.
www.BOLCHAZY.com

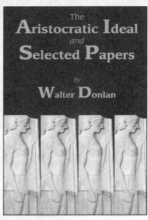